Medieval Londoners

Essays to mark the eightieth birthday of Caroline M. Barron

Medieval Londoners

Essays to mark the eightieth birthday of Caroline M. Barron

Edited by

Elizabeth A. New and Christian Steer

UNIVERSITY OF LONDON PRESS
INSTITUTE OF HISTORICAL RESEARCH

Published by

UNIVERSITY OF LONDON PRESS
SCHOOL OF ADVANCED STUDY
INSTITUTE OF HISTORICAL RESEARCH
Senate House, Malet Street, London WC1E 7HU

Available to download free at http://www.humanities-digital-library.org
or to purchase at https://www.sas.ac.uk/publications

ISBN
978-1-912702-14-5 (hardback edition)
978-1-912702-15-2 (PDF edition)
978-1-912702-16-9 (.epub edition)
978-1-912702-17-6 (.mobi edition)

INSTITUTE OF HISTORICAL RESEARCH | SCHOOL OF ADVANCED STUDY UNIVERSITY OF LONDON

This publication has been made possible by a grant received from the
late Miss Isobel Thornley's bequest to the University of London.

Caroline Barron at the 2019 Harlaxton Medieval Symposium.
Photograph: © Catherine Rendón.

Contents

Notes on contributors

CHARLOTTE BERRY completed her PhD at the Institute of Historical Research in 2018 with a thesis entitled 'Margins and marginality in fifteenth-century London'. She is currently a research assistant at the Goldsmiths' Company. Her research focuses on urban neighbourhoods, social structure and marginality.

JULIA BOFFEY is professor of medieval studies in the department of English at Queen Mary University of London. Her interests include Middle English verse, especially lyrics and dream poetry; and the relationships between manuscript and print in the late fifteenth and early sixteenth centuries, especially in London.

J. L. (JIM) BOLTON is a professorial research fellow in the school of history at Queen Mary University of London. His research interests are late medieval international trade and banking and the medieval money supply. He is currently bringing the Borromei Bank Research Project to its conclusion.

CLIVE BURGESS is a reader in medieval history at Royal Holloway, University of London, who has worked and published mainly on late medieval urban belief and behaviour. He concentrated first on late medieval Bristol but in his time at Royal Holloway has also worked on London's archives, naturally benefiting from Caroline Barron's encouragement. He has looked particularly at parish life and at the achievements of parishioners on the eve of the Reformation.

MARTHA CARLIN is professor of history at the University of Wisconsin-Milwaukee. Her research focuses on medieval towns, especially London and its suburbs, and on everyday life in medieval England, including the history of food, work, shopping, the household, household technologies, correspondence and inns. In recent years her research has also turned up new evidence concerning the lives of Geoffrey Chaucer, John Gower and William Shakespeare.

JUSTIN COLSON is lecturer in the department of history at the University of Essex.

MATTHEW DAVIES is professor of urban history at Birkbeck, University of London, where he is also executive dean of social sciences, history and philosophy. His research focuses on late medieval and early modern cities and especially London's crafts, guilds and government; and he has published extensively on these topics. He currently directs 'Layers of London: mapping the city's heritage', a major collaborative public-engagement project funded by the Heritage Lottery Fund and other bodies and based at the Institute of Historical Research.

STEPHEN FREETH was keeper of manuscripts at Guildhall library from 1986 until 2007, responsible for the archives of many of the city of London's parishes, livery companies, charities, businesses and other organizations. He has long been interested in medieval tombs and monuments, especially brasses, and is a vice-president of the Monumental Brass Society. He is currently archivist or historical adviser to three livery companies: the Merchant Taylors, Vintners and Feltmakers.

VANESSA HARDING began as a medievalist – her PhD thesis on the port of London in the fourteenth century was examined by Caroline Barron in 1983 – but now works on medieval and early modern London. Her research focuses on London's built environment, its demography, the London family, disease and death. She co-chairs the Medieval and Tudor London Seminar, which Caroline Barron founded in 1975.

JULIAN LUXFORD is a professor of art history at the University of St. Andrews and a specialist on late medieval English art. He is particularly interested in the art and architecture of the monastic orders and also medieval drawings.

JOHN A. McEWAN, BA (University of Western Ontario), MA, PhD (Royal Holloway, University of London) specializes in the history of medieval Britain. He is based at Saint Louis University, where he is associate director of the Centre for Digital Humanities. His research focuses on social organization, local government and visual culture in London, c.1100–1350.

ELIZABETH A. NEW is senior lecturer in history at Aberystwyth University. Her current research interests include London in the later middle ages, ideas of identity, Christocentric piety and the material culture of devotion and seals and sealing practices in medieval England and Wales, and she has published widely in these areas.

MATTHEW PAYNE is the keeper of the muniments at Westminster abbey and has written widely on early Tudor London and Westminster.

JOHN SCHOFIELD, whose PhD was supervised by Caroline Barron, was an archaeologist at the Museum of London from 1974 until 2008. He has written about the archaeology and buildings of London from Roman times to 1666. He is cathedral archaeologist at St. Paul's cathedral and secretary of the City of London Archaeological Trust.

CHRISTIAN STEER is honorary visiting fellow in the department of history at the University of York. His PhD thesis, supervised by Caroline Barron, was on 'Burial and commemoration in medieval London, c.1140–1540' (2013). He has published extensively on the lost tombs and epitaphs of medieval London.

ANNE F. SUTTON is the author of *The Mercery of London: Trade, Goods and People 1130–1578* (2005) and many articles on medieval London, the Mercers and Merchant Adventurers, with particular interest in the Yorkist period and Richard III. She is co-author/editor of *The Privileges of the Merchant Adventurers of England 1296–1483* (2009), *Richard III's Books* (1997), *The Hours of Richard III* (1990) and *The Coronation of Richard III* (1983).

List of figures and tables

Frontispiece: Caroline Barron at the 2019 Harlaxton Medieval Symposium.

Map: London showing the parish churches, religious houses, Old St. Paul's and major landmarks *c.*1520.

Figures

Tables

Abbreviations

BL	British Library, London
BRUC	A. B. Emden, *A Biographical Register of the University of Cambridge to 1500* (Cambridge, 1963)
BRUO (to A.D. 1500)	A. B. Emden, *Biographical Register of the University of Oxford to A.D. 1500* (3 vols., Oxford, 1957–9)
BRUO (A.D. 1501–1540)	A. B. Emden, *Biographical Register of the University of Oxford to A.D. 1501–1540* (Oxford, 1974)
Cal. Letter Bks. A, B, C, etc.	*Calendar of the Letter Books preserved among the Archives of the Corporation of the City of London*, ed. R. R. Sharpe, A–L (11 vols., London, 1899–1912)
CCR	*Calendar of Close Rolls* (46 vols., London, 1892–1963)
CIPM	*Calendar of Inquisitions Post Mortem* (London and Woodbridge, 1904–)
CPMR	*Calendar of Plea and Memoranda Rolls of the City of London 1323–1482*, ed. A. H. Thomas and P. E. Jones (6 vols., Cambridge, 1926–61)
CPR	*Calendar of Patent Rolls* (54 vols., London, 1891–1916)
CUL	Cambridge University Library
LMA	London Metropolitan Archives
ODNB	*Oxford Dictionary of National Biography*, ed. H. C. G. Matthew and B. Harrison (60 vols., Oxford, 2004)
OED	*Oxford English Dictionary*
PROME	*Parliament Rolls of Medieval England 1275–1504*, ed. C. Given-Wilson et al. (16 vols., Woodbridge, 2005)
STC	A. W. Pollard and G. R. Redgrave, *A Short-Title Catalogue of Books Printed in England, Scotland, and Ireland and of English Books Printed Abroad,*

	1475–1640, 2nd edn. revised and enlarged by W. A. Jackson, F. S. Ferguson and K. F. Pantzer (3 vols., London, 1986–91)
TNA	The National Archives of the UK

Acknowledgements

This special collection of essays has been produced to celebrate the eightieth birthday of Caroline M. Barron, emeritus professor of the history of London at Royal Holloway, University of London. There are many to whom our grateful thanks are due. First and foremost, we thank each of our contributors not only for their essays but also for dealing with our queries quickly, professionally and with good humour. We likewise owe a debt of gratitude to Clive Burgess, David Harry, Sue Powell and Joel Rosenthal, and our anonymous reader, for their comments, encouragement and specialist advice during the production of this volume; to Giles Darkes for providing the map of medieval London; to Richard Asquith for producing the index; and to each of the institutions cited here for reproduction permissions. We also thank Philip Carter and Julie Spraggon of the Institute of Historical Research, and Emily Morrell and Kerry Whitston of University of London Press, for their guidance during the publication process. This volume has been a well-kept secret from the birthday girl and we thank our fellow conspirators for their discretion, as we also thank the Barron family, Katie and Leo, Helen, Will and Seren, and David, with whom it has been a pleasure to plot. Finally, we thank Caroline Barron for all that she is, for her inspiration, friendship, boundless (and unstoppable) energy, encouragement, generosity and kindness. This volume is offered with gratitude and with love.

Elizabeth A. New   Christian Steer
Aberystwyth University   University of York

Feast of St Gilbert of Sempringham, 2019

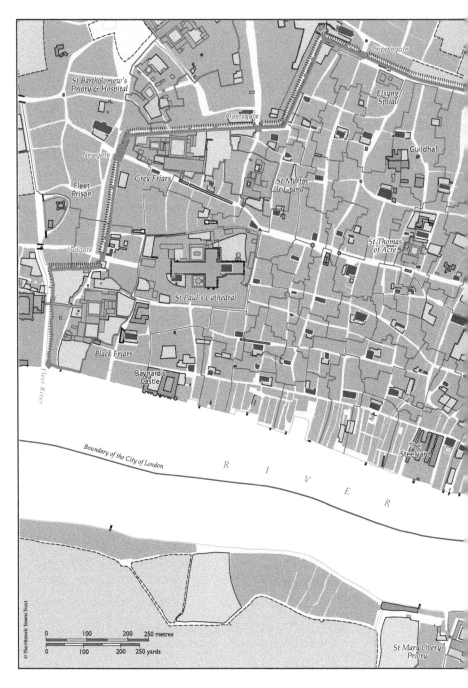

London showing the parish churches, religious houses, old St. Paul's and major landmarks *c.*1520. *Adapted from A Map of Tudor London* published by the Historic Towns Trust, 2018.

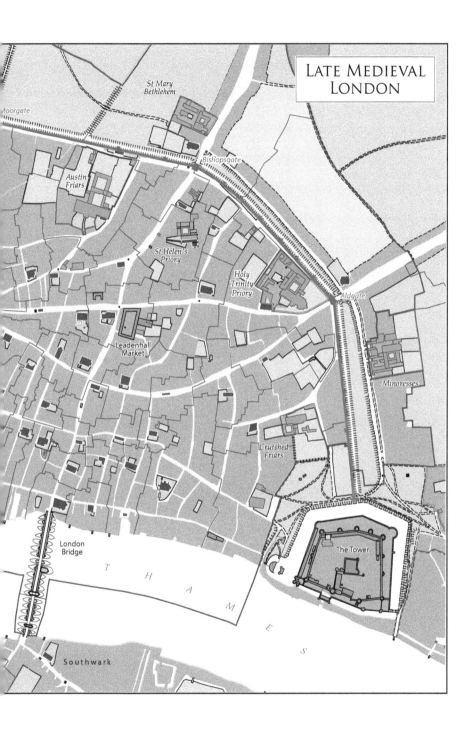

LATE MEDIEVAL
LONDON

St Mary
Bethlehem

Moorgate

Bishopsgate

Austin
Friars

St Helen's
Priory

Holy
Trinity
Priory

Aldgate

Leadenhall
Market

Minoresses

Crutched
Friars

The Tower

London
Bridge

T H A M E S

Southwark

Foreword

It is an honour to write this foreword to a volume dedicated to Caroline Barron. She is best known for her prolific scholarship on late medieval British history, especially the history of London and the history of women. Indeed, a search of the *Bibliography of British and Irish History Online* reveals eighty-five publications, ranging from 1968 to 2017. As testament to the enduring importance of her work, a selection of these papers has recently been gathered together.[1] Perhaps more important still has been Caroline's legacy through doctoral supervision and her generosity to early career historians. She has supervised thirty-three doctoral students to completion; and she has offered hospitality and accommodation in London to countless others needing to use the city's libraries and archives. In a clear demonstration of care for the well-being and educational experience of sometimes vulnerable doctoral students, Caroline often offered her expertise freely to ensure that postgraduate study was right for the individual: 'My policy was that when I wasn't certain that someone would be able to do it, or whether they had the funding, or domestic issues or other problems, what I would say would be: let me supervise you informally for a year – don't register – let's see how it goes. And if it's working out well – then register'. Her concern for the future of the discipline has seen Caroline direct her enormous energies into countless societies, institutes and projects, such as the British Association for Local History, the Harlaxton Medieval Symposium and the London Record Society. It is only fitting that this volume is to be published by the Institute of Historical Research. Caroline has given so much of her valuable time to the IHR: she has studied and lectured here; she is a driving force in the Friends of the IHR, which has offered so many opportunities to young scholars pursuing historical research; she serves on the IHR Trust; and she co-organizes one of the longest-running seminars at the IHR, the Medieval and Tudor London seminar. The IHR, and the discipline, owe her a great debt of gratitude.

Jo Fox
Director, Institute of Historical Research

---

[1] *Medieval London: Collected Papers of Caroline M. Barron*, ed. M. Carlin and J. T. Rosenthal (Kalamazoo, Mich., 2017).

Introduction: medieval Londoners

Elizabeth A. New

Caroline Barron leads the field on medieval London and her work on its politics, governance, economy and fabric has greatly enhanced our understanding of the late medieval city.[1] It is, however, her interest in and enthusiasm for the men and women who lived and worked in, or were visitors to, the capital, and her ability to inspire that interest and enthusiasm in others, which are perhaps her greatest gift to scholars and students alike.[2] This volume brings together a range of those who have been so inspired, whether as colleagues or students or through her publications, papers and conversations at the numerous seminars and conferences she attends; and is offered as a token of appreciation for such a pioneering and generous scholar.[3]

Medieval Londoners

The centrality of people as well as the built environment to the concept and reality of a medieval city was expressed by Saints Augustine of Hippo and

[1] C. M. Barron, *London in the Later Middle Ages: Government and People 1200–1500* (Oxford, 2004), is the standard text for the later medieval city. See also *Medieval London: Collected Papers of Caroline M. Barron*, ed. M. Carlin and J. T. Rosenthal (Kalamazoo, Mich., 2017), for a selection of her essays and articles, with a full bibliography of her work up until 2016.

[2] Caroline Barron's work has investigated those from the very highest to the lowest levels of London society. See, e.g., C. M. Barron, 'Searching for the "small people" of medieval London', *Local Historian*, xxxviii (2008), 83–94; C. M. Barron, 'The child in medieval London: the legal evidence', in *Essays on Medieval Childhood: Responses to Recent Debates*, ed. J. T. Rosenthal (Donington, 2007), pp. 40–53; C. M. Barron, 'Chivalry, pageantry and merchant culture in medieval London', in *Heraldry, Pageantry and Social Display in Medieval England*, ed. P. R. Coss and M. Keen (Woodbridge, 2002), pp. 219–41; *Medieval London Widows, 1300–1500*, ed. C. M. Barron and A. F. Sutton (London, 1994). A previous volume in her honour included essays focusing on Londoners but, as the title suggests, the overarching theme was somewhat different from the present collection: *London and the Kingdom: Essays in Honour of Caroline M. Barron*, ed. M. Davies and A. Prescott (Harlaxton Medieval Studies, n.s., xvi, Donington, 2008).

[3] The afterword to this volume by Clive Burgess highlights in particular Caroline's generosity as a colleague and teacher.

E. A. New, 'Introduction', in *Medieval Londoners: essays to mark the eightieth birthday of Caroline M. Barron*, ed. E. A. New and C. Steer (London, 2019), pp. 1–8. License: CC-BY-NC-ND 4.0.

Isidore of Seville, and their work continues to influence modern scholarship: the 'city' was, after all (according to Isidore), so named because of the *cives*.[4] When urban communities in western Europe started representing themselves through a communal seal – a medium that forces the distillation of identity into a small package of image and text – the motif quite often incorporated representations of citizens (and/or their leaders) in addition to, or in place of, architectural imagery or the depiction of their spiritual protector.[5] When considering modern historiography, studies of urban oligarchs and the power-politics of small, dominant groups within English towns and cities have, certainly since the late nineteenth century, been complemented by the investigation of citizens and burgesses.[6] From the mid twentieth century onwards, scholars broadened their investigations to consider those who lived and worked in towns but who were not officially citizens.[7] More recently, women, children, clergy and the religious and long-term residents and transient visitors from overseas have been incorporated into studies of English urban history.[8]

---

[4] The most relevant quotations from both Augustine and Isidore are cited in the original and in translation in C. Keen, 'Boundaries and belonging: imagining urban identity in medieval Italy', in *Imagining the City, Volume 2: The Politics of Urban Space*, ed. C. Emden, C. Keen and D. R. Midgley (Bern, 2006), pp. 65–86, at pp. 68–9. See also C. Frugoni, *A Distant City: Images of Urban Experience in the Medieval World*, trans. W. McCuaig (Princeton, 1991); and C. D. Liddy, *Contesting the City: the Politics of Citizenship in English Towns, 1250–1530* (Oxford, 2017), esp. ch. 3.

[5] See, e.g., M. Späth, 'The body and its parts: iconographical metaphors of corporate identity in 13th-century common seals', in *Pourquoi les sceaux? La sigillographie nouvel enjeu de l'histoire de l'art*, ed. M. Gill and J-L. Chassel (Lille, 2011), pp. 383–99. The representation of groups of people on town seals was, however, far less common in England than in most of western Europe (E. A. New, 'The common seal and civic identity in medieval London', in *Medieval Coins and Seals: Constructing Identity, Signifying Power*, ed. S. Solway (Turnhout, 2015), pp. 297–331, at pp. 302–3).

[6] Even J. Tait's unabashedly constitutional focus allowed room for a consideration of burgesses and citizens (J. Tait, *The Medieval English Borough: Studies on Its Origins and Constitutional History* (Manchester, 1936)). See also S. Reynolds, *Kingdoms and Communities in Western Europe 900–1300* (Oxford, 1984), ch. 6, for a thoughtful study of urban oligarchs in a European context.

[7] An important contribution in this regard was Elspeth Veale's essay about the range of people – both men and women – involved in manufacturing in later medieval London (E. M. Veale, 'Craftsmen and the economy of London in the fourteenth century', in *Studies in London History Presented to Philip Edmund Jones*, ed. A. E. J. Hollaender and W. Kellaway (London, 1969), pp. 133–54). It is, however, interesting to note that Liddy's recent study of English medieval towns, *Contesting the City*, focuses on urban politics and those with the freedom, perhaps reflecting the once-more dominant trends (of politics and the elites) in Anglophone, and especially British-based, history.

[8] For recent examples, see M. Kowaleski, 'The assimilation of foreigners in late medieval Exeter: a prosopographical analysis', in *Resident Aliens in Later Medieval England*, ed. W. M.

London, then as now, presents us with a melting pot of people, with men and women from across the realm and far beyond living and working in the city; nevertheless, identifying the 'Londoners' of the title of this volume is not as straightforward as it initially might appear.[9] Take, for example, the term 'citizen'. It is true that, by the late middle ages, the status of being a 'citizen' of London was clearly defined and carefully controlled.[10] In the late eleventh to early thirteenth centuries, however, when the polity of London was taking shape and becoming increasingly (self-)defined, 'citizen' was used alongside other terms and the nature of citizenship was still evolving.[11] Within the present volume, John McEwan's chapter, which looks in detail at the people and politics surrounding the reconstruction of London Bridge in the late twelfth century and its maintenance thereafter, touches upon these complexities of definition and highlights the ways in which the bridge helped Londoners – lay and cleric, men and women, as well as 'citizens' – to forge a civic identity.[12]

In the earlier period especially, but throughout the middle ages, an additional complication, even when considering just the citizens, is the fact

---

Ormrod, N. McDonald and C. Taylor (Turnhout, 2017), pp. 163–79; C. Hill, 'Merchants' wives and widows: networking in Norwich', in *The Medieval Merchant: Proceedings of the 2012 Harlaxton Symposium*, ed. C. M. Barron and A. F. Sutton (Harlaxton Medieval Studies, n.s., xxiv, Donington, 2014), pp. 111–26.

[9] According to the *OED*, the term 'Londoner' for an inhabitant of London was first recorded in *c*.1460 ('Londoner, n.', OED online, March 2019, Oxford University Press, <http://www.oed.com/view/Entry/109952> [accessed 20 Dec. 2018]). Helen Bradley provides a useful short summary of the varied nature of the origins of Londoners in her discussion of trade between Southampton and London (H. Bradley, 'Southampton's trading partners: London', in *English Inland Trade 1430–1540: Southampton and its Region*, ed. M. Hicks (Oxford, 2015), pp. 65–80, at p. 66).

[10] The developing definition and control of citizenship through the mechanisms of craft and merchant guilds is discussed in detail in, e.g., Barron, *London in the Later Middle Ages* (esp. ch. 9); and B. A. Hanawalt, *Ceremony and Civility: Civic Culture in Late Medieval London* (Oxford, 2017), ch. 5. The evolving nature of 'citizenship' in England's main towns is discussed in Liddy, *Contesting the City*; while David Harry looks in detail at the increasing control over the franchise by a small elite in the later middle ages (D. Harry, *Constructing a Civic Community in Late Medieval London: the Common Profit, Charity and Commemoration* (Woodbridge, 2019), esp. chs. 2, 3 and 4). I am grateful to Dr. Harry for sharing a pre-publication draft of this book with me.

[11] William FitzStephen loftily declared that, while the inhabitants of other towns are called citizens, in London '*barones dicuntur*' [they are called barons] (F. M. Stenton, *Norman London: an Essay. With a Translation of William Fitz Stephen's Description by H. E. Butler and a Map of London under Henry II* (London, 1934), p. 27). For discussion of the terms used for the inhabitants of London in the high middle ages, see, e.g., Tait, *Medieval English Borough*, pp. 256–9; S. Reynolds, 'The rulers of London in the twelfth century', *History*, lvii (1972), 337–57, at p. 346; New, 'Common seal and civic identity', p. 305.

[12] J. McEwan, 'Charity and the city: London Bridge, *c*.1176–1275' in this volume.

that such men very often came from outside the city, thus giving them identities and commitments beyond the capital.[13] Anne Sutton's detailed analysis of mayor Nicholas Alwyn in this volume provides us with insights into the life (and afterlife) of a leading Londoner with strong ties elsewhere.[14] Despite success in the capital, Sutton demonstrates that Alwyn retained close connections with his native Lincolnshire and that he took great care to preserve his memory in both his original and adoptive homes.

As the case of Alwyn makes plain, and unlike developments in many other major European cities, no powerful or wealthy dynasties dominated London in the fourteenth and fifteenth centuries – as a result both of circumstance and deliberate choice. A consequence of this is that even those involved in civic governance, and who might have been outstanding in terms of both material wealth and political influence, looked to other ways of ensuring their memory. For example, one of Caroline Barron's earliest publications sought to bring Richard Whittington into historical focus by highlighting his lifetime achievements and his *post mortem* generosity to his adoptive city.[15] The number of citizens who died without surviving children, or whose surviving relatives lived elsewhere or moved away, provided perhaps a spur for those seeking remembrance in late medieval London. In their chapters in this volume, Stephen Freeth and John Schofield, Julian Luxford and Christian Steer all explore, through careful investigation of remarkable sources, the care and attention paid by wealthier men and women to establishing physical and spiritual commemoration in London, preserving memories for many generations.[16]

Many laymen living and working in medieval London were not citizens, with Matthew Davies noting that non-citizens formed a clear majority. Furthermore, Vanessa Harding makes the important point that it is often difficult for us to tell from the sources who was a citizen and who was not, with the inference that the same was true for contemporaries unless neighbours of those in question.[17] These points are made in a number of chapters in

---

[13] J. McEwan, 'Horses, horsemen, and hunting: leading Londoners and equestrian seals in the late twelfth and early thirteenth centuries', *Essays in Medieval Studies*, xxii (2005), 77–93, esp. at p. 85.

[14] A. F. Sutton, 'Nicholas Alwyn, mayor of London: a man of two loyalties, London and Spalding'.

[15] C. M. Barron, 'Richard Whittington: the man behind the myth', in Hollaender and Kellaway, *Studies in London History*, pp. 197–250.

[16] S. Freeth and J. Schofield, 'John Reynewell and St. Botolph Billingsgate'; J. Luxford, 'The testament of Joan FitzLewes: a source for the history of the abbey of Franciscan nuns without Aldgate'; C. Steer, 'Souls of benefactors at Grey Friars church London'.

[17] M. Davies, 'Aliens, crafts and guilds in late medieval London'; and V. Harding, 'Families in later medieval London: sex, marriage and mortality', both in this volume.

this collection. Justin Colson, for example, brings together leading and lesser citizens and non-citizens in a portrait of a riverside hostelry.[18] Quite a large proportion of non-citizens would officially have been classified as 'foreign' (that is, from elsewhere in the realm) or 'alien' (outside the realm), although many such long-term residents might well have considered themselves Londoners. Within the present volume, Davies's chapter provides an overview of the life and contribution of such foreigners and aliens in medieval London, while Matthew Payne's investigation of the Bardi traders provides us with revelations about international trade and personal connections through close reading of an underappreciated source.[19] Jim Bolton's chapter considers interpersonal international exchange from the alien point of view, providing insights into connections forged through a notary, a man both part of a Europe-wide network but also very much a Londoner.[20]

Throughout her work, Caroline Barron has emphasized the need to consider women and children when discussing the people of medieval London, even if these Londoners are often rather more challenging to investigate.[21] The records may not be as good as for men, and especially men with the freedom, but evidence concerning the lives of female Londoners, in particular, can be gleaned, adding to our understanding of the medieval city, as demonstrated by a number of contributors in this collection. Women and children are foregrounded in Harding's study of marriage and families of the 'middling sort', which yields welcome insight into the rich and complex lives of early Tudor Londoners.[22] Julian Luxford focuses on the extant original will of a wealthy widower and uses forensic investigation of this document to reveal networks of friendship and patronage connected through the Minories.[23] Women of middling and lower status are the main players in Charlotte Berry's investigation of spatial and social networks and mobility within the crowded city and of the importance attached to reputation even among the less well established.[24]

---

[18] J. Colson, 'A portrait of a late medieval London pub: the Star inn, Bridge Street'.

[19] M. T. W. Payne, 'Bankers and booksellers: evidence of the late fifteenth century English book trade in the ledgers of the Bardi bank'.

[20] J. L. Bolton, 'William Styfford (fl. 1437–1466): citizen and scrivener of London and notary imperial'.

[21] Perhaps her most influential publication in this regard is C. M. Barron, 'The "golden age" of women in medieval London', *Reading Medieval Studies*, xv (1989), 35–58. See also C. M. Barron, 'The education and training of girls in fifteenth-century London', in *Courts, Counties and the Capital in the Later Middle Ages*, ed. D. E. S. Dunn (Stroud, 1996), pp. 139–53.

[22] Harding, 'Families in later medieval London'.

[23] 'Minories' is here used to denote the convent of the Minoresses as well as its inhabitants.

[24] C. Berry, '"Go to hyr neybors wher she dwelte before": reputation and mobility at the London Consistory Court in the early sixteenth century', this volume.

The general term 'medieval Londoners' should also include the men and women in holy or religious orders who made up an important proportion of the city's population. Many of London's priests and religious were local or had local connections and one, the prior of Holy Trinity, was part of the civic establishment, as *ex officio* alderman of Portsoken ward.[25] Whether local or not, the *oratores*, parish priests and (in particular) the mendicants were a familiar and integral part of the population of medieval London. The chapters by Freeth and Schofield, Luxford and (particularly) Steer remind us that lay Londoners were close confidants of secular and religious clergy. They relied on these neighbours for practical as well as spiritual support. Members of the Church from outside London also interacted with men and women in the city and its suburbs, as demonstrated by the fascinating case of disputed land and the Londoner charged with resolving it, as explored by Martha Carlin.[26]

As highlighted by the three sections of this collection ('Living in the city', 'The lure of London' and 'Londoners remembered'), men and women in the medieval city lived, worked, prayed, played and politicked, and eventually died and were commemorated together in a relatively small space; and many studies of the capital and its inhabitants have commented upon this close-quarter living, where rich and poor, good and not-so-good would have encountered each other daily. Sometimes groups of like-minded Londoners, perhaps friends and certainly acquaintances, can be identified from personal records, such as the manuscript at the heart of Julia Boffey's chapter.[27] The wills and testaments of Joan FitzLewes (Luxford), Nicholas Alwyn (Sutton) and various benefactors of the Grey Friars (Steer) can, with the usual caveats about such documents, also be used to provide glimpses of social networks. More formal records are another valuable way of investigating the daily lives of medieval Londoners, from disputes, acrimony and romance (Berry and Harding), through trade-related interaction and conviviality (Colson)

---

[25] For the origins of London priests and religious, see, e.g., V. Davis, *Clergy in London in the Late Middle Ages: a Register of Clergy Ordained in the Diocese of London Based on Episcopal Ordination Lists 1361–1539* (London, 2000). Despite Langland's dim view of them, the majority of chantry chaplains in St. Paul's cathedral actually came from the diocese of London (M.-H. Rousseau, *Saving the Souls of Medieval London: Perpetual Chantries at St. Paul's Cathedral, c.1200–1548* (Farnham, 2011), pp. 110–12). For the prior of Holy Trinity as alderman of Portsoken, see *The Cartulary of Holy Trinity, Aldgate*, ed. G. A. J. Hodgett (London Rec. Soc., vii, 1971), introduction, esp. pp. xiii–xviii; J. McEwan, 'The aldermen of London, c. 1200–80: Alfred Beaven revisited', *Trans. London and Middlesex Archaeol. Soc.*, lxii (2012 for 2011), 177–203, at pp. 183, 185.

[26] M. Carlin, 'Palaeography and forgery: Thomas D.'s *Book of the Hartshorn in Southwark*', in this volume.

[27] J. Boffy, 'Household reading for Londoners? Huntington Library MS. HM 140'.

and legal and historical investigations (Carlin), to international networks (Bolton, Davies and Payne). Material remains of medieval London are few but they, too, can reveal much about the lives of men and women in the city (Freeth and Schofield).

There are, alas, no portraits in the modern sense to accompany our sources about medieval Londoners. The illustrations of mid fifteenth-century London aldermen, proudly displaying their robes of office and armorial bearings associated with them, are representations of these powerful men rather than true-to-life images.[28] Moreover, they are images of the political elite of the city – Londoners, certainly, but of a rarefied sort. Rather less well known, and very slightly more representative of at least the upper levels of London society, are the series of illustrations of benefactors to St. Alban's abbey associated with the city, some of whom grace the cover of this volume. St. Alban's would no doubt have been familiar to most Londoners, dominating as it did the main route into the city from the north, a prestigious, wealthy site of pilgrimage to the shrine of Britain's proto-martyr.

The abbey's *Liber benefactorum* was begun by Thomas Walsingham, the prolific and talented monk-chronicler of the abbey, in *c*.1380 and, in addition to kings, prelates and nobles dating back to Offa, he included details and stylized pictures of many less illustrious benefactors in St. Alban's and further afield, including London.[29] As well as two bishops of London (Gilbert Foliot and Ralph Baldock), at least twenty-six Londoners were named as benefactors to the abbey: these include the mayor Sir John Philipot, buried in Grey Friars;[30] John Barton the elder, city recorder;[31] Reginald Kentwood, dean of St. Paul's;[32] John Lovekyn, canon of the church of St. Mary Cripplegate (Elsingspital);[33] John Shawe, vintner;[34] Adam Rous,

---

[28] LMA, SC/GL/ALD/001 and discussed by Barron, 'Chivalry, pageantry and merchant culture', pp. 234–5.

[29] BL, Cotton Nero D vii. I am grateful to Christian Steer for drawing my attention to the London content of this manuscript and we are both grateful to James Clark for a list of the Londoners commemorated within it. For a discussion of the benefactor pictures, see J. G. Clark, 'Thomas Walsingham reconsidered: books and learning at late-medieval St. Albans', *Speculum*, lxxvii (2002), 832–60, at pp. 847–8.

[30] See Steer, 'Souls of benefactors'.

[31] Barron, *London in the Later Middle Ages*, pp. 174 n. 11, 175, 356.

[32] Kentwood also patronized his cathedral and All Souls' College, Oxford (N. Ramsey, 'The library and archives to 1897', in *St Paul's: the Cathedral Church of London 604–2004*, ed. D. Keene, A. Burns and A. Saint (New Haven, Conn. and London, 2004), pp. 413–25, at p. 415).

[33] BL, Cotton Nero Dvii, fo. 108.

[34] LMA, DL/C/B/004/MS09171/002, fos. 378, 381.

surgeon, along with his wives Beatrix and Joanna;[35] William de Bury, fishmonger; and Sabina Semme. In a number of cases lively and engaging images accompany the text. Philipot is represented as a well-dressed, middle-aged man with a neat, pointed beard, holding a bag presumably filled with money.[36] Adam Rous, by contrast (perhaps because he was not a merchant), is shown offering up a sealed document, representing a land endowment, his wives Beatrix and Juliana peering over his shoulder, dainty circlets adorning their respectably veiled heads.[37] Canon Lovekyn is carefully depicted in his clerical dress, proffering a bag.[38] While not portraits and representing only the wealthier strata of society, these images capture something of the diversity of the inhabitants of London in the middle ages.

The people of medieval London were indeed a diverse group, some born in the city and others being drawn from across the realm and far beyond. For some London became the sole focus of their lives, while others retained or developed networks and loyalties that spread far and wide. The rich evidence for the medieval city, including a constant supply of archaeological, material and documentary discoveries, means that the study of London and its inhabitants remains a vibrant field, even if these sources can often be challenging and the men and women we seek to investigate sometimes remain frustratingly elusive. Through the work of Caroline Barron and others, including the contributors to this volume, however, we can catch glimpses of medieval Londoners in all their variety.

---

[35] Adam's second wife Juliana survived him and held a tenement in Dowgate which passed to St. Alban's abbey after her death. For the will of Adam Rous, see LMA, CLA/023/DW/01/108 (13); his inquisition *post mortem* <https://www.british-history.ac.uk/inquis-post-mortem/vol16/pp61-72> [accessed 29 Jan. 2019].

[36] BL, Cotton Nero D vii, fo. 105v.

[37] BL, Cotton Nero D vii, fo. 104v.

[38] BL, Cotton Nero D vii, fo. 108.

I. Londoners in the city

1. Families in later medieval London: sex, marriage and mortality

Vanessa Harding

In the 1970s Caroline Barron and the late Valerie Pearl began to teach an undergraduate paper, 'London: urban society, 1400–1700', as part of the University of London's BA degree in history. After Valerie Pearl left for Cambridge, Caroline reformulated the paper as 'London: urban society, 1400–1600' and continued to teach it until, and even beyond, her retirement. Literally hundreds of students must have taken this paper over the years, including several of the contributors to this volume; some of us have also taught it, either alone or in collaboration with her, and benefited from its wide-ranging approach and content. The syllabus evolved over the years, reflecting changing scholarship and new trends and interests, but its long focus remained, embodying the view that 'medieval London' did not end in 1485 or 1500 or even 1540 and emphasizing that social, political and economic change needed to be considered in perspective as well as in detail. The long view and comparative context are important as we consider 'medieval Londoners' and their characters; and experiences and points of reference well outside the period may not be out of order.

By way of complement to biographical and prosopographical approaches to 'medieval Londoners', this chapter takes a more general look at an important aspect of medieval Londoners' lives: marriage and family, including their demographic chances. It concentrates on Londoners of what would come to be called the 'middling sort': citizens and their families, those who left traces in the records as litigants, testators, parishioners and local officials. All the Londoners studied in this volume lived their lives in the social and demographic realities discussed here; and if some escaped the problems personally, London's close-knit neighbourhoods and communities ensured awareness of others' lives and issues.

The chapter focuses on the family in the period around 1500, partly for reasons of source survival and partly to avoid too generalized a picture. However, the agenda for the enquiry was prompted by looking at a later period, *c*.1700, when marriage and family life were believed to be in some

V. Harding, 'Families in later medieval London: sex, marriage and mortality', in *Medieval Londoners: essays to mark the eightieth birthday of Caroline M. Barron*, ed. E. A. New and C. Steer (London, 2019), pp. 11–36. License: CC-BY-NC-ND 4.0.

kind of crisis.[1] Contemporary writers and more recent historians have singled out for comment a number of problems in the 1690s, ranging from the less serious but indicative – such as declining observance of official marriage requirements – to the more serious ones of marital breakdown and child abandonment, vagrancy and criminality. Crisis in the family was set against, and in part explained by, a sense of crisis in society as a whole.[2] As with other themes such as the social and economic rights of women, the vigour of civic institutions or popular religion, posited decline or crisis in the later sixteenth and seventeenth centuries seems to suppose some more golden period in earlier decades or centuries.[3] But some at least of these issues can be identified in later medieval London, along with a significant level of concern: sexual misconduct; questionable marriage practices; licentious behaviour; irreligion (whether failures of the clergy or heretical beliefs); coupled with seemingly oppressive taxation and concerns about immigration. Was the London family in the early Tudor period any more robust, or less stressed, than in the late Stuart age? Were the circumstances of London life around 1500 more favourable to domestic stability and wellbeing? And were the concerns expressed around 1700 less a sign of particular crisis than a reflection that marriage and the family are always a focus of anxiety and pessimistic commentary?

The documentation for the enquiry is quite rich and varied and the secondary literature extensive. The chapter draws on individual lives, such as those detailed in Caroline Barron's and Anne Sutton's *Medieval London Widows*,[4] and on wills, a particular interest of the honorand of this volume. It benefits enormously from studies using contemporary London church court records, notably by Richard Wunderli and Shannon McSheffrey.[5]

---

[1]   See also V. Harding, 'Families and households in early modern London, *c.*1550–1640', in *The Oxford Handbook of the Age of Shakespeare*, ed. M. Smuts (Oxford, 2017), pp. 596–615.

[2]   G. King, 'Natural and political observations upon the state and condition of England' (1695), in *Seventeenth-Century Economic Documents*, ed. J. Thirsk and J. P. Cooper (Oxford, 1972), pp. 770–84, at p. 777; M. Kitch, 'Capital and kingdom: migration to later Stuart London', in *London 1500–1700: the Making of the Metropolis*, ed. A. L. Beier and R. Finlay (London, 1986), pp. 224–51, at pp. 224–5; R. B. Shoemaker, *Prosecution and Punishment: Petty Crime and the Law in London and Rural Middlesex, c.1660–1725* (Cambridge, 1991), p. 15.

[3]   E.g., A. Vickery, 'Golden age to separate spheres?: a review of the categories and chronology of English women's history', *Hist. Jour.*, xxxvi (1993), 383–414.

[4]   *Medieval London Widows, 1300–1500*, ed. C. M. Barron and A. F. Sutton (London, 1994); also A. F. Sutton, *Wives and Widows of Medieval London* (Donington, 2016).

[5]   R. Wunderli, *London Church Courts and Society on the Eve of the Reformation* (Cambridge, Mass., 1981); *Love and Marriage in Late Medieval London*, ed. S. McSheffrey (Kalamazoo, Mich., 1995); S. McSheffrey, *Marriage, Sex and Civic Culture in Late Medieval London* (Philadelphia, Pa., 2006). See also R. A. Houlbrooke, *Church Courts and the People during the English Reformation* (Oxford, 1979); M. Ingram, *Church Courts, Sex and*

Records of the city's orphanage procedures were another important source.[6]

London in 1500

There are specific features of London's society and economy in the period around 1500 which need to be borne in mind in any consideration of the family and family structures. In the long term, between *c*.1380 and 1550, the framing dates for which we can make population estimates, London's population grew quite substantially, marking a much more positive trend than the country as a whole and the urban sector in general. England's population in the mid sixteenth century may have been at around the same level as in the 1370s, or lower; Alan Dyer's figures for the urban experience suggest that the total population of the fifty-seven largest provincial towns declined by twelve per cent between 1377 and 1524.[7] London, however, had increased in size over the same period. The total population of the city, Southwark and Westminster in 1380 was probably around 40–45,000; in 1550 the population of the built-up area may have been around 60–70,000, possibly as much as 80,000, its probable maximum before the Black Death.[8] It is unlikely that this represents a slow but steady growth over a long period; it is possible that population growth was negligible or even negative until the second half of the fifteenth century, but evidence from rents suggests that it was accelerating quite rapidly before the mid sixteenth century.[9] It seems likely, therefore, that the population of London in 1500 was not much greater than it had been in 1380 – perhaps in the region of 50–55,000 – and it seems fair to assume that the early Tudor city was less crowded than before the Black Death, with more open space between and behind buildings as minor or unlettable properties were allowed to decay.[10]

Marriage in England, 1570–1640 (Cambridge, 1987); L. Giese, *Courtships, Marriage Customs, and Shakespeare's Comedies* (New York and Basingstoke, 2006); and M. Ingram, *Carnal Knowledge: Regulating Sex in England, 1470–1600* (Cambridge, 2017).

[6] *Cal. Letter Bks. L*; C. H. Carlton, *The Court of Orphans* (Leicester, 1974); B. A. Hanawalt, *Growing up in Medieval London: the Experience of Childhood in History* (Oxford, 1993).

[7] A. Dyer, *Decline and Growth in English Towns, 1400–1640* (Basingstoke, 1991), pp. 56–9.

[8] C. M. Barron, *London in the Later Middle Ages: Government and People, 1200–1500* (Oxford, 2004), p. 45; V. Harding, 'The population of London, 1550–1700: a review of the published evidence', *London Jour.*, xv (1990), 111–28.

[9] G. Rosser, *Medieval Westminster, 1250–1540* (Oxford, 1989); *London Bridge: Selected Accounts and Rentals*, ed. V. Harding and L. Wright (London Rec. Soc., xxxi, 1994).

[10] D. Keene, *Cheapside before the Great Fire* (London, 1985); cf. D. J. Keene and V. Harding, *Historical Gazetteer of London Before the Great Fire Cheapside; Parishes of All Hallows Honey Lane, St Martin Pomary, St Mary Le Bow, St Mary Colechurch and St Pancras Soper Lane* (London, 1987), *British History Online* <http://www.british-history.ac.uk/no-series/london-gazetteer-pre-fire> [accessed 31 Oct. 2018].

Although London had begun to spread, it was still a comparatively small and compact city, surrounded by fields and gardens.[11] John Stow's famous recollection of his youth in the 1530s – being sent to fetch milk hot from the cow in Goodman's Fields a few minutes' walk from Aldgate – recorded a London soon to disappear.[12]

Given high urban mortality rates, London's demographic growth depended on migration. In the late fifteenth and sixteenth centuries, young men were flooding to London to take up apprenticeships in the city companies, as the city's employment opportunities expanded. Between 1486 and 1491 the Merchant Taylors' Company, clearly expanding as the London cloth industry grew, enrolled on average sixty-eight apprentices a year; of those whose place of origin can be traced most came from the north Midlands and beyond. Lesser companies may have had smaller recruitment fields, but the range of London's reach is still remarkable.[13] The only surviving city freedom registers for the sixteenth century, for 1551–3, record 1,100 young men entering the freedom of the city in those years, most of whom would have been bound apprentice in the mid 1540s or earlier. Only seventeen per cent came from London or had London fathers; the rest were migrants from the provinces and not predominantly the home counties, either.[14] Despite these numbers, however, London's structures of apprenticeship and guild control offered young male migrants a path to citizenship and establishment, providing training, discipline, a framework of legal protection and the creation of a network of associates and possible patrons. Apprentices were socialized within a paternalistic framework of household order and invested in the ethos of citizenship and civic authority.

Not all migrants necessarily wished, or could afford, to obtain citizenship. The medieval city distinguished between citizens and 'foreigns', the latter comprising both settled Londoners who were not citizens and English migrants who had likewise not become citizens. Foreigns were meant to work in unskilled trades only and were debarred from participation in

---

[11] M. D. Lobel, *The British Atlas of Historical Towns: the City of London from Prehistoric Times to c.1520*, iii (2nd edn., Oxford, 1991). A new edition of the *c.1520* map of London has recently been produced: *A Map of Tudor London: England's Greatest City in 1520* (Historic Towns Trust Town and City Historical Maps, Oxford, 2018).

[12] *A Survey of London by John Stow*, ed. C. L. Kingsford (2 vols., Oxford, 1908), i. 126.

[13] *The Merchant Taylors' Company of London: Court Minutes 1486–93*, ed. M. Davies (Stamford, 2000), pp. 31–4; S. L. Thrupp, *The Merchant Class of Medieval London, 1300–1500* (Ann Arbor, Mich., 1948), pp. 389–92; J. Wareing, 'Changes in the geographical distribution of the recruitment of apprentices to the London companies, 1486–1750', *Jour. Hist. Geog.*, vi (1980), 241–9.

[14] S. Rappaport, *Worlds within Worlds: Structures of Life in Sixteenth-Century London* (Cambridge, 1989), pp. 78–9.

local democracy and administration, though they were not exempt from taxation.[15] In practice, given a shortage of labour in the fifteenth century, many citizen craftsmen employed or worked alongside foreigns, who made an essential contribution to the city's economy.[16] It is often hard to tell whether the ordinary Londoners mentioned in many sources were citizens or not. As London expanded, however, in the late fifteenth and early sixteenth centuries, craft guilds and companies began to police the rules restricting foreigns' activities more closely, complaining in 1494 of the influx of 'Foreyns journeymen' who took their employment without acknowledging guild control.[17] Part of the problem was the high level of the guilds' own entry fees, which deterred men from joining guilds and taking up citizenship. The city perceived the advantages of bringing more of the population into citizenship and, first on its own and then in obedience to acts of parliament in 1531 and 1536, ordered a reduction in entry fees. This seems to have resulted in a major increase in guild membership and citizenship – annual admissions to twelve companies increased by sixty-nine per cent over the next two decades. By the middle of the sixteenth century 'approximately three-quarters of London's men were freemen'.[18]

Women migrants to London are often hard to trace: they did not often obtain apprenticeships and an individual's entry to metropolitan society is not usually recorded. If there was a shortage of labour in fifteenth-century London, it is likely that female migrants would be drawn in to help meet demand and there are some examples of country-born girls apprenticed in London.[19] There were numerous female domestic servants and it would be surprising if many of these were not migrants. But the huge demand for domestic servants that developed in later seventeenth-century London was not yet apparent. Not only was London much smaller, but the traditional

---

[15] *Cal. Letter Bks. L*, p. 156; Rappaport, *Worlds within Worlds*, pp. 31–6.

[16] *Cal. Letter Bks. L*, pp. 203, 295, 302; *Merchant Taylors' Company of London: Court Minutes*, p. 40 and *passim*; *Records of the Worshipful Company of Carpenters*, iii. *Court Book, 1533–1573*, ed. B. Marsh (Oxford, 1915), pp. 12, 15, 16.

[17] *Cal. Letter Bks. L*, pp. 301–2 (quotation) and pp. 254, 284, 291, 294, 298, 306, 308, 312, 319–20; M. Davies, 'Governors and governed: the practice of power in the Merchant Taylors' Company in the fifteenth century', in *Guilds, Society and Economy in London, 1450–1800*, ed. I. A. Gadd and P. Wallis (London, 2002), pp. 67–83, esp. pp. 74–6.

[18] Davies, *Merchant Taylors' Court Minutes*, p. 31; Rappaport, *Worlds within Worlds*, pp. 47–9, 53. By 'London's population', Rappaport seems to have meant the city plus immediate suburbs but not the whole metropolis.

[19] S. Hovland, 'Girls as apprentices in late medieval London', in *London and the Kingdom: Essays in Honour of Caroline M. Barron: Proceedings of the 2004 Harlaxton Symposium*, ed. M. Davies and A. Prescott (Harlaxton Medieval Studies, n.s., xvi, Donington, 2008), pp. 179–94.

family economy of household/workshop production may have limited the need for hired female labour.[20]

Migrants to London were clearly drawn by its opportunity-rich society and economy. In the second half of the fifteenth century London began to capture an increasing proportion of England's export trade, especially in cloth, as this concentrated on the London-Antwerp axis. In 1450 about forty per cent of the wool export trade passed through London and just over forty per cent of cloth exports. By 1500 London was exporting about the same amount of wool, but its annual cloth exports had risen from 17,000 cloths in 1450 to 44,000, a rise of 150 per cent, or nearly sixty per cent of a rapidly rising national total. By 1520 London cloth exports had reached 63,000, or sixty-five per cent of the total; by 1550, at 112,000 cloths a year, they constituted nearly ninety per cent of the country's total. The annual value of London's import trade likewise rose from about £50,000 in the 1470s to c.£80,000 around 1500 and c.£140,000 in the 1530s.[21] Huge fortunes were being made, by London Merchant Adventurers in particular, and if this did not necessarily percolate through London society – since the bulk of the trade was essentially in undyed broadcloths woven outside London – it nevertheless had some impact. By the 1520s London's contribution to direct taxation was ten times that of the next English city, Norwich, and equal to the combined assessment of more than thirty provincial towns.[22]

For the ordinary artisan, the economic situation must also have seemed good. Wages had stabilized at a fairly high level following a century of labour shortage. In the second half of the fifteenth century a craftsman's or labourer's wage bought more than at any time in the sixteenth or seventeenth centuries. And although prices were rising, the drift was gradual: only twenty-two per cent between the 1490s and the early 1540s, or about half

[20] For examples of female servants, see *London Consistory Court Wills, 1492–1547*, ed. I. Darlington (London Rec. Soc., iii. 1967), nos. 6, 7, 37, 114, 118, 130, 161, 178, 183, 184, 228, 232, 238. Cf. P. J. P Goldberg, 'Marriage, migration, and servanthood: the York cause paper evidence', in *Woman is a Worthy Wight: Women in English Society, c.1200–1500*, ed. P. J. P. Goldberg (Stroud, 1992), pp. 1–15; P. J. P. Goldberg, *Women, Work, and Life Cycle in a Medieval Economy: Women in York and Yorkshire, c.1300–1520* (Oxford, 1992), pp. 195–202. Peter Earle argued that the changing nature of both men's and women's employment in the later 17th century increased the need for domestic service (P. Earle, *A City Full of People: Men and Women of London 1650–1750* (London, 1994), pp. 110–3).

[21] *England's Export Trade, 1275–1547*, ed. E. M. Carus-Wilson and O. Coleman (Oxford, 1963); B. Dietz, 'Antwerp and London: the structure and balance of trade in the 1560s', in *Wealth and Power in Tudor England: Essays Presented to S. T. Bindoff*, ed. E. W. Ives, R. J. Knecht and J. J. Scarisbrick (London, 1978), pp. 186–203; B. Dietz, 'Overseas trade and metropolitan growth', in Beier and Finlay, *London 1500–1700*, pp. 114–40.

[22] J. C. K. Cornwall, *Wealth and Society in Early Sixteenth-Century England* (London, 1988), pp. 64–5; Dyer, *Decline and Growth*, pp. 62–3.

a per cent per annum.[23] London wages were normally a quarter to a third higher than in the provinces, an obvious attraction to potential migrants, and this differential was retained even as the population began to grow.[24]

Early Tudor London certainly had its problems. Poverty and disease existed, and vagrancy. In 1518 the aldermen issued 772 licences to beg to people 'so impotent, aged, feeble, or blind that they are not able to get their living by labour and work'.[25] This figure can only represent a portion of the poor, limited to those seeking aid and thought to deserve it, but even so Steve Rappaport thought it indicated a poverty level of about six per cent, significantly less than the ten to twelve per cent indicated by surveys in the mid and late sixteenth century.[26] Henry VII's foundation of the Savoy hospital in 1505 significantly increased hospital provision in London beyond that offered in the still-extant older foundations. It was a fairly generously endowed attempt to deal with both poverty and sickness as social problems: offering accommodation to a hundred poor men, it provided beds, linen, medicines, nursing care and professional medical attendance.[27] Despite being quite well provided with hospitals, London was not a healthy place to live. Mortality is hard to calculate with any certainty and we may underestimate the severity of the late medieval epidemics because they fall between the devastation of the fourteenth-century plagues and the impressive documentation of the plagues of the 1550s and later. Numbers of wills proved – the nearest indication of elevated mortality totals – spiked in 1479, 1498–1501, 1504, 1513, 1518 and 1521.[28] Some of these epidemics were plague, but the sweating sickness first hit England in 1485, recurring in 1508, 1517, 1528 and 1551.[29] We cannot count the dead in these epidemics, but contemporary writings give some sense of the impact of 'pestilence'. The *Great Chronicle* reports that in the 1479–80 epidemic there was 'an huge mortalyte & deth of people ... To the grete mynysshyng of the people of

---

[23] The average daily wage of the London craftsman in the period between 1457 and 1471 was 8*d*, the labourer's 5*d* (Rappaport, *Worlds within Worlds*, pp. 130–1).

[24] Rappaport, *Worlds within Worlds*, p. 85.

[25] *Corporation of London Journal*, 11 (now LMA, COL/CC/01/01/011), fo. 337–8v, quoted by Rappaport, *Worlds within Worlds*, pp. 168–9.

[26] Rappaport, *Worlds within Worlds*, p. 169; see also I. W. Archer, *The Pursuit of Stability: Social Relations in Elizabethan London* (Cambridge, 1991).

[27] C. Rawcliffe, *Medicine and Society in Later Medieval England* (Stroud, 1995), pp. 165, 169, 209–10.

[28] P. Slack, *The Impact of Plague in Tudor and Stuart England* (London, 1985), p. 147, although he warns that 'the inadequacies of the probate evidence prohibit any attempt to measure the severity as well as the frequency of epidemics before 1540' (p. 48).

[29] G. Thwaites, M. Taviner and V. Gant, 'The English sweating sickness, 1485 to 1551', *New England Jour. Med.*, cccxxxvi (1997), 580–2.

all maner of agys'; in 1501 there was again 'grete deth In London and othir partis of this Realm'.[30] Testators referred to 'this present time of sickness' and made fall-back provision in case their appointed executors should not survive.[31] Early Tudor London was not all rosy, but arguably many aspects of life there were better than they were to be one or two centuries later.

Sex and marriage

If the social problems of the 1690s identified by late seventeenth-century commentators were blamed in part on wider economic and moral issues, do the somewhat more favourable conditions of life in London c.1500 mean that it was free from similar problems? Were the prospects for a stable and happy domestic and family life significantly better?

If we start with irregular marriage practices, then these can certainly be found in fifteenth-century London. One seventeenth-century problem was the increasing privacy of marital contracts. Publicity – as in the publication of banns and the performance of the marriage service in the couple's church – was an important safeguard against dubious or irregular marriages and against the possibilities of self-divorce and bigamy. But an increasing number of couples were seeking marriage by licence in the later seventeenth century and there were numerous locations where marriages could be made legally but clandestinely. Literally thousands of couples chose to be married not in their parish church but in one of a handful of privileged parishes or in the liberty of the Fleet. The result was that a person's marital status might be confused and could more easily be concealed and there is plenty of testimony to suggest that this happened.[32]

In early Tudor London irregularities and uncertainties centred on the mismatch between customary practices, legal requirements and the Church's pressure for oversight of all marriages. Customary marriage, in which the right words said anywhere were enough to establish an indissoluble bond, had not yet been universally replaced by Church marriage, in which the making of the contract was supervised and validated by the presence of clergy and community. Consequently, there was some space for dispute about whether a valid marriage had been contracted or not; there were more opportunities for contest, denial and evasion if the marriage had not been solemnized in a church and before reliable witnesses. And as Shannon

---

[30] *The Great Chronicle of London*, ed. A. H. Thomas and I. Thornley (London, 1938), pp. 226, 294.

[31] LMA, DL/C/B/004/MS09171/8, fo. cciii.

[32] J. Boulton, 'Itching after private marryings? Marriage customs in seventeenth-century London', *London Jour.*, xvi (1991), 15–34.

McSheffrey has pointed out, there were 'inherent tensions' between the individual's freedom to contract a binding marriage and 'the societal pressures to marry for family advantage and according to community norms'.[33]

The London church courts heard a number of cases in which the parties sought a ruling on whether a valid marriage existed. Both women and men could be the suitor or complainant. Agnes Whitingdon sued John Ely in 1487. She claimed a valid marriage had been contracted; he said that he had talked about it, but only conditionally, until he knew how much her father (who was not at the time in London) would give her. Agnes's witnesses, on the other hand, testified that he had spoken words of present consent, 'by my faith and troth, ... I take you to my wife', one evening in the shop of Agnes's employer; and further that he had offered her the clothes of his deceased wife and ordered a wedding gown for her.[34] In a case fifteen years earlier Rose Langtoft had contested Robert Smyth's claim that a valid marriage existed between them. According to Robert's witnesses, she spoke the words of consent actually in the sickroom of a neighbour's wife. Rose denied this and brought witnesses to say she could not have been in the place and at the time Robert's witnesses alleged she made the promise because she had not left the shop all afternoon. Subsequently, however, she relented – how willingly we do not know – and admitted she had so spoken and was therefore bound.[35]

Wunderli counted sixty-three 'validation' cases in the commissary court in the three years 1511 to 1513.[36] The numbers are not very great, but the pleadings are suggestive of a wider culture in which the preliminaries to marriage were eminently negotiable and in which serial relationships and perhaps even trial marriages – in the sense of a medium-term sexual relationship – were possible. It may be that a certain degree of flexibility or negotiability was, in fact, necessary and helpful: the declining observance of officially sanctioned marriage practices in the late seventeenth century could have been a reaction to a more rigid system whose assumptions – permanence, non-negotiability, patriarchal authority and economic responsibility, wifely subservience – were not in tune with the realities of

---

[33] McSheffrey, *Marriage, Sex and Civic Culture*, p. 21. For what follows the discussion leans heavily on R. Wunderli's analysis of the church court proceedings in *London Church Courts*; and on S. McSheffrey's useful edition of extracts from the cases in *Love and Marriage*.

[34] McSheffrey, *Love and Marriage*, pp. 56–9; McSheffrey, *Marriage, Sex and Civic Culture*, pp. 40–1.

[35] McSheffrey, *Love and Marriage*, pp. 59–65; McSheffrey, *Marriage, Sex and Civic Culture*, pp. 92–3.

[36] Wunderli, *London Church Courts*, p. 120. See also Giese, *Courtships, Marriage Customs*.

contemporary urban life. Wunderli indeed speculated that some of the validation of marriage suits in the pre-Reformation period might have been 'informal divorce cases from previous spouses', that the parties were seeking to exclude claims based on a prior relationship by obtaining a ruling that a valid marriage existed with the present partner.[37]

Formal divorce was nevertheless impossible if a valid contract existed.[38] Because marriage had to be entered into freely, the allegation of compulsion was grounds to query its validity. In 1475 William Rote sought an annulment of his contract with Agnes Wellys because he said he had been forced into it at dagger-point by her angry father.[39] It is not clear whether, in fact, he managed to have the contract annulled, but it seems hardly likely to have been a successful marriage. Only a small number of cases relate to the breakdown of unquestionably valid marriages – culminating in the expulsion of a wife from the matrimonial home or the formal suit (by the wife) for separation on grounds of cruelty. A wife had to be in justifiable fear of her life to obtain the court's backing in such cases, but Eleanor Brownynge seems to have been able to demonstrate this. She was threatened once by her husband in a tavern in Lombard Street with a dagger and a witness said she jumped 'the length of four men' to escape from him. On a later occasion he pursued her down the street, brandishing a dagger and threatening to kill her. She was wearing only her tunic and had her hair loose and streaming behind her, suggesting a domestic dispute that had escalated out of control. Under these circumstances, although the courts could not divorce the couple they could enjoin a legal separation and ensure that the wife received at least some of the assets of the marriage.[40]

While the church court records cannot show, or at least not directly, how many people, finding themselves in unbearable but indissoluble marriages, simply walked away from them, as they may have done in the seventeenth century,[41] there is certainly evidence for marital disharmony and alienated affections. A large number of suits brought before the church courts in the late middle ages concerned adultery, sexual relations between a married woman and another man. Numbers varied by year, but the commissary

---

[37] Wunderli, *London Church Courts*, pp. 120–1.

[38] Wunderli, *London Church Courts*, pp. 121–2.

[39] McSheffrey, *Love and Marriage*, pp. 81–2; McSheffrey, *Marriage, Sex and Civic Culture*, pp. 1–4.

[40] McSheffrey, *Love and Marriage*, pp. 82–3; McSheffrey, *Marriage, Sex and Civic Culture*, pp. 140–1.

[41] F. Dabhoiwala, 'The pattern of sexual immorality in seventeenth and eighteenth-century London', in *Londinopolis: Essays in the Social and Cultural History of Early Modern London*, ed. P. Griffiths and M. Jenner (Manchester, 2000), pp. 86–106.

court heard 506 adultery cases in the two years 1471 to 1472, 603 in eighteen months in 1492 to 1493. Not all of these came from metropolitan London, but the great majority did. The number of cases relative to the population of London seems quite high – in a city of approximately 40–50,000 people around 1500 there could have been 12–15,000 married couples – and obviously by no means all instances of adultery led to prosecution. Adultery cases formed a higher proportion of all cases in London than in the rural deaneries of Middlesex and Barking.[42] It seems to have been a common belief that the presence of foreigners (often single males travelling on some kind of business) and the numerous unemployed or underemployed clergy who thronged London made a significant contribution to the level of illicit sexual activity in the city. The fifteenth-century visitation articles of the bishop or ordinary included the pessimistic enquiry, 'whether the parson, vicar or chaplains ... be incontinent or defamed with any woman, namely with any wedded woman, or have in parsonage or any other house, woman suspect'.[43] Priests were indeed quite often in the dock, though it appears that the church courts were more lenient with them than the secular courts, which were also taking a hand in such cases.

Wunderli shows that although adultery cases 'flooded the court' in the late fifteenth century, conviction rates were low. Conviction entailed the enforcement of punishment, penance and/or compensation or child support, but even if few were convicted, adultery prosecutions served a social purpose. Norms and sanctions had been declared and their observation probably supported. It is notable that not all adultery suits were instance cases brought by the injured party: some were brought by neighbours or instituted on grounds of common fame, again suggesting that it was collective norms, not just the rights of a particular spouse, that were at issue.[44]

Fornication was not such a serious 'crime', but the victim, if any, was again society; it was usually society that prosecuted. A few couples were apparently reported for having sex between making a marriage contract and solemnizing it in church. This seems to have been a 'crime' created by the Church's increasing insistence on solemnization in church as the critical event in making a marriage.[45] More common, however, was fornication between couples who had no intention of marrying. Some long-term

[42] Wunderli, *London Church Courts*, pp. 84–8.

[43] *The Customs of London, Otherwise Known as Arnold's Chronicle: Containing, among Divers Other Matters, the Original of the Celebrated Poem of The Nut-brown Maid*, ed. F. Douce (London, 1811), p. 274.

[44] Wunderli, *London Church Courts*, pp. 84–8.

[45] McSheffrey, *Love and Marriage*, pp. 84–5; McSheffrey, *Marriage, Sex and Civic Culture*, pp. 113, 160–1.

relationships between priests and women – concubinage or living in sin, rather than casual sexual encounters – also came to light. But fornication prosecutions were only about half as common as adultery suits: in 1471–2 there were 266 fornication cases as opposed to 506 adultery; in 1492–3, 263 fornication as opposed to 603 adultery. Conviction rates were again low, though higher than for adultery, perhaps because more of the accused were prepared to confess.[46] However, while 'respectable' Londoners clearly used the courts and legal processes to help enforce communal norms, it does not appear that it was the middling sort imposing their moral judgment on the poor, as may have been the case in the seventeenth-century reformation of manners campaigns.[47] Paupers, in fact, were rarely prosecuted in these courts; and while there was certainly strong sanction against insulting or slandering the city's rulers, people of many ranks were accused of sexual misconduct: citizens, merchants and even an alderman.[48]

The wardmote inquest was an important forum in which sexual misdemeanours came to light and it shows us the level of local interest in the activities of neighbours. The articles of the inquest, recorded in the early fifteenth century, required the jury to present 'any woman of lewd life or common scold or common bawd or courtesan ... resident in the ward'.[49] The wardmen of Aldersgate responded in 1510 with a string of complaints against Nicholas Browne for keeping misrule in his house, both men and women. They claimed that his wife was a 'mis-woman of her body', that priests and courtiers resorted to his house at unlawful hours in the night and that he kept a 'quen' (quean, harlot) in his house. They presented Lovington's wife for keeping a married woman in her house to whom Laurence Micholl, a married man, resorted. Master Swafield – a name that implies some social standing – was suspected of keeping ill rule in his own house with a certain woman with whom he had had an illegitimate child some time previously. Stephen Watts was said to have two wives, one in Cornwall and the other in the parish of St. Anne Aldersgate.[50] These accusations run the gamut

---

[46] Wunderli, *London Church Courts*, pp. 88–92, 144–5.

[47] Shoemaker, *Prosecution and Punishment*, pp. 238–72; cf. M. Spufford, 'Puritanism and social control', in *Order and Disorder in Early Modern England*, ed. A. Fletcher and J. Stevenson (Cambridge, 1985), pp. 41–57.

[48] Wunderli, *London Church Courts*, p. 44; McSheffrey, *Love and Marriage*, pp. 84–8.

[49] *Liber Albus: the White Book of the City of London, compiled A.D. 1419, by J. Carpenter, Common Clerk, R. Whitington, Mayor*, ed. H. T. Riley (London, 1861), pp. 290–2. Cf. *CPMR 1413–37*, pp. 117–41, pp. 150–9. See also Wunderli, *London Church Courts*; C. E. Berry, 'Margins and marginality in fifteenth-century London' (unpublished University of London PhD thesis, 2018).

[50] *The Records of Two City Parishes: a Collection of Documents Illustrative of the History of SS. Anne and Agnes, Aldersgate, and St. John Zachary, London, from the Twelfth Century*, ed. W. McMurray (London, 1925), pp. 29–30.

from misrule to professional bawdry, from bastard-bearing to bigamy. Presentments made at the wardmote could be taken up as office cases in the church courts but, as noted above, it is unlikely that many, let alone all, of these offences were successfully prosecuted.

Another source of evidence was simple gossip and tale-bearing. John Palmer happened upon William Stevenes and Juliana Saunder in bed one afternoon in August 1471 and told the story to the parish chaplain, to the holy-water clerk of the church, to the priest of another parish, the wardmote inquest 'and others'; and he may also have deposed in writing to the commissary court. But prosecution sparked by ill fame is complemented by the other great business of the church courts, defamation and especially sexual slander, and in fact John Palmer came to court as defendant in a slander case brought by William Stevenes, not as a prosecutor.[51] Common fame or rumour was a real, almost tangible thing that in itself justified interference or even indictment, but, equally, individuals could defend their own fame by bringing prosecutions for slander against those who spread ill-reports of them. Laura Gowing has illuminated the world of sexual slander in Elizabethan London;[52] the contest between honour and defamation was still very much a part of London life in the later seventeenth century, but it was already an active area in the fifteenth.

Defamatory words had in principle to be spoken maliciously and against someone not already of ill fame; and to accuse him or her of a crime or punishable offence. Sexual slanders made up a high proportion of cases: in 1493, 116 of 143 defamation cases were wholly or partly centred on sexual slanders. Plaintiffs cited what may seem casual insults shouted in the street – 'strong whore', 'strong harlot', 'priest's whore' – and more detailed and specific accusations – 'this is where you did it', 'you have a child in your belly if ever I had one' – and, of course, the gossipers. A woman accused in this way was literally devalued in the marriage market, while a man was defamed if his wife was accused of bawdry or adultery, as much as if he himself were.[53] Defamation cases illustrate the interaction of a number of issues: the importance of a person's name and public perception; the construction of a woman's honour as primarily sexual and of a man's as encompassing the sexual behaviour of his wife; the sometimes aggressive moral surveillance of neighbours, arising from the sense of a common ownership of moral values;

---

[51] McSheffrey, *Love and Marriage*, pp. 87–8; McSheffrey, *Marriage, Sex and Civic Culture*, p. 152.

[52] L. Gowing, *Domestic Dangers: Women, Words and Sex in Early Modern London* (Oxford, 1996).

[53] Wunderli, *London Church Courts*, pp. 76–80, 90; McSheffrey, *Love and Marriage*, pp. 86–7.

and what Wunderli refers to as 'pre-Reformation Londoners' ... great ... concern ... with sexual norms and sexual misbehaviour'.[54]

The high proportion of sexual misdemeanours and sexual slanders among the cases heard by the church courts in late medieval London could be interpreted as evidence of a society in moral disarray in which standards were lax and misconduct common; or as one successfully policing itself. The latter seems more likely; and that these prosecutions served a useful purpose in proclaiming and supporting moral norms without, it would appear, being overly punitive or repressive. A large number of cases were inconclusive; convicted offenders were appropriately but not severely punished. Public penance, compensation and apology allowed the contrite to purge an offence and resume normal life. Londoners used the legal options available to them in a number of instrumental ways, exploiting the process to their own ends to confirm a marriage, exclude rival claims and assert their honour against impeachment.

However, the church courts dealt also with more professional forms of sexual misconduct. Casual fornication and adultery shaded into bawdry and prostitution. In defamation cases it is not clear whether calling someone a whore implied she was a common prostitute or just unchaste, but in some cases specific allegations of procuring and prostitution had been made. The city's wardmote articles obviously assumed a connection, or perhaps a slippery slope, between individual unchastity and professional prostitution, indicting 'any woman of lewd life or common scold or common bawd or courtesan'.[55] The city's leaders believed that professional prostitutes contaminated ordinary people. In a vehement proclamation against 'the stynkyng and horrible Synne of Lechery' in 1483, they charged 'Strumpettes mysguyded and idil women daily vagraunt and walkyng about by the streetes and lanes of this said Citee of London and suburbes of the same' with 'provokyng many othere persones unto the said Synne of Lechery'. Men and women heretofore 'weldisposed, daily fall to the said myschevous and horrible Synne'.[56]

These are strong words – and it is not the only time they are used – but in fact the prosecution of pimps and prostitutes seems to reveal the limits of moral policing in the metropolitan context. The church courts were notably unsuccessful either in obtaining convictions or in changing behaviour. Wunderli notes that of 1,030 individuals charged with procurement or bawdry in select years between 1471 and 1513, only seven confessed, but

---

[54] Wunderli, *London Church Courts*, p. 80.
[55] Riley, *Liber Albus*, pp. 290–2.
[56] *Cal. Letter Bks. L*, p. 206.

a larger number were suspended or excommunicated for contumacy. Prosecution of prostitutes was hardly more successful. Only ten prostitutes confessed out of 377 accused.[57] Wunderli's description of the life of pimp and prostitute Mariona Wood, frequently charged but never in practice inhibited from plying her trade in Portsoken over seventeen years, indicates how ineffective the court's sanctions were.[58] Contemporaries and, indeed, the seventeenth-century moralists might have characterized her as immoral and incorrigible; modern readers might consider economic necessity, desperation or a lack of alternatives as part of the picture. Wunderli argues that the high failure rate of prosecutions in the church courts may indicate that Londoners were turning to secular courts to police sexual offences,[59] but perhaps they merely felt that having denounced bad characters to the wardmote inquest they had done their bit and the responsibility now lay elsewhere. Nevertheless, when someone was punished, it was exemplary and seemingly memorable. The *Great Chronicle* recorded in February 1500 that a flax-wife named Margaret Clitherow was set in the pillory in Cornhill for a common bawd 'and aftir banished the toun for evyr'.[60]

The city on the whole preferred to export troublemakers rather than reform them. Its remedy for the plague of strumpets was to drive them from the city and to forbid anyone to harbour them. In effect, they marginalized the problem and, as is well known, the suburbs of London harboured numerous stews and brothels, from Cock Lane in the west to Portsoken in the east and especially south of the river. There were eighteen or more stewhouses or brothels in Southwark in 1506 and the bishop of Winchester's court- and pipe-rolls of the turn of the century record numerous presentations and fines – effectively, licences to operate – of stewholders, pimps and singlewomen.[61] The *Great Chronicle* records that in 1506 'the stews or common bordell beyond the water, for what hap or consideration the certainty I know not, was for a season inhibited and closed up. But it was not long before they were set open again'.[62] Southwark remained a place of sexual opportunity and ill fame and a source of complaint and anxiety to the city, but, as the final closure of the stews in 1546 demonstrated, metropolitan prostitution was not to be suppressed by edict or ordinary prosecution.

[57] Wunderli, *London Church Courts*, pp. 100–1, 146–7.

[58] Wunderli, *London Church Courts*, p. 99.

[59] Wunderli, *London Church Courts*, pp. 101–2.

[60] Thomas and Thornley, *Great Chronicle*, p. 289.

[61] M. Carlin, *Medieval Southwark* (London, 1996), pp. 209–19; J. B. Post, 'A fifteenth-century customary of the Southwark stews', *Jour. Soc. Archivists*, v (1977), 418–28. Cf. R. M. Karras, *Common Women: Prostitution and Sexuality in Medieval England* (Oxford, 1996).

[62] Thomas and Thornley, *Great Chronicle*, p. 331.

Early Tudor Londoners' sexual lives and marital relations were, therefore, as complicated as in any era, but problems, it appears, were contained. There was widespread respect for marriage and observance of its restrictions, as well as acknowledgement of authority, both domestic and civic. Norms were proclaimed and sometimes enforced, but the system had many loopholes. Concern about sexual misdemeanours and some enthusiasm for policing the behaviour of others were accompanied and moderated by readiness to compromise and seek conciliation – or, in the case of prostitution, by reluctance to push the process to the utmost.

Mortality

In the fifteenth century as well as in the seventeenth, however, human agency was not the only factor shaping the experience of marriage and family life. The harsh realities of disease and death were constantly reshaping the metropolitan population. Even when marriages were comparatively happy and settled, they were still fragile and often short-lived and the likelihood of bringing a whole family of offspring to adulthood – or of living to see that – was limited.

Despite recurrences of the sweating sickness and plague, London in 1500 was probably a safer place to live than it was in 1700, when both had disappeared. It seems probable that from 1540 to the 1640s 'at least in the absence of plague London may have been able to maintain a balanced demography' in that, epidemics apart, births matched or occasionally exceeded deaths, though probably not by a great deal.[63] This 'balanced' phase probably began much earlier than 1540. The historical demographer Roger Finlay pointed to evidence for deteriorating life expectancy in London over the course of the seventeenth century.[64] Explosive population growth entailed increased settlement densities, more overcrowding and poorer accommodation and environmental quality, but a range of other factors also contributed: increasing levels of poverty; the susceptibility of migrants to urban diseases; child-care practices such as wet-nursing; perhaps also health policies in relation to plague. Changing patterns of disease must also be considered, as smallpox and respiratory diseases became major killers, the latter plausibly linked to deteriorating air quality.

In the late seventeenth century, for every well-recorded long-term marriage – immortalized on monuments or by contemporaries or descendants – there

---

[63] C. Galley, *The Demography of Early Modern Towns: York in the Sixteenth and Seventeenth Centuries* (Liverpool, 1998), pp. 16–7.

[64] R. Finlay, *Population and Metropolis: the Demography of London 1580–1650* (Cambridge, 1981), p. 109.

were numerous unions cut short by death and often leaving no descent. We cannot calculate the duration of most marriages before the advent of parochial registration in 1538, but there is plenty of evidence for turnover: testators who mention two or more spouses; individual cases where a sequence of marriages is documented; more tangentially the evidence of the city's orphanage court. The case studies in Caroline Barron's and Anne Sutton's *Medieval London Widows* included women who married two, three or even four times and some of these marriages were very brief. Thomasyne Percyvale's first marriage, for example, probably lasted not more than three or four years; her second, less than a year, though her third lasted over thirty years.[65] In a sample of fifty-five wills of Londoners proved in the commissary court of London in 1499–1500, at least five male testators had been married more than once. It is possible that the numbers of second or third marriages were higher, since it is not always clear whether a reference is to a deceased wife or wives and some deceased spouses may simply have been omitted.[66] Remarriage, if it took place, was often quite speedy: Barbara Hanawalt found that over half of citizens' widows with under-age children (subject, therefore, to the jurisdiction of the city's court of orphans) between 1309 and 1458 had remarried by the time they came before the court to give surety for their children's estates, usually within a year.[67] John Bishop buried his wife in the Pardon Churchyard of St. Dunstan in the East in late 1495; before midsummer 1496 'John Byschoppe's odyr wyffe' was buried there too.[68] Though remarriage was frequent, widowhood could be a very long-term state. The married life of some of Barron's and Sutton's medieval London widows formed only a short fraction of their life span. Thirteen widows experienced on average twenty-six years of widowhood; five were widows for over thirty years; and one for as long as fifty-nine years.[69] Widows certainly formed a significant proportion of London's population in the fifteenth century, as they did in the seventeenth.

One feature resulting in part from the short duration of many marriages was an overall low fertility rate. Even with speedy remarriage – which cannot always have been the case – a woman's childbearing potential was interrupted and the survival of children who lost a father or mother must have been compromised. In the seventeenth century the statistician Gregory

---

[65] Barron and Sutton, *Medieval London Widows*, esp. M. Davies, 'Dame Thomasine Percyvale, "The Maid of Week" (d. 1512)', pp. 185–206; A. F. Sutton, 'Serious money: the benefits of marriage in London, 1400–1499', *London Jour.*, xxxviii (2013), 1–17.

[66] LMA, DL/C/B/004/MS09171/008, fos. 183–207.

[67] Hanawalt, *Growing up in Medieval London*, p. 96.

[68] LMA, P69/DUN1/B/001/MS04887, fo. 9v et. seqq.

[69] Barron and Sutton, *Medieval London Widows*, passim.

King noted that 'each marriage in London produceth fewer people than in the country'. He attributed this in part to 'the more frequent fornications and adulteries' and 'a greater luxury and intemperance', as well as 'a greater intenseness of business', implying that this was in some way a moral failure, not just a natural consequence of urban mortality. His conclusion, however – and the tone in which he expressed it – echoed the lament of William Caxton that 'in this noble cyte of london it [a family name and lineage] can unnethe contynue unto the thryd heyre or scarcely to the second', even though in other cities families could trace their lineage back 'for v or vi hondred yere and somme a thousand'.[70]

Although examples of large families are easily found in wills, memorials and orphanage cases, individual chances of survival were evidently low. Levels of infant mortality are impossible to trace before the age of baptismal registration, but the urban penalty – increased mortality in even quite modest centres of population – means that they were unlikely to be significantly better than those prevailing a century later, when nearly half of all children born in London did not survive to age fifteen.[71]

Wills are not a reliable source for assessing medieval child mortality, though quite a few do mention the burial-place of 'my children'. But we can obtain some impression of the scale of mortality from parish accounts, at least in those parishes where the parish received something for all or most burials. In the single surviving lightwardens' account for St. Andrew Holborn parish for 1477–8, twenty-eight burials are noted, possibly a little low for a parish of that size. At least ten of these were children: Arnold's child, Herry Prank's child, Milnepelle's son, the weaver's child in Gray's Inn Lane.[72] In St. Dunstan in the East the churchwardens' accounts for 1498–9 record payments for five adult burials and four children: three fathers paid to bury their children in the Pardon Churchyard and a fourth for a torch for the burial of his child. In 1500–1 eleven adult burials are recorded and five children. One of the fathers, Master Ysak (Isaac), paid also for a four-hour knell of the great bell at 3s 4d. Isaac buried another child in 1502–3; and Master Tate, who had buried one child in 1500–1, buried his eldest son in 1501–2.[73] Longer runs of accounts also show the repeated toll on individual

[70] *The Prologues and Epilogues of William Caxton*, ed. W. J. B. Crotch (Early English Text Soc., o.s., clxxvi, London, 1928), pp. 77–8.

[71] R. Finlay and B. Shearer, 'Population growth and suburban expansion', in Beier and Finlay, *London 1500–1700*, pp. 37–59, at pp. 49–50.

[72] C. M. Barron and J. Roscoe, 'The medieval parish church of St Andrew Holborn', *London Topographical Record*, xxiv (1980), 31–60, at pp. 56–7.

[73] LMA, P69/DUN1/B/001/MS04887, fo. 9v et seqq. Not all burials were liable for a fee, so the actual totals must be higher.

families. The records of St. Mary at Hill, which seem to be very full, noted that John Clerk or Clark buried a daughter in 1477–9 and three children in 1487–8. Harry Vavasour buried a child in 1489; his wife paid for the burial of a son and one of his servants in 1492–3. John Awthorpe, churchwarden in 1501–2, recorded the receipt of 6s 'of me, John Awthope, for the burial of 3 of myn owne chyldryn'.[74]

The inevitability of child mortality was implicitly acknowledged in the differential charges parishes made for burying them. Their smaller bodies took up less room and it was common to charge half the adult rate for the laystalls or burial-places of children. In 1498–9 St. Mary at Hill determined that the clerk should receive 8d for making a grave in their Pardon Churchyard for a man and 4d for a child.[75] St. Mary Woolchurch charged half price in church for children and 4d, as opposed to 6d, in the churchyard;[76] St. Martin Outwich in 1545 set its rate for a grave at 8d for adults and 4d for 'Innocents'.[77] St. Mary at Hill also authorized the clerk to take 4d for a knell of the little bell for a child and 8d for an adult, but St. Mary Woolchurch charged 4d for a knell of the least bell 'for man woman or child'.[78] But the fact that we do have records of children's burial in more privileged places, or with lights, torches and bells, demonstrates that even a high rate of child mortality did not lead to indifference or casual disregard.

Records of the city's orphanage procedures offer a complementary perspective on survival rates. For the fourteenth and fifteenth centuries together, Barbara Hanawalt calculated that of 631 city orphans whose fate is known, thirty-three per cent died under age.[79] Of eight children orphaned in 1495, for example, only five survived to adulthood. Elias and Elena, orphans of Richard Bodley, late grocer, came of age or married, but their brother John died under age; Richard and Alice, orphans of Richard Dakers, late tailor, survived, but their sister Elizabeth died; Agnes, daughter of William Tenacres, survived and inherited her brother William's share of their father's estate when he died under age.[80] Fathers often – with pessimistic realism – provided for the possibility that their heirs might die under age, arranging that the children should be each other's heir, or that a proportion of a deceased child's legacy should be devoted to pious uses. Henry Patenson left

[74] *Medieval Records of a London City Church*, ed. H. Littlehales (Early English Text Soc., o.s., cxxviii, London, 1905), pp. 78, 128, 146, 183, 245.

[75] Littlehales, *Medieval Records of a London City Church*, p. 231.

[76] BL, Harley MS. 2252, fo. 164.

[77] LMA, P69//MTN3/B/004/MS06842, fo. 3 et seqq.

[78] *Medieval Records of a London City Church*, p. 231; BL, Harley MS. 2252, fo. 163.

[79] Hanawalt, *Growing up in Medieval London*, p. 57.

[80] *Cal. Letter Bks. L*, pp. 314–5.

his daughter Elizabeth 10 marks for her marriage; if she died under age, it was to go to her brother, but if he too died under age Henry's wife Elizabeth was to have half and spend the remainder on a chalice and paten to be given to Our Lady of Walsingham for prayers.[81]

The end result of this mortality of children, as Caxton noted, was that London's population – and he surely meant the established, noteworthy families – was not reproducing itself in the male line. Family names died out, something that is easily visible in lists of aldermen, for example. Sylvia Thrupp calculated that medieval London merchants – surely the most favoured class demographically – left on average only one direct male heir and that fewer than eighty-five per cent of these lived long enough to have a chance of reproducing themselves.[82] Of 141 lay testators in the consistory court of London in the early to mid sixteenth century, only forty per cent mentioned their own children in their testaments.[83] It is possible that fewer than half of all marriages resulted in surviving offspring. London was growing between 1450 and 1550 by migration and not by natural increase.

Consideration of the family in medieval or early modern London has to take account of the immense impact of migration. The influx of young men skewed the age- and sex-distribution of the capital's population considerably and the large numbers of apprentices contributed to problems of order. Apprentices participated in anti-alien riots in the fifteenth century and in the disturbances of Evil May Day in 1517 (when their targets included brothels).[84] But they were firmly – if not inescapably – bound into structures of authority and patriarchal discipline and integrated into the households of their masters. And in a society that was hardly producing enough children of its own, they filled both an economic and an emotional need.

A great many men and women in later medieval London had no lineal descendants to whom to pass their skills and business capital and needed to find other ways of transmitting them to the next generation. It is not surprising that other kinds of relationship – collateral descent, kinship and apprenticeship – figured largely in the inter-generational transmission of skills and capital. The most significant of these was the master-apprentice one, a surrogate father-son relationship explicitly centred on the transmission of skills and work opportunity. More common than the bequest of tools and goods to any family member was the bequest to a servant or apprentice. Often a widow inherited and continued her late husband's business; she

---

[81] LMA, DL/C/B/004/MS09171/008, fo. 197v.

[82] Thrupp, *Merchant Class of Medieval London*, pp. 199–200, 203.

[83] Darlington, *London Consistory Court Wills, passim.*

[84] Thomas and Thornley, *Great Chronicle*, p. 188; D. Wilson, 'Evil May Day 1517', *History Today*, lxvii (2017), 66–71.

would then be the one to pass it on to the apprentice. One widow specified that her apprentice be allowed to choose his own master and to have the shop, tools and his chamber for a year; another left the apprentice the use of her house and hangings. And apprentices were often held in affection, bequeathed personal goods other than tools and in many ways regarded as inheriting the persona of the deceased master.[85] Members of the family in the sense of the household unit, they also became part of the family in a more literal sense. Henry Lussher left 10 marks 'in good and sufficient wares' to 'John Dane which was my apprentice and now is my servant and to Alice Rumbold daughter to my wife if they be complet together as man and wife in way of marriage'.[86] John Robotom, draper, left 20s to each of his six children under age and 20s to his apprentice when he came out of his years. All the residue, including presumably his stock, debts and other capital, he left to his wife Dorothy.[87] Just a year after his death, however, Dorothy, apparently by then some three months pregnant, married the former apprentice, now himself a master.[88]

Parents lost children, but, as already implied, children lost parents, too. Many wills indicate that the children named were under age; and the city's court of orphans had an important role to play in safeguarding the inheritance and wellbeing of the children of deceased citizens. The court's very existence was an acknowledgement of the fragility of life and that many fathers would not see their children grow to adulthood. Thrupp calculated that of ninety-seven merchants who died between 1448 and 1520, the median age at death was forty-nine to fifty.[89] Since a man could not marry until he came out of his apprenticeship, normally in his mid twenties, and would probably not have done so immediately, it is very likely that some of his children – if he had any – would still be under twenty-one by the time he reached fifty.

The under-age or unmarried children of a deceased citizen came under the protection of the common serjeant, who inventoried their inheritance, committed it and the children to one or more guardians and took bonds for the repayment of the estate when the children should come of age or marry. Orphanage business takes up an enormous amount of the city's

[85] V. Harding, 'Sons, apprentices, and successors in late medieval and early modern London: the transmission of skills and work opportunities', in *Generations in Towns*, ed. F.-E. Eliassen and K. Szende (Cambridge, 2009), pp. 53–68.

[86] LMA, DL/C/B/004/MS09171/008, fo. 200v.

[87] Darlington, *London Consistory Court Wills*, no. 237.

[88] *The Parish Registers of St Michael Cornhill, 1546–1754*, ed. J. L. Chester (Harleian Soc., Register Section, vii, 1882), pp. 5, 74.

[89] Thrupp, *Merchant Class of Medieval London*, p. 194.

recorded activity, since bonds and custody awards were regularly registered in the city's main record books, the *Letter Books*. Between 1470 and 1497 the aldermen dealt with orphanage matters on 315 occasions (relating to perhaps a hundred families); between 1500 and 1530 they accepted 620 recognizances (relating to perhaps 300 families). The pressure of business is reflected in the establishment in 1492 of a formal annual meeting to review and reaffirm the sureties for the orphans' estates.[90] Orphans were often committed to their mother, with or without a second husband. In due course, either the orphan himself or a female orphan's husband acknowledged receipt of the inheritance. The situation offered opportunities for exploitation, either of the inheritance or of the child, but the city was a fairly careful guardian. Children could not be made wards of someone in the line of inheritance, who might have an interest in their death. It was forbidden to marry a city orphan without the city's permission, presumably to prevent heirs being forced into disadvantageous and exploitative contracts and simple misalliance.[91] The majority of marriages sanctioned by the city for the daughters of deceased merchants were to men of the merchant class or above.[92]

Paternal anxiety is expressed, not only in provision for the deaths of some or all of the children but in identifying a suitable guardian or in charging the widow to look after them. Henry Elveden noted in 1498 that he and his wife Joyce had three children 'of our twey bodies lawfully begotten' in nine years of marriage (though only two seem to have survived): he desired Joyce to be 'specially good mother to [them], to help them after her power'.[93] Most men with under-age children left a widow, even if she was not the children's mother; in some cases there was an adult brother or sister who may have been expected to take an interest. Because married women so rarely made wills, we have little sense of their emotions on leaving their children to the care of their father or even to a stepfather. Elinor Fynimor (d. 1500) probably expected her parents, both of whom were still alive, to take care of her son, to whom she left the residue of her goods 'to find him to school'. She did not call herself a widow or mention a husband, which could imply that she was unmarried, in which case the choice of parents seems natural.[94]

Comparatively few widow testators seem to have left underage children, which may be an indication of the likelihood, even necessity, of remarriage

[90] Carlton, *Court of Orphans*, pp. 20, 25, 36.
[91] Carlton, *Court of Orphans*, pp. 18–19. Cf. *Cal. Letter Bks. I*, p. 141.
[92] Thrupp, *Merchant Class of Medieval London*, p. 28.
[93] LMA, DL/C/B/004/MS09171/008, fo. 192v.
[94] LMA, DL/C/B/004/ MS09171/008, fo. 199.

for such women. As Hanawalt noted, use of the child's patrimony while it was under age would certainly have been an attraction to a second husband.[95] Dying husbands rarely took steps to impede their wife's remarriage and city companies probably encouraged widows to remarry within the craft to maintain its solidarity and wealth. But it may in any case have been that young widowed mothers, whose children were under the supervision of the court of orphans, did not need to make a will for the settlement of their estate.

One striking phenomenon in seventeenth-century London was the large number of single-parent households. In one parish in 1695, for example, St. Katherine Coleman, there were numerous partial or broken families. Fifteen households with children were headed by widows or single women and three by single men, while fourteen widows or single women lodgers and two single male lodgers had children. Single parents made up over twenty per cent of all parents.[96] This was well above the mean for the city as a whole, but there is a strong likelihood that single parenthood was an increasing feature of city life in the seventeenth century as marriages fractured or dissolved under stress and remarriage became less common. There is no comparable source for the 1490s, but it seems unlikely that this was such a problem then. It seems rare for widowed men and women, at least of the middling or citizen sort, to remain single for long if they had young children. Either they remarried or, perhaps equally often, the child or children may not have survived.

Another problem in the late seventeenth century that may be specific to that period was child abandonment. This was probably a long-running issue in early modern London, but it seemed to be spiralling out of control in the 1680s and 1690s: Valerie Fildes estimated that approximately 1,000 children a year were abandoned in London in the 1690s. This huge problem seems to have been the result of increasing poverty, broken families (warfare made a serious contribution) and the stresses of urban life.[97] Though neither poverty nor distress was absent from London in 1500, if the capital was both economically buoyant and struggling to reproduce itself there may not have been so many unwanted births. There seems also to have been a culture of

---

[95] Hanawalt, *Growing up in Medieval London*, p. 96.

[96] LMA, COL/CHD/LA/04/01/042. See also D. V. Glass, 'Introduction', in *London Inhabitants Within the Walls* (London Rec. Soc., ii. 1966), pp. ix–xxxvii. For further analyses, see P. Baker and M. Merry, '"For the house, herself and one servant": family and household in late seventeenth-century London', *London Jour.*, xxxiv (2009), 205–32.

[97] V. Fildes, 'Maternal feelings re-assessed: child abandonment and neglect in London and Westminster, 1550–1800', in *Women as Mothers in Pre-industrial England: Essays in Memory of Dorothy McLaren*, ed. V. Fildes (London, 1990), pp. 139–78.

care, perhaps because the problem was manageable. Londoners internalized the Church's exhortation to perform works of corporal mercy and to care for the widow and orphan; and it is striking how many instances of effective adoption of poor children or alms children are brought up in even a brief trawl of wills and biographies. John Clovier in 1495 left a pair of sheets and 6s 8d to 'a young child found by me of alms called after my name';[98] Thomas Portar left 3s 4d to 'my poor child' in 1500.[99] The anonymity of these children is perhaps a little chilling, but the wealthy widow Alice Claver (d. 1489) left 40s each to Alice 'my mayde that was gevyn me to find of almes' and Edward 'whom I find in almes for Goddis sake called my childe'.[100] Thomasyne Percyvale was bringing up five such children at the time she made her will in 1503. The boys were to be educated for the Church or apprenticed; the girls were to be bound to good masters at the age of fourteen, but in the meantime, all were to be provided with 'mete drynk and lernyng'.[101]

Crisis or coping?

The issues discussed above – marital irregularities, sexual misconduct, the mortality of parents and children – might well suggest that the family in London was under quite serious stress in 1500. But in most of these cases it appears that the problem was limited or mitigated in some way. The family provided a flexible and enduring structure in London society; and late medieval Londoners responded to the strains under which they lived by strengthening the connections that existed and forging new relationships. 'Family values' cannot be equated with a hard-and-fast patriarchal family unit, with an insistence on 'real' or biological parents and a propensity to view anything less as dysfunctional. They were expressed in a more collaborative and supportive networking. London custom supported family values of this kind in the sense that it accepted the fragility of the nuclear unit and sought to mitigate the effects of that fragility. The 'custom of London' had several different connotations, but it specifically protected both widow and children against disinheritance, insisting that the unadvanced children should receive a one-third share of the estate and the widow likewise. It protected orphans against harm and exploitation and guaranteed their accession to their inheritance in due course. It guaranteed the widow's

---

[98] LMA, DL/C/B/004/MS09171/008, fo. 190v.

[99] LMA, DL/C/B/004/MS09171/008, fo. 199v.

[100] A. F. Sutton, 'Alice Claver, silkwoman (d. 1489)', in Barron and Sutton, *Medieval London Widows*, pp. 129–42, at pp 138–9.

[101] Davies, 'Thomasyne Percyvale', p. 202.

future residence in the marital home beyond the meagre forty days offered by common law. The husting court heard pleas of dower and of execution of testament, which helped widows and heirs to obtain their rights against executors; widows' claims for dower had a high rate of success. Although London had no official dowry fund as many European cities did, many Londoners included 'poor maids' marriages' among their benefactions. In a different way, a familial or fraternal ideal was manifested in the numerous fraternities and brotherhoods in virtually every church in London, to which Londoners clearly attached great affection and importance.[102]

This chapter suggests that the London family was a loose and ever-changing nexus, both a domestic entity and a more extended network, providing vital support and continuity. If we read late medieval wills with pessimistic eyes, we are struck by the loss of husbands and wives, the feared deaths of children, the large proportion of marriages that produced no surviving issue. But if we are more optimistic, we can interpret the evidence in a more positive way. The premature death of a spouse or children was often followed by their replacement by surrogates. The London commissary court wills of the late fifteenth and early sixteenth centuries document an array of significant relationships beyond the nuclear family. Testators named brothers, sisters, their spouses, their sons and daughters, cousins, the wife's own children by a former marriage, her brothers and sisters and their children, even a deceased wife's god-daughter. In several instances these were the heirs, not just casual beneficiaries; while one's own issue was preferred, collateral descendants were acceptable substitutes. And the net stretched wider: alms children filled a gap in the households of older or childless parents. Godchildren were remembered; and the rector of St. Michael Bassishaw left legacies to two 'spiritual sons'.[103] And, as discussed above, apprentices filled an important gap in the affective as well as the business lives of Londoners.

However, even if later medieval London was resilient in the face of demographic and social stress, there was some continuity of concern over the centuries. The French visitor Henri Misson, in the late seventeenth century, commented that the English (and he evidently had most of his experience in London) were too affectionate and indulgent with their children, 'always flattering, always correcting, always applauding what they do', whereas 'to keep them in awe is the best way to give them a good

---

[102] C. M. Barron, 'The parish fraternities of medieval London', in *The Church in Pre-Reformation Society*, ed. C. M. Barron and C. Harper-Bill (Woodbridge, 1985), pp. 13–37.

[103] Darlington, *London Consistory Court Wills*, nos. 46, 75, 77, 84, 148, 155, 187; LMA, DL/C/B/004/MS09171/008, fo. 203.

turn in their youth'.[104] But 200 earlier William Caxton had lamented that although London children started out well – 'fare ne wyser ne bet bespoken children in theyre yongthe ben nowher than there ben in london', they did not turn out so: 'at their full rypyng there is no carnel ne good corn founden, but chaffe for the moost parte'.[105]

---

[104] H. de Valbourg Misson, *M. Misson's Memoirs and Observations in his Travels over England ... Dispos'd in Alphabeticall Order, Written originally in French and Translated by Mr Ozell* (London, 1719), p. 33.

[105] Crotch, *Prologues and Epilogues of William Caxton*, pp. 77–8, quoted by Thrupp, in *Merchant Class of Medieval London*, p. 191.

2. A portrait of a late medieval London pub: the Star inn, Bridge Street

Justin Colson

One of Caroline Barron's articles set out to find the 'small people' of medieval London, drawing upon late fourteenth-century scrivener Thomas Usk's distinction between the 'worthy persons and the small people'.[1] Usk was referring to the supporters of John of Northampton, especially the lesser artisans and craftsmen, and yet, perhaps counter-intuitively, those of such relatively humble status, but who did not run afoul of the authorities, are less well documented than those even further down the social spectrum. The most marginal individuals, such as fraudsters, prostitutes and petty criminals, can be found throughout London's late medieval court records. At the upper levels of urban society, members of London's 'merchant class', defined by Sylvia Thrupp as the liverymen of the greater companies, tend to be documented well enough to build comprehensive and meaningful biographies.[2] This is especially true when our focus is restricted, as it often tends to be, to that even narrower subset of merchants who sought and achieved political office as common councilmen, aldermen and mayors. The medieval Londoners for whom it is hardest to build biographies are those who fell between the two extremes of fortune and notoriety: the artisans, retailers and members of the mercantile companies who never made it to the ranks of the livery or the top of the league tables of international trade.[3] This chapter seeks to build on Caroline Barron's inquiry into 'the small people' and to construct something of a 'biography' of a group of middling people in late medieval London. Rather than focusing upon an individual

---

[1] C. M. Barron, 'Searching for the "small people" of medieval London', *Local Historian*, xxxviii (2008), 83–94. See also F. Rexroth, *Deviance and Power in Late Medieval London* (Cambridge, 2007); R. M. Wunderli, *London Church Courts and Society on the Eve of the Reformation* (Cambridge, Mass., 1981).

[2] S. L. Thrupp, *The Merchant Class of Medieval London, 1300–1500* (Chicago, Ill., 1948), pp. 1–52; see also, e.g., A. F. Sutton, 'Nicholas Alwyn, mayor of London: a man of two loyalties, London and Spalding' in this volume.

[3] Barron, 'Searching for the "small people"', pp. 83–8.

J. Colson, 'A portrait of a late medieval London pub: the Star inn, Bridge Street', in *Medieval Londoners: essays to mark the eightieth birthday of Caroline M. Barron*, ed. E. A. New and C. Steer (London, 2019), pp. 37–54. License: CC-BY-NC-ND 4.0.

or an institutionally defined group of individuals who practised the same trade or who were members of the same parish, this chapter explores the history of one inn and the people connected with it over the course of the fifteenth century. Inns provided a unique combination of hospitality for travellers and sociability for locals, apparently avoiding some of the negative associations of other drinking establishments, such as alehouses (a distinction discussed below). Examining a range of documents, especially those which were witnessed by, or otherwise had the involvement of, innkeepers, gives a new insight into the local sociability and networks of the 'middling' strata of medieval London society.

Uses of inns and taverns

The social role of drinking establishments in the late medieval period has received rather less attention than might be expected, and medieval London's inns have, as yet, received no dedicated comprehensive studies. Although there are some valuable general studies of inns, taverns and alehouses in the middle ages, this chapter will also draw on the more extensive literature on the cultural history of drinking, and of drinking places, in the early modern period to help to build a rich picture of the varied uses of the semi-public, semi-private spaces of taverns and inns.[4]

The tripartite division between inns, which provided accommodation and a full hot-food service; taverns, which sold wine; and alehouses, which sold only ale, is well rehearsed, although in practice the boundaries could be a little blurred.[5] It certainly seems to have been the case that alehouses often catered to travellers and inns often entertained locals, even if taverns might have maintained control over the retailing of wine. In London especially, inns and taverns had developed a notable sideline as restaurants during the fifteenth century, catering to the nobility, organizations and merchants.[6]

---

[4] Discussions of the archaeological remains and extant fabric of medieval inns are, by contrast with social and cultural studies, quite numerous. For a still-useful general survey of inn buildings in medieval England, see W. A. Pantin, 'Medieval inns', in *Studies in Building History: Essays in Recognition of the Work of B. H. St. J. O'Neil*, ed. E. M. Jope (London, 1961), pp. 166–91; for London, Ralph Treswell's surveys provide valuable evidence of pre-Great Fire inns: *The London Surveys of Ralph Treswell*, ed. J. Schofield (London Topographical Soc., cxxxv, London, 1987).

[5] P. Clark, *The English Alehouse: a Social History* (London, 1983), pp. 5–15. John Hare noted that while 'not everyone would have agreed on the borderline cases' between inns and alehouses, medieval sources did try to distinguish the different types of establishment (J. Hare, 'Inns, innkeepers and the society of later medieval England, 1350–1600', *Jour. Med. Hist.*, xxxix (2013), 477–97, at p. 480).

[6] M. Carlin, '"What say you to a piece of beef and mustard?" : the evolution of public dining in medieval and Tudor London', *Huntington Libr. Quart.*, lxxi (2008), 199–217, at p. 210.

The reputations for respectability of the different types of establishment also seem to have been less clear-cut than might be imagined. Historians have perhaps too often tended to assume that medieval drinking houses were somewhat seedy environments.[7] It is true that Judith Bennett's account of women's roles in brewing and selling ale emphasized the association of ale-selling with corruption, dishonesty and, if not actual prostitution, then at least sexual suggestion and flirtation.[8] However, the social world of the tavern was much more complex.[9] In practice, many of those joining in the most boisterous drinking games included figures of authority, such as the parish constable noted as having attempted to drink two gallons of ale from a stone pot, and having passed out for the whole of the next day, in Layer Marney, Essex, in 1604.[10]

Many of the most negative anecdotes relate to alehouses, and it would seem as though inns were the more respectable drinking establishments. Most obviously, they were much larger, requiring greater capital to own and operate, and therefore tended to be run by more respectable landlords than the frequently somewhat marginal alehouse keepers, who often improvised a normal domestic space into a 'public house'. John Hare suggested that, by the sixteenth century at least, provision of locked chambers for guests was a key feature of inns, with even those in provincial towns sometimes providing upwards of a dozen guest rooms, while Beat Kümin calculated that early modern inns had on average forty to fifty beds.[11] Travel accounts from before 1500 reported that elites including prelates, diplomatic envoys and high-ranking pilgrims routinely stayed at inns.[12] Respectable men and women of knightly and gentry families also patronized inns, with both the Stonors (who, interestingly, let their own property and instead stayed in public inns) and Pastons staying in such establishments in London.[13] Older studies have implied that the respectability of inns in the middle ages declined during the early modern period, although both Kümin and Hare

[7] R. Mazo Karras, *Common Women: Prostitution and Sexuality in Medieval England* (Oxford, 1996), p. 72.

[8] J. M. Bennett, *Ale, Beer and Brewsters in England: Women's Work in a Changing World, 1300–1600* (Oxford, 1996), pp. 123–44.

[9] B. Hanawalt, *Of Good and Ill Repute: Gender and Social Control in Medieval England* (Oxford, 1998), p. 105.

[10] M. Hailwood, *Alehouses and Good Fellowship in Early Modern England* (Woodbridge, 2014), pp. 171–2.

[11] Hare, 'Inns', p. 481; B. Kümin, 'Public houses and their patrons in early modern Europe', in *The World of the Tavern: Public Houses in Early Modern Europe*, ed. B. Kümin and B. A. Tlusty (Aldershot, 2002), pp. 44–62, at p. 47.

[12] Kümin, 'Public houses', p. 50.

[13] C. M. Barron, *London in the Later Middle Ages* (Oxford, 2004), p. 59.

suggested that this model required a lot more nuance: there was no shortage of 'respectable' opportunities for men and women to attend, or indeed to run, taverns and inns in the sixteenth and seventeenth centuries, as there had been in the fourteenth and fifteenth.[14] There are, however, plenty of indications that not all medieval inns were as 'respectable' as the contrast with alehouses might suggest. Erasmus's discussion of inns throughout Europe was certainly less than flattering, highlighting again the importance of a female host of 'handsome of carriage' and the somewhat questionable attitude to service (especially in Germany), where eighty or ninety people of every social rank were made to eat together in a single sitting and change was rarely given at the reckoning.[15] While there were undoubtedly differences between inns and alehouses, they were certainly nuanced.

Nonetheless, there were important ways in which inns and taverns particularly served unambiguously legitimate social functions in pre-modern cities. Phil Withington has argued that legitimate sociability and 'keeping company' were integral to the establishment of corporate and civic identities and solidarities; and while haunting taverns too much was to be avoided, they were still appropriate venues for respectable sociability.[16] What was, and was not, acceptable in terms of the use of drinking establishments was socially and contextually specific. Drinking with one's peers was absolutely routine and integral to the mechanisms of social capital for the elites, but was confined to inns and taverns. The boisterous drinking of the poor in alehouses was always much more suspect.[17] The legitimacy of a visit to a tavern or inn depended upon its purpose: if there was any serious purpose, it was perfectly legitimate for anyone of any status or sex to visit a drinking house. Yet haunting taverns for its own sake was certainly seen as a danger: Thomas Dekker's satirical *Gull's Hornbook* (1609) suggested ironically that the man who 'desires to be a man of good reckoning in the city ... take his continual diet at a tavern, which out of question is the only rendezvous of boon company'.[18] It is also important to remember that not only were there a multitude of legitimate reasons for respectable men and women to visit all manner of drinking houses, including alehouses, but that in practice any

---

[14] Kümin, 'Public Houses', pp. 55–6; Hare cited the New Inn at Gloucester, which had its own tennis court ('Inns', p. 481). The Pastons stayed at the George at St. Paul's wharf, where the innkeeper Thomas Green and his wife were trusted enough by the family to receive and forward messages and parcels for them (Barron, *London*, p. 59).

[15] *The Colloquies of Erasmus*, ed. N. Bailey (2 vols., London, 1878), i. 286–93.

[16] Hailwood, *Alehouses*, p. 56; P. Withington, *The Politics of Commonwealth: Citizens and Freemen in Early Modern England* (Cambridge Social and Cultural Histories, iv, Cambridge, 2005), pp. 127–37.

[17] Hailwood, *Alehouses*, pp. 55–7.

[18] *The Gull's Hornbook by Thomas Dekker*, ed. R. B. McKerrow (New York, 1971), p. 69.

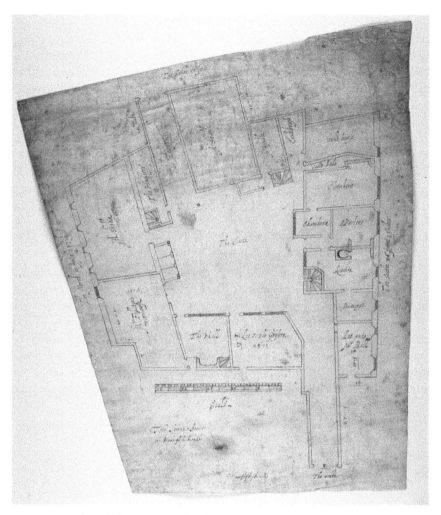

Figure 2.1. Plan of the Star Inn, dated to *c*.1645. London Metropolitan Archives, City of London (COLLAGE: the London Picture Archive, ref CLC/L/FE/H/003).

one such establishment would host any number of 'companies' of drinkers, all engaged in their own conversations, business or drinking games.[19]

A wide range of activities which took place within inns and taverns could be classed as legitimate forms of sociability. According to Clark, both taverns and inns were 'places for business to be done; investments arranged, lawyers and physicians consulted'.[20] From the early seventeenth century

[19] Hailwood, *Alehouses*, pp. 180–1.
[20] Clark, *English Alehouse*, p. 13.

dedicated tavern societies used the private rooms available within a tavern or inn to provide particular forms of sociability, such as the *Convivium Philosophicum* which met at the Mitre tavern around 1611.[21] This use of inns and taverns for organized cultural activities was nothing new. Anne Sutton has convincingly argued that the Tumbling Bear on Cheapside was the meeting place of the fraternity known as the Puy, which met during the late thirteenth and early fourteenth centuries to compose a new *chant royale*.[22] The socially prestigious Jesus guild, which met in St. Paul's cathedral from the mid fifteenth to mid sixteenth centuries, also made extensive use of inns and taverns, including in 1514 when the assistants of the guild convened at the Mitre in Cheapside for the 'makyng of the ordenances'.[23] Inns and taverns could, then, certainly be quite respectable places. Indeed, the inn that features most prominently in Chaucer's *Canterbury Tales*, the Tabard, was explicitly described as a 'gentyle tavern' and was a place in which a wife, a prioress and a monk all saw fit to stay.[24]

The important place of the inn in the social and economic life of the city also emerges from sixteenth-century theatre. The anonymous *Famous Victories of Henry V*, widely considered to be Shakespeare's source for *Henry IV* and *Henry V*, offered a lively description of the 'old tavern' on Eastcheap.[25] Shakespeare developed this image of the prince's affray in a way that transposed the Boar's Head of his own era into the medieval period for, as John Stow was at pains to point out, there was no tavern on Eastcheap at that time, only cookshops.[26] Hostess Quickly sets out her case

[21] M. O'Callaghan, 'Tavern societies, the inns of court, and the culture of conviviality in early seventeenth-century London', in *A Pleasing Sinne: Drink and Conviviality in Seventeenth-Century England*, ed. A. Smyth (Studies in Renaissance Literature, xiv, Cambridge, 2004), pp. 37–51, at p. 39.

[22] A. F. Sutton, 'The "Tumbling Bear" and its patrons: a venue for the London Puy and mercery', in *London and Europe in the Later Middle Ages*, ed. J. Boffey and P. King (London, 1996), pp. 85–110, at pp. 85–95.

[23] Oxford, Bodleian Library, MS. Tanner 221, fo. 35v; E. A. New, 'The cult of the Holy Name of Jesus in late medieval England, with special reference to the fraternity in St. Paul's cathedral, London' (unpublished University of London PhD thesis, 1999), pp. 230, 390. The Jesus Guild also owned a tavern, the Bull's Head in St. Martin's Lane, which they sold in 1507 with the explicit intention of acquiring a guildhall, although this never happened (MS. Tanner 221, fo. 14; New, 'Cult of the Holy Name', pp. 205–6).

[24] For a useful historicization of the pilgrims and insightful discussions of Chaucer himself and of Harry Bailly, innkeeper of the Tabard, see M. Carlin, 'The Host', in *Historians on Chaucer: the 'General Prologue' to the Canterbury Tales*, ed. S. Rigby (Oxford, 2014), pp. 460–80.

[25] *The Famous Victories of Henry the Fifth: Containing the Honourable Battell of Agin-court: As it was Plaide by the Queenes Maiesties Players* (London, 1598) (*STC* 13072).

[26] N. Levine, *Practicing the City: Early Modern London on Stage* (New York, 2016), p. 26; *A Survey of London by John Stow*, ed. C. L. Kingsford (2 vols., Oxford, 1908), i. 216–7.

against Falstaff in *Henry IV Part 1* with what Nina Levine has described as an 'outrageously detailed account of the material circumstances' to give authority and authenticity to her claim: 'Thou didst swear to me upon a parcel-guilt goblet, sitting in my Dolphin chamber, at the round table, by a sea-coal fire'.[27] Levine argued that Shakespeare's use of the tavern setting 'delineates a world whose ethics are rooted as much in the business practices of London's middling sort as the holiday festivities of popular culture' and, furthermore, emphasized the place of credit and centrality of contracts in that world.[28] In theatre, the tavern or the inn stood for the social world of London and the commercial mind-set that went with it; there was no contradiction between the tavern as place of mischief and of business.

Barbara Hanawalt referred to the medieval tavern as a 'permeable domestic space', where gendered work replicated that of a domestic house: wives and daughters oversaw the running of the house and supervised servants, while husbands supervised guests and looked after provisioning. Female employees, and even daughters and wives, were at risk of being pimped, while ordinary female patrons were not beyond suspicion.[29] Again, this was highly contextual: women's use of public space was 'neither simple nor free' but certainly could include taverns and inns.[30] Laura Gowing has persuasively argued that while the late medieval and earlier early modern periods might not have seen the inclusiveness and parity between the sexes that the theory of the growth of 'separate spheres' after 1650 has implied, gendered spaces were certainly permeable.[31] A woman's place might have been in the household, but that was not synonymous with the physical limits of the house. Indeed, witness testimonies described women routinely moving around the streets, shops and inns and taverns of their neighbourhoods.[32]

Meanwhile, Shannon McSheffrey's analysis of matrimonial litigation in the London Consistory Court has suggested that, outside of homes and churches, drinking houses such as inns, taverns and alehouses were the most common locations for the making of marriage contracts. The testimonies describing such marriages, whether testifying for or against, do not appear to have made any judgement as to the drinking house having been unsuitable or disreputable. Indeed, McSheffrey argued that, especially for

---

[27] W. Shakespeare, *Henry IV Part 2*, ed. by S. Greenblatt et al., in *The Norton Shakespeare* (New York, 1997), II. i. 79–81; Levine, *Practicing the City*, p. 42.

[28] Levine, *Practicing the City*, p. 33.

[29] Hanawalt, *Of Good and Ill Repute*, pp. 106–9.

[30] L. Gowing, '"The freedom of the streets": women and social space, 1560–1640', in *Londinopolis: Essays in the Cultural and Social History of Early Modern London*, ed. by P. Griffiths and M. S. R. Jenner (Manchester and New York, 2000), pp. 130–53, at p. 145.

[31] Gowing, '"Freedom of the Streets"', pp. 133–4.

[32] Gowing, '"Freedom of the Streets"', pp. 139–45.

those of middling and lower status, the tavern served as a home away from home. Marriages were, she argued, most often contracted and announced to those closest to the couple in a domestic or quasi-domestic space before being announced more widely.[33] While courtship in taverns was common, in the form of eating and drinking together, the actual formal contracting of marriage was no less common – guests and witnesses were specially gathered together in a public space. Those contracting marriage in a tavern were not seeking to escape the patriarchal authority of the household, but were more likely simply to have lacked a suitable space of their own. At no point in the testimonies did women try to claim that they had not been drinking in a tavern, suggesting there was nothing disreputable about it, although it would still have been more common for women to visit only in the company of men.[34] There was no cultural objection to such a venue: 'In a world in which the sacred was immanent, medieval people saw nothing unusual about undertaking a sacrament "before God" in a space that we might regard as obviously profane'.[35] The defining factor in the choice of an appropriate venue for an exchange of wedding contracts was accessibility: propriety depended upon visibility. Thus, a tavern, like the hall of a prosperous household or a church, was a social centre, full of people, and was thus an eminently suitable location for the exchange of a contract because of the ready supply of witnesses.

Marriages were far from the only contracts routinely drawn up in the tavern or inn. In market towns and smaller cities drinking establishments could invariably be found near marketplaces and inns themselves were often the site of economic exchange, both legitimate and underhand.[36] It was also common for larger provincial inns to act as forerunners of county halls from the later sixteenth century, playing host to courts and administrative meetings.[37] Nor was Chaucer's parish clerk doing something unusual in using the tavern as venue for his charters of land:

[33] S. McSheffrey, *Marriage, Sex, and Civic Culture in Late Medieval London* (Philadelphia, Pa., 2006), pp. 129–30.

[34] McSheffrey, *Marriage, Sex, and Civic Culture*, pp. 133–4.

[35] Hanawalt, *Of Good and Ill Repute*, p. 105; S. McSheffrey, 'Place, space, and situation: public and private in the making of marriage in late-medieval London', *Speculum*, lxxix (2004), 960–90, esp. at pp. 973, 983–5.

[36] Hare, 'Inns', pp. 481–2. Hare noted that buying and selling within inns and taverns was forbidden in many places but could be part of regulated exchange, as in Exeter, where legitimate cloth sales occurred in the Eagle and the New inns.

[37] A. Everitt, 'The English urban inn 1560–1760', in *Perspectives in English Urban History*, ed. A. Everitt (London, 1973), pp. 91–137, at pp. 109–10.

Wel koude he laten blood, and clippe ans shave,
And maken a charter of lond or acquitaunce

...

In al the toun nas brewhous ne tavern
That he ne visited with his solas,
Ther any gaylard tappestere was.[38]

The wide range of business activities routinely carried out in inns and taverns often led to conflict; and the role of a successful taverner or innkeeper entailed a large part of mediation – not least as they were legally required to act as *paterfamilias* for those (and their property) under their roof.[39] The language used to describe Chaucer's innkeeper Harry Bailly is evocative of statutes and ordinances; and Martha Carlin has proposed that contemporary audiences would have identified the host in the *Canterbury Tales* with 'the Southwark MP and innkeeper of the same name'.[40] Hanawalt concluded that the successful innkeeper, just like Chaucer's Harry Bailly, required 'a ready wit heightened by some education, sharp eyes, a physical appearance and strength adequate to overcome resistance, and a certain presence and seeming gentility of manner'.[41] Alan Everitt also highlighted the importance of early modern innkeepers' roles as proto-bankers, retaining cash and administering credit on behalf of regular patrons.[42]

London's inns and taverns simultaneously stood comparison with those of provincial English towns, but were quite distinct in other ways. While many inns could be found in the central marketplaces of the city, such as Cheapside, there was a much stronger tendency for inns to be located near, or even outside, the gates, as land values forced the space-hungry inns out from the centre from as early as the fourteenth century.[43] In terms of their physical form, though, medieval London taverns and inns were more similar to their provincial counterparts. While there was a tradition of taverns and social drinking spaces occupying cellars, as has remained common in the Germanic world, in London the main drinking spaces of taverns and inns tended to concentrate on the ground floor. When Ralph Treswell surveyed three small taverns in 1610, all had their drinking rooms

---

[38] G. Chaucer, 'The clerk's prologue and tale', in *The Canterbury Tales*, ed. L. D. Benson (3rd edn., Oxford, 1988), pp. 68–77, at p. 70, ll. 3326–36.
[39] Hanawalt, *Of Good and Ill Repute*, pp. 13–5.
[40] Carlin, 'The Host', p. 472.
[41] Hanawalt, *Of Good and Ill Repute*, p. 117.
[42] Everitt, 'English urban inn', pp. 109–10.
[43] C. Barron noted that in 'Southwark and Westminster by 1400 inns were ubiquitous' (Barron, *London*, p. 59).

on the ground floor.[44] The physical form of inns most obviously varied from taverns in terms of the provision of stabling facilities and accommodation, increasingly in the form of private rooms, on upper floors.[45] The inn that we take as our case study, the Star on Bridge Street, provides an example of an inn serving the travelling public but emerges most clearly as a social space for the local community.

The Star inn

The inn known as 'le Sterre' was a large tenement in the north of the parish of St. Margaret Bridge Street, just a few moments' walk from London Bridge. It spanned the whole area between Bridge Street to the west and Pudding Lane to the east, and from the cemetery of St. Margaret's to the south to the parish boundary to the north. The Star is exceptionally well documented because it passed into the ownership of the Fishmongers' Company in 1505 and a complete collection of original deeds survive in the Fishmongers' collection at the Guildhall library.[46] This tenement was one of numerous drinking establishments along Bridge Street which also included the Kings Head, the Bell and the Castle on the Hoop in the parish of St. Magnus; and the Hotelar, formerly known as the Brodegate; and the Sun on the Hoop in St. Margaret Bridge Street.[47] Tenements known as 'on the hoop' tended to be alehouses, their title apparently originating in the adoption of a metal hoop, as used in beer barrels, as a frame for their sign, whereas taverns and inns had no particular theme to their names.[48]

The fact that the Star formed part of the institutional property portfolio of the Fishmongers' Company has meant that not only the fifteenth-century deeds survive, but also detailed surveys. Unusually, plans for the Star exist in both pre- and post-Great Fire forms. The first plan, catalogued by the London Metropolitan Archives as dating from c.1700, has been identified by Dorian Gerhold as having a much earlier date (see Figure 2.1).[49] This plan depicts one room in the south-west corner of the inn as let to a John Ball, ironmonger. He had leased the shop to the south of the inn gateway that abutted this room in 1617 and hired the room in question before 1639,

---

[44] Schofield, *London Surveys*, p. 15 and nos. 43, 50, 51.

[45] J. Schofield, *Medieval London Houses* (London, 1995), p. 54; Hare, 'Inns', p. 481; Schofield, *London Surveys*, p. 15 and nos. 3 and 4. C. Barron observed that while 'providing bed and breakfast … was an important part of the innholder's job, the stabling and feeding of horses were probably even more important' (Barron, *London*, p. 59).

[46] LMA, Fishmongers' Company Deeds, CLC/L/FE/G/179/MS06696.

[47] *CPMR 1413–1437*, pp. 139–40, 158–9.

[48] M. Ball, *The Worshipful Company of Brewers: a Short History* (London, 1977), p. 63.

[49] LMA, CLC/L/FE/H/003.

but had left by 1645, establishing the dating of the plan.[50] The plan was evidently drawn up in connection with the request of the lessee, William Molins, to rebuild the east (Pudding Lane) side of the inn when the Company required him to provide a 'draughte' of his plans. This plan shows a complex layout of uses and sub-tenancies. Beyond Ball's second room or shop, the southern range included the kitchen and buttery, two chambers and stores for both wood and coal. Stables were found at the east side, one of them reaching all the way to Pudding Lane, but mainly separated by a fifteen-foot gap occupied by separate shops. Next to the eastern gateway a room with a spiral staircase was referred to as 'the Hoastrey', while the main hall, with large fireplace and elaborate windows, was directly opposite. Another well-lit room was let to the Grocers' Company and a warehouse in the north-western corner was let to one Mr. Fellton. Molins requested to rebuild in order to provide small chambers upstairs 'for want thereof looseth many guests', suggesting that the original medieval form of the inn with communal accommodation had survived until this point.[51]

The second plan is part of the Fishmongers' Company plan book, still kept at Fishmongers' hall and securely dated to 1686. The passageway from Pudding Lane had been re-aligned to give a continuous line of five shops, noted as having been rebuilt by the lessee of the inn, to the north of the passageway. To the west, the shop facing Fish Street Hill to the south of the main gateway was now included as part of the plan.[52] The area around the central yard was dominated by a large stable to the north and a smaller one to the east, with stairs alongside leading up to the main accommodation areas of the inn, spread over two extra storeys on all sides, including a substantial projection over the yard and offering no fewer than thirty-three chambers.[53] The southern range included another shop in what had been Ball's room, a kitchen and buttery and a parlour and a chamber in what had been the wood and coal stores. The grandest parlour, with a large fireplace, and the tap-house were on the west range within the yard. The Star's central location was more constrained than that of most other London inns, but its lessees clearly did their best to maintain the facilities that were expected of a metropolitan inn, catering to both travellers and Londoners.

---

[50] D. Gerhold, *London Plotted: Plans of London Buildings c.1450–1720*, ed. S. O'Connell, London Topographical Soc., clxxviii (London, 2016), p. 173.

[51] Gerhold, *London Plotted*, pp. 173–4.

[52] Gerhold, *London Plotted*, p. 175.

[53] Gerhold, *London Plotted*, p. 175.

The Whaplodes, the Fishmongers and the Star inn

While the earliest extant visual depictions of the inn are firmly seventeenth century, it was nonetheless thoroughly documented in earlier periods. The chronology of the ownership of the tenement, revealed through the virtually unbroken sequence of deeds, quitclaims, leases, indentures, receipts and acknowledgements, is, as such documents generally are, complex and detailed, particularly on legal ownership. There were at least nineteen transactions in the century from 1403 to 1505, with four of these having occurred within the same year (1498). The longest period of stable tenure of the property, thirty-two years, occurred between 1456 and 1488, perhaps representing the lowest point in the 'slump' of the fifteenth-century economy.[54] The Star's fifteenth-century history began with the death of Walter Doget, a fishmonger, in 1403 and its sale by his son and executor, John, to a consortium of local merchants. At this time it was occupied by a brewer, Robert Forneux.[55] At some point before 1425 this group sold the tenement on to another group of locals, including the rector of St. Margaret's, Henry Shelford. At this point the Star first entered the hands of Robert Whaplode, a hosteller and one of this consortium of 1425, who presumably occupied it and traded there.[56] Following Whaplode's death in the 1430s, his co-investors conducted a series of leases and grants of rents upon the property before selling it to a further consortium, comprising chaplains, clerks, country gentlemen, and even a royal justice, in 1442.[57] These transactions, involving many parties as both grantors and grantees, are particularly ambiguous, potentially representing either a genuinely collaborative investment purchase, or a kind of mortgage. London does not seem to have seen the same kind of official mortgage often seen in the cities of the Low Countries, which were often backed by religious houses. Instead it appears to have been routine for lenders to have been listed among the grantees in a transaction and then gradually recording quitclaims until a single owner was left.[58] Several patterns emerge from the late medieval

---

[54] D. Keene, *The Walbrook Study: a Summary Report: Social and Economic Study of Medieval London* (London, 1987), pp. 19–20.

[55] LMA, CLA/023/DW/01/131 (45).

[56] LMA, CLC/L/FE/G/179/MS06696, folder 1, item 16.

[57] The grantees were Henry Fane, gentleman, of Hadlowe in Kent; Alexander Colepepper, esquire; Reginald Pekham, esquire; William Palley, stockfishmonger; and Thomas Reynold of Hadlew, yeoman (LMA, CLC/L/FE/G/179/MS06696, folder 2, item 6).

[58] This appears to have been a covert way of arranging a mortgage and is also discussed in J. L. Bolton, 'Was there a "crisis of credit" in fifteenth-century England?', *Brit. Numismatic Jour.*, lxxxi (2011), 144–64, at p. 156. London and other English cities did not see the widespread use of formal and explicit mortgages, which were common in many continental cities (C. Van Bochove, H. Deneweth and J. Zuijderduijn, 'Real estate and mortgage finance

history of the Star and its owners which neatly illustrate some wider trends in London's late medieval property market and patterns of tenure. For example, while occupation of a tenement by a single householder might remain stable for many years, this had little relation to the ownership of that property, which could change much more frequently. Furthermore, while a single household may have occupied and used a property, ownership seldom rested with any one individual, or even with family or company-related groups of individuals.

The Star was leased to another group of fishmongers in 1488 which included William Whaplode, son of Robert, the hosteller who had been an owner from 1425.[59] In 1498 the remnant of the 1442 owners, Edmund Watton, a gentleman from Addington in Kent, sold the tenement to a further group comprising William Palley, a stockfishmonger, and several gentlemen from Kent for the considerable sum of 230 marks. One of the Kent gentlemen, all seemingly connected with the village of East Peckham, was Sir Alexander Culpepper, participant in the October 1483 rising against Richard III, who served as sheriff of Kent in 1500 and 1507 and was the father of Thomas Culpepper, gentleman of the privy chamber who was executed as the supposed lover of Queen Katherine Howard.[60] Such gentry investment in the urban land market was surprisingly common in this period and provides an interesting counterpoint to the typical narrative of London wealth being exported to the shires as mercantile dynasties 'come of age' as gentry families. After numerous intermediate quitclaims and grants, the Kent gentlemen Richard Broke, Reginald Pekham and Alexander Culpepper sold the Star to the Fishmongers' Company, in the form of its twelve feoffees, in 1505. Among the feoffees was none other than William Whaplode, who was still tenant under the terms of the lease of 1488; and although he was free of the Fishmongers' Company, the Star was undoubtedly in use as an inn.[61] It is therefore interesting to observe the well-documented tendency for successful and aspirational members of minor companies to 'trade up' when apprenticing their children. Here, within the immediate social world, the dominant local company was chosen but, in practice, traditional family business interests prevailed.

The connections between the Fishmongers' Company and the Whaplode family are particularly illuminating as to how personal and institutional

---

in England and the Low Countries, 1300–1800', *Continuity and Change*, xxx (2015), 9–38.

[59] LMA, CLC/L/FE/G/179/MS06696, folder 1, item 13.

[60] LMA, CLC/L/FE/G/179/MS06696, folder 2, item 6; P. Fleming, 'Culpeper family (*per. c.*1400–*c.*1540)', in *ODNB* <https://doi.org/10.1093/ref:odnb/52784> [accessed 28 Apr. 2009].

[61] LMA, CLC/L/FE/G/179/MS06696, folder 1, item 1.

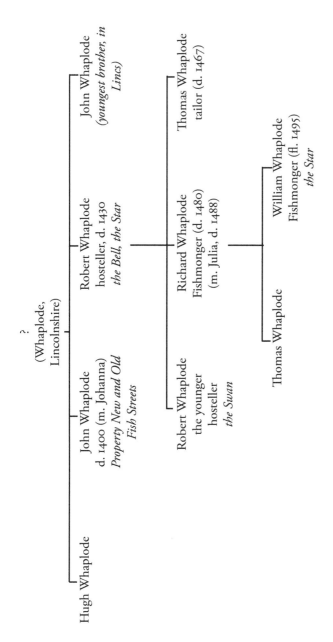

Figure 2.2. Family tree of the Whaplodes of Bridge Street, reconstructed from wills and deeds.

networks intersected in the late medieval city. Brothers John and Robert Whaplode, from the village of that name near Spalding in Lincolnshire, arrived in London in the closing decades of the fourteenth century. Undoubtedly exploiting his east coast connections, John became a successful fishmonger and owned lands in the parishes of St. Margaret Bridge Street and in St. Nicholas Cole Abbey in what would later be known as New and Old Fish Street respectively. John died in 1400 and appears to have been childless; at least some of his property found its way to his brother, Robert, who was a hosteller in the parish of St. Margaret. Robert was indicted in the wardmote inquests of 1421 for 'selling their ale within their hostels in hanaps [cups], and not in sealed measures according to the mayor's proclamation', as hosteller at the Bell and in 1423 both there and at the Star.[62] His son, also Robert, was hosteller at the Swan at this time. All three taverns were located in Bridge Street, the venue of London's main fish market. The elder Robert, while a hosteller, counted prominent local fishmongers among his associates, including Thomas Dursle and William Downe, to each of whom he left a money rent from his properties.[63] Robert Whaplode apprenticed his oldest son, Richard, to a fishmonger, undoubtedly making use both of family connections and those he had built up by acting as host at an inn which was inevitably patronized by members of Fishmongers' Company. Richard's son William then continued the precedent set by his father, becoming a Fishmonger.

Far from being simply another tavern, the Star appears to have had a particular place in the history of the Fishmongers' Company. Like most other victualling trades in medieval London, the markets for fish were situated on eastern and western hills of the city. This meant that for many fishmongers their day-to-day life was concentrated upon one market or the other and contacts between each branch were limited to the defence of their corporate liberties through the court of halimote.[64] The division between the Fishmongers of New and Old Fish Streets ran so deep that civic proclamations were explicitly addressed to 'the Masters of the Fishmongers of the one Street and the other'.[65] Individual Fishmongers were equally aware of the distinction and their bequests to their brethren were phrased to make it very clear that they did not intend their generosity to extend

---

[62] *CPMR 1413–1437*, pp. 139, 158.

[63] LMA, CLA/023/DW/01/159 (13).

[64] For a more detailed discussion, see J. Colson, 'London's Forgotten Company? Fishmongers, their trade and their networks in later medieval London', in *The Medieval Merchant: Proceedings of the 2012 Harlaxton Symposium*, ed. C. M. Barron and A. F. Sutton, Harlaxton Medieval Studies, n.s., xxiv (Donington, 2014), pp. 20–40.

[65] LMA, COL/CC/01/01/01, journal of the common council, i, fo. 51v.

to fishmongers of the other market. John Snoryng of St. Nicholas Cole Abbey, for example, bequeathed some silverware to the 'brotherhood and fraternity of the Fellowship of Fishmongers in Old Fishstreet of London' in 1490.[66] Intensely local, market-based identity was clearly important in the lives of the Company and it is tempting to conclude that the Star might have functioned as the *de facto* hall for the Fishmongers' Company in Bridge Street by the time it was leased to the trustees of the Company in 1488, before the establishment of the current hall in Stockfishmonger Row following the consolidation of the companies under ordinances drawn up in 1508.[67] Priscilla Metcalf, historian of the Fishmongers' halls, has suggested that this connection may have originated with a separate 'regulars' table', or *Stammtisch*, in the tavern.[68] The prime location in the midst of the fish market and the family connection of the Whaplodes certainly meant that the Star was integral to the life of the market and its users in the Fishmongers' Company and beyond.

Robert Whaplode and local networks

The place of the inn and its proprietors in the social world of Bridge Street, its market and its dominant company becomes even clearer when we look at evidence for other forms of social interaction. Witnessing was integral to the verification of exchanges and the documents that recorded them in the pre-modern world, but also played a wider social role in cementing local relationships. Acting as a witness was, in the words of Craig Muldrew, 'a casual, and normal, part of daily activity, and was one of the duties of neighbourliness'.[69] While it might seem a rather abstract or impersonal act, Christine Carpenter has not been alone in arguing that the position of responsibility invoked through witnessing, together with glimpses of the contexts in which such documents were drawn up, makes their value as a marker of a social relationship clear.[70] The witnessing of deeds relating to properties within the parish of St. Margaret Bridge Street during the

---

[66] TNA, PROB11/8, fos. 207v–2078v.

[67] For details of the merger of the companies, see J. N. Colson, 'Negotiating merchant identities: London companies merging and dividing, c.1450–1550', in *Medieval Merchants and Money: Essays in Honour of James L. Bolton*, ed. M. Allen and M. Davies (London, 2016), pp. 2–20, at pp. 9–10.

[68] P. Metcalf, *The Halls of the Fishmongers' Company: an Architectural History of a Riverside Site* (Chichester, 1973), p. 12.

[69] C. Muldrew, 'The culture of reconciliation: community and the settlement of economic disputes in early modern England', *Hist. Jour.*, xxxix (1996), 915–42, at pp. 926–7.

[70] C. Carpenter, 'Gentry and community in medieval England', *Jour. Brit. Stud.*, xxxiii (1994), 340–80, at pp. 368–9.

first half of the fifteenth century (when enrolment in the court of husting was more prevalent) gives a detailed picture of relationships in property transactions. The vast majority of witnesses, and especially the most prolific, were members of the Fishmongers' Company, which is an expected reflection of the social and economic characteristics of the neighbourhood.[71]

However, conspicuous among the Fishmonger witnesses was one member of a minor trade who in fact witnessed more local deeds than any other person: none other than Robert Whaplode, hosteller and tenant of the Star inn on Bridge Street. Whaplode's prominence in the local deeds as a witness represented his role as landlord: it is indicative of the kinds of local social networks, just as found by the Clarks in their study of early modern Canterbury.[72] It seems likely that, as Chaucer described, the physical process of validating written exchanges often took place within the hostelry and the innkeeper was called upon as a witness. The combination of the location of the inn and the intensely local nature of the Fishmongers' Company in the earlier fifteenth century combined to create a special place for this hosteller which was perpetuated and even intensified over the course of the following century. Despite acting as churchwarden of St. Margaret's in 1404,[73] Robert Whaplode never attained civic office, but was clearly prosperous when considered in a local context: viewed from the street up, rather than the civic government down, he was certainly significant. If the Star was anywhere near as large and complex a business as it was in the plans of the seventeenth century, it would certainly have been a significant business to run.

The nature of medieval record-keeping ensures that the Londoners we know most about are those with great status and wealth or those who attracted the attention of the courts; and this has understandably led historians to focus upon the extremes of urban society: those in civic government or those constituting the 'underclass'. While the records of the middling sort of late medieval London society might be sparse, this case study has shown how it is possible to examine their lives in a broader sense. Innkeepers, like the lower-status merchants and moderately prosperous

---

[71] This is based upon an analysis of all deeds registered in the hustings court between 1400 and 1450 relating to the parish of St. Margaret Bridge Street. They are discussed further in J. Colson, 'Local communities in fifteenth century London: craft, parish and neighbourhood' (unpublished University of London PhD thesis, 2011), pp. 279–89.

[72] P. Clark and J. Clark, 'The social economy of the Canterbury suburbs: the evidence of the census of 1563', in *Studies in Modern Kentish History: Presented to Felix Hull and Elizabeth Melling*, ed. N. A. Y. Detsicas (Maidstone, 1983), pp. 65–86.

[73] The only reference to Whaplode's role as a churchwarden is a passing reference in a will proved in the commissary court (LMA, DL/C/B/004/MS09171/2, fo. 47v).

artisans that appear to have formed their social milieu, frequently crossed paths with the 'merchant class', mayors and aldermen, but also possessed their own rich social lives and connections throughout the city. Taverns and inns provide a lens through which to view the range of social activities, from guild meetings to witnessing deeds, which middling-status late medieval Londoners conducted within their neighbourhoods. While it might not be possible to build a full biography of Robert Whaplode, a moderately prosperous but far from notable victualler, by examining the inn through which he and his family built a connection with their local community and local economy, a light has been cast into this stratum of late medieval London society, who might not be the 'small people' but certainly have been neglected.

3. Household reading for Londoners? Huntington Library MS. HM 140[*]

Julia Boffey

The reading matter available to members of prosperous lay households in late medieval London has attracted productive attention in a number of recent studies. Some of these have foregrounded the range of favoured texts, which included chronicles in the *Brut* tradition, poems by Chaucer and his successors and works of spiritual instruction and practical advice in both prose and verse.[1] Other investigations have concentrated on the production and material features of manuscripts available to London readers, looking, for example, at common-profit collections, at anthologies composed of distinct booklets and at the personnel at work in the book trade.[2]

[*] In this chapter the following abbreviations have been used: *DIMEV* for *The DIMEV: an Open-Access, Digital Edition of 'The Index of Middle English Verse'*, compiled L. R. Mooney, D. W. Mosser and E. Solopova, with D. Thorpe and D. H. Radcliffe <http://www.dimev. net>; and *NIMEV* for J. Boffey and A. S. G. Edwards, *A New Index of Middle English Verse* (London, 2005).

[1] See, e.g., L. M. Matheson, 'National and civic chronicles in late fifteenth-century London', in *The Yorkist Age: Proceedings of the 2011 Harlaxton Symposium*, ed. H. Kleineke and C. Steer (Harlaxton Medieval Studies, n.s., xxiii, Donington, 2013), pp. 56–74; *Chaucer and the City*, ed. A. Butterfield (Chaucer Studies, xxxvii, Cambridge, 2006); S. Lindenbaum, 'London texts and literate practice', in *The Cambridge History of Medieval English Literature*, ed. D. Wallace (Cambridge, 1999), pp. 284–309; M. Connolly, 'Books for the "helpe of euery persoone þat þenkiþ to be saued": six devotional anthologies from fifteenth-century London', *Yearbook English Stud.*, xxxiii (2003), 170–81; A. Appleford and N. Watson, 'Merchant religion in fifteenth-century London: the writings of William Litchfield', *Chaucer Rev.*, xlvi (2011), 203–22; S. Kelly and R. Perry, 'Devotional cosmopolitanism in fifteenth-century England', in *After Arundel: Religious Writing in Fifteenth-Century England*, ed. V. Gillespie and K. Ghosh (Medieval Church Studies, xxi, Turnhout, 2011), pp. 363–80.

[2] W. Scase, 'Reginald Pecock, John Carpenter and John Colop's "common-profit" books: aspects of book ownership and circulation in fifteenth-century London', *Medium Aevum*, lxi (1992), 261–74; L. R. Mooney, 'Locating scribal activity in late medieval London', in *Design and Distribution of Later Medieval Manuscripts in England*, ed. M. Connolly and L. R. Mooney (York, 2008), pp. 183–204; L. R. Mooney, 'Scribes and booklets of Trinity College, Cambridge, MSS. R. 3. 19 and R. 3. 21', in *Middle English Poetry: Texts and Tradition: Essays in Honour of Derek Pearsall*, ed. A. Minnis (Woodbridge, 2001), pp. 241–66;

J. Boffey, 'Household reading for Londoners? Huntington Library MS. HM 140', in *Medieval Londoners: essays to mark the eightieth birthday of Caroline M. Barron*, ed. E. A. New and C. Steer (London, 2019), pp. 55–70. License: CC-BY-NC-ND 4.0.

The distinctive commercial and cultural energies of London necessarily shaped some of the characteristics of its reading public, a significant proportion of whom were prosperous, educated laypeople keen to buy and in some cases commission both manuscripts and printed books. The interests of this sector have been explored by, among others, Caroline Barron, who has paid special attention to London merchants and to the works owned and read in their households.[3]

The surviving manuscripts that can be associated with this mercantile milieu are in many cases compilations of several works, sometimes the product of assembling separate booklets or fascicles.[4] MS. HM 140 in the Henry E. Huntington Library in San Marino, California, is one such collection.[5] Among its diverse contents are some works likely to have interested London merchants and prosperous householders: *The Libelle of English Policy*, for instance, dealing with commercial regulation and trade routes; and some *Advice to Apprentices*, aimed at the junior members of mercantile households.[6]

C. P. Christianson, 'Evidence for the study of London's late-medieval book-trade', in *Book Production and Publishing in Britain 1375–1475*, ed. J. Griffiths and D. Pearsall (Cambridge, 1989), pp. 87–108; C. P. Christianson, *A Directory of London Stationers and Book Artisans 1300–1500* (New York, 1990).

[3] C. M. Barron, 'What did medieval London merchants read?', in *Medieval Merchants and Money: Essays in Honour of James L. Bolton*, ed. M. Allen and M. Davies (London, 2016), pp. 43–70; C. M. Meale, '*The Libelle of Englyshe Polycye* and mercantile literary culture in late-medieval London', in *London and Europe in the Later Middle Ages*, ed. J. Boffey and P. King (Turnhout, 1995), pp. 181–227; A. Moss, 'A merchant's tales: a London fifteenth-century household miscellany', *Yearbook of English Stud.*, xxxiii (2003), 156–69; A. F. Sutton, 'The acquisition and disposal of books for worship and pleasure by mercers of London in the later middle ages', in *Manuscripts and Printed books in Europe 1350–1550: Packaging, Presentation and Consumption*, ed. E. Cayley and S. Powell (Liverpool, 2013), pp. 95–114; K. L. Scott, 'Past ownership: evidence of book ownership by English merchants in the later middle ages', in *Makers and Users of Medieval Books: Essays in Honour of A. S. G. Edwards*, ed. C. M. Meale and D. Pearsall (Cambridge, 2014), pp. 150–77.

[4] For some examples, see J. Boffey and C. M. Meale, 'Selecting the text: Rawlinson C. 86 and some other books for London readers', in *Regionalism in Late Medieval Manuscripts and Texts: Essays Celebrating the Publication of 'A Linguistic Atlas of Late Mediaeval English'*, ed. F. Riddy (Cambridge, 1991), pp. 143–69.

[5] The manuscript has been digitized in full: <http://cdm16003.contentdm.oclc.org/cdm/ref/collection/p15150coll7/id/19150> [accessed 23 July 2018]. The most recent description is by D. Mosser, *A Digital Catalogue of the Pre-1500 Manuscripts and Incunables of 'The Canterbury Tales'*, 2nd edn. <http://mossercatalogue.net/results.php?location=&repository=&manuscript=Ph4&edition=&search=SEARCH> [accessed 23 July 2018].

[6] *DIMEV* 5509/*NIMEV* 3491 and *DIMEV* 976/*NIMEV* 596. See Meale, '*Libelle*', for the *Libelle*'s London circulation (recently extended by an argument that, whatever its circulation, the *Libelle*'s author 'is less obviously metropolitan than is often supposed' (M. Bennett, '*The Libelle of English Policy*: the matter of Ireland', in *The Fifteenth Century XV. Writing, Records, and Rhetoric*, ed. L. Clark (Woodbridge, 2017), pp. 1–21, at p. 6).

Descriptions of the compilation have indicated other connections to London in the form of various of the names inscribed in it.[7] Since the manuscript as it now exists was compiled from distinct units, however, some careful analysis is needed in order to establish precisely how much of it might have originated in London or have been in the hands of London readers. This chapter will attempt an account of these matters as a prelude to exploring the appeal of some of the manuscript's contents and extending what is known about the identities and affiliations of the individuals whose names are recorded in it.

Opinions have differed about the number of units brought together to form the manuscript as it now exists.[8] The first of the sections (current fos. 1–92), made up of six gatherings, each constructed of paper with inner and outer strengthening bifolia of parchment, is mostly taken up with a copy of Lydgate's *Lives of SS. Alban and Amphabell* (fos. 1–67).[9] The rest of this section is filled with shorter poems by Lydgate and Chaucer, almost all explicitly oriented towards the cultivation of Christian virtues: Chaucer's *Clerk's Tale*, seemingly offered here as a parable about the virtue of constancy and rounded off with his short poem, 'Truth'; Lydgate's *Prayer upon the Cross*; and finally three more Lydgate items: 'Midsomer Rose', 'Song of Vertu' and the first section of his *Testament*.[10] Only Chaucer's *Complaint of Anelida*, a love complaint here extracted from the narrative framework in which it is sometimes found, interrupts what seems an explicit concern with cultivating properly devout and virtuous conduct.[11] The likelihood that this unit of the manuscript originally had an independent existence, perhaps in an unbound state or in a simple and flimsy wrapper, is suggested by its very grubby opening leaf and the fact that the last leaf of its final gathering has been cut away, perhaps because it was damaged.[12]

---

[7] The details in J. M. Manly and E. Rickert, *The Text of 'The Canterbury Tales'* (8 vols., Chicago, Ill., 1940), i. 433–8 are confirmed in C. W. Dutschke et al., *Guide to Medieval and Renaissance Manuscripts in the Huntington Library* (2 vols., San Marino, Calif., 1989), i. 185–90; and in Mosser, *Digital Catalogue*.

[8] The nineteenth-century binding (dated 1835 by Dutschke et al.) obscures much about the early bringing together of the manuscript's component parts. For some analysis of the manuscript's construction, see W. McClellan, 'A codicological analysis of the quire structure of MS HM 140 and its implications for a revised ordinatio', *Text*, ix (1996), 187–98.

[9] *DIMEV* 5966/*NIMEV* 3748.

[10] *DIMEV* 6414/*NIMEV* 4019; *DIMEV* 1326/*NIMEV* 809; *DIMEV* 6132/*NIMEV* 3845; *DIMEV* 3058/*NIMEV* 1865; *DIMEV* 663/*NIMEV* 401; *DIMEV* 3937/*NIMEV* 2464 (other excerpts from *Testament* were in circulation).

[11] *DIMEV* 4949/*NIMEV* 3670, placed here between the *Prayer upon the Cross* and *Midsomer Rose*.

[12] Gatherings 3 and 4 of this section have been bound in reverse order, which may also suggest that they were only loosely kept together for part of their early existence.

This section offers no clues about its place of origin. It has some of the features of a planned anthology made up of gatherings of uniform size and structure and copied by scribes who worked in collaborative stints. As has been noted, though, the scribal collaboration becomes erratic towards its conclusion; and there may be grounds for supposing that this section was not produced in a commercial context in a centre such as London but more likely in a household or community of some kind where a number of resident scribes were able to share small stints of copying.[13] Some descriptions of the manuscript have tentatively suggested that this section might be identifiable as the 'newe boke of Inglisse, the which begynnyth with the lyffe of Seynt Albon and Amphiabell and other mony dyvers lyfez and thynges in the same boke', bequeathed in 1459 by Sir Thomas Chaworth of Wiverton (Notts.) to his relative Robert Clifton; but, as has been recently noted, the watermarks in the paper of this section of MS. HM 140 suggests manufacture well into the second part of the fifteenth century, after Chaworth's death in 1459.[14] The hands also seem datable to the later fifteenth century. It remains unclear where this part of the manuscript originated and when exactly it was brought together with the other booklets with which it is now bound.

Immediately following this section in the manuscript's current binding is a unit made up of three paper gatherings (fos. 93–123), all differently sized. A secretary hand different from any of the hands in the preceding section, although seemingly not far from them in terms of date, has copied a verse *Life of Job* onto some of the leaves (fos. 93v–96v), but most remain blank apart from some added notes.[15] If there was ever a plan to insert further contents into this section it was never implemented. Possibly because the *Life of Job* seems somehow to echo Lydgate's *Lives of SS. Alban and Amphabell* in the preceding part of the manuscript,

---

[13] W. McClellan, 'The transcription of the "Clerk's Tale" in MS HM 140: interpreting textual effects', *Stud. in Bibliography*, xlvii (1994), 89–103. McClellan supplied an analysis of the hands (pp. 91–3) and noted a suggestion made to him by Ralph Hanna that 'production features of the manuscript indicate that it might have been produced in a private household, not a commercial shop' (p. 92, n. 7). Mosser noted linguistic forms characteristic of the central Midlands in some of the scribal stints (*Digital Catalogue*).

[14] G. Cole and T. Turville-Petre, 'Sir Thomas Chaworth's books', in *The Wollaton Medieval Manuscripts: Texts, Owners and Readers*, ed. R. Hanna and T. Turville-Petre (Woodbridge and Rochester, 2010), pp. 20–9, at pp. 25–6.

[15] *DIMEV* 3551/*NIMEV* 2208. See G. N. Garmonsway and R. R. Raymo, 'A Middle English metrical life of Job', in *Early English and Norse Studies Presented to Hugh Smith in Honour of his Sixtieth Birthday*, ed. A. Brown and P. Foote (London, 1963), pp. 77–98; and C. Hume, '*The Life of Job*: Bible translation, poem or play?', *New Medieval Literatures*, xviii (2018), 211–42. I am most grateful to Dr. Hume, who kindly allowed me to read her article before publication.

some commentators on MS. HM 140 have assumed that the first two sections of the manuscript were connected from an early point.[16] But this is unsupported by any evidence of shared paper stocks or scribes, or by the pattern of later annotations entered by particular individuals into both of these two parts. On the other hand, there are persuasive reasons for supposing that the *Life of Job* section was from an early stage associated with the third and currently final part of the manuscript, an enormous single paper gathering (fos. 124–70) containing items copied in several different hands. These include *The Libelle of English Policy* and *Advice to Apprentices*, both in verse; the story of Apollonius, in Latin prose; an English prose life of St. Ursula and the 11,000 virgins; and some short prose items of spiritual instruction. This final large gathering and the *Life of Job* section contain annotations in the same early sixteenth-century hand (on fos. 98 and 167, for example); and the paper of the outer bifolium of the large final gathering is of a stock that matches some of the paper in the *Life of Job* section. Both would therefore seem to have been together from an early stage. Since these are the sections containing annotations that make reference to Londoners, it is worth considering if and how their contents may reflect identifiably London-centric interests.

The longest item in the large single gathering forming the third section is *The Libelle of English Policy*, a *libellus* or 'little book', apparently compiled in a series of versions that came into circulation between late 1436 and a date sometime after June 1441 and dealing in over 1,000 lines of verse with English trade with the countries of Europe. Its concern with Anglo-Burgundian relations and the need to safeguard the English stronghold of Calais suggests that it would have been of immediate interest to a merchant audience; and indeed the work seems to have retained its appeal over many decades, well beyond the set of circumstances which prompted its composition. Notes or other forms of evidence in five of the fifteen complete or nearly complete surviving manuscripts point to owners from mercantile circles with London connections; and the copy in MS. HM 140 may be one further copy from such a milieu.[17]

---

[16] See, e.g., S. Lerer, who reads the whole manuscript as a demonstration of 'formal and thematic coherence' (S. Lerer, *Chaucer and his Readers: Imagining the Author in Late-Medieval England* (Princeton, N.J., 1993), pp. 100–16, at p. 101); and L. Staley, who offers a more cautious assessment (L. Staley, 'Huntington 140: Chaucer, Lydgate and the politics of retelling', in *Retelling Tales: Essays in Honor of Russell Peck*, ed. T. Hahn and A. Lupack (Cambridge, 1997), pp. 293–320).

[17] Meale, '*The Libelle*', pp. 206–27. The version in MS. HM 140, classified among those descending from one produced between (?)9 Dec. 1437 and 6 June 1441, has close relatives in Oxford, Bodleian Library MS. Rawlinson poet. F 32; and BL MS. Cotton Vitellius E X and Additional MS. 40673, all apparently of London provenance. Mercantile ownership has

The short poem now known as 'Advice to Apprentices' (fos. 167v–168) is even more explicit in its address to members of urban households.[18] Offered as 'doctryne' for 'children and yong men' learning a craft in a master's urban household, these instructions counsel predictable forms of good behaviour: early rising; cleanliness; good table manners; punctual attendance at work; and the cultivation of properly humble and respectful conduct towards master and mistress. The perils of city life loom threateningly in its advice to 'flee suspeciows weyes' and bad company and to avoid the forms of riotous living that involve cards, gaming, swearing and lechery. In its recommendations to 'Lyve with your felisship peisibly', 'By and selle truly', 'Gette noo goode vntruly' it nods explicitly to the mercantile milieux for which the young apprentice readers were being shaped. No other copy of this poem has survived and it could well be a one-off, brought into being by someone conscious of the need for an easily memorable and carefully targeted code of conduct for urban youth. The text is based on a widely circulating, endlessly adaptable set of instructions known as the 'Precepts in –ly', usually taking the form of a rough list of one-line nuggets of advice and in many instances roughly jotted down by manuscript readers who used some inviting empty space to record injunctions probably often learned by heart. Although there is considerable variation across the different surviving versions, particularly in relation to length and to devotional or secular focus, no other surviving text targets an apprentice audience. It seems possible that this version, carefully wrought in six-line stanzas, was conceived specially for a particular community, household or group.

In her exploration of what London merchants read, Caroline Barron has drawn attention to the prominence of copies of the *Legenda aurea* among books mentioned in bequests or surviving with notes of early ownership.[19] The inclusion of an English account of the life St. Ursula and the 11,000 virgins translated from the *Legenda* in the third section of MS. HM 140 may reflect this taste. Stories from the *Legenda* had a wide circulation in

---

also been suggested for the copies in Boston Public Library MS. 1519; and London, Society of Antiquaries MS. 101.

[18] The only edition of this version is that in *Reliquiae Antiquae*, ed. T. Wright and J. O. Halliwell (2 vols., 1841–3), ii. 223–4. Other versions of the 'Precepts in –ly' include *DIMEV* 553/*NIMEV* 317; *DIMEV* 560/*NIMEV* 324; *DIMEV* 4810/*NIMEV* 905.77; *DIMEV* 2415/ *NIMEV* 1436.44; *DIMEV* 4444/*NIMEV* 2794.99; *DIMEV* 4810/*NIMEV* 3087; *DIMEV* 4840/*NIMEV* 3102. There is useful discussion of the different versions in *The Commonplace Book of Robert Reynes of Acle: an Edition of Tanner MS 407*, ed. C. Louis (New York, 1980), pp. 393–4. Felicity Riddy explores some other works addressed to young members of urban households in 'Mother knows best: reading social change in a courtesy text', *Speculum*, lxxi (1996), 66–86.

[19] Barron, 'What did medieval merchants read?', p. 44.

English in the context of the *South English Legendary*, a verse translation dating, in its earliest form from the late thirteenth century, and the fifteenth-century prose *Gilte Legende*, based on the French of Jean de Vignay. The narrative in MS. HM 140 was not taken from either of these but represents an independent translation of the life of St. Ursula that survives in only one other witness, Southwell Minster MS. 7, where it accompanies John Mirk's *Festial* and a selection of other saints' lives.[20] Studies of the cult of St. Ursula in England have drawn attention to the confusion of the legend of Ursula the virgin martyr with a story recounted in Geoffrey of Monmouth's *Historia regum Britanniae* of the British woman who perished with her female companions en route to Brittany, where she was to marry Prince Conanus.[21] The gradual elision of the two stories came to give Ursula special status as a British saint, addressed in the fifteenth century by Lydgate in a prayer as one of the company of 'Brytoun martirs, famous in parfitnesse' and celebrated in early Tudor spectacle and pageantry.[22]

MS. HM 140's life of St. Ursula concludes with a verse stanza advising how to secure grace with the saint's help, some Latin versicles and responses and a Latin prayer, all perhaps suggesting address to readers somehow actively involved in Ursula's cult.[23] During the fifteenth and early sixteenth

[20] For an edition (with the Latin of the *Legenda*), see G. N. Garmonsway and R. R. Raymo, 'A Middle-English prose life of St Ursula', *Rev. English Stud.*, n.s., ix (1958), 353–61. This article does not take account of the version in Southwell Minster MS. 7, on which see M. Görlach, 'A second version of the Huntington prose legend of St. Ursula', *Rev. English Stud.*, n.s., xxiv (1973), 450–1; V. Edden, *The Index of Middle English Prose. Handlist XV: Manuscripts in Midland Libraries* (Cambridge, 2000), pp. 54–7; and S. Nevanlinna and I. Taavitsainen, *St Katherine of Alexandria: the Late Middle English Prose Legend in Southwell Minster MS 7* (Cambridge, 1993), pp. 49–54. On versions of the life of St. Ursula, see W. Marx, 'St Ursula and the eleven thousand virgins: the Middle English *Legenda Aurea* tradition', in *The Cult of St Ursula and the 11,000 Virgins*, ed. J. Cartwright (Cardiff, 2016), pp. 143–62. Dr. Marx kindly provided me with a copy of his chapter, for which I am most grateful.

[21] E. J. Bryan, 'Ursula in the British history tradition', in Cartwright, *Cult of St Ursula*, pp. 119–41.

[22] For Lydgate's prayer, see *The Minor Poems of John Lydgate*, ed. H. N. MacCracken (Early English Text Soc., e.s., cii and o.s., cxcii, 2 vols., London, 1911 and 1934), i. 144. Ursula's role in early Tudor pageantry is discussed by C. Sanok, *New Legends of England: Forms of Community in Late Medieval Saints' Lives* (Philadelphia, Pa., 2018), pp. 237–73.

[23] See further, L. S. Chardonnens and C. Drieshen, 'A Middle English version of Saint Ursula's prayer instruction in Nijmegen, Universiteitsbibliotheek, HS 194', *Stud. in Philology*, cx (2013), 714–30 (the English stanza in MS. HM 140, *DIMEV* 1185/*NIMEV* 720 is transcribed here on p. 727 and is also in Wright and Halliwell, *Reliquiae Antiquae*, ii. 224). The English verse life of St. Ursula commissioned by Lady Margaret Beaufort from Edmund Hatfield, monk of Rochester, and printed by Wynkyn de Worde *c*.1509 (*STC* 24541.3) concludes with similar Latin material.

centuries St. Ursula's following was especially strong among merchants whose activities gave them links with Cologne, the location of both her tomb and important relics. The London church of St. Mary Axe (also known as St. Mary Pellipar) near Leadenhall Street, whose patrons were the Skinners' Company, was dedicated to her; and the church of St. Lawrence Jewry near the Guildhall had a Fraternity of St. Ursula, members of which were among the many mercers who lived in this area (a copy of a printed indulgence from c.1520 for confraternity members survives).[24] Early sixteenth-century records of pageants of St. Ursula, one of which was the responsibility of members of the Drapers' Company, suggest that her story was well known; and the inclusion of her legend in MS. HM 140 may reflect acquaintance with performance as well as with narrative accounts. The manuscript's verse *Life of Job* has recently been analysed by Cathy Hume as 'written to accompany mimed action of a fairly elaborate kind', perhaps at a guild feast, and it is tempting to imagine that St. Ursula's legend might have been celebrated in a similar context.[25]

The other narrative copied in this section of the manuscript, the Latin *Apollonius of Tyre*, shares with the genre of the saint's life a concern with faith and virtuous conduct in the face of vicissitudes. Medieval references to the story, which had a wide circulation in Latin and in many European vernaculars, suggest that it was thought of variously as a romance, a history and an exemplum, or indeed as an amalgam of all three.[26] It presumably came the way of the compilers of MS. HM 140 as a free-standing tale, although by the later fifteenth century its reputation had been increased by its inclusion among the exemplary stories collected in the *Gesta Romanorum*, a tale collection with a wide European circulation.[27] Its appearance in

[24] On St. Mary Axe, originally dedicated to St. Mary the Virgin and St. Ursula and the 11,000 virgins, see *A Survey of London by John Stow*, ed. C. L. Kingsford (2 vols., Oxford, 1908), i. 160 and ii. 296; on St. Lawrence Jewry see A. F. Sutton, *The Mercery of London: Trade, Goods and People 1130–1578* (Aldershot, 2005), p. 195. Sanok has much interesting information on 'urban Ursulas' and includes an illustration of the indulgence (printed by Wynkyn de Worde, *STC* 14077c.59, BL frag, C.18.e.2(33)) (Sanok, *New Legends of England*, pp. 247–50).

[25] Hume, '*The Life of Job*', p. 236. In August 1523 the Drapers' Company was responsible 'for making of a newe pagent of Saynt Ursula' (A. Lancashire, *Records of Early English Drama: Civic London to 1558* (3 vols., Toronto, 2015), ii. 414).

[26] E. Archibald, *Apollonius of Tyre: Medieval and Renaissance Themes and Variations* (Cambridge, 1991), provides an English translation and a Latin text, the latter based on that of *Historia Apolloni Regis Tyri*, ed. G. A. A. Kortekaas (Medievalia Groningana, iii, Groningen, 1984). The European reception of the story is discussed by E. Archibald and by G. A. A. Kortekaas, 'The Latin adaptations of the "Historia Apollonii regis Tyri" in the middle ages and Renaissance', *Groningen Colloquia on the Novel*, iii. ed. H. Hofmann (Groningen, 1990), pp. 103–37.

[27] P. Bright, 'Anglo-Latin collections of the *Gesta Romanorum* and their role in the cure of

MS. HM 140 may also owe something to the fact that it was one of the earliest narratives to circulate widely in printed form, with free-standing Latin versions available by the very late 1460s and translations into various European vernaculars appearing in subsequent decades (testimony to some sense among printers that it would be a commercial success); it also had a wide printed circulation in its context in the *Gesta Romanorum*.[28] Thematic connections between *Apollonius* and the *Life of St. Ursula* are not obvious, beyond their shared inclusion of sea journeys, but it may be significant that MS. HM 140's version of the life of St. Ursula is shaped to include a heavenly marriage between Ursula and her earthly suitor, an element perhaps reflecting the family reunification that concludes Apollonius's story.[29]

The collection of short prose items that concludes the final section of MS. HM 140 serves to consolidate its generally pious flavour. Copied here in several different hands, all the items survive in other copies. The so-called *Profits of Tribulation* circulated widely, surviving in at least fifteen other manuscripts, and is found in the company of other, longer works of religious instruction for laypeople.[30] An item on *The Benefits of Reading the Psalter* survives elsewhere, not only in the manifestly pious context of books of hours: it also made its way into a collection of recipes and charms.[31] The prose text known as *Seven Things Necessary for Pardon*, evidently some form of advertisement for the Syon pardon, survives in another copy, one with demonstrable London connections: Oxford, Corpus Christi MS. 237.[32]

---

souls', in *What Nature Does Not Teach: Didactic Literature in the Medieval and Early Modern Periods*, ed. J. F. Ruys (Turnhout, 2008), pp. 401–24.

[28] Incunabule versions are listed in the British Library's *Incunabula Short-Title Catalogue* <https://data.cerl.org/istc/_search> under *Apollonius de Tyro* and *Gesta Romanorum* [accessed 23 July 2018]. The earliest free-standing Latin printed version is from 1474, printed in Utrecht.

[29] On Ursula's heavenly marriage, see Sanok, *New Legends of England*, pp. 252–4. Kortekaas noted that versions of the Apollonius story in the *Gesta Romanorum* usually conclude with a gesture towards a moralization, as customary in *Gesta* exemplary narratives ('Latin adaptations', p. 105). The text in MS. HM 140 ends with the family reunification, at a point equivalent to Archibald, *Apollonius*, paragraph 49 (p. 174), but has no moralization.

[30] 'Here begynnyth a litell short Tretis that tellith howe that there were vj maistres'; see P. S. Jolliffe, *A Check-List of Middle English Prose Writings of Spiritual Guidance* (Toronto, 1974), item 2c, for a list of manuscripts.

[31] London, Lambeth Palace, MS. 186 and London, Victoria and Albert Museum, MS. Reid 45; Oxford, Bodleian Library, MS. Ashmole 1447 (2). See O. S. Pickering and V. M. O'Mara, *The Index of Middle English Prose. Handlist XIII: Manuscripts in Lambeth Palace Library, including those formerly in Sion College Library* (Cambridge, 1999), p. 15.

[32] 'Here folowen seven thynges whiche a man or womman must haue for to be able to gete pardon' (Jolliffe, item E5). See K. A. Rand, 'The Syon pardon sermon: contexts and texts', in *Preaching the Word in Manuscript and Print in Late Medieval England: Essays in Honour of Susan Powell*, ed. M. W. Driver and V. O'Mara)Sermo, xi, Turnhout, 2013), pp. 317–49. MS.

Even though the contents of the second and third sections of MS. HM 140 may indicate London connections, the scribes and earliest owners left no obvious information about their identities or places of residence. The number of blank leaves and the variety of different hands may indicate that the sections resided for some years in a place where different people could make additions as desirable texts became available: a household seems a likely possibility. Some of the added notes are precisely datable, however, and these supply information on the whereabouts of the second and third sections of the manuscript during the third decade of the sixteenth century. The researches of John M. Manly and Edith Rickert, who were primarily interested in the manuscript's copy of Chaucer's *Clerk's Tale*, produced identifications of some of the individuals named in these notes and situated MS. HM 140 in the hands of readers associated with Henry VIII's court and with the council of Princess Mary.[33] The likelihood that such readers would have been interested in the manuscript's contents, and especially in the poems of Chaucer and Lydgate, has proved attractive,[34] but this account of the manuscript's early history clearly needs some adjustment, since its Chaucer and Lydgate section may not have been conjoined to the other parts in the early sixteenth century. Nonetheless, the findings of Manly and Rickert can serve as the starting point for further investigation of the early readers or owners of the second and third sections of the manuscript, bringing into focus individuals connected to civic and company circles in London and also to some of the offices of the court.

One name that appears in both the *Life of Job* section of the manuscript and in its large final gathering is that of a 'William Marshall' (on fos. 98, 160, 166v, 167, 170v). On folio 167 Marshall's name appears at the start of a note about a grievance concerning a sum of money, recording an incident of 9 December 1521 in which 'Master Breges' assured 'John Skot' that someone (probably the writer and hence Marshall himself) 'sholde ley & rote in presen'; the note goes on to recount that on 12 December Breges repeated the same words to 'Nycolas Slendon'. While Manly and Rickert did not follow up Marshall, they identified 'Master Breges' as John Brydges, master of the wardrobe in 1521 and 1530, and 'John Skot' as John Skut,

---

Corpus 237 includes (along with several saints' lives and *The Pilgrimage of the Soul*) Lydgate's *Dance macabre*, headed 'The daunce of powlys', and 'The maner of offering in the cyte of london'; for a description, see R. M. Thomson, *A Descriptive Catalogue of the Medieval Manuscripts of Corpus Christi College, Oxford* (Cambridge, 2011), pp. 121–2.

[33] Manly and Rickert, '*The Canterbury Tales*', i. 436–8.

[34] For the wider context, see, e.g., S. Lerer, *Courtly Letters in the Age of Henry VIII: Literary Culture and the Arts of Deceit* (Cambridge, 1997); and G. Walker, *Writing under Tyranny: English Literature and the Henrician Reformation* (Oxford, 2005), pp. 56–99.

queen's tailor.[35] But although royal service may have been one element of the acquaintance between these individuals, it seems important not to overlook that they were also a group of Londoners associated by craft. John Skut, first recorded in 1519 as tailor to Katherine of Aragon, would indeed serve all of Henry VIII's queens; but he was also a prominent merchant tailor, warden of the Company in 1527 and master in 1536.[36] Nicholas Slendon, identifiable as a tailor of London at a date close to 1521, might well have known Skut through a company association and is documented as bringing an action for debt against William Marshall.[37] The various individuals identifiable as 'Master Breges' include not only the king's tailor, John Bridges,[38] but also Sir John Bridges or Brugge, an important merchant and member of the Drapers' Company, who served as an alderman and then as mayor in 1520 to 1521 and was a member of parliament; he was knighted in 1521 and on these grounds and those of his company role would have warranted the title 'master'.[39] Quite how William Marshall might have offended these people in 1521 is unclear. He describes himself in another note in MS. HM 140 as 'armerar' (fo. 98) and may have been the man described in records as a 'wire-seller' of London, who was in 1524 retained by the captain of a ship named the George 'to serve in the war'.[40]

---

[35] The identification of Skut (Manly and Rickert, *The Canterbury Tales*, i. 437) is supported by references in *Letters and Papers, Foreign and Domestic, of the Reign of Henry VIII*, ed. J. S. Brewer, J. Gairdner and R. H. Brodie (23 vols. in 38 (1862–1932) and in *Privy Purse Expenses of the Princess Mary*, ed. F. Madden (London, 1831), p. 266 for the years 1530–47. Breges or Bridges is taken to be the individual mentioned in *Letters and Papers*, iii (1). 502 and v. 320.

[36] See M. Hayward, *Dress at the Court of Henry VIII* (Leeds, 2007), p. 322; *The Great Wardrobe Accounts of Henry VII and Henry VIII*, ed. M. Hayward (London Rec. Soc., xlvii, 2012), pp. xxix, xxxv; and M. Hayward, 'Skut, John (fl. 1519–1547), tailor', *ODNB* <https://doi.org/10.1093/ref:odnb/93736> [accessed 24 July 2018].

[37] TNA, C 1/442/39: Slendon named as plaintiff in a case brought against William Michell of London, armourer, 1515–18; he is also named in C 1/442/38 and C 1/347/20.

[38] Hayward, who noted that he was in royal service from 1516 to 1559 (*Dress*, p. 322).

[39] See the *History of Parliament* biography by H. Miller at <http://www.historyofparliamentonline.org/volume/1509-1558/member/brydges-%28brugges%29-john-1470-1530> [accessed 23 July 2018]. A less likely candidate as 'Master Breges' is Walter Brydges, groom of the chamber to Princess Mary, 1525–37 (Madden, *Privy Purse Expenses*, index, p. 215).

[40] *Letters and Papers*, iv (2), g. 86 (3), 34. Other cases from 1520 to 1530 involving William Marshall are documented in TNA, C 1/547/12 (action against William Marshall by John Fardyng of London, merchant tailor, for an unpaid debt); TNA, C 1/546/83 (action by Marshall and Richard Moniam, draper, against a mercer and a merchant stranger); TNA, C 1/574/12 (action taken against Marshall by John Smyth, skinner, and [William?] Rogiers, wax-chandler, both of London); TNA, C 241/282/85 (action taken by Robert Smith, citizen and merchant, to reclaim a debt from Marshall). It seems unlikely that William Marshall, armourer, is to be identified with the William Marshall who was clerk to the chief baron of

Armourers in London worked closely with other artisans and seem often to have identified with several different crafts during the course of their working lives; their affiliations depended partly on whether they were linen armourers, producing padded garments, or were concerned rather with the production of plate armour or chain mail.[41] Many had close contacts with the royal wardrobe and it is hardly surprising to find Marshall in the circles of skilled craftsmen and merchants who worked in and around this office. Another note in MS. HM 140 in Marshall's hand, undated, records 'the … profettes of scavagyng gaderid [by] Robard Actun and wylliam marshall', and 'indytementes of vnlawfull pamentes chymneyis and pentesis don by the warmvthe queste and the aldyrman of the warde' (fo. 166v).[42] Marshall evidently undertook with an associate some local tasks relating to the enforcement of building regulations, under the purview of the wardmote; and was involved in 'scavaging', collecting the taxes imposed on foreign merchants who were obliged to find local hosts to act as their sponsors or brokers.[43] His associate Robert Acton, identified by Manly and Rickert as a groom of the chamber by 1518 and a gentleman usher by 1528, was also a saddler, someone whose expertise and craft associations might have intersected with those of William Marshall; in this capacity Acton was king's

---

the exchequer in 1527 and in the 1530s a writer and translator of reformist works. On this individual, see A. Ryrie, 'Marshall, William (d. 1540?), printer and translator', in *ODNB* <https://doi.org/10.1093/ref:odnb/18153> [accessed 16 Jan. 2019]; D. E. Rhodes, 'William Marshall and his books, 1533–1537', *Papers Bibliograph. Soc. America*, lviii (1964), 219–31; and W. Underwood, 'Thomas Cromwell and William Marshall's Protestant books', *Hist. Jour.*, xlvii (2004), 517–39.

[41] M. Mercer, 'Kings' armourers and the growth of the armourers' craft in early fourteenth-century London', *Fourteenth-Century England VII*, ed. J. S. Hamilton (Woodbridge, 2014), pp. 1–20; B. Kirkland, '"Now thrive the Armourers": the development of the armourers' crafts and the forging of fourteenth-century London' (unpublished University of York PhD thesis, 2015). Linen armourers were assimilated into the Merchant Taylors' Company (M. Davis and A. Saunders, *The History of the Merchant Taylors' Company* (Leeds, 2004), pp. 11–3 and 49–52). I am very grateful to Christian Steer for alerting me to relevant studies of armourers and to Elizabeth New for discussion of linen-armourers.

[42] 'scavagyng', collecting a toll on merchant strangers (OED *scavage*, n., 1); 'pamentes', pavements (OED *pament*, n., 1); 'warmvthe queste', wardmote inquest (OED *wardmoot*, n., compounds, C2).

[43] On these responsibilities of the wardmote, see C. M. Barron, *London in the Later Middle Ages: Government and People 1200–1500* (Oxford, 2004), pp. 21–7, 247–8. For scavaging, see further S. Ogilvie, *Institutions and European Trade: Merchant Guilds 1000–1800* (Cambridge, 2011), p. 173; and N. Middleton, 'Early medieval port customs, tolls and control on foreign trade', *Early Med. Europe*, xiii (2005), 313–58. It is possible, although less likely, that the term 'scavaging' here refers to the forms of street-cleaning for which local wards appointed 'scavengers' (Barron, *London*, pp. 125 and 262; E. Sabine, 'City cleaning in medieval London', *Speculum*, xii (1937), 19–43).

saddler from 1528 until his death in 1558, by which time he had advanced to a number of important positions.[44] The names of the taxpayers on their list (John More, John Pachet, Richard Lyne, Thomas and Richard Alen, Nicolas Krystin and John Barton, along with 'the cutlar nexte the flowirdeluse' and 'myghhell the ffrutrar') include those of several other men who probably had connections similar to those of Acton and Marshall. Thomas Alen, for example, may have been the skinner who supplied lambskins to the royal wardrobe in 1510 and 1511; his will, made in 1524, refers to a son, Richard Alen, and names as a witness Richard Lyne, waxchandler: two of the names on Marshall's list.[45] The Nicolas Krystin on the list may have been the draper of that name who gained the freedom of the company in 1528 and was living in the parish of St. Michael Cornhill when he made his will in 1551.[46]

Chronologically the latest of the notes that Marshall added to MS. HM 140, the only one in which he describes himself as 'armerar' (fo. 98), records his delivery on 16 December 1527 of an 'obligation' and a 'supplication' signed by 'my lorde of exetores hand & master doktar borneles hande', together with a letter of attorney made by Richard Base, notary, to Richard Johnson, citizen, haberdasher and yeoman of the chamber to Lord Ferrers. The letters confirm that Johnson will receive at Bewdley, 'or at ane othar plase were my lade prynses konsell lyethe', a debt owed to Marshall by another armourer, William Carter, for a horse bought by Marshall on Carter's behalf from Richard Welles of Stratford at Bow. As Manly and Rickert noted, some of the individuals named here were connected to the household of Princess Mary, specifically to the council in the Marches that was attached to it during the years that Mary spent in Wales.[47] 'My Lord of Exeter' was

<hr />

[44] Manly and Rickert, 'The Canterbury Tales', i. 37, citing Letters and Papers, iv, index. See Hayward, Great Wardrobe Accounts, pp. 215, 280; Hayward, Dress, pp. 27, 276, 332, 339–40; and the History of Parliament biography by D. F. Coros <http://www.historyofparliamentonline. org/volume/1509-1558/member/acton-robert-1497-1558> [accessed 23 July 2018].

[45] Hayward, Great Wardrobe Accounts, pp. 93–4, 106, 108–10, 124, 152; Thomas Allen 'of the royal household' is mentioned in Letters and Papers, iii. 50 (Jan. 1519). The will of Thomas Aleyn (TNA, PROB 11/21, fos. 200–200v) mentions his birth in the parish of St. Clement and arrangements for his burial in what had become his local parish of St. Martin Ludgate. A 'Richard Alen' is noted among those serving in the office of the beds at the Field of the Cloth of Gold (Letters and Papers, iii. 246).

[46] TNA, PROB 11/34, fo. 184r–v.

[47] D. Loades, Mary Tudor: a Life (Oxford, 1989), pp. 36–76 and (for a list of household members) pp. 348–51; W. R. B. Robinson, 'Princess Mary's itinerary in the marches of Wales 1525–1527: a provisional record', Hist. Research, lxxi (1998), 233–52; J. L. McIntosh, From Heads of Households to Heads of State: the Pre-Accession Households of Mary and Elizabeth Tudor, 1516–1558 (New York, 2009), pp. 46–72; and J. L. McIntosh, 'A culture of reverence: Princess Mary's household 1525–27', in Tudor Queenship: the Reigns of Mary and Elizabeth, ed. A. Hunt and A. Whitelock (New York, 2010), pp. 113–26.

John Veysey or Voysey, bishop of Exeter and at this point in charge of Mary's council;[48] 'Master doktar bornele' was Peter Burnell, Princess Mary's almoner and treasurer;[49] 'My Lord feres' was Walter Devereux, Lord Ferrers, steward of the household and councillor to the princess.[50] But Marshall's points of contact with Princess Mary's council were men like himself: Richard Johnson, a London citizen and haberdasher attached at this point to Lord Ferrers's household, and William Carter, another armourer.[51]

The other individuals named in the manuscript are not easily identifiable. Manly and Rickert suggested that the William Turner who left a Latin note (fo. 101) and wrote 'This is master Turneris Boke testes John dolman Jamys Crock' (fo. 170v) was master of the robes for Henry VIII; others have believed him to be the physician and botanist, also dean of Wells, who died in 1568.[52] Another possible candidate is the William Turner, skinner, who died in 1533 and was commemorated in the church of St. Mildred Poultry, possibly to be identified as the man of the same name who served as groom of the toils (hunting nets) during the 1530s.[53] The second part of the manuscript, at the very least, seems to have stayed in London for some years. Other notes made in informal sixteenth-century hands in this section include one that refers to 'maister John hammulttone duyllyng in

---

[48] See N. Orme, 'Veysey [formerly Harman], John (c. 1464–1554), bishop of Exeter', in *ODNB* <https://doi.org/10.1093/ref:odnb/28262> [accessed 24 July 2018]; and Loades, *Mary Tudor*, pp. 40–1.

[49] Called John Burnell by Manly and Rickert, *The Canterbury Tales*, i. 436, following a reference in *Letters and Papers*, iv (1), no. 2331; but see *BRUO (to A.D. 1500)*, i. 316.

[50] See H. A. Lloyd, 'Devereux, Walter, first Viscount Hereford (c. 1489–1558), administrator and nobleman', in *ODNB* <https://doi.org/10.1093/ref:odnb/7567> [accessed 24 July 2018]; and Loades, *Mary Tudor*, pp. 39–41, 185.

[51] A 'William Armourer', possibly William Carter, is listed among those supporting the council in the Marches in 1525 (Loades, *Mary Tudor*, p. 351). Richard Johnson may be the citizen and haberdasher of the parish of All Hallows Barking whose will was proved in 1539 (LMA, DL/C/B/004/MS09171/010, fo. 336). William Marshall also made the note 'Md that I william marshall hathe R of Thomas' (fo. 170v) and was probably responsible for a series of informal memoranda about rental of a property (fo. 160).

[52] A. J. Kempe, *Historical Notices of the Collegiate Church or Royal Free Chapel and Sanctuary of St. Martin le Grand, London* (London, 1825), p. 113; Garmonsway and Raymo, 'St Ursula', p. 353; W. R. D. Jones, 'Turner, William (1509/10–1568), naturalist and religious controversialist', *ODNB* <https://doi.org/10.1093/ref:odnb/27874> [accessed 24 July 2018]; and the *History of Parliament* biography by T. F. T. Baker and A. D. K. Hawkyard <http://www.historyofparliamentonline.org/volume/1509-1558/member/turner-william-1512-68> [accessed 24 July 2018].

[53] The monument was noted by John Stow (Stow, *Survey of London*, i. 262). His will, made in 1536, is TNA, PROB 11/25/574. References to William Turner, groom of the toils, are in Hayward, *Dress*, p. 280 and *Great Wardrobe Accounts*, pp. 214, 280.

seint Jeyllis // parishe with ought cripulgat' (fo. 123v);[54] and another naming 'Henry Diszell … Citiz. and stationer of London' (fo. 114), who must have been the Henry Disle (fl. 1563–80) who was both a bookseller and a member of the Drapers' Company.[55] At some point before the late eighteenth or very early nineteenth century the three sections that make up the manuscript as currently compiled reached the collection of the antiquarian Richard Gough, himself a Londoner.[56] It may be the case that some, if not all, of the component sections stayed in the vicinity of London during the intervening years.

London interests are marked in MS. HM 140 in a variety of ways. A number of items in what are now its second and third sections (notably the short texts of religious instruction) had an attested London circulation. Some of these contents, especially the *Libelle of English Policy* and the *Advice to Apprentices*, would clearly have been of interest to readers who were themselves merchant householders or were close to people from such circles. Others, such as the *Life of Job* and the *Legend of St. Ursula and the 11,000 Virgins*, would have interested those involved in the pious activities sponsored by London guilds and fraternities or taking place in London parishes. The raft of informal notes added to the second and third sections of the manuscript in the early sixteenth century, particularly those by William Marshall, indicate that by this point these sections were certainly in the hands of individuals with London connections. Some of the people mentioned in these notes were associated with the royal wardrobe and the household of Princess Mary; but they also seem likely to have been affiliated through the crafts they practised – as tailors, drapers, haberdashers, skinners, wire-makers; and through these same crafts to have forged connections with various of the offices of court. None of the notes left in the second and third sections of the manuscript comments on its contents; and it is quite possible that these contents went unread during the sixteenth century as annotators simply used available writing surfaces to record business matters they wanted to remember. As so often, it is impossible to know what kinds of value were attached by readers to the texts that passed through their

---

[54] It has not proved possible to identify a John Hamilton of the parish of St. Giles Cripplegate, but there may be a London connection for the name 'Thomas ?masun' (fo. 113v): Stow noted a monument to a draper of this name in the church of St. Giles Cripplegate (Stow, *Survey of London*, i. 299).

[55] See *The London Booktrades: a Biographical and Documentary Resource* <http://lbt. bodleian.ox.ac.uk/mediawiki/index.php/LBT/07877> [accessed 23 July 2018].

[56] See R. H. Sweet, 'Gough, Richard (1735–1809), antiquary', in *ODNB* <https://doi. org/10.1093/ref:odnb/11141> [accessed 24 July 2018]; and for wider context, R. Sweet, 'Antiquaries and antiquities in eighteenth-century England', *Eighteenth-Cent. Stud.*, xxxiv (2001), 181–206.

hands. On the evidence of their content and known circulation, though, most of the texts brought together in the second and third sections of MS. HM 140 had a lively contemporary appeal in the late fifteenth century. Furthermore, the indications that texts were copied at different points by different hands into the third section suggest that this part, at least, enjoyed some kind of use. Whether readers continued to engage with the contents of the manuscript into the 1520s and beyond, as they used its empty space to record personal memoranda, is harder to fathom. Even though the saints' lives and the instructions for pious living might have seemed unattractive reading during the decades of religious reform, other of the manuscript's contents would not necessarily have lost their appeal. Parts of MS. HM 140 may have remained household reading for Londoners over many decades.

4. Palaeography and forgery: Thomas D.'s
*Book of the Hartshorn in Southwark**

Martha Carlin

In the summer of 1479 William Waynflete, bishop of Winchester (*c.*1400–86), was in the fifth year of a rather desultory dispute over title to a piece of property in Southwark, across the River Thames from the city of London. In June of that year one 'Thomas D.', who described himself as Waynflete's 'servant' (*serviens*), put together a book of evidence bearing the title *Liber de la Hertys Horne in Suthwerk* (*Book of the Hartshorn in Southwark*). This compilation was a legal brief of sorts in which Thomas D. rehearsed the history of the dispute, transcribed dozens of relevant documents concerning the ownership and tenancy of the property, and gave a précis and analysis of both the bishop's case and that of his adversary. What did he discover and who was Thomas D.?

The *Liber de la Hertys Horne* is a loosely stitched booklet in the archives of Magdalen College, Oxford.[1] It consists of eighteen paper folios in a

---

* Earlier versions of this chapter were presented long ago at Caroline Barron's seminar on medieval London, Institute of Historical Research, University of London, 30 April 1981; at the annual conference of the Western Association of Women Historians, Huntington Library, San Marino, California, 15 April 1984; and at the 25th International Congress on Medieval Studies, University of Western Michigan, Kalamazoo, 12 May 1990. My deep thanks are due to Caroline Barron for facilitating my access to the Fastolf Papers in Magdalen College, Oxford when I was working on my doctoral dissertation on medieval Southwark. I am also very grateful to Brenda Parry-Jones, at that time the Magdalen College archivist; Christopher Woolgar, formerly cataloguer of the archives at Magdalen College and now of the University of Southampton; the late A. G. (George) Rigg of the Centre for Medieval Studies, University of Toronto; and the late Leonard Boyle, OP, formerly of the Pontifical Institute of Mediaeval Studies in Toronto and subsequently prefect of the Vatican library, for their assistance, advice and encouragement when I was first working on the material in this chapter; and to Charlotte Berry, Magdalen College archivist, for her very helpful assistance when I went to the college in June 2018 to take the photographs used here.

[1] Thomas D.'s text is Oxford, Magdalen College Archives, MS. Southwark 204. In future citations, all manuscripts designated 'Southwark' (e.g., 'Southwark 204') are in the Magdalen College Archives, Oxford. All Magdalen College documents are cited by courtesy of the President and Fellows of Magdalen College.

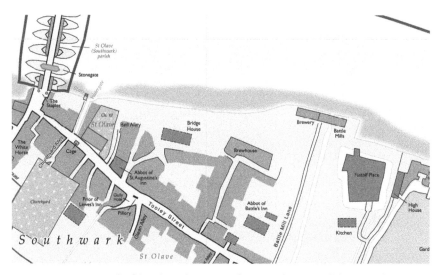

Figure 4.1. Detail of Southwark, *c*.1520, showing the sites of the Hartshorn property and of Sir John Fastolf's house. From *A Map of Tudor London* (British Historic Towns Atlas, in association with The London Topographical Society, 2018). Reproduced by courtesy of The Historic Towns Trust.

parchment wrapper, written in ink by Thomas D., with a few entries in a smaller contemporary hand. Its compilation was prompted by a dispute between Bishop Waynflete and the abbot of Lesnes (or Lessness), Kent, over title to a property known as the *Hertishorne* (Hartshorn) or *Bukhede* (Buckhead). This property lay in Southwark near the southern end of London Bridge, and extended in length from Tooley Street on the south to the Thames on the north, and in breadth from the parish churchyard of St. Olave on the east to a dock called the 'Watergate' on the west (see Figure 4.1). The site originally formed part of the Southwark estate of the Warennes, who were earls of Surrey from 1088 to 1347.[2]

In 1440 the site of the Hartshorn was acquired by Sir John Fastolf (1380–1459) and two co-feoffees, and in 1449 it came into Fastolf's sole possession. Fastolf developed a considerable estate in Southwark and built himself a large moated mansion house on the riverside there in an area known as Horselydown, opposite the Tower of London (see Figure 4.1).[3] He paid £161

[2] On the Warenne estate in Southwark, see M. Carlin, *Medieval Southwark* (London, 1996), pp. 28, 30, 107–8. The site of the Hartshorn is no. 228 on the plan and gazetteer of Tooley Street and Bermondsey Street in Fig. 7 (p. 35).

[3] On Fastolf's Southwark estate, which he built up between 1439 and his death in 1459, see M. Carlin, 'The urban development of Southwark, *c*.1200 to 1550' (unpublished University of Toronto PhD dissertation, 1983), pp. 252–4 (the Boar's Head), 310–7, 324–37 (the Horselydown estate and mansion house), 368–70 (the Hartshorn). For an overview of

13*s* 4*d* for the Hartshorn, a very considerable sum. The property contained shops and a wharf, and its location adjoining the dock and near the foot of London Bridge must have been a valuable one.[4] When Fastolf, a childless widower, died in 1459, the contest over the disposal of his vast estate began immediately and lasted for years.[5] The claimants included, among others, the Pastons, of epistolary fame, and Fastolf's friend and feoffee Bishop Waynflete, at that time (1456–60) chancellor of England, who himself had a grand riverside palace and manor in Southwark, and who in 1470 became the sole executor of Fastolf's will. Waynflete ultimately acquired much of Fastolf's valuable estate in Southwark, and in 1471 he obtained title to the Hartshorn.[6]

In 1474, as we learn from Thomas D., Waynflete's title to the Hartshorn was challenged by the abbot of Lesnes, a small house of Augustinian canons near Erith in Kent. Thomas describes the opening scenes of the dispute in these words:

> Be it remembered that in Michaelmas term in the 14th year of the reign of King Edward IV [1474] a certain [blank] abbot of Lesnes near Dertford in Kent, through the mediation of the bishop of Chester (*per mediacionem episcopi Cestrensis*),[7] delivered at Horseydoun'[8] to the lord bishop of Winchester a certain

---

Fastolf's properties, see Carlin, *Medieval Southwark*, pp. 52–5, 56 n. 162, 132–3.

[4] The site was surveyed for Magdalen College in 1684 and measured roughly 46 ft east-west by 115 ft north-south (Carlin, 'Urban development of Southwark', pp. 368–70).

[5] On an aspect of the Pastons' part in this dispute, see K. H. S. Wyndham, 'An Elizabethan search: the Norfolk Pastons and the Tower archives', *Archives*, xiv (1980), 211–6. On Fastolf, see G. L. Harriss, 'Fastolf, Sir John (1380–1459), soldier and landowner', in *ODNB* <https://doi.org/10.1093/ref:odnb/9199> [accessed 28 Jan. 2019]; and D. E. Thorpe, 'Writing and reading in the circle of Sir John Fastolf (d. 1459)' (unpublished University of York PhD thesis, 2011).

[6] J. Rose, 'Medieval estate planning: the wills and testamentary trials of Sir John Fastolf', in *Studies in Medieval Legal History in Honour of Paul Brand*, ed. S. Jenks, J. Rose and C. Whittick (Leiden, 2012), pp. 299–326; BL, Additional Charter 18,249 (probate of Fastolf's will, 5 May 1469); Southwark 76, 80, 207, B.20(6) (Warenne ownership); Southwark 6 C., 103 (Fastolf); Southwark 24 C., 82, 107, 111, 112, 7 C., 104, 53 C. (Waynflete).

[7] It was not uncommon for the bishop of Coventry and Lichfield to be styled bishop of Chester in the later medieval period (*Handbook of British Chronology*, ed. E. B. Fryde et al. (3rd edn., London, 1986), p. 53 n.; *A Survey of London by John Stow*, ed. C. L. Kingsford (2 vols., Oxford, 1908), ii. 92–3; *The Gentleman's Magazine*, lxi (2 vols., 1791), i. 323, ii. 1170. Richard Scroop (or Le Scrope), who was bishop of Coventry and Lichfield from 1386 to 1398, is called bishop of Chester in TNA, E 40/11372 (Ancient Deeds, ser. A). Alternatively, perhaps *Cestrensis* here is a slip for *Cicestrensis* (Chichester). In 1474 the bishop of Coventry and Lichfield was John Hales; the bishop of Chichester was John Arundel (Fryde et al., *Handbook of British Chronology*, pp. 254, 239). It has not been possible to trace a connection between either of them and Lesnes or its abbot. Lesnes abbey lay in the diocese of Rochester (*Roffensis*).

[8] Horselydown: Waynflete had possession of Fastolf's moated mansion there (Southwark A.17).

old charter (*quandam veterem Cartam*) by which he pretended (*pretendebat*) to have title by right of his said monastery to the tenement of the said bishop of Winchester called le Bukhed or le Herteshorne in Suthwerk near the church of St. Olave. He prayed the same lord bishop of Winchester to inspect his evidences touching the said tenement and do what was just for him and his house, or else compound with them for cash, according to his conscience, by which the abbot was willing to be ruled, etc. And soon afterward the same abbot died [fo. 15v].

Following this entry, Thomas transcribes the 'certain old charter' that the abbot delivered to Waynflete, calling it a 'copy of the pretended charter' (*Copia carte pretense*). It is an undated but ostensibly mid thirteenth-century grant by which Andrew le Ferun, for the salvation of his own soul and that of his wife Wymarca, and of the souls of his ancestors and 'successors' (*successorum*), gives to God and to the church and canons of Lesnes all the land with houses built upon it that Andrew had bought from Henry Jukell in the parish of St. Olave in 'Southwerc' (the abutments given are those of the Hartshorn property), together with three acres of marshland in 'Hrederhedere' (Rotherhithe). Magdalen College still possesses the alleged original of this deed of Andrew le Ferun (Southwark 125; see Appendix I), that is, the very document that the abbot delivered to Waynflete in the autumn of 1474. We shall return to it later.

There the matter evidently rested for two years, at which time the late abbot's successor revived the claim. Thomas reported:

> Be it remembered that in Michaelmas term in the 16th year of the reign of King Edward IV [1476], at Horseydon', a certain [blank] abbot of Lesnes, successor of the aforesaid abbot, with his counsel, asked the lord bishop of Winchester to return to him the aforesaid charter of Andrew le Ferun, which his predecessor had delivered to the same bishop, or else to compound with him for his title to the aforesaid tenement. And to strengthen his title the same abbot then delivered to the said bishop copies of the charters of Henry Jukell and of Mark, abbot of Lesnes, as follows [fo. 15v].

The abbot who initiated the abbey's claim to the Hartshorn in 1474 and died soon after would have been John Colman (abbot 1460–74); his successor was Abbot William (surname unknown).[9] This account is followed by

---

[9] For lists of the abbots, see *The Heads of Religious Houses: England and Wales, I. 940–1216*, ed. D. Knowles, C. N. L. Brooke and V. M. C. London (2nd edn., Cambridge, 2001), p. 171; II. *1216–1377*, ed. D. M. Smith and V. C. M. London (Cambridge, 2004), pp. 409–10; III. *1377–1540*, ed. D. M. Smith (Cambridge, 2008), pp. 264–5. A note on the dorse of TNA, SC 11/357 records that sub-prior J. Colman was elected abbot on the feast of St. Katherine the Virgin (25 Nov.) 1460.

transcriptions of the abbot's two copied charters. The first (Southwark 77[1]; see Appendix I) is an undated grant by Henry Jukell to Andrew le Ferun of the Hartshorn property, in return for a payment (*gersuma*) of 2 marks (26s 8d) in cash and an annual quitrent of 20s. The second (Southwark 110[3]; see Appendix I) is a lease by Abbot Mark and the convent of Lesnes to Robert Chesewyk, citizen and fishmonger of London, of the same property, which Andrew le Ferun had given to the house in pure alms. The lease was for a term of eighty years beginning at Michaelmas, at a rent of £10 a year. It was dated at the monastery of 'Ledes' (Leeds priory, Kent), the Friday after the feast of St. Lucy the Virgin 1299 (18 December); and the witnesses included Helias Russell, then mayor of London, and Luke de 'Leovyng' and Richard de Campes, then sheriffs. These witnesses were to be used by Thomas D. in his attack on the authenticity of this charter and we shall return to them as well.

Following the alleged lease from Abbot Mark is another note on the dispute:

> Again, the same abbot then affirmed in writing to the same bishop that he had account rolls in his monastery by which it appeared that in the 13th year of the reign of King Richard II [1389–90] a certain John Cheswyk, fishmonger of London, was their tenant and farmer of the aforesaid tenement, etc., and he paid them in that same year ten pounds for the aforesaid tenement [fo. 16r].

This alleged tenant's surname (Cheswyk) and occupation (fishmonger), the amount of his rent (£10) and the date (1389–90) imply that his tenure represented a continuation of the eighty-year lease allegedly granted by Lesnes to Robert Chesewyk in 1299.

This concludes the abbots' case, at least insofar as Thomas D. presented it. It appears to rest on three documents and some unspecified financial accounts (see Appendix I). These consisted of one allegedly original charter (Southwark 125: Andrew le Ferun to Lesnes Abbey), undated, but seemingly of the thirteenth century; a copy of another charter (Southwark 77[1]: Henry Jukell to Andrew le Ferun), also undated but supposed to be of the thirteenth century; a copy of a lease (Southwark 110[3]: Lesnes abbey to Robert Chesewyke), dated 18 December 1299, in the year that Elias Russell was mayor of London and Luke de 'Leovyng' and Richard de Campes were sheriffs; and a claim by the abbot in writing (Southwark 110[3], note 1) that he had account rolls at his monastery that proved that one John Cheswyk, fishmonger of London, was renting the Hartshorn property from Lesnes abbey in 13 Richard II (1389–90) for £10 a year.

In contrast, Thomas D. provided in support of bishop Waynflete's claim copies or précis of some thirty-five charters, which traced the ownership of the Hartshorn property from the mid thirteenth century to 1449, when it was purchased by Fastolf. The originals of all these charters still survive in the Magdalen College archives and they all appear to be authentic.[10]

The remainder of Thomas D.'s brief, and the most interesting portion of the text, consists of his analysis of the abbots' case, and the reasons for which he considered it to be invalid and Waynflete's case to be sound (Southwark 204, fos. 16–18, translated in full in Appendix II). Thomas attacked the abbots' claim by challenging both the validity and the authenticity of their written evidences and the existence of the second abbot's alleged, but unproduced, account rolls. He did this by using five types of evidence.

The first of these was legal evidence: Thomas claimed that, according to one of Waynflete's charters (Southwark 61; see Appendix I), Henry Jukell purchased only an annual rent of 4s from the site of the Hartshorn and not the property itself. Therefore, he argued, Jukell was not entitled to sell the land to Andrew le Ferun, as claimed in the abbot's second charter (Southwark 77[1]: see Appendix I). Thomas also argued that Jukell would not have sold to le Ferun for 2 marks the land whose rent alone Jukell had purchased for 2½ marks.[11] Thomas recited thirty-five charters that traced the descent of the Hartshorn property for 250 years and made no mention of Lesnes abbey.

Coupled with this legal evidence, Thomas used negative evidence to challenge two of the second abbot's alleged documents. The alleged grant from Jukell to le Ferun, he said, was produced only in copy and the bishop was given no original of the deed to examine. Thomas himself travelled to Lesnes abbey in May 1479 to investigate the truth of the abbot's claims and to view the account rolls that the abbot had claimed to have there and which allegedly contained proof that the abbey had owned the Hartshorn in 13 Richard II (1389–90). But, said Thomas, when he arrived at the abbey and demanded to see the account rolls, the abbot showed him 'various writings' but said that he was unable to find the account rolls at that time. Thomas wrote that it was his firm belief that even if such rolls ever were to be found, they would not be found to be authentic.

Thomas did further research, this time in search of historical evidence, to discredit the abbots' claim. He went to London to consult the civic records

---

[10] The originals are Southwark 61, 78, 49, 81, 109, 54, 124, 127, 126, 117, 93, 85, A.6, 101, 91, 95, 97, 88/89, 22 B., 122, 23 B., 102, 24 B., 114, 8 B./65 C., 92/64 C., 99/63 C., 121/62 C., 84/61 C., 118, 86, 90, 87, 6 C. and 209. (References such as '99/66 C.' signify two separate documents, generally an original and copy, but sometimes an original and counterpart.)

[11] Thomas failed to note, however, that in Southwark 61 Jukell acquired the 4s annual rent for a payment of 2½ marks down plus a yearly quitrent of 6d, whereas in the abbot's alleged charter (Southwark 77[1]) the price (*gersuma*) of the land was only 2 marks, but the annual quitrent was to be 20s, forty times the amount of the quitrent for the 4s rent.

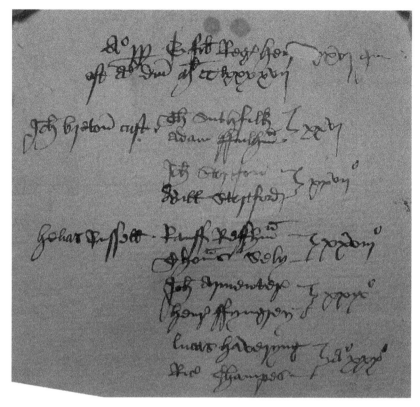

Figure 4.2. List of the warden, mayor and sheriffs of London, 26–30 Edward I, made in 1479 by Thomas D. from records in the London Guildhall. Magdalen College, Oxford, MS. Southwark 204, fo. 15A (photograph © Martha Carlin, reproduced by courtesy of the President and Fellows of Magdalen College).

in Guildhall, the seat of the city's government, where he looked up the dates of the mayor Elias Russell and the sheriffs Luke de 'Leovyng' and Richard de Campes (Champs, Champes). He made a list, based on his research at Guildhall, of the warden, mayor and sheriffs of London for the years 26–30 Edward I. The list was written on a narrow strip of paper, sewn askew into Southwark 204 between folios 15 and 16 (Figure 4.2).

According to the witness list in the alleged copy of the lease by Abbot Mark (Southwark 110[3]), the mayor Elias Russell and the sheriffs Luke de 'Leovyng' and Richard de Campes were all serving concurrently in December 1299. In fact, as Thomas pointed out, this was not the case: Russell was indeed mayor in that year (he served from October 1299 to October 1301), but it was not the year in which Luke and Richard were sheriffs. Thomas D.'s list (Figure 4.2) is as follows:

'In the 26th year of the reign of King Edward the son of King Henry, which is AD 1297'

[*Warden or mayor*]	[*Sheriffs*]	[*Regnal year*]
John Breton, warden	Thomas Suthfolk and Adam Fulham	26
	John Stortford and William Stortford	27
Helias Russell [mayor]	Rauff Refham and Thomas Sely	28
	John Armenter and Henry Fyngrey	29
	Luke Haveryng and Richard Campes	30

However, Thomas's list is also defective: he omitted one mayor (Henry le Waleys, who served from April 1298 until October 1299) and his regnal years are incorrect. In his discussion (Southwark 204, fo. 17) Thomas said that in December, 28 Edward I (1299), the sheriffs were Ralph Reffham and Thomas Sely and that Haveryng and Campes were sheriffs 'in AD 1301, etc.' In fact, Sely and Reffham were sheriffs from 29 September 1298 to 28 September 1299 (26–27 Edward I). They were succeeded by John de Armenters and Henry Fyngrye, who served from 29 September 1299 to 28 September 1300 (27–28 Edward I); and they in turn were succeeded by Haveryng and Campes, who served from 29 September 1300 to 28 September 1301 (28–29 Edward I). The confusion evidently experienced by all parties no doubt arose from the fact that sheriffs of London served from 29 September (Michaelmas) of one year to 28 September of the next; the mayor from 28 October (the feast of SS. Simon and Jude) to the following 27 October; and Edward I's regnal years ran from 20 November to the following 19 November. In other words, both the mayor and the sheriffs were elected near the end of one regnal year but served the bulk of their term in the next regnal year.

The correct sequence of mayors and sheriffs for these years is as follows:

Date	Warden (W) or mayor (28 Oct.–27 Oct.)	Sheriffs (29 Sept.–28 Sept.)	Regnal year (20 Nov.–19 Nov.)
1296–7	John le Breton (W)	Adam le Blund of Fulham and Thomas of Suffolk	24–25
1297–8	John le Breton (W) (until April 1298); Henry le Waleys (beg. April 1298)	John de Storteford and William de Storteford	25–26
1298–9	Henry le Waleys	Richer de Refham and Thomas Sely	26–27
1299–1300	Elias Russell	John de Armentiers and Henry de Fyngrie	27–28
1300–1	Elias Russell	Richard Campes and Lucas de Havering	28–29
1301–2	John le Blund	Peter de Bosenho and Robert le Callere[12]	29–3

Moreover, Luke's surname was not 'de Leovyng' but 'de Haveryng'; this was another suspicious aspect of the abbot's document, although Thomas D. failed to mention it.

The fourth type of evidence that Thomas employed was diplomatic evidence, which he used to challenge the grant by Andrew le Ferun (Southwark 125). He reported that the seal and parchment of this alleged original charter seemed to date from the reign of Henry III or earlier, but that 'the lettering in that charter appears black and fresh and not old, and as if it were written within the last twenty years' (fo. 16v).

Thomas used similar arguments in his criticism of the authenticity of Abbot Mark's lease to Robert Cheswyk dated 1299. Apparently, Thomas had seen an alleged original of this lease. As only a copy (Southwark 110[3]) was handed over to Waynflete in Michaelmas term 1476, it seems likely that the alleged original indenture was among the 'various writings' that the abbot showed to Thomas during Thomas's visit to Lesnes in May 1479.[13] Thomas criticized

---

[12] A. Lancashire, *Mayors and Sheriffs of London, 1190–1558* <https://masl.library.utoronto.ca/search.html> [accessed 1 Dec. 2018]; printed in C. M. Barron, *London in the Later Middle Ages: Government and People* (Oxford, 2004), Appendix I: 'The mayors and sheriffs of London 1190–1558' (pp. 308–55, at p. 324). Regnal years supplied by M. Carlin.

[13] The alleged original indenture does not survive among the muniments at Magdalen College and it has not proved possible to trace it elsewhere. For Thomas's description of it, see Appendix II, at the end of fo. 16v.

it on the grounds that, although the wax and seal, inscribed with Robert Cheswyk's name and arms, appeared to be genuinely old and authentic, 'still the hand and writing of the same charter seem to be manifestly suspect'. Therefore, he concluded, some 'cunning forger' (*subtilis fabricator*) had taken a genuine charter of Robert Chesewyk and, retaining the seal, had erased the original text of the charter 'with cunning waters' (*cum aquis subtilibus*) and in its place forged the alleged lease by Abbot Mark.[14]

The latter arguments link up very closely with the fifth type of evidence that Thomas used: palaeographic evidence. Some argument from palaeographic grounds is implied in his rejection of Abbot Mark's lease to Robert Cheswyk because its 'hand and writing' seemed 'manifestly suspect'. He became much more explicit, however, in his discussion of the grant by Andrew le Ferun (Southwark 125). After condemning the ink of that charter as too fresh to date from the thirteenth century, he went on to say that 'if one carefully notes the form of the writing of the script in that charter, it will appear false, because the script is like a "text" or "set" hand. And such was not the manner of writing in the olden days' (fo. 16v).[15] And indeed this is so. The hand of this document is strongly suggestive of a date in the fifteenth century, not the thirteenth, although there are attempts to archaize some of the letters and place-names (Figures 4.3 and 4.4).

There are, for example, bifurcated ascenders in a number of places; and some of the capital letters have two or more horizontal strokes on or through the ascenders, as do the exaggerated 7-shaped *et* abbreviations. Other archaizing touches are the spelling of the names *Hrederhedere* for Rotherhithe and *Southwerc* for Southwark. The usual spelling of Rotherhithe in the thirteenth century was some form of *Rotherhegh*, becoming *Retherheth(e)* in mid century. Southwark was usually spelled *Suwerk* or *Suwerc* at that period, becoming *Sutwerk*. The first syllable was never spelled *South-* in the thirteenth century.[16] Unquestionably late elements include the 'double-barrelled, straight-sided' lower-case 'A', typical of the late fourteenth and especially the fifteenth century, and the late capital 'W'.[17]

---

[14] In 1308 Robert, son of Gilbert de Cheswyk, sometime fishmonger of London, occurs as the owner of a different Southwark property, which he had inherited from his father (TNA, CP 40/171, rot. 37d (Trinity term 1308)) <http://aalt.law.uh.edu/E2/CP40no171/bCP40no171dorses/IMG_0899.htm> [accessed 4 Jan. 2018].

[15] '*Ac eciam si bene notetur forma scripture littere in illa carta apparebit ficta quia littera est quasi textus siue set honde. Et non fuit talis modus scribendi ex antiquo tempore*'. On writers of text hand, see G. Pollard, 'The Company of Stationers before 1557', *Library*, 4th ser., xviii (1937), 1–38, at pp. 5–11.

[16] See *The Place-Names of Surrey*, ed. J. E. B. Gover, A. Mawer and F. M. Stenton (English Place-Name Soc., xi, Cambridge, 1934), pp. 28–30.

[17] For this information I am very grateful to the late Andrew Watson of University College, London.

Figure 4.3. Magdalen College, Oxford, MS. Southwark 125
(photograph © Martha Carlin, reproduced by courtesy of the
President and Fellows of Magdalen College, Oxford).

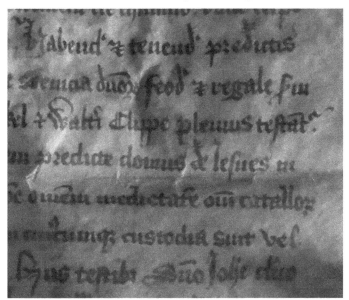

Figure 4.4. Magdalen College, Oxford, MS. Southwark 125, with
detail (photograph © Martha Carlin, reproduced by courtesy of
the President and Fellows of Magdalen College, Oxford).

About the rival claimants and the validity of their respective claims, what can be known? The abbey of Lesnes was founded by Richard de Lucy in 1178. It was dedicated to St. Thomas the Martyr, the first foundation in England in honour of Becket.[18] In the lists of its known abbots there is no mention of an abbot named Mark c.1299, as mentioned in the alleged lease by that abbot to Robert Cheswyk.[19] The abbots of Lesnes seem to have been a somewhat shady as well as shadowy lot. Gross financial and moral misconduct and breaches of the Rule, often with charges laid specifically to the abbot's door, were cited in episcopal visitations of 1283, 1299, 1336, 1340 and 1349, and there were further charges of misgovernance and even outright fraud in the fourteenth and early fifteenth centuries. The abbey became so impoverished and debt-ridden through the maladministration of its abbots that the king sequestrated it in 1402. In the same year the Commons complained in parliament that the abbot of Lesnes, together with certain other unnamed abbots and priors, was selling corrodies, annuities and pensions, *pur grandes et excessives somes* – cash down – under their common seals, to *diverses poveres lieges* of England. These prelates were then purchasing protections from the king that allowed them to default on the payments while making them immune from action at common law.[20]

As to the claim by the abbots of Lesnes to the Hartshorn, a title allegedly dating back to the thirteenth century: there is no mention of any such holding in the abbey's taxation of 1291, nor in a valuation of the abbey's possessions made in 1403, nor in a list of the abbey's income properties made in June 1472, only two years before the abbey first laid claim to the property.[21] In fact, apart from the 'pretended' charters dismissed by Thomas D., there is no record that the abbey ever owned any property in Southwark at all.

Bishop Waynflete's title rested on much firmer ground. The thirty-five charters that Thomas D. cited, together with others that also survive among the Magdalen College muniments,[22] establish an almost unbroken chain

---

[18] C. N. L. Brooke and G. Keir, *London 800–1216: the Shaping of a City* (London, 1975), p. 219.

[19] The only Abbot Mark occurs between 1219 and 1223 (Smith and London, *Heads of Religious Houses*. ii, pp. 409–10).

[20] *The Victoria History of the County of Kent*, ed. W. Page (3 vols., London, 1908–32) (hereafter *VCH Kent*), ii. 165–6; TNA, SC 8/22/1095; summarized in *Parliament Rolls of Medieval England*, ed. C. Given-Wilson et al. (Woodbridge, 2005), 'Appendix: September 1402', no. 19; and printed in full in *Rotuli Parliamentorum* (7 vols., London, c.1767–83, 1832), iii. 520; A. W. Clapham, 'The history and remains of the Augustinian abbey of Lesnes', *Trans. St. Paul's Ecclesiol. Soc.*, vii (1911), 1–13.

[21] *VCH Kent*, ii. 166; TNA, SC 11/357, SC 12/9/37.

[22] The additional charters, which date from c.1265 to 1440, are Southwark 11 B., 100, 128, 18 B., 123, 116, 105/106, 96, 115, 12 B. and 72. It is not clear whether Thomas omitted them

of ownership of the Hartshorn property from the middle decades of the thirteenth century to its conveyance by Waynflete to Magdalen College in the winter of 1482 to 1483.[23] Waynflete's title seems to have been secure; the abbot of Lesnes apparently dropped his claim.

What of the identity of the author of this brief, the mysterious Thomas D.? We know from his work that he was a trusted servant (*serviens*) of Waynflete and that he was able and conscientious, experienced in dealing with legal documents and prepared to analyse them in terms of their technical nature, provisions, forms of dating and authentication, and also their seal, ink and script. He used the civic archives at Guildhall to research the sequence and dates of London's mayors and sheriffs, and did not hesitate to go to Lesnes and interrogate the abbot in his own abbey in attempting to view the abbot's alleged but unproduced account rolls. This information, together with our knowledge of his first name and surname initial, makes it possible to identify Thomas D. as Thomas Danvers of Waterstock, Oxfordshire.

Thomas Danvers was the eldest son of John Danvers and his second wife Joan Bruley. He was born *c*.1422 and died, aged about eighty, in 1502. The Danvers family were closely associated with William Waynflete and Thomas became 'an intimate member' of Waynflete's household and the bishop's closest associate and friend.[24] Thomas and his younger brother William, who became a judge, appear as principals or witnesses in many of the charters pertaining to lands in Southwark that Waynflete obtained from the Fastolf estate.[25] Thomas Danvers is mentioned in connection with Waynflete in a number of the Paston letters of the 1460s and 1470s and is the author of one of them.[26] He served from 1476 or 1478 until 1486 as treasurer of Wolvesey, the bishop's palace in Winchester and the seat of his exchequer. The treasurer of Wolvesey was the bishop's diocesan receiver-general and the office was equivalent in rank and importance to that of chancellor of the bishop's household.[27] A letter of *c*.1477 to Waynflete from

---

through oversight or because he thought them superfluous. There is a copy of one further charter in Magdalen College archives, 'Evidences of Southwark (Unclassified Estates)', fos. 32v–33r.

[23] In addition to the charters cited above, see for the period 1449–97 Southwark 201, 50 A., 113, 107, 112, 120, 7 C., 82/111, 104, 53 C., 207, B.29(3), 21/45, 28, 28 C., 76, 80 and B.20(6).

[24] F. N. Macnamara, *Memorials of the Danvers Family* (London, 1895), pp. 155, 158; V. Davis, *William Waynflete: Bishop and Educationalist* (Woodbridge, 1993), pp. 130, 142.

[25] Southwark 24 C., 68 C., 26, 6, 8, 7, 60 C., 40 C., 57 C., 12 and 14.

[26] *Paston Letters and Papers of the Fifteenth Century*, ed. N. Davis (2 vols., Oxford, 1971 and 1976), i. 430, 596; ii. 378–79, 424, 583.

[27] Davis, *William Waynflete*, p. 121. Davis dated Danvers's period as treasurer from 1478 to 1486 (p. 121, n. 16), but he appears already to be holding the office in the Winchester pipe

the chancellor and regents of Oxford University referred to Danvers as one of the bishop's *fidelissimis familiaribus*.[28]

From the 1450s Waynflete employed Thomas Danvers in his arrangements for the foundation and endowment of Magdalen College, and perhaps it was in this connection that Thomas was called in to lend his expertise to the Hartshorn controversy, for the property was to pass to the college in a few years' time.[29] Several letters from Danvers to president Richard Mayhew of Magdalen survive; they date from c.1469 to c.1494 and contain references to Waynflete and to business affairs and lawsuits connected with Waynflete and the college.[30] These letters furnish conclusive proof of Thomas Danvers's identification as Thomas D. Not only do the hands match, but so, too, does the distinctive flourish with which Danvers finished off the initial 'D' of his surname in one of his letters to Mayhew, which is identical to that of Thomas D. (Figures 4.5 and 4.6). In much the same fashion Danvers also initialled a letter to John Paston II.[31]

In addition to his services to Waynflete and Magdalen College, Thomas Danvers became a prominent landowner in Oxfordshire.[32] He was a justice of the peace for the counties of Oxford and Hampshire and represented in parliament the Wiltshire boroughs of Downton and Hindon, of which Waynflete, as bishop of Winchester, was lord: Downton in 1459 (at Coventry); Hindon in 1467–8 (at Westminster and Reading); and Downton again in 1470–1, 1472–5, 1478, 1483 and 1484 (all at Westminster). Thomas Danvers also seems to have been, at least for a time, a resident of Southwark. On 28 January 1493 Magdalen College obtained a lease (Southwark 47) from the prior of St. Mary Overy's in Southwark of a tenement within the priory close. This tenement was described as lying between the house of a glazier on the east and the tenement in which Thomas Danvers, esq., 'now dwells' on the west. Danvers would have been about seventy years old at the time. In 1501, together with his brother William and nephew John Danvers of Dauntsey, he

---

roll for 1476 (Winchester, Hampshire Archives, Bishopric of Winchester pipe rolls, 11M59/B1/205 (formerly Eccles. II/155840), last 3 fos. (1476)).

[28] R. Chandler, *The Life of William Waynflete, Bishop of Winchester* (London, 1811), pp. 364–5.

[29] Davis, *William Waynflete*, p. 144; Southwark 28, 28 C., 76 (1482–7).

[30] Magdalen College, MS. 367, nos. 18–21.

[31] Cf. the signature *'per me Thomam Danvers manu proprie'* on a receipt in BL, Add. Chart. 20,329; and Danvers's letter to John Paston II, signed with his characteristic flourished 'T.D.', in BL, Add. MS. 34,889 (letter dated 29 Jan. 1467; printed in Davis, *Paston Letters*, ii. 378–9). The use of initials in documents was very common; the Paston letters contain many examples in addition to the letter signed by Danvers.

[32] *The Victoria History of the County of Oxfordshire* (18 vols., London, 1907–), viii, ed. M. D. Lobel, p. 152; see also pp. 62–3.

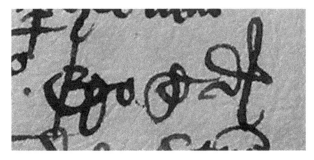

Figure 4.5. Thomas Danvers's distinctive initial 'D', Magdalen College, Oxford, MS. Southwark 204, fo. 17v, line 14 (1479) (photograph © Martha Carlin, reproduced by courtesy of the President and Fellows of Magdalen College, Oxford).

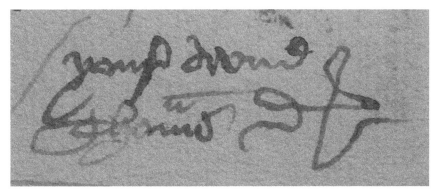

Figure 4.6. Thomas Danvers's initial 'D', Magdalen College, Oxford, MS. 367/21 (*c*.1490–96) (photograph © Martha Carlin, reproduced by courtesy of the President and Fellows of Magdalen College, Oxford).

was knighted on the occasion of Prince Arthur's marriage.[33] In the codicil to Waynflete's will he received a bequest of 40 marks, the same amount that the chief executor was to have.[34] In his own will, made on 1 November 1501, about ten months before his death, Thomas directed that his property in Longstock, Hampshire, be disposed to the cathedral priory of Winchester for prayers for his own soul and that of Bishop Waynflete, who had died in 1486.[35]

---

[33] Macnamara, *Memorials*, pp. 158, 164; Davis, *William Waynflete*, p. 130.

[34] Chandler, *Life of William Waynflete*, pp. 382–4.

[35] Thomas Danvers's will (TNA, PROB 11/13/303, formerly reg. Blamyr, fos. 93v–94) was proved at Lambeth on 26 Sept. 1502. It is printed in full in *Some Oxfordshire Wills*, ed. J. R. H. Weaver and A. Beardwood (Oxfordshire Record Soc., xxxix, 1958), p. 75. He died childless on 10 Sept. 1502 and was survived for 9 years by his second wife, Dame Sybil (Macnamara, *Memorials*, pp. 165, 169–73).

Thomas Danvers also was a half-brother of the attorney Robert Danvers (*c*.1400–67), who, in order to trap a forger in a title dispute in 1432, resorted to some forgery himself. Robert Danvers, who was acting as counsel for one of the claimants, was able by his ruse to expose the forgery of the other party and so won his case. He was to become a famous judge and so, perhaps, was able to pass on his analytical and forensic expertise to his young half-brother Thomas.[36] Robert Danvers also served first as common sergeant and then as recorder of London, which may explain Thomas's knowledge of and access to the municipal records at Guildhall.[37]

Forgery, even forgery perpetrated or instigated by abbots, is nothing new. The eleventh and twelfth centuries were particularly rife with ecclesiastical *spuria*.[38] Pope Innocent III (1198–1216), alarmed at discovering that forged *bullae* were being produced in Rome in his own name and that of his predecessor Celestine III, issued decretals on how to detect false documents by checking for a false or re-used seal, erasures that altered a genuine text, the phrasing (*stylus dictaminis*) and the form of the script (*forma scripture*).[39] In England, major producers of forgeries included Westminster abbey, Christ Church, Canterbury and St. Augustine's, Canterbury,[40] but many other religious houses, large and small, also created false documents. In 1364, for example, the abbot of Stoneleigh in Warwickshire was found to

---

[36] The details of Robert Danvers's case are given in L. C. Hector, *Palaeography and Forgery*, (Borthwick Institute of Historical Research: St. Anthony's Hall Publications, xv, London and New York, 1959), pp. 16–8. Robert Danvers served Archbishop Henry Chichele in arranging for the endowment of All Souls College, Oxford, much as Thomas Danvers later was to serve Bishop Waynflete in the endowment of Magdalen College (Macnamara, *Memorials*, pp. 102–16).

[37] Robert Danvers was common sergeant of London by 1439 and recorder from 1442 to 1450. He was an MP for Oxfordshire in 1436 and for London in 1445 and a justice of the common bench from 1450 until his death in 1467. In 1465 he was knighted on the occasion of Elizabeth Woodville's coronation (Macnamara, *Memorials*, pp. 103–10). The municipal records at Guildhall were kept apart from the public library collection there (C. M. Barron, *The Medieval Guildhall of London* (London, 1974), pp. 31–5, 49 n. 100).

[38] On medieval forgery in general, see *Fälschungen im Mittelalter. Internationaler Kongreß der Monumenta Germaniae Historica, München, 16.–19. September 1986* (Monumenta Germaniae Historica Schriften, xxxiii, 5 vols., Hanover, 1988); and A. Grafton, *Forgers and Critics: Creativity and Duplicity in Western Scholarship* (Princeton, N.J., 1990).

[39] A. Hiatt, *The Making of Medieval Forgeries: False Documents in Fifteenth-Century England* (London and Toronto, 2004), p. 26.

[40] C. N. L. Brooke, 'Approaches to medieval forgery', *Jour. Soc. Archivists*, iii (1968), 377–86, at pp. 379–80, citing the reference to the 'factory of forgeries' at Westminster in J. Tait, 'An alleged charter of William the Conqueror', in *Essays in History Presented to R. L. Poole*, ed. H. W. C. Davis (Oxford, 1927), pp. 151–67, at pp. 158–9 n. 2; S. E. Kelly, 'Some forgeries in the archive of St. Augustine's abbey, Canterbury', in *Fälschungen im Mittelalter*, iv. 347–69; cf. R. Southern, 'The Canterbury forgeries', *Eng. Hist. Rev.*, lxxiii (1958), 193–226.

have recovered illegally certain abbey tenements from their tenant by means of a deed 'which had been erased and forged' by one of the monks, acting under the abbot's orders.[41]

L. C. Hector, in *Palaeography and Forgery* (1959), explored the subject of medieval and post-medieval forgery and the contemporary detection of it. Hector examined the broad range of techniques employed by medieval forgers, from simple erasures to seal substitutions and such sophisticated ploys, and how these were detected and challenged. He believed, however, that medieval forgers and those who challenged their work displayed little or no palaeographical knowledge of how modes of scripts had changed from generation to generation. Apart from one or two inconclusive examples, the earliest firm evidence that Hector found for such knowledge was among the late sixteenth-century officials of the treasury of the receipt (the custodians of the *Domesday Book*). He concluded that, '[o]utside the ranks of official specialists of this kind we could hardly expect Mabillon to have been thus anticipated'.[42]

Hector's position was, perhaps, too extreme, since, for example, post-conquest scholars were well aware of the difficulties of reading documents written in Anglo-Saxon script (*manu Saxonica*)[43] and medieval examples of deliberate archaizing of scripts did occur. Documents forged at St. Augustine's, Canterbury (1060s) and at Evesham abbey (probably 1150s), for example, imitated earlier hands.[44] In the early fifteenth century Thomas of Elmham, who wrote a history of the priory of St. Augustine, Canterbury, copied out four of the abbey's so-called 'earliest' documents, reproducing them in rough facsimile as well as in the handwriting of his own time, for the benefit of posterity. He did this, however, for antiquarian motives and

---

[41] *Select Cases in the Court of King's Bench under Edward III*, ed. G. O. Sayles (Selden Soc., lxxxii, 6 vols., London, 1965), vi, 134–5.

[42] Hector, *Palaeography and Forgery*, p. 13 and *passim*. This is in direct opposition to T. F. Tout's view that medieval forgers routinely tried to imitate bygone scripts (T. F. Tout, 'Medieval forgers and forgeries', *Bull. John Rylands Libr.*, v (1918–20), 208–34; repr. in T. F. Tout, *The Collected Papers of Thomas Frederick Tout* (3 vols., Manchester, 1932–4), iii. 117–43, especially at pp. 123–8). Hector makes no reference to this claim or this article, although several of the most interesting forgery cases he cites were discussed by Tout. Jean Mabillon, OSB (1623–1707) founded the disciplines of palaeography and diplomatic with his publication of *De Re Diplomatica Libri VI* (Paris, 1681).

[43] E.g., in the late eleventh century Abbot Ingulf of Crowland took some of the abbey's Mercian charters, which had, he said, long been 'neglected and despised, because of the barbarous characters in which they were written', and gave them to the cantor so that he could teach the younger monks how to read the script (Hiatt, *Making of Medieval Forgeries*, p. 37, citing *Historia Croylandensis*, ed. W. Fulman (2 vols., Oxford, 1684), i. 98, and *Ingulph's Chronicle of the Abbey of Croyland*, trans. H. T. Riley (London, 1854), p. 201).

[44] Hiatt, *Making of Medieval Forgeries*, p. 23.

evinced no suspicion that his four documents were themselves forgeries of the late eleventh century.[45] Some archaized forgeries were poorly done. The prior of Canterbury, who 'came near to drowning in spurious title deeds', had one charter, a supposedly original grant of lands by King Alfred, in which 'the script moves from a pastiche of the ninth century to the thirteenth in five lines or so, and stays there'.[46] On the other hand, in the fourteenth century the nunnery of Wix in Essex produced two forgeries of a charter of Henry II that imitated twelfth-century script, one so successfully that it was reproduced as a genuine document in a modern catalogue.[47]

The Hartshorn controversy provides insights into how a title conflict might be disputed outside the courts in fifteenth-century England and reveals the extent of archival research and professional expertise that this might entail. It is especially intriguing to find an account of the use of palaeography as well as diplomatic to argue a case in the 1470s, two centuries before Jean Mabillon's pioneering publication of *De re diplomatica* in 1681. Thomas D.'s *Liber de la Hertys Horne in Suthwerk* (Southwark 204) presents an array of evidence, analyses and arguments that reflect its compiler's exhaustive title search in the muniments collection of Bishop Waynflete, his research on the dates of London's mayors and sheriffs in the Guildhall archives, his attempted examination of the muniments at Lesnes abbey and his familiarity with the wax, seals, inks and scripts of the thirteenth century. The watertight case that he built on behalf of his patron William Waynflete and his demolition of the rival claim of the abbot of Lesnes, including by discrediting two of the abbot's documents on palaeographical grounds, are an impressive testament to the labour and expertise of that shrewd and industrious man of affairs, and sometime resident of Southwark, Thomas D.

---

[45] A. Gransden, 'Antiquarian studies in fifteenth-century England', *Antiquaries Jour.*, lx (1980), 75–97, at p. 79; see also M. Hunter, 'The facsimiles in Thomas Elmham's history of St. Augustine's, Canterbury', *Library*, 5th ser., xxviii (1973), 215–220; and Hector, *Palaeography and Forgery*, pp. 13–4.

[46] M. Brett, 'Forgery at Rochester', in *Fälschungen im Mittelalter*, iv. 397–412, at pp. 406, 408.

[47] H. Jenkinson, with revisions by P. M. Barnes and L. C. Hector, *A Guide to Seals in the Public Record Office* (Public Record Office Handbooks, i, 2nd edn., London, 1968), 'Forgery', 29–31, at pp. 29–30 and 30 n. 1. See also Brooke, 'Approaches to medieval forgery', p. 381; and Grafton concerning Giovanni Nanni, a papal theologian of the late 15th century who faked inscriptions and texts (*Forgers and Critics*, pp. 28, 55). Grafton comments that Nanni's techniques (which included the use of an archaic script) were known in classical antiquity and 'rediscovered' in the 15th century (p. 55).

Appendix I

Summaries of the documents discussed above
(All in the Magdalen College Archives, Oxford)

SOUTHWARK 125 *(allegedly original deed; copies in Southwark 77[2], 110[2] and 108)*

Grant, in pure and perpetual alms, by Andrew le Ferun, for the salvation of his soul and that of his wife Wymarca, and of his ancestors and 'successors' (*successorum*), to God and to the church of Blessed Thomas the Martyr of Lesnes and to the canons there, of all the land that he bought of Henry Jukell in the parish of St. Olave in 'Southwerc' with houses and other appurtenances, lying between the cemetery of St. Olave on the east and the 'Watergate' on the west, and extending in length from the royal highway to the Thames; and also three acres of marshland with appurtenances, enclosed with ditches, which he bought of Walter son of William Clippe in the vill of 'Hrederhedere' opposite the land of Blakeman, of which the east end extends to 'Gatefeld' and the west to the royal highway. To have and to hold forever, for the services to the lords of the fees and the royal service. In addition, for the salvation of his soul and the emendation of the said house of Lesnes, Ferun grants to the canons in pure alms a moiety of all of his chattels, both movables and immovables, when he dies. Witnesses: dom. John the clerk, William the goldsmith (*Aurifabro*), Martin de Ponte, Anselinus son of Walter Clippe, Gerold de Castell', and many others. Undated. Round red seal depicting St. Christopher carrying the Christ child, with illegible inscription.

SOUTHWARK 61 *(original deed)*

Grant by William de Budely, son of Edward de Budely, to Henry Jukel, his heirs or assigns, of four shillings of annual quitrent in the parish of St. Olave 'de Sutwerk', to be taken of Ysabella de Budely and her heirs from the land that she held of William between the cemetery of St. Olave and the 'Watergate', rendering *6d* per annum to William and his heirs for all services. Henry has given William 2½ marks (33*s* 4*d*) in silver as payment (*gersumam*). Undated. Witnesses: Hervey son of Fulcher, Benet son of Luke, William the vintner (*Vinit'*), Robert de Boclande, Reginald the baker (*pistore*), Alexander the baker (*pistore*), Richard Walkelin, Robert de Codinetone, Walter the sacrist, William Chaloner, Ralph de Berkinge, Richard Ailard, Elys son of Godard, Norman de Sutwerk, Christian the clerk, and many others. Round green seal (broken) depicting a winged quadruped, inscribed 'S . . . . . . Edwardi'.

SOUTHWARK 77(1) (copy; a later copy is Southwark 110[1])

Copy of an alleged charter by which Henry Jukell grants to Andrew le Ferun all his land with appurtenances lying between the cemetery of St. Olave on the east and the Watergate on the west, and extending in length from the royal highway to the Thames, with everything in stone and wood, in buildings and all things. To have and to hold to le Ferun and his heirs or anyone to whom they should wish to give, sell, or bequeath the property, except the said church of St. Olave, for an annual quitrent to Jukell and his heirs of 20*s* for all services. If le Ferun, his heirs or assigns should wish to sell, Jukell and his heirs may buy the property for one gold bezant less than anyone else (*propriores erimus omnibus alijs de uno bisancio auri*). Le Ferun has given Jukell a payment (*gersumam*) of 2 marks (26*s* 8*d*). Undated. Witnesses' names omitted.

SOUTHWARK 110(3) (copy)

Alleged copy of an indenture by Abbot Mark and the convent of Lesnes by which they demise and let to farm to Robert Chesewyk, citizen and fishmonger of London, all their land with buildings and other appurtenances that Andrew le Ferun gave them in free alms, in the parish of St. Olave '*in Suthwerc in suburbio London*', between the cemetery of St. Olave on the east and the Watergate on the west, and extending from the royal highway to the Thames. To hold to Robert, his heirs, executors, [and assigns], from Michaelmas (29 September) for a term of eighty years, for an annual rent of £10 sterling, paying the rents and services to the king and the lords of the fee, and maintaining the property in good repair. Dated at the monastery of 'Ledes', Friday next after the feast of St. Lucy the Virgin, AD 1299 (18 December). Witnesses: Helias Russell, mayor of London; Luke de Leouyng and Richard de Campes, sheriffs; John de Ponte; John de Sancta Anastasia; William de Gradu; Matthew de Stell'; Norman *blundo*; William Thomas, clerk; and many others.

Notes in fifteenth-century hands appended to Southwark 110(3):

(1) [*In the same hand as the lease*] John Chesewyk, fishmonger of London, held 'le Hertishorne in Southwerk' to farm at an annual rent of £10 in 13 Richard II, as appeared in an account roll made in that year.

(2) [*In Thomas D.'s hand*] According to sworn evidence, John Okley and Alice his wife, daughter and heir of Ralph Wayte, were in possession of 'le Hertishorne in Southwerk' by inheritance in 13 Richard II. It is also established (*compertur est*) by evidence that, from the time of Edward II to that of Henry VI, others were in possession of the said tenement and there is no mention of the title of the said abbot.

Appendix II

Full translation of Thomas D.'s analysis of the Hartshorn case
(Magdalen College Archives, Southwark 204, folios 16–8)

[fo. 16] Here follow the considerations by which it appears that the said abbot of Lesnes has no right or title to the said tenement of Le Bukhed or le Hertishorne

First, because as appears by the first evidence of the lord [bishop] [Southwark 61], the said Henry Jukell long before only purchased of William son of Edward de Budely an annual rent of four shillings issuing from the said land between the church of St. Olave and the Watergate, which Isabella de Budely then held etc. And thus then the same Henry was lord of the said rent, etc., and not of the said land or ground (*et non terre siue fundi predict*). And if so, then his said charter made to Andrew le Ferun of the said land [*Southwark 77(1)*] is of no value.

Second, if one closely inspects that pretended charter of Andrew le Ferun made to the monastery of Lesnes [Southwark 125], it will appear false and counterfeit, because it is a charter, as is clear from the seal and [fo. 16v] parchment, of an earlier date, namely, of the time of King Henry III or earlier, and nevertheless the lettering in that charter appears black and fresh, and not old, and as if it were written within the last twenty years. And also, if one notes well the form of the writing (*forma scripture littere*) in that charter it will appear false, because the script is like a 'text' or 'set' hand (*quia littera est quasi textus siue set honde*). And there was no such manner of writing in olden days (*Et non fuit talis modus scribendi ex antiquo tempore*).

Item, if the said Henry and Andrew were contemporaries of King Henry III or King John or earlier, etc., and this is proved by the charter of the said William de Budely made to the said Henry of the said annual rent, etc. [*Southwark 61*], therefore the charter of the said Andrew [Southwark 125] is false or very suspect, because it is newly written.

Item, be it remembered that the lord bishop of Winchester never saw that charter by which it is pretended that the said Henry Jukell gave to the said Andrew the said land etc. [Southwark 77(1)], but only a copy of it, delivered to him by the said present-day (*modernum*) abbot of Lesnes. And that charter similarly appears to be false and counterfeit, for the following reason: because, as appears by the said pretended copy, the said Andrew gave to the said Henry Jukell for the purchase of the entire land and tenement aforesaid, which are of the value of ten pounds per annum, only two marks etc., whereas the same Henry gave, as is clear from the said charter of William Budely [Southwark 61], two-and-a-half marks for the purchase of the annual rent of four shillings.

Item, it seems and appears that the pretended demise made by Abbot Mark of the monastery of Lesnes to Robert de Cheswyk of the aforesaid tenement for a term of eighty years [Southwark 110(3)] is false and counterfeit for the following reasons:

First, because, although the words 'Robert Cheswyk', with arms, are inscribed on the seal of that indenture, and the wax of the seal is very old, still the hand and writing of the charter seem manifestly suspect. And thus it appears that perhaps some cunning forger (*subtilis fabricator*) took a certain old charter of one Robert Cheswyk and with cunning waters (*cum aquis subtilibus*) erased everything that had been written within it, and afterward re-wrote, fabricated and falsified (*finxit*) that demise of the said Abbot Mark.

[fo. 17] Second, it is proved infallibly that the said pretended demise of Abbot Mark is false, because at the end of the pretended charter is written: 'Given Friday next after the feast of St. Lucy the Virgin, AD 1289 [*recte* 1299], with Helias Russell then mayor of London, Luke de Leouyng and Richard de Campis then sheriffs', etc. And as is proved by the records in the Guildhall of the city of London, on the feast of St. Lucy the Virgin, in the month of December, AD 1299, it was the 28th year of the reign of King Edward, the son of King Henry III, with Elias Russell then being mayor of London, and Ralph Reffham and Thomas Sely then being the sheriffs of London, etc. But it is true that one Luke Haueryng and Richard Campes were sheriffs of London in AD 1301 etc. Therefore, the said charter of demise is very suspect and false.

Third, the said charter of demise of Abbot Mark is proved to be false because, for a long time, and years before and after the said pretended demise (as it pretends to have been made, namely, near the feast of St. Lucy the Virgin, AD 1289 [*recte* 1299], which was the 28th year of the reign of King Edward the son of King Henry, as said above, etc.), the said abbot and convent were not seised of the said tenement etc., because one William Barnewell and Agatha his wife, and Peter Long of Suthwerk and Matilda his wife, as in dower right of their wives, as daughters and heirs – together with their two other sisters – of one William Froys, were seised of all the said land and tenement between the church of St. Olave and the Watergate, as by hereditary descent after the death of the said William Froys, who died seised thereof, as is clear from the charter of the said Peter Long, of which the date is the 25th year of the reign of King Edward the son of King Henry [Southwark 78, dated 29 August 1297]. And also one William de Horkesley, glazier (*vitrearius*), and Katherine his wife, by feoffment of Isabella wife of John de Malton', another of the daughters and heirs of the said William Froys, and Robert [fo. 17v] Graspeys and Johanna his wife, the fourth of the daughters and heirs of the said William Froys, were peacefully and hereditarily seised of the said land and tenement near the church of St. Olave after the death of the said William Froy[s] their father, who died seised thereof, as is clear from their charters – of which copies are written in the present booklet (*quaterno*) – which are dated in the 15th and 16th years of the reign of King Edward the son of King Edward [Southwark 49, dated 7 March 1322; and Southwark 81, dated 24 May 1323], without counter-claim (*absque reclamacione*) by any predecessor of the said abbot of Lesnes.

Item, whereas the present-day (*modernus*) abbot of Lesnes, by his written bill, as said above, has alleged that a certain predecessor of his as abbot of the said monastery was seised of an annual rent of ten pounds for the said land, let to farm to one John Cheswyk, fishmonger of London, and received by the hands of the said John etc., as would appear by account rolls of the 16th [*recte* 13th] year of the reign of King Richard II: upon this, now, on the first day of the month of May, in the 19th year of the reign of King Edward IV [1479], I, T.D., servant of the said lord bishop of Winchester, and by his command, going then to the said monastery of Lesnes to investigate the truth of the premises, etc., when the said current abbot showed to me, the said Thomas, divers writings on his part, I demanded of him to see the account rolls of his said monastery for the 13th year of the reign of King Richard II previously alleged by him to my lord the bishop, etc. He responded to me that he did not know where to find them at that time, etc. But I firmly believe that he will never find them to be authentic (*vera*), etc., and this is proved by the reason that he who wishes to inspect well this this booklet (*quaternum*) will see that in the said 13th year of the reign of King Richard II, one John Okley and Alice his wife, and many and divers others whose state the said lord bishop now has, for the entire time of the said King Richard II were seised peacefully of the said land and tenement, without counter-claim or title of any predecessor of the said abbot of Lesnes [Southwark A.6, dated 24 July 1389].

[fo. 18] Item, to conclude all, and to undermine (*ad enervandum*) all and every title of the said abbot to the said tenement and land, I affirm that from the time of William de Budely, who was the owner of the said land and tenement before the time of King Henry III or of King John his father, or earlier, until the month of June, in the 19th year of the reign of King

Edward IV [1479], namely for 250 years and more, the lord bishop of Winchester, and those whose state the same bishop now has in the said land and tenement, were thus peacefully seised without disturbance by any predecessors of the said abbot of Lesnes. And the present-day abbot, as I firmly believe, is unable to prove (*nescit probare*) that any of his predecessors was in seisin of the said tenement or of any part of it for 250 years and more.

5. 'Go to hyr neybors wher she dwelte before': reputation and mobility at the London Consistory Court in the early sixteenth century

Charlotte Berry

In the summer of 1521 a woman named Agnes Cockerel was expelled from her home in the London parish of St. Sepulchre without Newgate.[1] Agnes was not the kind of woman that respectable Londoners wanted living on their street. She was described as a prostitute 'a brothel of her taylle' (fo. 101) and 'a crafty dame' (fo. 100).[2] In response, she launched a defamation case at the London Consistory Court. The case provides a rare perspective on the workings of expulsion as a punishment and the wider relationship between reputation and mobility at the end of the middle ages.

The parties and witnesses to the case were a thoroughly ordinary crowd of medieval Londoners: a widow and her apprentice; a young fletcher; a capper and his wife; and Agnes, who described herself as a midwife. Caroline Barron has written of the difficulty of recovering the lives of the 'small people' of late medieval London, citizens with some foot on the low rungs of the civic ladder, and the 'smaller', marginalized people excluded from citizenship and sometimes forced to leave the city itself.[3] The ordinary 'small' people, and occasionally the marginalized 'smaller' people, appeared as witnesses in consistory court cases, giving narrative depositions which included many incidental details about their day-to-day lives and personal histories. They appeared as witnesses alongside those of higher status and members of the clergy. The records are thus a valuable resource for the range

---

[1] All references to and quotations from the case of Cockerel *contra* Beckett are taken from *Consistory Court Deposition Book, 1520–24* (LMA, DL/C/0205, fos. 99–102v).

[2] The phrase implies that she sold sex. Brothel was, in this period, a word for a prostitute. 'Tail' could refer to the posterior or genitals: 'brothel, n.' and 'tail, n.1', *OED Online* <http://www.oed.com/view/Entry/23789>, <http://www.oed.com/view/Entry/197067> [accessed 3 Jan. 2019].

[3] C. M. Barron, 'Searching for the "small people"' of medieval London', *Local Historian* xxxviii (2008), 83–94, at pp. 85–6.

of experiences they represent and shed light on how both the comfortably off and the less wealthy were perceived by their neighbours.

This chapter exploits the richness and depth of social description in consistory depositions as a starting point to explore the themes of mobility and reputation among late medieval Londoners. Reputation was important for Londoners of all social levels; for the better off, defence of their reputation was crucial to maintaining access to influential social networks and financial credit.[4] A bad one could, as will be discussed, result in expulsion from the neighbourhood. Moreover, the city contained a multitude of neighbourhoods in which it was impossible for every Londoner to be known. In the case of Cockerel *contra* Beckett, which is discussed at length in this chapter, a landlady suspicious of her new tenant's reputation was told to 'go to hyr neybors wher she dwelte before' (fo. 99v). As this phrase implies, it was within the neighbourhood that a person's character was known. Mobility across the many social spaces contained within the city could arouse suspicion and those who moved could face difficulties in establishing their good character among their new neighbours.

Consistory court depositions as evidence for mobility

The consistory court was the highest church court within London, held by the bishop of London. It heard suits relating to canon law: disputes over tithes, marriages, marital separation and defamation were among the most common cases. Unlike lower ecclesiastical courts, most suits were brought by a named aggrieved party, although cases could also be brought *ex officio* by order of the court itself.[5] Each party presented a series of witnesses (deponents) who made witness statements (depositions) regarding the disputed events surrounding a case. Depositions were made in response to a series of articles and interrogatories. The articles set out the facts of the case as they were seen by that party. The interrogatories similarly set out the facts according to the defendant. Each was designed by canon lawyers to draw out information which gave credence to either party's narrative.[6] Both articles and interrogatories often asked witnesses questions not just about the material of the case, but also about their knowledge of the opposing party's witnesses, their places of residence and reputation within

---

[4] H. Robb, 'Reputation in the fifteenth century credit market; some tales from the ecclesiastical courts of York', *Cult. and Soc. History*, xv (2018), 297–313, at pp. 307–10.

[5] On the process of the consistory and its difference to other ecclesiastical courts, see R. M. Wunderli, *London Church Courts and Society on the Eve of the Reformation* (Cambridge, Mass., 1981), pp. 7–15.

[6] S. A. McDonough, *Witnesses, Neighbors, and Community in Late Medieval Marseille* (New York, 2013), p. 40.

the community. Unlike in a modern court, local gossip about a person or a series of events, often termed their 'fame', was materially important in the consistory and other ecclesiastical courts.[7] All that survives of the London Consistory Court in this period are its deposition books, meaning that we know neither the outcome of the cases nor the precise arguments of either party, other than what can be inferred from the witness statements. However, the depositions, with their myriad of incidental detail about daily life, personal history and social relations, are a rich seam of material for social historians.

Martin Ingram's study of the regulation of sex in England made extensive use of the London consistory records, demonstrating their importance as documents of legal and communal punishment and control.[8] As records of individual voices depositions are problematic, being mediated through both the requirements of the court and the anticipatory 'pre-construction' of witnesses themselves.[9] Moreover, as Shannon McSheffrey has argued, they offer no direct window into the events described, but instead a series of narratives calculated to appear plausible in court.[10] Nonetheless, ecclesiastical court depositions are very useful records for mobility and migration in England owing to the fact that, unlike in secular courts, witnesses were regularly required to provide details of their age and places of past and present residence. Such sources have been well used by early modern historians and, to a lesser degree, by late medievalists to study mobility, but are yet to be widely exploited for this theme by urban historians or those studying London before the late sixteenth century.[11]

---

[7] T. S. Fenster and D. L. Smail, 'Introduction', in *Fama: the Politics of Talk and Reputation in Medieval Europe*, ed. T. S. Fenster and D. L. Smail (Ithaca, N.Y., 2003), pp. 1–11; McDonough, *Witnesses, Neighbors, and Community*, pp. 49–50.

[8] M. Ingram, *Carnal Knowledge: Regulating Sex in England, 1470–1600* (Cambridge, 2017).

[9] T. Johnson, 'The preconstruction of witness testimony: law and social discourse in England before the Reformation', *Law and Hist. Rev.*, xxxii (2014), 127–47.

[10] S. McSheffrey, *Marriage, Sex and Civic Culture in Late Medieval London* (Philadelphia, Pa., 2006), p. 12.

[11] P. Clark, 'Migration in England during the late seventeenth and early eighteenth centuries', in *Migration and Society in Early Modern England*, ed. P. Clark and D. Souden (London, 1987), pp. 213–52; L. R. Poos, *A Rural Society after the Black Death: Essex 1350–1525* (Cambridge, 1991), pp. 164–5; J. Whittle, 'Population mobility in rural Norfolk among landholders and others c.1440–c.1600', in *The Self-Contained Village?: the Social History of Rural Communities, 1250–1900*, ed. C. Dyer (Hatfield, 2006), pp. 28–45; P. J. P. Goldberg, *Women, Work and Life Cycle in a Medieval Economy: Women in York and Yorkshire c.1300–1520* (Oxford, 1992), pp. 217–63; L. B. Smith, 'A view from an ecclesiastical court – mobility and marriage in a border society at the end of the middle ages', in *From Medieval to Modern Wales: Historical Essays in Honour of Kenneth O. Morgan and Ralph A. Griffiths*, ed. R. R. Davies and G. H. Jenkins (Cardiff, 2004), pp. 64–80.

What make the consistory depositions such important sources for mobility comes down to two factors: the social range of witnesses and the extraordinary detail of the depositions. Witnesses ranged in status from servants and watermen to merchants and gentlemen. In some cases parties might have manipulated an event itself to engineer a persuasively high-status set of witnesses, particularly in the making of marriage contracts.[12] However, ultimately what the court required was a detailed account of an event and deponents who had sufficient knowledge of the circumstances of a dispute. Thus, witnesses were often of lower status or occupied menial positions in a household.[13] Under canon law the testimony of paupers was supposed to be ineligible.[14] Nonetheless, in London, as has been noted in similar records at Marseilles, parties seem to have made their own judgments about who was a suitable witness.[15] Witnesses frequently were described, or described themselves, as 'an honest pauper'.[16] There was thus a deal of negotiation about who was sufficient to appear, permitting the wide social range of deponents. This also led to potential for cases to become protracted as multiple counter-witnesses were called to depose about the status of other deponents rather than the particulars of the case.[17]

As well as these insights from others, deponents also gave much information about themselves. Witnesses were often asked to give histories of previous residences and even place of birth. This was especially the case when witnesses had only been resident for a short time: those living in a parish for two years or less often gave a history of their previous two or three parishes. The deposition book in which Agnes Cockerel's case appears, DL/C/207, seems to coincide with a period when the London Consistory Court was especially diligent in its recording of places of birth. As Table 5.1 shows, nearly three-quarters of witnesses in sampled cases from this deposition book provided their place of birth, compared with barely a fifth in the previous book. This diligence was perhaps influenced by Cardinal

---

[12] McSheffrey, *Marriage, Sex and Civic Culture*, pp. 116–20.

[13] McSheffrey, *Marriage, Sex and Civic Culture*, p. 197.

[14] McDonough, *Witnesses, Neighbors, and Community*, p. 52.

[15] McDonough, *Witnesses, Neighbors, and Community*, pp. 52–4.

[16] See, e.g., the description of Thomas Plowghe as 'an honest pauper' (LMA, DL/C/207, fo. 268); Henry Fit, Richard Thompson and James Adene are described as 'honest paupers' (LMA, DL/C/208, fo. 38v); 'John Broke is an honest person save that he is reputed as a pauper' (LMA, DL/C/207, fo. 255); Helen Elys described herself as poor but honest (LMA, DL/C/208, fo. 65v).

[17] S. McSheffrey, 'Liberties of London: social networks, sexual disorder, and independent jurisdiction in the late medieval English metropolis', in *Crossing Borders: Boundaries and Margins in Medieval and Early Modern Britain*, ed. K. J. Kesselring and S. Butler (Leiden, 2018), pp. 216–36, at pp. 219–21.

Wolsey's drive against immorality in London and its surroundings in the late 1510s, which included a crackdown on vagrancy.[18]

Table 5.1. Proportion of deponents with place of birth
recorded in consistory court deposition books.[19]

Deposition book	Period covered	Total of witnesses in selected cases	Number naming place of birth	% with place of birth given
DL/C/0205	1467–76	60	4	6.70%
DL/C/A/001/ MS09065, MS09065B	1487–96	51	3	5.90%
DL/C/0206	1510–6	84	15	18.10%
DL/C/0207	1520–4	97	71	73.20%
DL/C/0208	1529–33	109	51	46.80%
Total	–	401	144	36%

Crucially, we can also connect these histories of mobility with detailed understanding of the social status of parties and witnesses and the *fama* which circulated about them among their neighbours. *Fama*, that which was said about someone, was not peripheral to a case, but was an essential component of the evidence presented in medieval courts.[20] Sometimes the defence of reputation or justification of a perceived insult was the explicit purpose of a case, as with defamation. Often information about status and reputation made its way into the records incidentally as parties gathered counter-witnesses who opposed not just what a witness had said but also their entitlement to depose. Movement itself was sometimes used as a sign of insufficient status to depose, as will be seen. The depositions can therefore give us a sense of the workings of reputation for a relatively wide spectrum of people and so indicate how movement around the city (thus away from localized gossip networks) might affect *fama* in varied ways.

[18] Ingram, *Carnal Knowledge*, pp. 156–60.
[19] Cases were gathered for my doctoral research into the connection between social and spatial marginality in the city of London. The cases chosen all focussed on events and people living in the city of London, rather than the wider diocese. The selection of cases included all those relating to the extramural parishes as well as others which featured low-status witnesses and shed particular light on mobility or the workings of communal punishment (C. Berry, 'Margins and marginality in fifteenth-century London' (unpublished University of London PhD thesis, 2018), pp. 169–73).
[20] Fenster and Smail, 'Introduction', p. 3.

June 1521: St. Sepulchre without Newgate

Agnes Cockerel's case was a defamation suit against John Beckett, capper, and his wife Elizabeth, of the extramural parish of St. Sepulchre without Newgate. According to the chantry certificates of 1548, St. Sepulchre was London's most populous parish with 3,400 recorded communicants.[21] It was a sprawling parish to the north-west of London's walls which extended from near Ludgate in the south into Clerkenwell beyond the jurisdiction of the city at its north. Although suburban, it was quite intensively developed, influenced by the busy route from London to Westminster as well as the presence of West Smithfield market.[22] Central to the case was a move from this extramural neighbourhood into the centre of the city, prompted by Agnes Cockerel's expulsion. In geographic terms this move was a fairly short one. However, in its apparent attempt to outrun her poor reputation, it reveals that social knowledge might not (or could be anticipated not to) circulate between the extramural and intramural parts of London.

The origins of the feud which caused the incident of defamation are a little obscure; the circumstances suggest that the Becketts were in some way involved in Agnes's expulsion from the ward and had perhaps been her landlords. Witnesses were questioned about a series of events surrounding the expulsion. These began with an argument witnessed by John Gruege, a fletcher. While sitting working in his shop opposite John Beckett's house in late June 1521 Gruege saw a passionate dispute between Agnes Cockerel, John and Elizabeth. While standing in the door of Beckett's shop, Cockerel 'said openly and in an audible voice and an evil and angry manner' to John Beckett 'thow pyllery knave and papyr face knave I shall make the to were a papyr and make the over dere of a grote and to shytt in thy wyndowes and I have done with the' (fo. 99). Most of her insults suggested John was a liar and alluded to suing him: to 'wear a paper' meant to wear a badge of criminal conviction.[23] To make Beckett 'overdear of a groat' would perhaps mean to reduce him to poverty.[24] 'Make the … to shytt in thy wyndowes' is

---

[21] *London and Middlesex Chantry Certificate 1548*, ed. C. J. Kitching (London Rec. Soc., xvi, 1980), p. 8.

[22] See Map 2 and the map of the parishes of London *c.*1520 in M. D. Lobel, *The City of London from Prehistoric Times to c.1520* (Oxford, 1989).

[23] 'paper, n. and adj. 8', *OED Online* <http://www.oed.com/view/Entry/137122> [accessed 3 Jan. 2019].

[24] Overdear usually meant that a given item was too expensive. The *OED* cites Taverner's 1539 translation of Erasmus's proverbs as using the phrase 'ouer dere of a farthyng' to mean that something was too costly at that price. Agnes Cockerel's statement, as reported, makes little sense if 'the' (John Beckett) was to be made too expensive so perhaps 'dere' is meant in the sense of being fond ('overdear, adv. and adj.' and 'dear, n. 5a', *OED Online* <http://www.oed.com/view/Entry/134468> [accessed 6 Jan. 2019]).

a more cryptic, if entertaining, threat. Perhaps Cockerel meant she would expose Beckett's alleged duplicity for the world to see, or perhaps it was meant literally as an allusion to the indignities of the poverty to which she would reduce him by her legal suit. In response, Beckett told her to leave, saying 'gete the hens dame, I pray the hens or ells wyll I' and his wife added 'I defye the dame. I sett not by thy malesse thow art known well, I nowe what though arte' (fo. 99). These threats may be examples of pre-construction of depositions by consistory witnesses, as identified by Tom Johnson.[25] With their convenient avoidance of specific accusations or defamatory language, they are perhaps versions of the words spoken modified to protect the Becketts in court.

This exchange appears to have coincided with Agnes Cockerel's departure from the neighbourhood. The expulsion itself was only described in hearsay by witnesses, who were inconsistent on whether she had been expelled from the ward or from the parish.[26] Expulsion was a mechanism of civic justice, usually ordered by the alderman of a city ward.[27] However, the parish of St. Sepulchre lay almost entirely within the ward of Farringdon Without (bar a very small portion outside the city's jurisdiction), so witnesses may have regarded the effect of expulsion from either as the same. John Gruege deposed on Cockerel's behalf, but his deposition seems unlikely to have done much to help her case since he told the court the grounds for her expulsion. Not only did he provide the only witness to her insults against the Becketts, he also told the court that the Becketts' alleged defamation had done minimal damage to Cockerel's reputation. Her reputation was not damaged, he said, because she had been expelled on account of her evil conversation and because many people called her a woman of ill fame.[28] The expulsion followed a search made of Agnes's house at night, probably led by the ward constables but conducted by a mixed group of neighbours.[29] An arrest was made on account of undefined suspicious activity found to

---

[25] Johnson, 'The preconstruction of witness testimony', p. 143.

[26] Richard Holand deposed that John Beckett said 'she was putt ought of thys warde' (fo. 101) but John Gruege deposed that '*Agnes fuit expulsatur extra eandem parochiam*' (Agnes was expelled from that parish) (fo. 100).

[27] Ingram, *Carnal Knowledge*, pp. 223–4.

[28] '*dicit quod bona fama ipsius Agnetis minime est lesa occasione prolacionis verborum superiorum per eum depositorum ut credit quia dicit quod eadem Agnes fuit expulsata extra eandem parochiam propter malam conversacionem suam… et quod audivit de diversis personis quod fuit mulier male fame*' (He says that the good fame of Agnes is minimally damaged on occasion of the expression of the words deposed by him above as he believes, because the same Agnes was expelled from the parish due to her evil conversation … and that he heard from diverse people that she was a woman of ill fame) (LMA, DL/C/0207, fo. 100).

[29] Ingram, *Carnal Knowledge*, p. 222.

be going on, most likely sexual given the accusations against Cockerel and her male servant discussed below. This is the only point where Gruege's deposition is favourable to the party he supposedly appeared for, as he suggests her servant Robert Dyngley was arrested and taken to the Counter jail alone, whilst Cockerel could not be found.[30] Another witness said Agnes had also been arrested. In either case, the outcome was that Agnes Cockerel and Robert Dyngley found themselves expelled and looking for a new place to live.

About two weeks later Alice Bayly, a sixty-nine-year-old widow of the central London parish of St. Mary Woolnoth, arrived at the Becketts' house. She was accompanied by her apprentice, Richard Holand, and another man called David. Both Bayly and Holand had been born in Denbigh in north Wales and young Richard's accent was perhaps still strong, since Gruege described him as 'foren' (fo. 99v).[31] Bayly approached John Beckett as he worked in his shop and asked him whether he knew 'Maystres Cockerel the midwyff' (fo. 99v) who had recently lived in that neighbourhood. Beckett said he did but, according to Holand, he would say no more in the street and instead invited Bayly to 'come nere and drynke'.

In the Becketts' house there followed a discussion about Agnes Cockerel's character. Bayly explained that, 'I have letten her a howse off myn and I wolde be glade to knowe off what conversation she wer' (fo. 102). As Gruege's reference to Cockerel's 'evil conversation' (*malam conversacionem*) (fo. 100) suggests, conversation was loaded with the double meaning of both the kind of words she spoke and the manner in which she conducted her life. She had taken a penny from Cockerel as surety for her rent but had been concerned by rumours about the ill fame of Agnes and her servant, Robert Dyngley. This would suggest that Cockerel's poor reputation was remarkably widespread given the distance between St. Sepulchre and St. Mary Woolnoth parishes (Figure 5.1). However, Cockerel may simply have been unlucky. Widow Bayly's apprentice Richard Holand was aware of Agnes's poor reputation from years before 'when she was at Tourney' (fo. 100) and it may have been he who alerted Bayly to the rumours.

John Beckett was initially evasive, telling Bayly to 'go to hyr neybors wher she dwelte before at Holborne Crosse' (fo. 99v). Holborn Cross lay within St. Sepulchre parish, although John's wording suggests that despite this it was considered a separate neighbourhood.[32] This detail suggests the

---

[30] Counter or compter was a term for a prison, of which there were two described by this name in the city (at Poultry and Bread Street).

[31] See the discussion of this term below.

[32] Neither the street where the Becketts lived nor where Agnes Cockerel lived is ever mentioned in the depositions.

Figure 5.1. Parishes of London *c*.1520 with locations from Cockerel *contra* Beckett. Base map produced by the Centre for Metropolitan History, Institute of Historical Research, with boundary adjustments by Justin Colson.

multiple social worlds which might exist within a large extramural parish. Agnes Cockerel had apparently moved in disgrace before. At length, both John and Elizabeth Beckett were persuaded to speak. They told Bayly that she had been deceived in letting to Cockerel, since 'Dyngley her servaunt kepyth her' (fo. 102) and that she was a prostitute, a 'brothel of her taylle' (fo. 101).[33] Dyngley was evidently seen as involved in her sexual transgressions, although whether this was a commercial arrangement or, as Martin Ingram reads the case, an illicit relationship, is ambiguous.[34] The reference to Dyngley keeping her could suggest anything from allowing her to have extramarital sex in the household to the operation of a brothel.[35] In any case, the implication is that Dyngley was not governed as a servant ought to be but had some kind of power over Agnes gained through sex, either as a pimp or as a lover. The ambiguity of the language is highly suggestive of the challenge a female-headed household with a male servant

[33] See n. 2.
[34] Ingram, *Carnal Knowledge*, pp. 221–2.
[35] R. H. Helmholz, 'Harboring sexual offenders: ecclesiastical courts and controlling misbehavior', *Jour. Brit. Stud.*, xxxvii (1998), 258–68.

posed to early sixteenth-century norms of social control. The Becketts also warned Bayly about Cockerel's reliability as a tenant and that Bayly ought to be wary 'that she do not pute yow clene ought of your howse for ye shall fynde hyr a crafty dame' (fo. 100).

We have no way of knowing the judgment in Agnes Cockerel's case, nor the specific questions and allegations put to deponents. Although we do not know the precise contentions of Agnes's case, it seems clear from the response of witnesses that she sued the Becketts for what they told Alice Bayly, her prospective landlady. Presumably, those words cost Agnes the lease of her new home. Neither Agnes herself nor the Becketts were examined, unlike in other cases, which may suggest a swift conclusion. However, the outcome of the case is of far less importance than what it suggests about the workings of reputation or *fama* in London neighbourhoods and the difficulties, in an oral society, that movement around the city posed.

Agnes's case concerned compelled movement but also, in its detail, voluntary migration. Agnes Cockerel herself had probably lived in two places in the parish of St. Sepulchre without Newgate. She had most likely only moved to her latest house about six months before being expelled in June 1521, given that, during his deposition in November, John Gruege claimed to have known her about a year. It is perhaps not surprising that John Beckett could refer to Agnes having previous neighbours within the same parish, given its size as outlined above. St. Mary Woolnoth, the London parish where Alice Bayly's house lay, by contrast covered a very small area in heart of the city along Lombard Street, a busy commercial route. It was described as having 300 communicants in 1548, compared with St. Sepulchre's 3,400.[36] Although only a short walk away, one would pass through more than ten other parishes in travelling between the two. It also seems that Agnes had moved greater distances in the past. Richard Holand referred to having known Agnes at 'Turney': this was probably Tournai, on the boundary between Hainault and Flanders. From 1513–9 the city was under English rule as part of Henry VIII's claim to the French crown. Holand's claim to have known Agnes seven or eight years before the date of the case (1521) would place them both in the city during its English occupation.[37] She was evidently no stranger to migration and apparently took her poor reputation with her wherever she went.

Some careful reading of the depositions therefore reveals Agnes Cockerel's highly mobile life, but she was not alone in this. We have already seen that Richard Holand and Widow Bayly, his mistress, were both born in

---

[36] Kitching, *London and Middlesex Chantry Certificate*, pp. 23–4.

[37] C. S. L. Davies, 'Tournai and the English crown, 1513–1519', *Hist. Jour.*, xli (1998), 1–26.

north Wales. Twenty-nine-year-old Holand must have been a well-travelled man, having gone from Wales to London via Tournai. Within London itself he had also moved, living with Bayly in St. Mary Woolnoth during his apprenticeship and then, between the events of the case and his deposition, moving to St. Giles Cripplegate on the northern edge of the city. Widow Bayly also moved after Holand's apprenticeship, to the parish of St. Michael Bassishaw. Since she was sixty-nine years old, Holand was perhaps her last apprentice and her move may signal her retirement from tailoring.

Like most late medieval town dwellers, Londoners were a very mobile group; high urban mortality rates meant that most residents had been born elsewhere and migrated to the city.[38] Nonetheless, attitudes to those perceived as 'outsiders' could be hostile, particularly at times of communal tension. Locative insults such as 'skotts drab' and 'Lumberd knave' featured in consistory cases, where they were used to defame aliens (that is, non-English immigrants).[39] As Laura Gowing has argued of such insults in a slightly later period, they symbolically exiled the target from the city, undermining their right to local belonging.[40] Xenophobia was a recurrent aspect of London society, from the violence against the Flemish in the 1381 rising to attacks on alien property on 'Evil May Day' in 1517, just four years before the events of the case discussed here. Richard Holand was referred to as a 'foren' by a witness in the Cockerel case who did not know him, a term with a specific legal meaning in a civic context. 'Foreigns' were those who visited or lived in the city and practised an occupation but were not citizens.[41] However, Holand was an apprentice at the time of the incidents described so the use of the term in relation to him was inaccurate in a strict legal sense. Instead, it suggests how perceptions of belonging were subjective and mutable. Holand's highly mobile life, from Wales to London via Tournai, perhaps left traces in his accent that might have led others to assume he was a 'foreign'. However, suspicion around mobility was not just directed at those believed to be of legally foreign or alien status. Mobility around the city could itself be a cause for suspicion.

---

[38] M. Kowaleski, 'Medieval people in town and country: new perspectives from demography and bioarchaeology', *Speculum*, lxxxix (2014), 573–600, at pp. 583–7.

[39] LMA, DL/C/0207, fo. 58; LMA, DL/C/0207, fo. 229v.

[40] L. Gowing, *Domestic Dangers: Women, Words and Sex in Early Modern London* (Oxford, 1996), p. 67.

[41] See M. P. Davies, 'Citizens and "foreyns": crafts, guilds and regulation in late medieval London', in *Between Regulation and Freedom: Work and Manufactures in European Cities, 14th–18th Centuries*, ed. A. Caracausi, L. Mocarelli and M. Davies (Newcastle upon Tyne, 2018), pp. 1–21.

Social knowledge and mobility

One of the remarkable aspects of Agnes Cockerel's case is that she brought it at all. She claimed defamation against the Becketts for statements about her character when, as far as the witnesses were concerned, the neighbourhood had already decided she was of 'evil conversation'. The mechanisms of ward justice had already acted: the constables had made search, Robert Dyngley and possibly Cockerel had been led to the Counter prison and an order had been made to expel her. Expulsion from the ward was a standard punishment for those who persistently flouted civic authority, more serious than imprisonment and far more common than exemplary trials before the mayor.[42] The ward was the lowest level of civic government, where the priorities of the ruling elite of the city met the concerns and initiative of local residents.[43] Decisions over whom to expel appear to have been made by the ward's alderman rather than local officers or wardmote juries, although it was probably their knowledge and advice which identified potential targets.[44] It is quite striking that throughout the late medieval period the routine means of dealing with offenders remained within the ward itself and generally did not require the expelled to abjure the city completely, other than during concerted morality drives by the civic government and crown.[45] This suggests that the primary nuisance caused by persistent offenders was perceived to be that inflicted on neighbours, a problem which could be solved by moving people along.

Expulsion thus resolved the immediate problem caused by anti-social or disruptive people, especially for aldermen who found themselves petitioned by ward inhabitants demanding they get rid of particular individuals.[46] However, like Agnes Cockerel, those who were expelled might simply move to another part of the city. Margaret Morgan alias Smyth, a witness in a consistory case in the late fifteenth century, had allegedly been expelled from both city wards and an ecclesiastical precinct on multiple occasions.[47] This series of punishments served to deny Margaret a settled existence and reaffirmed her pariah status through repeated expulsion.[48]

[42] Ingram, *Carnal Knowledge*, pp. 223–4.

[43] C. M. Barron, *London in the Later Middle Ages: Government and People, 1200–1500* (Oxford, 2004), pp. 121–7.

[44] E.g., a consistory witness named Richard Trussyngton was said to have been indicted by his neighbours at the wardmote for being quarrelsome but that the alderman had spared him expulsion because he found surety for his future good behaviour (LMA, DL/C/207, fo. 268v).

[45] Ingram, *Carnal Knowledge*, pp. 231–7.

[46] See, e.g., the deposition of Fulk Pygott, 21 Jan. 1533 (LMA, DL/C/0208, unnumbered folio).

[47] 'Deposition of Margaret Smyth, 4 November 1491', *Consistory Database* <http://consistory.cohds.ca/obj.php?p=982> [accessed 11 June 2018].

[48] Ingram, *Carnal Knowledge*, p. 226.

We can also read the movements of Agnes and Margaret as attempts to outrun their *fama* and find a new place to settle where their reputations might be unknown. In a city of roughly 50–60,000 inhabitants,[49] no one could be known by everyone and knowledge about reputation was generated and circulated within neighbourhoods, of which there were many. London contained over 100 parishes within the jurisdiction of the civic government alone; and in some places a sense of neighbourhood might be even more acute, as suggested by witnesses in consistory depositions. In a case originating in the liberty of the priory of St. John of Jerusalem at St. John's Street near Smithfield Market, a butcher engaged in a bitter dispute with his neighbour exclaimed to his rival's wife, 'thow skotts drab I will bere never a shert to my back but I will have thy husband owte of this strete'.[50] The victim was cast as both an unwanted foreigner and a neighbourhood pariah. Whether by street, parish or precinct, Londoners conducted their social lives to a great degree within the small area around their home and methods of punishment reflected this.

Martin Ingram described early sixteenth-century London as a 'surveillance society', where gossip was used as a means of bringing offences to the attention of authorities.[51] However, it is only within the densely connected social spaces of the neighbourhood, or even the street, that such surveillance could be carried out. Outside them it was impossible for tabs to be kept on every potential malefactor. Medieval conceptions of status were rooted in *fama*, the talk about an individual that 'continually adjusts honor and assigns rank or standing',[52] and thus in the gossip which flowed around neighbourhoods but might struggle to reach beyond their boundaries.[53] Any sense of London as a surveillance society has to be qualified by the inherent limitations of relying on highly localized networks of social knowledge. When Londoners moved around, the flaws in the system could be exposed.

This is an important context for the actions of the Becketts, as portrayed by the deponents. All three deponents agreed that their words were not spoken maliciously; and there is a marked caution in the manner in which John and Elizabeth Beckett approached discussing Agnes Cockerel's reputation with a stranger from another neighbourhood. John took great pains first to move the discussion from the shop to the more private space of

---

[49] V. Harding, 'The population of London, 1550–1700: a review of the published evidence', *London Jour.*, xv (1990), 111–28, at pp. 112–17.

[50] LMA, DL/C/0207, fo. 58.

[51] Ingram, *Carnal Knowledge*, p. 194.

[52] Fenster and Smail, 'Introduction', pp. 3–4.

[53] E. Spindler, 'Marginality and social relations in London and the Bruges area, 1370–1440' (unpublished University of Oxford DPhil thesis, 2008), pp. 220–7.

the house interior. In the proceeding discussions both he and Elizabeth are presented as hesitant in substantiating Agnes's bad fame, even attempting to send Alice Bayly to ask her previous neighbours at Holborn Cross before they would speak. Their hesitancy suggests they feared the repercussions of speaking ill of Cockerel, namely the prospect of a defamation case (a fear which proved to be well-founded). By speaking to Bayly the Becketts were in effect acting as linchpins between two parish networks of knowledge about reputation, passing information about Cockerel which was well-attested locally to someone who was unfamiliar in the neighbourhood. It is this element of the case that can be inferred as the motivating factor in Cockerel's attempt to prosecute the Becketts, despite all the evidence of how uncontroversial the fact of her poor reputation and expulsion was within St. Sepulchre parish. It suggests that knowledge which in one place was treated as commonly known fact could be portrayed as defamatory when removed from the social context which legitimated it. In another defamation case, also originating in the parish of St. Sepulchre, a deponent from the neighbouring parish of St. Bride responded to a question about the fame of the case that 'he has nothing to depose because he is unknown in that area'.[54] Despite living just a short distance from the parish where the events had occurred, he was not part of the neighbourhood gossip network which generated and circulated *fama* of people and events. It seems likely that, in moving to the centre of the city, Agnes sought to exploit this 'knowledge gap' between neighbourhoods just as she may have tried to do previously in her move around St. Sepulchre. Thus, the fact that Agnes brought a defamation case seems to have little to do with contesting the grounds for her expulsion and more to be an attempt to hamper the spread of poor *fama* around the city.

Indeed, it was not just those with poor reputations who might seek to use this gap to their advantage. Evidence from a different kind of consistory case, those centring on marital separation and spousal abuse, suggests that moving outside the area in which one was known in London could be a useful strategy for women in desperate circumstances. For many women abused by their husbands their first support network was probably within the parish itself, as Tim Reinke-Williams has noted for early modern London.[55] However, as he makes clear, this depended upon standing in good stead with the community; when a woman lacked a good local reputation, mobility may have been the only option available. Prolonged violence may

---

[54] LMA, DL/C/0208, fo. 105v.

[55] T. Reinke-Williams, *Women, Work and Sociability in Early Modern London* (Basingstoke, 2014), pp. 130–1.

also have driven some women away, even when they had local friends, simply to avoid discovery; a number of cases show neighbours were willing to intercede on the part of women who subsequently moved.[56] Certainly, a common feature of these cases was that an abused wife was driven not just to leave the family home, but also the neighbourhood.

Agnes Corbe, for instance, moved to St. Giles Cripplegate in 1516 after she remarried to a man who severely beat her.[57] Both of Agnes's husbands appear to have been butchers and the parish she left, St. Nicholas Shambles, was one of three centres of the city's meat trade. Two of her male servants who deposed in the case remained in the parish but had found new masters among the local butchers in the months between Agnes's flight and the case coming to the consistory. Butchers were one of the most occupationally clustered trades in the city and Agnes's decision to leave the parish may reflect an attempt to escape the local social network in which her husband would have been well-known.[58] Nonetheless, her experience in the butchery trade perhaps helped her in setting up a new household, as she was able to take her female servant with her to St. Giles.[59] Elizabeth Spenser, who also suffered cruel treatment at the hands of her husband Edmund, appears to have moved in the opposite direction, from an extramural parish into the city centre, to escape. The two witnesses in the separation case she brought against Edmund recall their separate dwelling places, Edmund at St. Clement Danes to the west of the city and Elizabeth at London Stone (probably the parish of St. Swithin) in the eastern city centre.[60] Unfortunately, Edmund seems to have found her, as both the witnesses recalled Edmund drawing his dagger to threaten her at each house.

It is notable that in the cases of Elizabeth Spenser, Agnes Corbe and Agnes Cockerel, all chose to cross the city walls to find new accommodation and in doing so all appear to have attempted, in some way, to evade public fame. They appear to have calculated that the social distance between centre and periphery offered them some protection: for Spenser and Corbe from the attention of their abusive husbands; and for Cockerel from knowledge of her expulsion. We can only speculate as to whether the suspicion aroused

---

[56] See, e.g, Spenser *contra* Spenser (LMA, DL/C/208, fos. 16v–17, 39v).

[57] LMA, DL/C/206, fo. 466.

[58] On the social networks of occupationally clustered craftsmen, see J. Colson, 'Commerce, clusters, and community: a re-evaluation of the occupational geography of London, c.1400–c.1550', *Econ. History Rev.*, lxix (2016), 104–30, at pp. 114–7.

[59] Women commonly knew their husbands' trades well enough to train apprentices and continue in the trade after his death and this is probably the case for Agnes Corbe (LMA, DL/C/206. fos. 467–8).

[60] LMA, DL/C/208, fos. 16v, 39v.

by Cockerel's arrival in her new parish was also experienced by the other women in their search for new accommodation. Perhaps a woman like Agnes Corbe, with experience in an established trade, found it easier to convince others of her suitability as a tenant. Cockerel had told her new landlady she was a midwife, perhaps in an attempt to suggest both financial stability and a legitimate means of supporting herself. Certainly by the later part of the century midwives could be highly respected figures with clients across the city and suburbs and a good reputation which extended beyond their own parish.[61] It may have been true that Agnes was a midwife, but if not it was perhaps a plausible story for a single woman looking to rent a new house. Poor reputation and the suspicious behaviour of occupying tenants posed an embarrassing risk to the reputation of the property owner.[62] Mobility outside the social space in which one's reputation was established thus presented difficulties in finding a place to live even as it offered women an escape from very different social problems.

Crossing the boundary between neighbourhoods might mean passing between different social worlds alive with rumour and gossip about their inhabitants. These were spaces of intense personal scrutiny. This situation produced both, at a local level, the surveillance society suggested by Martin Ingram and, across the city, possibilities for the evasion of social networks and social knowledge while remaining in the same settlement. Moreover, moving from the city within the walls to extramural neighbourhoods, or vice-versa, seems to have offered an additional level of social distance useful to those who needed to escape their *fama*.

'Men wer glad that they wer ryd of yow'

In essence, mobility around the city enabled people to evade one of the primary means of urban social control: the close observation of neighbours. It also transgressed ideals of social control as rooted in the stability of the household. The household was central both to the self-image of burgesses and to the system of security and policing maintained by the civic authorities. All residents of the city were expected to be sworn to keep the peace within their ward through the frankpledge system, whereby adult males were responsible for the actions of women, children, servants and apprentices within their household.[63] This reliance on the subsuming of

[61] D. E. Harkness, 'A view from the streets: women and medical work in Elizabethan London', *Bull. Hist. Med.*, lxxxii (2008), 52–85, at p. 70.

[62] Helmholz, 'Harboring sexual offenders', p. 260.

[63] S. Rees Jones, 'Household, work and the problem of mobile labour: the regulation of labour in medieval English towns', in *The Problem of Labour in Fourteenth-Century England*, ed. P. J. P. Goldberg, W. M. Ormrod and J. Bothwell (York, 2000), pp. 33–53.

dependent individuals within a household confirmed its status as a site of patriarchal social control; wise governance of the household was a cornerstone of ideal masculinity for well-to-do Londoners.[64] However, it was a norm which was at odds with the realities of urban life. Sarah Rees Jones has argued that the frankpledge system entrenched difficulties for the working poor.[65] It was a system which presumed stability of residence within the household and which took no account of impermanent living arrangements. The development of small alleyway houses and chambers for rent in the late medieval city provided accommodation for a large group of urban poor including labourers, journeymen, single women, widows and others who were not subsumed into this household model of social control. She has also suggested this was politically important for the divisions between citizens and others in the medieval town. This kind of living arrangement was also impermanent, often based on tenancies at will and sub-tenancy rather than long-term lease-holding.[66] Andrew Wareham has argued that in the seventeenth century this group of Londoners were highly mobile and capable of moving at very short notice when hearth-tax collectors were due to assess their household.[67] Moreover, the movement of the poor was increasingly considered problematic in the late fifteenth and early sixteenth centuries. From the 1470s onwards there were an increasing number of statutes and frequent civic and royal proclamations against vagrancy; punishment of vagrants became noticeably harsher between the 1510s and 1530s.[68] At the transition from the medieval to early modern periods mobility, especially that of the poor, was increasingly considered problematic and liable to attract suspicion.

The movement of Agnes Cockerel into a new neighbourhood evidently attracted enough suspicion for her background to be checked. The ideal of the stable household, combined with the fact that expulsion enforced mobility for the socially undesirable, sometimes put less affluent newcomers to a parish under suspicion. As part of the vetting of their suitability to depose in the court, witnesses were usually asked to give an account of where they had lived. If they had been present in their current parish for less than two years they were often asked to give a history of residences, sometimes

---

[64] S. McSheffrey, 'Man and masculinity in late medieval London civic culture: governance, patriarchy and reputation', in *Conflicted Identities and Multiple Masculinities: Men in the Medieval West*, ed. J. Murray (New York, 1999), pp. 243–78, at pp. 245–66.

[65] Rees Jones, 'Household', pp. 143–4, 149–50, 151–2.

[66] S. Rees Jones, *York: the Making of a City 1068–1350* (Oxford, 2013), p. 273.

[67] A. Wareham, 'The unpopularity of the hearth tax and the social geography of London in 1666', *Econ. Hist. Rev.*, lxx (2017), 452–82, at p. 464.

[68] M. K. McIntosh, *Poor Relief in England, 1350–1600* (Cambridge, 2012), pp. 43–4, 121–3.

extending all the way back to their birth. In the prevailing climate of suspicion, witnesses were alert to the aspersions that could be cast on their character by dint of their movement. On occasion they manipulated their presentations of themselves to the court, casting themselves as reliable and respectable people by smoothing over histories of mobility. Henry Wylsher or Wyther, a tailor who appeared as a witness at the consistory court in January 1533, said he lived temporarily in the parish of Hendon but before that had been resident in Totteridge, both in Middlesex, for five years. A counter-witness asserted that he was not a man of sufficient means to be considered a reliable witness because he is 'a tailor, having no fixed abode … but he goes here and there wherever he can get his living'.[69] Elizabeth Weston, a twenty-seven-year-old servant called as a witness in 1512, went to great lengths to explain part of her residence history. She said she was born in Cockermouth in Cumberland but had lived in the parish of St. Martin in the Fields, Westminster, for eight years, with the exception of nine months spent in the service of a man called Newton in St. Dunstan in the West in London. Elizabeth went on to explain that she had only departed St. Martin's 'to fulfil her position in the service of a good man' and that she left his service after nine months by mutual agreement.[70] This was far more detail about a past residence than most other witnesses gave and suggests a certain anxiety on Elizabeth's part about how her movement around the city would be perceived and how it could affect her reputation. Perhaps she sought to pre-empt assumptions that she had breached her service contract or even that the nine months away from her parish were related to an illicit pregnancy. In the act of witnessing, these deponents had to defend their reputations and assert their sufficient status to give testimony. They thus sought to explain or hide histories of movement which might be used by counter witnesses to denigrate them and their reputations. Those who moved to a new neighbourhood would not have wanted insinuations that circumstances like those of Agnes Cockerel had caused them to move.

While the poor, or women moving on their own, may have been particularly liable to such accusations, another case suggests that even those with quite a high social status could face hostility because of their movement. In May 1532 a meeting of 'certain of the parishioners' of St. Clement Eastcheap descended into acrimony when James Pott grumbled about being imposed with a greater assessment than usual after everyone else had agreed to the new charges for the parish clerk's wages.[71] Such a

---

[69] Deposition of John Hayward, 1 March 1533 (LMA, DL/C/0208, unnumbered folio).
[70] LMA, DL/C/0206, fo. 168.
[71] Deposition of Benedict Jackson, 8 July 1532 (LMA, DL/C/208, unnumbered folio).

meeting would have been made up of the better-off members of the parish who had a say in local decision making.[72] Pott's fellow parishioner John Hooke became so frustrated with Pott's complaints that he angrily proposed paying Pott's increase himself and removing Pott's wife from her accustomed pew in church 'rather then we wyll have all this brablyng'.[73] Hooke went on to exclaim 'ye made a brablyng her as ye have in other parishes as ye have com from'. Pott responded, '[What] parishes be that?'; and Hooke said, 'from St. Marten Orgor and St. [Christopher] at Stockes for ther men wer glad that they wer ryd of yow'.[74] In Pott's own testimony he claimed Hooke had accused him of being 'driven out of diverse parishes', perhaps an exaggeration of Hooke's intent but nonetheless suggestive of the stinging insult perceived in his words.[75] In his anger, it was to Pott's movement around the city that Hooke turned as an insult, focusing on an aspect of his life which could be reinterpreted as potentially suspicious. This case suggests mobility as a kind of liminal state, open to insinuation even for a member of the parish elite.

Of course, not everyone who moved would automatically come under suspicion. Neighbourhood migration was very common in late medieval and early modern London, albeit that the poor probably kept moving throughout their time in the city while others tended to move as a response to life-cycle changes such as household formation or widowhood.[76] Context is important in understanding when mobility might have had deleterious effects on reputation. For those with an obvious reason for movement, such as becoming master of their own household, the move was perhaps perceived positively and they could quickly be integrated into a new neighbourhood. Having social contacts gained through an occupation or company membership may also have helped. For instance, twenty-eight-year-old William Grene, a butcher, had moved from one community engaged in the preparation and sale of meat at St. Nicholas Shambles to another at the St. John's Street liberty about two years before he appeared at the consistory in February 1521. Despite being a relative newcomer, he was referred to respectfully as 'neybor Grene' and asked to

---

[72] C. Burgess, 'Shaping the parish: St. Mary at Hill, London, in the fifteenth century', in *The Cloister and the World: Essays in Medieval History in Honour of Barbara Harvey*, ed. J. Blair and B. Golding (Oxford, 1996), pp. 246–85.

[73] Deposition of John Knyll, 8 July 1532 (LMA, DL/C/208, unnumbered folio).

[74] Deposition of John Knyll.

[75] Deposition of James Pott, 15 Nov. 1532 (LMA, DL/C/208, unnumbered folio).

[76] J. Boulton, 'Neighbourhood migration in early modern London', in Clark and Souden, *Migration and Society*, pp. 107–49, at pp. 120–1; on neighbourhood migration and its relationship to life cycle in late medieval London, see C. Berry, 'Margins and marginality', pp. 195–8.

inspect some pig carcasses in a conversation recalled in his deposition.[77] For Grene, who had been a journeyman butcher before his move to St. John's Street, where he became a householder, his move and integration into a new neighbourhood would have been eased by occupational connections as well as the augmented social status gained by establishing his own household.

William Grene's situation contrasts with that of Agnes Cockerel, Agnes Corbe and Elizabeth Spenser. Unlike Grene, their mobility was not a positive choice which aimed to increase their social standing but was enforced by circumstance. Although they may well have been assisted by social networks not referred to in their depositions, choosing a new place to live was informed by the need to avoid public attention to their whereabouts. The basis of reputation in a locality and the fact of a mobile urban population meant that systems of social control and surveillance in London could only be partial. In the cases of both Agnes Cockerel and James Pott, it is evident that Londoners were aware of this gap and sought to exploit it for their own ends. For the former, it could be exploited by an individual as part of their management of their own reputation. For the latter, the gap allowed a man of apparently middling status to have insinuations cast on his past behaviour and the reasons for his movement around the city. The reliance on ward expulsions as a civic punishment may well have served to strengthen the potentially suspicious air surrounding movement, especially for women who were both disproportionately likely to be indicted at wardmotes and less able to challenge local decisions.[78]

Mobility across the walls

A final aspect to the case of Agnes Cockerel is her choice of home and her move from the extramural periphery of London to a parish at the heart of the walled city. While for William Grene a move across the walls came through occupational connections, Agnes's attempts to evade gossip of her expulsion suggests she was hoping for a lack of social connections between the two parishes. Indeed, extramural parishes had distinctive socio-economic characteristics, particularly in terms of the profile of occupations among their inhabitants and levels of uptake of citizenship, which meant that the social gap between intramural and extramural neighbourhoods may have been greater than that between other city parishes.[79]

---

[77] LMA, DL/C/207, fo. 33v.
[78] Ingram, *Carnal Knowledge*, p. 226.
[79] Berry, 'Margins and marginality', pp. 111–2.

For those travelling in the opposite direction, from city centre to suburbs, there may have been additional attractions beyond the walls. The precincts of religious houses and liberties exempt from civic jurisdiction were magnets for those making a living in prostitution or otherwise living at the very fringes of urban life. As Shannon McSheffrey has discussed in a detailed analysis of the consistory case in which Margaret Morgan appeared as a deponent, residents of the precincts had their own social networks which might extend across the liberties in the vicinity of London.[80] Movement into a precinct would seem a good option for those who had been formally expelled from a ward due to their immunity from civic jurisdiction. Under other circumstances, the enclosed nature of the precincts might provide a very physical form of protection. Eleanor Brownynge ran to the house of the sisters within the precinct of St. Bartholomew's hospital in spring 1473 when her husband Alexander chased her with a drawn dagger. The nuns admitted her and closed the door against Alexander, an action which, in the judgment of witnesses, saved her life.[81]

London offered the opportunity for its residents to move when necessary but retain access to the city's economy. Whether moving to a neighbourhood outside the walls or a walled precinct or, indeed, from such spaces to a city-centre parish, Londoners who needed to outrun their reputation or otherwise avoid detection could do so by moving less than a mile. Given that London was far larger than any other English town in the period, such an opportunity must have been rare elsewhere in the country. Nonetheless, we should not underestimate the challenges of maintaining such an existence, especially given the prejudice against ungoverned mobility. While the multiple social spaces of the city enabled those on the fringes of urban life to be flexible, anonymity was at best an ambiguous blessing in a society which valued *fama* as tool for the creation of hierarchy and affirmation of social relations.

Conclusion

Examination of the consistory depositions can offer more than just an understanding of moral misdemeanours and social control. Caroline Barron's work has given us a rich understanding of the framework of institutions which governed life in the late medieval city, but she has also explored the lives of individual Londoners both within and beyond the civic record. As this chapter has shown, the way that depositions centre on personal reputation for those of middling and lower status in the city

---

[80] McSheffrey, 'Liberties of London', pp. 223–4.
[81] LMA, DL/C/205, fo. 203r–v.

allows us to understand how they negotiated their place in urban society. Their lives were affected by interactions with civic and other forms of authority, but the authority they had to deal with most regularly was the court of neighbourhood opinion. The close observation of behaviour by neighbours which underpinned structures of social control and punishment was frustrated by the propensity of Londoners to move around. Leaving a neighbourhood could mean the loss of the social knowledge which anchored reputation and credit; mobility was a liberation of a kind but also a risky pursuit.

II. The lure of London

6. Aliens, crafts and guilds in late medieval London*

Matthew Davies

London has always been a city of migrants, its demographic and economic growth fuelled by immigration from the English regions and other parts of the British Isles and by periodic influxes of migrants from continental Europe and further afield. Migration therefore represents a long and continuous thread in the history of the capital that allows reflections not only on the history of particular communities (Italians, Huguenots, Greeks, Germans, Jews), but on the nature of the city itself as a place of life and work and as an entrepôt for peoples, ideas and commodities. This was certainly the case in the later middle ages, when it has been estimated that there were approximately 3,500 aliens in London at any one time, representing some six per cent of the post-Black Death population.[1] 'Alien' (*alienigena* in Latin) was the term that denoted someone born outside the realm; and in the case of London this differentiated them from 'foreign' (*forinsecus*), a term normally used (in this context) to describe a migrant from elsewhere in the realm who was not a citizen of London.[2] These and other terms were deployed by contemporaries in a variety of contexts – cultural as well as political and legislative – as part of efforts to identify, differentiate, characterize and restrict the activities and roles of aliens and, indeed, 'strangers' more generally.[3] What roles did aliens play in the economy and society of late medieval London? This chapter seeks to contribute to

---

* This chapter owes a huge amount to Caroline Barron's scholarship and friendship over many years and to her many contributions to our understanding of the diversity and activities of medieval Londoners. I am grateful to Bart Lambert, Elizabeth New, Joshua Ravenhill and Christian Steer for their comments on earlier drafts of this essay.

[1] J. L. Bolton, *The Alien Communities of London in the Fifteenth Century: the Subsidy Rolls of 1440 and 1483–4* (Stamford, 1998), pp. 8–9, revising S. L. Thrupp, 'Aliens in and around London in the 15th century', in *Studies in London History presented to P. E. Jones*, ed. A. E. J. Hollaender and W. Kellaway (London, 1969), pp. 251–74.

[2] Thrupp, 'Aliens in and around London', pp. 251–3.

[3] See, e.g., D. Pearsall, 'Strangers in late-fourteenth-century London', in *The Stranger in Medieval Society*, ed. F. R. P. Akehurst and S. C. Van D'Elden (Minneapolis, Minn., 1997), pp. 46–62.

discussion about the participation of aliens in the trades of the medieval city by focussing particularly on their links with guilds and by extension the nature and limits of those organizations' jurisdictions and roles. The argument here is that the roles of aliens, like other non-citizens, have generally been underplayed by historians and that a better understanding of those roles provides a richer sense of the nature of productive networks and the relationships between aliens, guilds and citizens – relationships often vividly expressed at moments of crisis.

Research on aliens in London in the period after the expulsion of the Jews in 1290 and before the establishment of the first Protestant stranger church in 1550 generally has focussed on two main areas. First, historians and projects have sought to produce accurate surveys of the numbers and types of aliens in the capital. Sylvia Thrupp pioneered research in this area, using the alien subsidy records and other sources to provide estimates of the numbers of aliens in the capital. Her figures have been modified since, first by Jim Bolton's work on the alien subsidy rolls for London from 1440 and 1483; and most recently through the detailed work on the subsidy rolls for England as a whole and on royal letters of protection and denization by the Arts and Humanities Research Council-funded *England's Immigrants* project.[4] Much of this work has been quantitative in nature, assessing the numbers of aliens by origin and by occupation, where such information exists, providing a valuable context for more qualitative research undertaken in the last few years, notably by the *England's Immigrants* team of researchers, which is transforming our understanding of the alien presence.[5]

Alongside the largely quantitative, 'top-level' work, research of a more qualitative nature has tended to focus on the most prominent and wealthiest migrants, notably the Italians and the merchants of the Hanse. Although relatively small in numbers compared with aliens from the Low Countries and German lands, the Italians were of undeniable importance because of their involvement in trade, banking and diplomacy; and studies by Michael Bratchel, Helen Bradley, Suzanne Dempsey and others have uncovered much about particular families (such as the Datini) and their networks.[6] Bradley's

---

[4] Bolton, *Alien Communities*, pp. 8–9; *England's Immigrants* <http://www.englandsimmigrants.com> [accessed 17 Aug. 2018].

[5] See especially *Resident Aliens in Later Medieval England*, ed. W. M. Ormrod, N. McDonald and C. Taylor (Tournhout, 2017); and W. M. Ormrod, B. Lambert and J. Mackman, *Immigrant England, 1300–1550* (Manchester, 2018). I am grateful to Bart Lambert for sharing the proofs of this important new contribution before publication.

[6] M. E. Bratchel, 'Alien merchant communities in London, 1500–50' (unpublished University of Cambridge PhD thesis, 1975); M. E. Bratchel, 'Italian merchants' organisation and business relationships in early Tudor London', *Jour. Eur. Econ. Hist.*, vii (1978), 5–32; M. E. Bratchel, 'Regulation and group consciousness in the later history of London's Italian

digital and hard-copy editions of the 'views of hosts' reveal in extraordinary detail the interactions between alien and non-alien merchants and the level and type of transactions in which they were involved. Interestingly, they reveal, in a politically hostile climate, the close relationships between London and alien merchants. Much more information about finance and trade has been revealed by studies of London merchants such as William Cantelowe and especially by the work of Bolton and his colleagues on the banking ledgers of the Borromei family in London and Bruges.[7] The role of the Hanseatic merchants in England, and particularly their presence in London at the Steelyard, have been another active area of research among scholars in the UK and on the Continent for more than a century, with more recent contributions from T. H. Lloyd, Stuart Jenks and others.[8]

When it comes to alien craftsmen and their English counterparts in London, attention has often focussed on moments of crisis rather than on in-depth analysis. In 1468, for example, the city of London authorities uncovered a plot hatched by a large group of artisans – mostly goldsmiths, skinners, tailors and cordwainers – to cross the River Thames to Rotherhithe on the south bank and, because 'the Flemings there take away the living of English people, [they] purposed to have cut off their thumbs or hands so that they should never after that have helped themselves by means of craft'.[9] This relatively well-known incident has often been cited in debates about the roles of, and reactions to, non-English migrants in the capital city in the later middle ages and especially the relationships between London craftsmen and their migrant counterparts. Others include the violence and hostility directed to Flemings during the 1381 revolt, the anti-Italian rioting of 1456 and, most famously, the 'Evil May Day' disorder of 1517 involving London apprentices. Much of this historiography has drawn on the vivid accounts in chronicles and other sources, which perhaps tend to skew our perceptions

merchant colonies', *Jour. Eur. Econ. Hist.*, ix (1980), 585–610; H. Bradley, 'The Italian community in London, 1350–1450' (unpublished University of London PhD thesis, 1992); H. Bradley, 'The Datini factors in London, 1380–1410', in *Trade, Devotion and Governance*, ed. D. J. Clayton, R. G. Davies and P. McNiven (Stroud, 1994), pp. 55–79; *The Views of the Hosts of Alien Merchants 1440–1444*, ed. H. Bradley (London Rec. Soc., xlvi, 2012). See also Matthew Payne's essay in the present volume.

[7] G. A. Holmes, 'Anglo-Florentine trade in 1451', *Eng. Hist. Rev.*, cviii (1993), 371–84; J. L. Bolton, 'London merchants and the Borromei bank in the 1430s: the role of local credit networks', in *The Fifteenth Century X. Parliament, Personalities and Power: Papers Presented to Linda S. Clark*, ed. H. Kleineke (Woodbridge, 2011), pp. 53–73.

[8] E.g., S. Jenks, 'Hansische Vermächtnisse in London, c.1363–1483', *Hansische Geschichtsblätter*, civ (1986), 35–111; T. H. Lloyd, *England and the German Hanse, 1157–1611* (Cambridge, 1991).

[9] LMA, COL/CC/01/01/007, fos. 178r–v.

because of their focus on 'extreme' events.[10] Similarly, attention has focussed on formal and legislative responses by governments and organizations, such as the alien subsidies of the late medieval period; different kinds of restrictions placed on alien economic activity by governments and guilds; and the petitions from the London crafts against the employment of alien and, indeed, other migrant labour that were sent to the city government and even to parliament in the later middle ages. Much of this lobbying took place at a time when guilds and civic authorities were especially conscious of the effects of economic recession on the opportunities available to their own members – at least in terms of these 'high level' interventions.[11]

The purpose here is to try to put the anti-alien rhetoric, legislation, violence and hostility into a wider context and to bring additional perspectives to bear on what are often polarized debates about control and conflict on the one hand and 'integration' and 'assimilation' on the other. Thrupp's assertion of a degree of mutual respect between aliens and other Londoners is not necessarily incompatible with scepticism from Bolton and others about her evidence for 'assimilation' in London.[12] Here, an important starting point is our relatively poor understanding of the world beyond the formal structures of the city, guilds and parish, the focus of most of the historiography. This is understandable, perhaps, given the nature of the sources, but nonetheless there is considerable potential to use existing sources to study the ways in which non-citizens – whether English or non-English residents – participated in the London economy and interacted

[10] J. L. Bolton, 'London and the peasants' revolt', *London Jour.*, vii (1981), 123–4; E. Spindler, 'Flemings in the peasants' revolt, 1381', in *Contact and Exchange in Later Medieval Europe: Essays in Honour of Malcolm Vale*, ed. H. Skoda, P. Lantschner and R. J. L. Shaw (Woodbridge, 2012), pp. 59–78; B. Lambert and M. Pajic, 'Immigration and the common profit: native cloth workers, Flemish exiles, and royal policy in fourteenth-century London', *Jour. Brit. Stud.*, lv (2016), 633–57 (modifying some of Spindler's conclusions); J. L. Bolton, 'The city and the crown, 1456–61', *London Jour.*, xii (1986), 11–24. For recent work on 'Evil May Day', see S. McSheffrey, 'Evil May Day, 1517: prosecuting anti-immigrant rioters in Tudor London', *Legal Hist. Miscellany*, xxx (2017) <https://legalhistorymiscellany. com/2017/04/30/evil-may-day-1517> [accessed 3 Jan. 2018].

[11] Ormrod, Lambert and Mackman, *Immigrant England*, pp. 32–5, 142; Bolton, *Alien Communities*, pp. 2–7; J. L. Bolton, 'London and the anti-alien legislation of 1439–40', in Ormrod, McDonald and Taylor, *Resident Aliens*, pp. 33–50; J. Lutkin, 'Settled or fleeting? London's medieval immigrant community revisited', in *Medieval Merchants and Money: Essays in Honour of J. L Bolton*, ed. M. Allen and M. Davies (London, 2016), pp. 137–55; M. Davies, 'Lobbying parliament: the London companies in the fifteenth century', *Parliamentary Hist.*, xxiii (2004), 136–48.

[12] Thrupp, 'Aliens in and around London', pp. 262–3; Bolton, 'Alien communities', pp. 39–40.

with each other as well as with formal institutions such as the guilds.[13] Recent work has begun to contribute to a more nuanced understanding of aliens in London society by using sources which tell us more about the lives and connections of the aliens themselves. These complement and enhance what we can learn from subsidy records, for example, or from moments of crisis such as 1381, 1456 or 1517, which, though important, are not the only lenses through which interactions should be explored.[14] The work of Bolton and others on the Borromei banks and of Bradley on the 'views of hosts' has been extremely important in shedding light on the relationships between London merchants and alien merchants and how they interacted in networks of international trade and finance.[15] Elsewhere, there has been a great deal of interest in the culture and practices of migrant communities in cities in Europe, much of it taking the form of further discussions about the ways in which migrants interacted with host communities by looking at the nature and effectiveness of institutional structures as well as cultural attitudes.[16] For London, Erik Spindler, for example, has explored the concept of 'portable communities' in London and Bruges, examining mental frameworks and communal structures that existed within transient populations.[17] Justin Colson's work on alien fraternities in medieval London has looked at the ways in which migrants established fraternities to foster and preserve identities, while at the same time (because they had to be located somewhere) interacting with London institutions such as the religious houses.[18] While most of these studies have concentrated on the upper strata of the alien community, they do at least provide some useful pointers and

---

[13] E.g., E. M. Veale, 'Craftsmen and the economy of London in the fourteenth century', in *The Medieval Town: a Reader in English Urban History 1200–1540*, ed. R. Holt and G. Rosser (London, 1990), pp. 120–40; C. E. Berry, 'Margins and marginality in fifteenth-century London' (unpublished University of London PhD thesis, 2018); M. Davies, 'Citizens and "foreyns": crafts, guilds and regulation in late medieval London', in *Between Regulation and Freedom: Work and Manufactures in European Cities, 14th–18th Centuries*, ed. A. Caracausi, M. Davies and L. Mocarelli (Newcastle, 2018), pp. 1–21.

[14] Ormrod, Lambert and Mackman, *Immigrant England*, ch. 10, 'Integration and confrontation'.

[15] Bolton, 'London merchants and the Borromei bank'; Bradley, *Views of the Hosts*.

[16] E.g., M. Boone, 'The desired stranger: attraction and expulsion in the medieval city', in *Living in the City: Urban Institutions in the Low Countries, 1200–2010*, ed. L. A. C. J. Lucassen and W. H. Willems (New York, 2012), pp. 32–45; *Gated Communities? Regulating Migration in Early Modern Cities*, ed. B. De Munck and A. Winter (Farnham, 2012).

[17] E. Spindler, 'Between sea and city: portable communities in late medieval London and Bruges', in *London and Beyond: Essays in Honour of Derek Keene*, ed. M. Davies and J. Galloway (London, 2012), pp. 181–200.

[18] J. Colson, 'Alien communities and alien fraternities in later medieval London', *London Jour.*, xxxv (2010), 111–43.

concepts to deploy when studying craftsmen and women further down the social and economic scale.

The history of the alien presence in London connects in significant ways with broader narratives and frameworks in urban and metropolitan history, but these have perhaps not been considered as much as they might have been. One of the characteristics of much of the work on medieval London is that it is overwhelmingly focused on citizens and their careers, trading activities, institutions, parishes and so on. In part, this of course reflects the nature of the sources – we do not have the richness of sources such as the Bridewell court records of the mid sixteenth century, for example, which are of immense value for studying social life, culture and economic activity beyond the formal structures of London society.[19] For the later middle ages most of our sources are those created by formal city institutions, which promoted citizenship through a rhetoric of inclusion and exclusion and idealized career paths and modes of production. This was particularly the case with the city companies or guilds, which created and promoted what one historian has termed a 'myth of the metropolitan experience', centred on apprenticeship and citizenship as the route to financial and social success.[20] Yet we need to remind ourselves that citizens were a distinct minority of Londoners – in fact, of a population of around 50,000 after the Black Death, it has been estimated that only about 4,000 were citizens – a quarter of the adult male population. Citizenship was intricately connected with the craft and merchant guilds: from the early fourteenth century onwards they were responsible for controlling apprenticeship, which was the most popular route to the freedom of the city.[21] As a result, economic activity in London has very often been studied and represented principally in relation to citizenship. Exceptions notably include work on women, such as Anne Sutton's work on silkwomen (though many of these were closely connected with members of the Mercers' guild), or Judith Bennett's study of the role of women in the brewing industry, both of which take us beyond formal

[19] E.g., the work of Paul Griffiths, such as *Lost Londons: Change, Crime and Control in the Capital City, 1550–1660* (Cambridge, 2008).

[20] This was in the context of a discussion about the afterlife of that migrant *par excellence*, Richard Whittington (J. Robertson, 'The adventures of Dick Whittington and the social construction of Elizabethan London', in *Guilds, Society and Economy in London, 1400–1800*, ed. I. A. Gadd and P. Wallis (London, 2002), pp. 51–66). For Whittington's career, see especially C. M. Barron, 'Richard Whittington: the man behind the myth', in Hollaender and Kellaway, *Studies in London History*, pp. 197–248.

[21] *Two Early London Subsidy Rolls*, ed. E. Ekwall (Lund, 1951), pp. 71–81; *CPMR 1364–1381*, pp. vii–lxiv; S. L. Thrupp, *The Merchant Class of Medieval London* (Ann Arbor, Mich., 1962), p. 50. For the rights and privileges of London citizens, see C. M. Barron, *London in the Later Middle Ages: Government and People 1200–1500* (Oxford, 2004), pp. 38, 77.

structures and into the wider world of work and retailing.[22] But in the main we still lack studies of work and production which look at the roles of non-citizens, and especially aliens, in productive networks and their interactions with these formal structures. We can usefully, for example, draw inspiration from the approaches and conclusions of early modern historians such as Lien Luu, who has studied aliens in early modern London through this kind of wider perspective on urban crafts, which in her case have allowed her to assess the role of alien skills and know-how in transforming the city's economy.[23]

Luu has made good use of guild records in her work and a second strand or framework that is useful here is research on the roles and functions of guilds themselves in urban society. This has been a lively area of debate over recent years, which has focused attention on the extent to which guilds either hindered or promoted innovation and entrepreneurship in the urban economy.[24] Looking beyond 'normative' legislative frameworks, some historians have emphasized the flexibility of guilds in practice, seen in their employment practices, selective and pragmatic enforcement of regulations and so on.[25] This is one way in which we might try to bring aliens and their work and skills more fully into the picture of industrial and economic development in late medieval London. Elspeth Veale, in one of her many important contributions to studies of the city's craftsmen, raised some key questions about economic and productive networks in the city and especially the significance of 'non-citizen' labour within the frameworks established by the guilds themselves.[26] Her work prompted this author's own examination

[22] E.g., A. F. Sutton, 'Two dozen and more silkwomen of fifteenth-century London', *Ricardian*, xvi (2006), 46–58; J. M. Bennett, 'Women and men in the brewers' gild of London *ca.* 1420', in *The Salt of Common Life: Individuality and Choice in the Medieval Town, Countryside and Church: Essays Presented to J. Ambrose Raftis on the Occasion of His 70th Birthday*, ed. E. B. DeWindt (Studies in Medieval Culture, xxxvi, Kalamazoo, Mich., 1995), pp. 181–232.

[23] L. B. Luu, *Immigrants and the Industries of London, 1500–1700* (London, 2005).

[24] E.g., S. R. Epstein and M. Prak, 'Introduction', in *Guilds, Innovation and the European Economy, 1400–1800*, ed. S. R. Epstein and M. Prak (Cambridge, 2008), pp. 1–24, at pp. 10, 23; *Technology, Skills and the Pre-Modern Economy in the East and the West: Essays Dedicated to the Memory of S. R. Epstein*, ed. M. Prak and J. Luiten van Zanden (Leiden and Boston, Mass., 2013).

[25] D. Keene, 'English urban guilds, *c.*900–1300: the purposes and politics of association', in *Guilds and Association in Europe, 900–1900*, ed. I. A. Gadd and P. Wallis (London, 2006), pp. 3–26.

[26] Veale, 'Craftsmen and the economy of London'. See also S. Rees Jones, 'Household, work and the problem of mobile labour: the regulation of labour in medieval English towns', in *The Problem of Labour in Fourteenth-Century England*, ed. J. Bothwell, P. J. P. Goldberg and W. M. Ormrod (York, 2000), pp. 133–53.

of how the London guilds considered English non-citizens, 'foreigns', which seems to suggest – perhaps unsurprisingly – that the complexities of the urban economy simply cannot be straightforwardly represented in terms of narratives of inclusion and exclusion. Indeed, reliance on non-guild labour and skills was a hallmark of London's economy, as it was for cities across Europe in the middle ages.[27] What roles did alien craftsmen occupy in relation to the city's guilds, beyond what is implied by anti-alien sentiment or indeed 'directed' by official pronouncements and legislation, even in times of crisis?

Research on the role of aliens needs to be integrated into some of these broader ways of studying cities in general and London in particular and especially its economic structures and modes of production beyond those which were defined narrowly by the city government and by the guilds. This could be a useful strand of future research on aliens in London and its suburbs: assessing the extent to which alien labour and skills underpinned certain trades and the ways in which guild policies and practices interacted with these wider economic ebbs and flows. For example, the second half of the fifteenth century saw a noticeable increase in anti-alien petitioning and legislation at guild, city and national level. What was behind this? How representative were these concerns of the needs of craftsmen on the ground and the availability of labour and skills? To make sense of this, or rather to contextualize it better, we need to understand structures of production and the dependencies they created, but also reactions to wider circumstances such as economic and demographic change and how they impacted on economic relationships.

Before discussing some of the evidence that might help to answer these questions, we need to start with a sense of the overall picture, as provided by the *England's Immigrants* project through its analysis of the alien subsidy records in particular.[28] This is very much an overview – much more detailed analysis of the London records has been written up by the project team online and in print.[29] The data from the alien subsidy records contain some 16,822 instances of resident aliens in the city of London in the later middle ages, with 836 in Westminster and 657 in Southwark (Tables 6.1, 6.2 and 6.3). The vast majority of the London resident aliens were listed in the tax assessments between 1441 and 1488, although the nature of the sources means that they were likely to exclude more 'transient' aliens as the subsidies

---

[27] Davies, 'Citizens and "foreyns"', p. 121.

[28] See the *England's Immigrants* database <https://www.englandsimmigrants.com/> [accssed 10 Feb. 2019].

[29] Lutkin, 'Settled or fleeting?'.

were based on households and residence.[30] Other sources, such as oaths and letters of denization, include a further 500 or so instances of aliens from across the late medieval period, but these have been excluded from the statistical analysis here as they are heavily weighted towards merchants rather than providing a cross-section of the alien population. Tables 6.1 to 6.3 indicate where information about gender or occupation is given; and also where 'nationality' is indicated, although it is important to note that in this context national labels could be both specific ('Lombard') but also rather broad: 'Theutonicus' and 'doche', referring to migrants from the Low Countries and German lands, for instance.

Table 6.1. Instances of resident aliens in the city of London, 1440–1549. Source: *England's Immigrants* database.

Total number of resident aliens in London	16,822
Male/female/unknown (%)	82.9/16.6/0.5
Nationality given	3,676
Geographical location in city given	8,039
Occupation given	2,569

As well as names, the data include characteristics of different kinds – nationality, location, occupation and so on – although these characteristics are particularly common in certain sources such as the subsidy of 1483 and are not uniformly present.[31] There is much to be gained by combining and analysing these characteristics and taking a broad view across the period, as well as by drawing out key changes over time. It is important to note at this point that we are working here with mentions or instances of aliens: some individuals crop up more than once in the various sources, for example across the alien subsidy records of the fifteenth century, and one would expect merchants to be more prominent and frequent in these sources. As a result, we are not dealing with 16,800 'individuals' in the city but 16,800 instances in the sources. However, with that caveat, it is nonetheless useful to aggregate the data to see what patterns emerge from them as a way of identifying characteristics and lines of further enquiry. This, in many ways, builds on the analysis of the alien subsidy rolls carried out by Bolton and published in 1998 and on Lutkin's analysis from 2016.[32]

---

[30] Lutkin, 'Settled or fleeting?', p. 139.
[31] On the variations between the subsidy returns, see Lutkin, 'Settled or fleeting?'
[32] Bolton, *Alien Communities*; Lutkin, 'Settled or fleeting?'

Table 6.2. Instances of residential aliens in Westminster,
1440–1549. Source: *England's Immigrants* database.

Total number of resident aliens in Westminster	761
Male/female (%)	93.5 / 6.5
Nationality given	70
Occupation given	415

Table 6.3. Instances of residential aliens in Southwark,
1440–1549. Source: *England's Immigrants* database.

Total number of resident aliens in Southwark	445
Male/female/unknown (%)	72 / 27 / 1
Nationality given	12
Occupation given	347

To start with, if we look at places of residence overall within the city of London, the pattern of distribution of mentions of aliens of all nationalities across London's wards can be visualized using a map (Figure 6.1). These, of course, are raw figures; ideally they would be 'normalized' using ward populations, but those are not easy to determine for this period. The maps also aggregate the figures from the 1441 and 1483 subsidy returns: these were not identical in terms of their scope; and cross-referencing between the two sets of records shows the way in which some aliens moved around the capital. Nonetheless, as Bolton and the *England's Immigrants* project have found, such a high-level visualization of the alien presence in fifteenth-century London reveals some important patterns. We can see, for example, that the central ward of Langbourn was most associated with aliens, followed by Tower, Farringdon Without and Broad Street, with uneven distribution across the city. It is possible to refine this picture slightly by taking into account the geographical sizes of wards (Figure 6.2). This appears to show even more of a concentration in the central and eastern wards. However, a significant caveat here is that some of the extramural parishes were not as fully built up as they were to become in the sixteenth century, so this overstates the contrast to a degree.

This broad pattern does, of course, raise questions about who these aliens in Langbourn and the other wards were. If we include 'nationality' as a characteristic, we can see that there are some clear differences. Figure 6.3 shows the distribution of Italians across the wards: Langbourn is again the most heavily populated ward, but there was a clear concentration in the

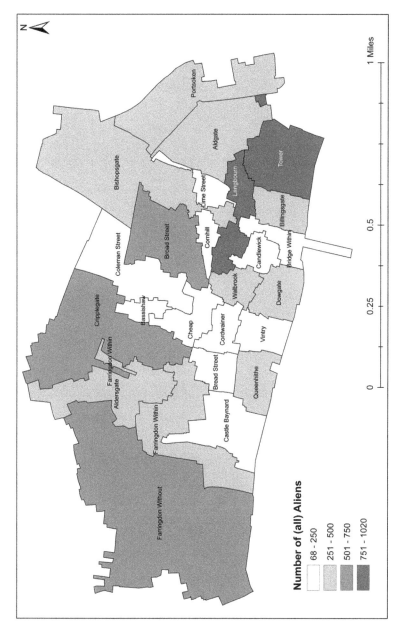

Figure 6.1. Geographical distribution of instances of aliens in fifteenth-century London. Source: *England's Immigrants* database. Mapping: Mark Merry/Centre for Metropolitan History.

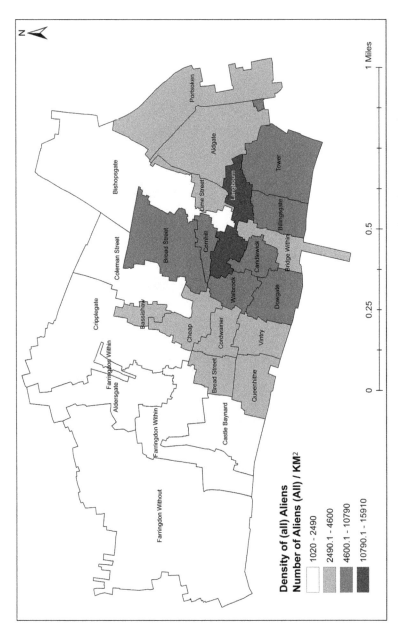

Figure 6.2. Geographical density (per km²) of instances of aliens in fifteenth-century London. Source: *England's Immigrants* database. Mapping: Mark Merry/Centre for Metropolitan History.

centre of the city. This ward contained Lombard Street and was well-known as a centre of activity for Italian merchants and bankers in the later middle ages.[33] If we turn to the northern Europeans, we can see a very different picture (Figure 6.4). In this case, there is a much greater presence in the peripheral areas of the city. We already know from studies by Bolton and Lutkin, and from analysis of the *England's Immigrants* data, that (to put it very simply) most of the Italians were merchants and most of the northern Europeans (mainly Teutonic/German) were craftsmen of different kinds. What we have is a classic picture of urban migration common to many other towns and cities in Europe: merchants congregating in the centres of power and finance, able to access individuals, markets and institutions, while migrant craftsmen were, in many cases at least, drawn to cheaper, marginal areas, where they attempted to set up shops and businesses. Portsoken and Aldgate to the east of the city, for example, were already taking on the socially and nationally diverse character which they were to retain throughout the early modern period. Once again, this analysis does not reflect variations over time and within the assessments: the exemption of the Italians from the 1483 subsidy, for example, was probably responsible for a sharp drop in the numbers of aliens in Langbourn ward in that year.[34]

The occupational structure of London's alien population is an important means of understanding their contribution to, and participation in, the city's economy – and especially how their activities mapped onto the trades practised by Londoners. Where occupations are mentioned (mostly in the 1483 subsidy rolls), we can see that there were large numbers of merchants in the city itself (or those with related mercantile occupations such as broker, factor, merchant's clerk), a fact which helps to explain the overall residential pattern there. Outside the city there were few merchants, at least in terms of occupations reported in the subsidy returns (see Table 6.4). Servants formed a large group in the three areas, being especially numerous in Westminster, and constituted around half of reported occupations in the city and in Southwark. The term 'servant' almost certainly covered a range of positions and relationships to householders, including apprentices (such as those of the goldsmiths discussed below), journeymen and live-in servants. A great many of these were the servants of fellow aliens, while others, particularly in London, may have been servants to citizens – and, as we shall see, this links very well with the evidence from the guilds. It is also important to emphasize the frequent instances of alien wives recorded in the subsidy returns as living with their householder husbands, especially migrants from

---

[33] For the residence patterns of Italian merchants, see Bradley, 'Italian community in London', pp. 13–62.

[34] Lutkin, 'Settled or fleeting?', p. 150.

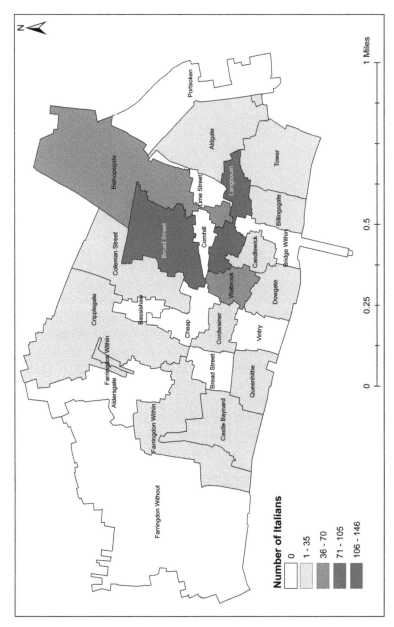

Figure 6.3. Geographical distribution of instances of Italians in fifteenth-century London. Source: *England's Immigrants* database. Mapping: Mark Merry/Centre for Metropolitan History.

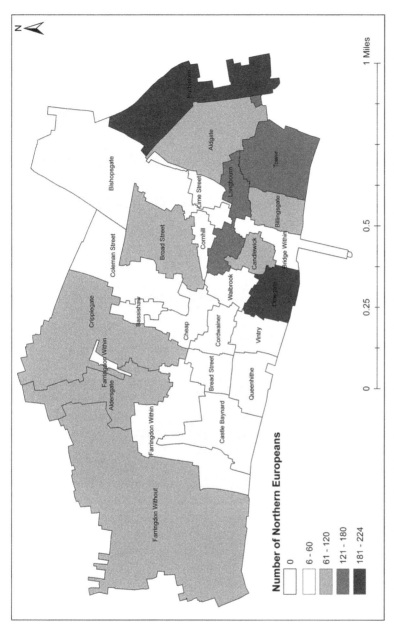

Figure 6.4. Geographical distribution of instances of northern European aliens in fifteenth-century London. Source: *England's Immigrants* database. Mapping: Mark Merry/Centre for Metropolitan History.

the Low Countries: like their native counterparts, many would have been involved in the household business or undertaken complementary activities such as brewing. As Table 6.4 shows, there were 476 instances of aliens in London with a specific occupational designation as craftsmen, not including the servants or the mercantile trades.

Table 6.4. London, Southwark and Westminster aliens by broad occupational group (mostly 1483). Source: *England's Immigrants* database.

	London	Westminster	Southwark
Servants and labourers	1313 (51% of stated occupations)	394 (95%)	228 (66%)
Mercantile	780 (30%)	0	0
Craftsmen	476 (18.5%)	21 (5%)	119 (34%)

In contextualizing the alien craftsmen of London, it is possible to use, as a rough comparator, Caroline Barron's analysis of the city's occupational structure as represented in the thousands of testators whose wills were proved in the commissary court of London (Table 6.5).[35] By comparing this picture with the distribution of aliens in the same categories it is clear that aliens were relatively more likely to be involved in the leather and clothing trades. Within these broad descriptors there are some significant patterns: a remarkable three-quarters of the alien metalworkers were goldsmiths, rather than the more typical mix of ironmongers, pewterers, cutlers and other crafts that we see among the host population. Historians such as Jenny Stratford and Jessica Lutkin have emphasized the valuable skills brought by alien goldsmiths; and their prominence in London raises some interesting questions (to be discussed later) about their relationships with native English goldsmiths and the London guild.[36] Eighty-three per cent of the leatherworkers were described as cobblers, cordwainers or shoemakers, emphasizing their manufacturing activities rather than involvement in the preparation of leather. While the overall proportion of victuallers is lower among aliens, more than fifty per cent of them in the city were beer-brewers: aliens had brought beer (rather than ale) brewing to London in the early fifteenth century and dominated it into the early sixteenth.[37] Finally, more

---

[35] Barron, *London in the Later Middle Ages*, p. 66.

[36] J. Lutkin, 'Goldsmiths and the English royal court 1360–1413' (unpublished University of London PhD thesis, 2008); J. Stratford, *Richard II and the English Royal Treasure* (Woodbridge, 2013).

[37] J. M. Bennett, *Ale, Beer and Brewsters in England: Women's Work in a Changing*

than three-quarters of those aliens stated as being involved in the clothing industry were designated as tailors or cappers.

Table 6.5. Comparison between the occupational structures of alien craftsmen in the city of London (mostly 1483) and craftsmen in the commissary court. Sources: *England's Immigrants* database; Barron, *London in the Later Middle Ages*, p. 66.

Occupational group	Commissary wills %	Aliens %	Difference %
Victualling	22.5	5.6	-16.9
Leather	11	15.5	4.4
Clothing	11.5	27.7	16.2
Metal working	13.4	13.9	0.5

We can see similar patterns to these in Southwark in particular, where several crafts were especially prevalent within the same broader categories: fifteen cordwainers (thirteen per cent of stated non-service occupations), fourteen tailors (twelve per cent), and eleven goldsmiths (nine per cent). Considered together, these figures provide us with a useful overview of the main sectors of the economy that we might look at more closely to understand some of the structural issues that might have underpinned attitudes and responses to aliens. These sectors reflect significant changes in consumer demand in the hundred years after the Black Death of 1348/9, which can also be seen in customs accounts – new clothing styles and dress accessories were especially significant, as were the skills brought by alien goldsmiths.[38]

The second part of this chapter will take a qualitative approach to the relationships between guilds and citizens on the one hand and alien workers on the other. This means trying to delve beneath anti-alien complaints and legislation and to look more closely at the evidence for production and participation within the trades in which aliens were numerically prominent. This is not to say that those complaints were not significant; and indeed the work of Caroline Barron, Jim Bolton and others has charted the ebbs and flows of anti-alien hostility and legislation – including, of course, measures such as the alien subsidies themselves. These were far from being the whole story of interactions between aliens and London's trades and inhabitants.

World, 1300–1600 (New York and Oxford, 1996), pp. 80–1. See also Ormrod, Lambert and Mackman, *Immigrant England*, pp. 127–39, for detailed discussion of the findings of the *England's Immigrants* project.

[38] These patterns are discussed in depth in Ormrod, Lambert and Mackman, *Immigrant England*, pp. 127–33.

The normative frameworks established by London's guilds are represented most clearly in the dozens of sets of ordinances that were drawn up and in many cases presented to the city government for approval from the early fourteenth century onwards. This period of activity reflected the growth of formal structures within London's crafts, which was itself both cause and consequence of the delegation by the mayor of the regulation of the trades to their leading representatives. Access to the freedom of the city via apprenticeship lay at the heart of this delegation.[39] Craft ordinances often tended to focus on formal structures, especially apprenticeship and qualification for the franchise, and sought to describe and promote an idealized career path, as well as defining the membership of the craft in terms of citizenship rather than the wider body of inhabitants who practised particular trades. Yet this does not mean that we cannot use ordinances, despite their normative function and character, to shed light on the roles of non-citizens. Despite the anti-alien and anti-foreign rhetoric of petitions and legislation, the rules and regulations of crafts often reveal a more nuanced picture. In the case of aliens, if one looks closely at craft ordinances there are a few useful points that emerge. First, aliens and 'foreigns' were often lumped together, in legislative terms at least – perhaps not surprising given that the primary distinction being made was between freemen and everyone else. Guilds in London tended to define the 'craft' or 'mistery' in two ways, depending on the context: first, in a narrow sense to mean just the freemen, but also in a much broader sense to include anyone who practised the trade: citizen, alien or foreign.[40] The Saddlers' ordinances of 1364 are fairly typical:

> Also that no alien or foreigner coming to the said city be allowed to keep house or shop, but that he be first examined by the four masters of the said mistery who are elected and sworn, whether he be able and sufficient to work in the said mistery or not. And if he be able and sufficient that they cause him to come before you to see if he can be acknowledged as good and sufficient for the common people as the franchise of the city demands, under the same penalty.

> Also if any such be found to be not able or experienced in the said mistery, be he foreigner or alien, let him be compelled by the four masters aforesaid to

---

[39] *CPMR 1364–81*, pp. ii, xxviii; E. M. Veale, 'The "great twelve": mistery and fraternity in thirteenth-century London', *Hist. Research*, lxiv (1991), 237–63; M. Davies, 'Crown, city and guild in late medieval London', in Davies and Galloway, *London and Beyond*, pp. 247–68, at pp. 251–3.

[40] M. Davies, 'Governors and governed: the practice of power in the Merchant Taylors' Company in the fifteenth century', in Gadd and Wallis, *Guilds, Society and Economy*, pp. 67–84.

serve other masters of the said mistery until he [be] able and sufficient for the common weal and also [become] free in the city, under penalty aforesaid.[41]

What is especially interesting – again in legislative/normative terms – is that the saddlers and other crafts specifically had mechanisms to allow aliens as well as foreigns to become freemen and to open shops, on the understanding that they should be examined as to their fitness to do so. In other words, there was, at that time at least, an acknowledgement of the involvement of aliens in manufacturing and a willingness to allow them to operate officially, subject to the scrutiny of the guilds' wardens.

However, what was acceptable in the mid to late fourteenth century – a period of labour shortages and increasing demand for consumer goods – seems to have been less so by the end of the fifteenth century, when economic and demographic conditions had changed. Instead of labour shortages, the effects of economic recession, while not undermining London's pre-eminence, meant that guilds were especially keen to preserve opportunities for their own members and took various measures to try and achieve this. Petitions against both aliens and foreigns became more common and matched the increase in rhetorical and legislative responses to migration seen in further alien subsidies and other measures. In 1484 parliament passed a statute which contained the complaint that alien craftsmen were arriving 'in greate noumbre and more than they have used to doo in daies passed' and attempted to impose a ban on the employment of aliens by fellow aliens and on aliens exercising any craft unless they were in the employ of subjects of the king.[42] Petitions and ordinances submitted to the mayor and aldermen for approval in the 1480s and 1490s suggest that some guilds wished to go even further, reflecting a sense of anxiety about opportunities for apprentices and freemen which may well indicate that London's population was beginning to grow again after a century of stagnation. Thus, the waxchandlers' ordinances of 1488 stated simply that: 'No foreyn or alien to be set on work in the Craft'.[43] The hurers (cap-makers) took a similar view: 'That no freeman of the Fellowship set an alien to work or to buy or sell in his shop, under penalty of 6s 8d'.[44]

---

[41] *Cal. Letter Bks. G, 1352–1374*, p. 142.

[42] Bolton, *Aliens*, pp. 35–40; *Statutes of the Realm … [1101–1713]*, ed. A. Luders et al. (11 vols., London, 1810–28), ii. 489–93; 'Richard III: January 1484', in *Parliament Rolls of Medieval England*, ed. C. Given-Wilson et al. (Woodbridge, 2005); *British History Online* <http://www.british-history.ac.uk/no-series/parliament-rolls-medieval/january-1484> [accessed 3 Jan. 2019].

[43] *Cal. Letter Bks. L*, p. 254.

[44] *Cal. Letter Bks. L*, p. 264.

Having gained a sense of how guilds formally regarded the work of aliens, and how that changed over time, we can now look in more detail at what their records tell us about the activities of aliens within particular crafts. The focus here is on two trades in which, as we have seen, aliens were especially numerous in the subsidy records and, crucially, for which extensive guild records survive: the London goldsmiths and tailors. The Goldsmiths in London were very closely associated with the aliens, both at the level of the royal court and in the city and country more generally. They were prized for their skills in working precious metals and as a result the guild made considerable efforts to reconcile the need to integrate them into networks of production (and indeed into the guild itself), with the need to ensure that they did not threaten opportunities for native-born servants, apprentices and freemen.[45] The Tailors were one of London's largest and most ubiquitous trades, providing clothing for all levels of society, from fine robes for courtiers down to second-hand clothing sold on stalls in London's markets. The king's tailor in the later middle ages had often been an alien, with Parisian tailors being especially popular, though native-born tailors were also appointed to that office.[46] Away from the royal court, as we have seen, it is clear from the alien subsidy rolls of 1483 and the records of the guild itself that alien labour and production formed a significant element in the clothing industry of late medieval London. With both the Goldsmiths and Tailors we have a combination of legislative records establishing the kind of normative frameworks with which we are perhaps most familiar, but also very detailed account and minute books which provide more nuanced insights into the ways in which regulations were, or were not, put into practice over time. The sources need to be treated carefully as they are not immune to the institutional perspectives and assumptions that come out more clearly in legislative sources, but they have much to offer, nonetheless. The same combination exists for some other guilds, the Brewers being the most obvious example of a craft with a significant alien element in the workforce. Alien brewers represented new skills and a new product – beer rather than ale – which remained associated with aliens well into the sixteenth century. Judith Bennett has drawn attention to the distinctive

---

[45] T. F. Reddaway and L. E. M. Walker, *The Early History of the Goldsmiths' Company, 1327–1509* (London, 1975); J. Lutkin, 'Luxury and display in silver and gold at the court of Henry IV', in *The Fifteenth Century IX. English and Continental Perspectives*, ed. L. Clark (Woodbridge, 2010), pp. 155–78; Ormrod, Lambert and Mackman, *Immigrant England*, pp. 127–39.

[46] M. Davies and A. Saunders, *The History of the Merchant Taylors' Company* (Leeds, 2004). On royal tailors, see, e.g., A. F. Sutton, 'George Lovekyn, tailor to three kings of England, 1470–1504', *Costume*, xv (1981), 1–12.

employment and service patterns of the alien beer brewers, in which male servants predominated, unlike the ale brewing workshops, which had a greater proportion of female servants. This both represented the importation of practices from the Low Countries, but also reflected the gender and age balance of migration more generally: relatively young and male in character. But she also noted, interestingly, that some alien brewers were becoming assimilated in the London Brewers' guild: in 1436, for example, a number of wealthy alien brewers contributed substantial sums for a guild levy raised to provide funds for troops to relieve the town of Calais, besieged by Philip the Good, duke of Burgundy. This may partly have been a way for alien brewers to demonstrate their loyalty to the crown at a time when it was being questioned: the same year rumours had been spread in London about the unwholesome nature of beer as a 'Dutch' product.[47] Nonetheless, it is one of several cases in which groups of aliens interacted with London guilds for mutual support and which should be set alongside instances of conflict, monitoring and exclusion.[48]

The records of the Goldsmiths and Tailors contain the names of dozens of alien craftsmen for the late fourteenth to early sixteenth centuries. Relatively few of these individuals are found in the alien subsidy records – partly a reflection of the infrequency of the subsidies themselves, but probably also of the mobility and transience of the alien population of London; and of patterns of service and employment within these trades which are difficult to reconstruct with snapshot sources. Broadly speaking, aliens appear in the records of these two guilds in two ways. First, they were fined by the guild for contravening ordinances of various kinds, whether to do with the quality of workmanship or other offences. Second, and especially in the Goldsmiths' guild, aliens appeared swearing oaths or paying fees that allowed them to participate in different ways in the craft, for instance by registering servants or opening shops.[49] Aliens were also fined for failing to observe those requirements. These broad categories remind us again of the 'institutional lens' through which we are looking, so care is needed when assessing this large quantity of information. Nonetheless, some notable patterns are visible.

---

[47] *Cal. Letter Bks. K*, p. 206. I am grateful to Joshua Ravenhill for this reference. For the ramifications of the political turmoil, see Ormrod, Lambert and Mackman, *Immigrant England*, pp. 140–1.

[48] Bennett, *Ale, Beer and Brewsters*, pp. 80–1.

[49] The analysis which follows draws especially on the Tailors' accounts, which run from 1398 to 1484 (with small gaps); and the accounts and minute books of the Goldsmiths. See CLC/L/MD/D/003/MS34048/001, 002, 003; *Wardens' Accounts and Court Minute Books of the Goldsmiths' Mistery of London 1334–1446*, ed. L. Jefferson (Woodbridge, 2003), *passim*; Reddaway and Walker, *Goldsmiths*.

To begin with, it is worth noting that, once again, the distinction in practice between aliens and foreigns (that is, English born inhabitants) is much less clear than one might assume from some of the rhetoric of petitions and other sources. In the records of the Tailors we can see a particularly interesting blurring of these distinctions – the terms alien or stranger (or their Latin and French equivalents) were hardly ever used. Instead, they just used the word 'foreign', even for people who seem, judging from their names, to be of non-English origin. Very occasionally they tried to separate people out, so there are instances of individuals who were labelled 'English foreigns', 'Dutch foreigns' and 'French foreigns'. But mostly it was just 'foreign' (Table 6.6).

Table 6.6. Terms used to describe aliens in the Tailors' guild records. Source: LMA, CLC/L/MD/D/003/MS34048/001, 002, 003 (Wardens' Accounts for the Tailors, 1398–1445, 1453–69, 1469–84).

Status	Alien (e.g., *alientes, alienigena*) Foreign (occasionally 'Dutch foreign' etc.)
Nationality/place of origin	Almain Brabant 'Dutch' French Fleming Irishman Jersey Lombard Norman Utrecht Venetian
Skills-related	Botcher Shaper Sower

The Goldsmiths, on the other hand, were usually much more explicit about these differences and used terms such as 'stranger', 'dutchman' or 'alien' far more often, although again there are exceptions.[50] It would be interesting to know why this was. It could simply be because alien goldsmiths were less numerous than tailors and so easier to keep tabs on in terms of names, locations and nationalities – the Tailors quite often did

[50] Jefferson, *Wardens' Accounts, passim.*

not give names, for example, whereas the Goldsmiths mostly did. It could also be something to do with the distinctiveness or otherwise of the skills which aliens in these two crafts brought with them: possibly tailoring skills were more 'generic' outside the senior echelons of the trade and hence aliens and foreigns had much more in common, whereas alien goldsmiths were especially highly prized for their skills, whether in London or at the royal court.[51]

The prominence of aliens in the clothing industry in London is well attested in the records of the Tailors' guild and in other sources, not just in the alien subsidy rolls but also in the few surviving wills of aliens and in wardmote and Church court records. As with other measures taken by the guilds and the city, one can see attempts to differentiate and limit the roles of aliens, while at the same time there is an implicit acknowledgement of interdependence. In terms of their official strategy, the primary (and ambitious) aim of the London Tailors' guild seems to have been to 'segment' clothing manufacturing in the city by trying to stop non-citizens, and especially aliens, from making new clothing and forcing them to concentrate on refurbishing old clothes. This was not a new idea and it related in part to concerns in the clothing and textile industries (and others too) about the mixing of old and new materials.[52] The separation of new and old commodities to avoid deceiving customers was reflected in a judgment made by the mayor and aldermen in 1409 that formally gave the Cordwainers the right to make new shoes, with the Cobblers restricted to refurbishing old shoes. Detailed specifications were laid down about the mixing of new leather with old, for example when putting a new sole on an old shoe. Interestingly, the judgment included the names of thirteen cobblers, divided into two groups of six English cobblers and seven aliens.[53] The occupational information collected by the *England's Immigrants* project has more than twice as many references to cobblers as to cordwainers – and, in fact, together these two shoemaking crafts constitute the largest cluster of occupational designations. It may well have been the case that aliens in the shoemaking industry were defined more closely by the second-hand trade rather than new work. In this and other cases, the guild structure in London reflected divisions between trades that were much more problematic in practice than in theory. The Tailors, by contrast, regulated the manufacture of both new and refurbished clothes – although that only dealt with the jurisdictional issue, not the concern about deception and

---

[51] Lutkin, 'Luxury and display'; Lutkin, 'Goldsmiths and the English royal court'; Reddaway and Walker, *Goldsmiths*; Stratford, *Richard II and the English Royal Treasure*.

[52] Davies, 'Citizens and "foreyns"', p. 19.

[53] *Cal. Letter Bks. I*, pp. 73–4.

confidence. Despite the practical challenges of implementing this policy of segmentation in the clothing trade, steps were taken by the Tailors to enforce it. Indeed, the overwhelming majority of fines the guild extracted from aliens in the fifteenth century were for 'new work', with very few relating to other aspects of the quality of the goods made and sold. For example, in 1427 a fine of 12*d* was received from 'Un dutyschman in birchenlane for [making] a new doublet'.[54] The guild tended to use the word 'forcyn' to denote unfree status generally and so it is not easy to separate out the aliens. Nonetheless, it is likely that many aliens were among those 'foreyns' fined for new work: in 1432–33, for example, 40*d* was extracted from 'un forein in holborn pur faisur de nove werke diversis foitz'. The addition of a lining of 'nove bokeram' to an old gown cost one botcher 2*s* in 1425–6.[55] It is worth noting, also, that the geographical distribution of these alien tailors was broad: although there were a number located on the eastern fringes of the city, others were identified as living in areas as diverse as Holborn, St. Margaret Pattens, Aldersgate, Thames Street, Dowgate, Fenchurch Street and elsewhere, in addition to unspecified taverns and hostels.[56]

There is another point of contrast here with the Goldsmiths, whose fines were much more likely to result from the detection of poor-quality workmanship – not surprising, given the relative value of the products and the high skill-levels involved. In the early 1430s fines were extracted from a number of alien goldsmiths, including two 'at le Horn', 'Joanne, Duchman in le spitelle' and 'une frensshman in le Tour'.[57] In 1441–2 Henry Luton, 'dutchman', was fined for making a sub-standard collar for the duke of Gloucester.[58] Poor quality clothing, on the other hand, could always be sold to someone, as long as the customer was not deliberately deceived by, for example, the mixing of old and new materials: the famous ballad 'London Lyckpeny' sees the narrator losing his hood to a thief outside Westminster Hall before finding it again on a stall in Cornhill 'where was mutch stolen gere'.[59] The roles of aliens within trades were therefore connected with characteristics such as product differentiation and the role of the consumer.

---

[54] LMA, CLC/L/MD/D/003/MS34048/001, fo. 181.

[55] LMA, CLC/L/MD/D/003/MS34048/001, fos. 159, 235.

[56] LMA, CLC/L/MD/D/003/MS34048/001, *passim.*

[57] Possibly the environs of the Tower of London, such as the precincts of St. Katherine's hospital, where 'Dutch' aliens are known to have congregated to avoid scrutiny by the city and the guilds. I am grateful to Joshua Ravenhill for this information.

[58] Jefferson, *Wardens' Accounts*, pp. 461, 521.

[59] J. Lydgate, 'London Lyckpeny', in *The Oxford Book of Late Medieval Verse and Prose*, ed. D. Gray (Oxford, 1985), pp. 16–9.

As we have seen, ordinances and petitions from the guilds suggest that their own members frequently employed skilled alien workers, whether because they were cheaper or because they had different or better skills, or a combination of the two. The alien subsidy rolls testify to the large number of alien servants in London in the later middle ages; and many of these would have worked with native citizen craftsmen, despite the tendency for leading alien goldsmiths, as well as other migrant craftsmen, to employ fellow aliens. Both the Tailors and the Goldsmiths, despite some of their ordinances and public pronouncements, set in place mechanisms to try to integrate aliens into their trades – an implicit recognition of the significance of their work and skills and, one could argue, of the need to allow guild members some flexibility in expanding their businesses and developing new products. In the case of the Goldsmiths this integration was carefully structured: as early as 1368 an alien goldsmith arriving in London was meant to spend seven years as a servant before being allowed to open a shop or become enfranchised and further requirements were introduced over the next century.[60] There was also much more of an emphasis in the Goldsmiths' records on aliens as masters of their own workshops than was the case in other guilds: substantial fees were paid by aliens wanting to run businesses and they had to appear before the wardens to swear an oath. In 1409, for example, John de Ghent and three other aliens came before the wardens and swore on a book to keep all the ordinances of the craft.[61] In most years covered by the fifteenth-century accounts there were three or four licences to trade granted each year in return for fees and oath swearing. The Goldsmiths had special oaths to be sworn by 'Dutchmen' which required them to take on English apprentices and not to employ other aliens or foreigns without permission. This says something about the delicate line that some guilds, at least, had to tread when they were dependent to a significant extent on alien skills and labour, but were under pressure to safeguard opportunities for native English apprentices and servants.[62] A few were even admitted to the freedom of the city, paying very hefty fines to the Goldsmiths for the right to be presented: in 1432–3 Godard Sotte, 'Dutchman', took the oath and paid the extraordinary sum of £50 to be a freeman.[63] The relatively small size of the goldsmiths' craft seems to have allowed the guild to have a greater knowledge of, and confidence in, some of the aliens who worked in the trade. In February 1434 the guild passed an ordinance which revealed concerns about the distribution of

[60] Jefferson, *Wardens' Accounts*, p. 113.
[61] Jefferson, *Wardens' Accounts*, p. 335.
[62] Jefferson, *Wardens' Accounts*, p. 363.
[63] Jefferson, *Wardens' Accounts*, p. 457.

substandard gold and silver by aliens. Their solution was to give the names of six trustworthy aliens, three of whom lived in Southwark, with whom guild members could buy and sell raw materials.[64] As a result, many alien goldsmiths were, like their counterparts in the brewing industry, regarded as quasi-members of the guild: the Goldsmiths also contributed to the 1436 levy for Calais; and in their case more than half the £34 raised came from 'dutchmen' in London, Southwark and Westminster – possibly, like the alien brewers, as a demonstration of loyalty to the crown. Therefore we have at least two cases in which alien craftsmen collectively contributed to guilds' civic obligations.[65] This suggests that the Goldsmiths, despite some concerns about competition and regulation, did indeed operate what Reddaway and Walker termed a policy of 'quiet absorption' of immigrants into the trade: in the 1450s and 1460s fifteen aliens presented thirty-two apprentices, mostly also aliens by origin.[66]

There are some similarities with the tailoring industry. Some aliens became freemen via the Tailors' guild: in 1427–8, for instance, John Chicheyard of Brabant paid £13 6s 8d and James Florence of Utrecht £18 to be freemen by redemption; the usual fee for English tailors was £3.[67] Again, they were relatively few in number and the emphasis was much more on selling licences to practice the trade, although no oaths had to be sworn. Like goldsmiths, alien tailors were also granted licences to hold shops and to employ a specified number of servants, though there seems to have been more flexibility in terms of numbers than with the alien goldsmiths, who were often restricted to one servant. The main difference is a greater emphasis on the employment of servants and journeymen by citizen tailors, which seems to have been ubiquitous and suggests a dependence on alien and foreign labour and skills. In 1425–6, for example, a large number of 'dutch foreign servants' were registered by freemen of the guild at the fairly hefty cost of 5s each.[68] In some cases fees were paid to employ alien servants for a specified number of weeks, but we can also see certain London tailors appearing every year to re-register the same alien servants – indicating continuity as well as transience in the alien population, something which Bolton and Lutkin also noted.[69] Sometimes the aliens themselves paid a fee to work as journeymen, indicating the perceived advantages of association with the formal craft even at that level: in 1432–3 a 'Dutchman' in Lombard

[64] Jefferson, *Wardens' Accounts*, p. 461.
[65] Jefferson, *Wardens' Accounts*, pp. 481, 485–7.
[66] Reddaway and Walker, *Early History of the Goldsmiths*, p. 128.
[67] LMA, CLC/L/MD/D/003/MS34048/001, fo. 182.
[68] LMA, CLC/L/MD/D/003/MS34048/001, fo. 160v.
[69] See especially Lutkin, 'Settled or fleeting?', pp. 150–3.

Street paid 8*d* to be covenanted with Alexander Farnell, a leading member of the guild who had been master in 1424–5.[70]

A range of terms was used in the Tailors' records to describe these aliens, with 'foreign' being the most common. Some are given a 'nationality' – Dutch, Fleming, French, Norman – or a place of origin such as Brabant or Almain. In combination we sometimes find occupational descriptors: the term 'shaper' is used frequently by the Tailors, a direct reference to the skills needed to cut cloth for clothing, while stitching skills were reflected in the label 'sower'. 'Botchers' were those who refurbished and sold second-hand clothing and were extremely numerous, as the guild sought to ensure that they stuck to their allocated market. Equally common (and interesting) is the frequent use of the term 'galleyman', used to describe Italians who came to London on galley ships. We know from the city records that galleymen were traders who arrived on ships in the port of London and sold small wares of various kinds in 'their accustomed shops'.[71] There was a similar presence in Southampton, as Alwyn Ruddock has noted. In both Southampton and London tailors seem to have been especially numerous among the galleymen: in 1406 the Southampton tailors asked the mayor for protection and as a result all foreign and galley tailors were forbidden to set up shop or to work in the town until they made a payment to the master of the craft.[72] Similarly in London, the guild required galleymen to obtain licences to make and sell clothing and to register their servants. In the 1420s, for example, the records generally list payments from the galleymen as a group, with the total fees received from them of between £3 and £7 per annum, but increasingly we have the names of individuals such as Nicholas de Georgio 'galyman shaper', who paid fees for himself and his servants in 1455.[73] Some galleymen appear to have been regular visitors to London, or else spent months or years in the city: in September 1488 Benedict de Cena, galleyman, paid 4*s* for two months for himself and his family and 2*s* for a further four months in November. He may then have left London, but in April 1491 he was back and agreed to pay 6*d* a week for two shops on an ongoing basis. Nicholas de Zachary paid for

---

[70] LMA, CLC/L/MD/D/003/MS34048/001, fo. 236v.

[71] *Cal. Letter Bks. L*, p. 278.

[72] See A. A. Ruddock, 'The merchants of Venice and their shipping in Southampton in the fifteenth and sixteenth centuries', *Papers and Proceedings of the Hampshire Field Club & Archaeological Society*, xv (1943), 274–91; A. A. Ruddock, 'Alien merchants in Southampton in the later middle ages', *Eng. Hist. Rev.*, lxi (1946), 1–17; A. A. Ruddock, 'The Flanders galleys', *History*, xxiv (1940), 311–17, at p. 314 (for the 1406 incident). I am grateful to Joshua Ravenhill for these references.

[73] LMA, CLC/L/MD/D/003/MS34048/001, fos. 55, 61, 68, 73, 81, 89, 95, 100v, 107v, 117v, 125v, 133, 142, 151, 159, 181.

himself and two servants in 1463 and then again in 1465.[74] It seems from the Tailors' records that galleymen did not just trade with goods they brought with them: apart from licences to buy and sell, the guild also fined many of them for making new clothes of various kinds as part of its drive to keep aliens to the second-hand trade.[75] There are also references to licences granted to aliens during 'le temps dez galeys' or 'le galetyme' – indicating that the arrival of fleets in London at particular times of the year heralded an influx of potential competitors, as well as increasing the supply of alien skilled labour.[76] However, judging from the frequency with which some individuals appear in the guild's records, many galleymen were in fact semi-permanent residents – perhaps staying for anything from a few months to a few years. Where did they live? Their generally temporary residence means that few, if any, would have been picked up in the alien subsidy rolls. John Stow, writing at the end of the sixteenth century, described Mincheon (now Mincing) Lane in London as follows: 'In this lane of olde time dwelled diuers strangers borne of Genoa and those parts, these were commonly called Galley men, as men that came vppe in the Gallies, brought vp wines and other merchandises which they landed in Thames street, at a place called Galley key'.[77] We do not know whether Mincing Lane was a hub for galleymen in the fifteenth century, as few locations are mentioned for them, but, as we have seen, Tower ward was one of the areas where aliens were especially well represented in the alien subsidy records (see Figures 6.1, 6.2 and 6.3). An inventory of the church of All Hallows Barking, in the east of the city, from 1452 listed 'ij candelstikkes of siluer', 'crosse plated with siluer and the fote of coper', 'ij chalys marked vppon the patyns that oon w^t B and th^t other with D', 'ij. clothes of gold' and 'j baner of white tartaryn wt an ymage of our lady' – all said to be 'of the yifte of the Galymen', suggesting connections with areas further east.[78]

Throughout these records anti-alien feeling and the rhetoric of exclusion and control are never far away – and indeed without it the documentary sources would be rather sparse, given the efforts of the Goldsmiths and

[74] *The Merchant Taylors' Company of London: Court Minutes 1486–1493*, ed. M. Davies (Stamford, 2000), pp. 114, 122, 181; LMA, CLC/L/MD/D/003/MS34048/001, fos. 242, 257. He was possibly related to the Genoese merchant Jacopo Zachary (listed wrongly as a Florentine), in a tax assessment of 1464 <https://www.englandsimmigrants.com/person/24124> [accessed 18 Aug. 2018]. I am grateful to Bart Lambert for this information.

[75] LMA, CLC/L/MD/D/003/MS34048/001, 002.

[76] LMA, CLC/L/MD/D/003/MS34048/001, fo. 181.

[77] *A Survey of London by John Stow*, ed. C. L. Kingsford (2 vols., Oxford, 1908), i. 129–38 (Tower ward).

[78] *Survey of London*, xii, *The Parish of All Hallows Barking. Part 1: the Church of All Hallows*, ed. L. J. Redstone (London, 1929), pp. 70–5.

Tailors to regulate the activities of aliens. What this chapter has tried to suggest, however, is that we can use records such as these to try to describe more comprehensively the roles played by aliens within some of the city's crafts, thereby contributing to a wider view of urban production and distribution that extends beyond the guilds and citizens. The frequent complaints made by guilds about aliens to the city government are not incompatible with this; and in deciding how far to regulate their trades in practice, the guilds had to grapple with internal dynamics and aspirations which were sometimes contradictory. We can see, for example, that aliens were especially prominent, and perhaps embedded, within certain trades and that in different ways guilds such as the Brewers, Goldsmiths and Tailors managed to tolerate or accommodate them – acknowledging the demand for their skills and labour services, but at the same time responding to pressure from those concerned about competition. More research is needed in order to contextualize and supplement these findings. Was it the case, for example, that crafts which were less dependent on alien skills and labour could afford to be less flexible and pragmatic in the enforcement of legislative restrictions? Aliens, whether temporary or settled, were very much part of the world of production, exchange and consumption in London and there is more to be learned about their activities within crafts and neighbourhoods in the city.

7. William Styfford (fl. 1437–66): citizen and scrivener of London and notary imperial*

J. L. Bolton

Written instruments made the economic and social world go round in fifteenth-century London as much as money, with which they were usually inextricably linked in one way or another.[1] They took many forms: wills; conveyances; leases; accounts; and bonds or obligations. These ranged from simple agreements that **A** would perform certain services for **B** by a certain date, to those with performance clauses that a specified sum would be paid in addition to the principal debt if the repayment terms were not met. Sometimes, although not always, such bonds had a seal attached which turned them into what was called a 'specialty'. Bonds were used for all manner of purposes, from securing marriage settlements and property transfers to almost any form of agreement where a formal and enforceable contract was needed.[2] These written instruments, with or without a seal, could also be produced as parol evidence in common law courts. As long ago as 1979 John Baker argued that such evidence remained largely unacknowledged in the records of pleading until the common law could refine its methods of acknowledging them through the action of *assumpsit*, mainly after 1450.[3]

The growth in the use of written instruments, and especially bonds, meant, of course, a parallel growth in the number of scriveners, scribes,

---

* I am grateful to Francesco Guidi Bruscoli for his usual assistance in checking my Italian translations.

[1] With apologies to Fred Ebb and John Kander, who wrote the music and lyrics for the musical *Cabaret*.

[2] M. Richardson, *Middle-Class Writing in Late Medieval London* (London, 2011), pp. 66–7.

[3] J. H. Baker, 'The law merchant and the common law before 1700', *Cambridge Law Jour.*, xxxviii (1979), 295–322, at pp. 302–6. Parol evidence followed a common-law rule that prevented parties who had settled their agreement in a final written document from later introducing other evidence, such as the content of oral evidence from earlier in the negotiations that was not referenced in the document. *Assumpsit* allowed action to be taken on a breach of an express or implied promise or contract not under seal.

J. L. Bolton, 'William Styfford (fl. 1437–66): citizen and scrivener of London and notary imperial', in *Medieval Londoners: essays to mark the eightieth birthday of Caroline M. Barron*, ed. E. A. New and C. Steer (London, 2019), pp. 149–64. License: CC-BY-NC-ND 4.0.

writers of court hand and notaries public who were involved in writing them. As the late medieval courts began to prefer written over oral evidence, so actions in the higher courts turned to the validity of the written instruments presented. Any mistakes or errors of phrasing in the documents could see the case thrown out and the plaintiff having to start the action again. The statute of additions of 1413 required all legal documents to give not only a person's name but also his legal occupation and place of abode and that made accuracy in recording all the more important.[4] So there emerged, mainly in London and Westminster but also in major provincial towns, scriveners trained to write the many different forms of deeds, bonds and letters that civil society increasingly needed. It is important to note that they worked for civil society. Papal notaries handled all matters ecclesiastical and were themselves trained and appointed by the Church. Book production became the work of a separate group of scriveners who eventually emerged as members of the Stationers' Company in London, leaving civil work to members of the Scriveners' Company. Much of what we know about the scriveners in late medieval London is drawn from their so-called *Common Paper*, edited by Francis W. Steer for the London Record Society.[5] Recently this has been the subject of a critical re-evaluation by Richard Firth-Green and his account of the early history of the Company differed from that given by Steer, although that is of no concern to us here. What can be taken from the document is the sense of fumbling attempts to control the scriveners in London in order to prevent fraud and malpractice, although they were not entirely successful in that. Oaths had to be sworn on admission to the Company and the 1497 ordinances give us the first inklings of what an apprentice was supposed to know on his enrolment and the measures to be taken if he did not. Then he was to be sent to a grammar school to be made completely erudite in the book of *pervula* (Latin grammar), genders, declensions, preterites (tenses), '*supynes Equivox*' (in Latin the ablative forms of a verbal noun) and synonyms, with the other petty books. This was to be done within the first four years of the apprenticeship, on pain of a fine of £5.[6]

There has been a considerable amount of recent published work demonstrating the important role played by scriveners and notaries in

---

[4] 1 Henry V, cap. 5; *Statutes of the Realm*, ii (London, 1816), p. 171.

[5] *Scriveners' Company Common Paper 1357–1628*, ed. F. W. Steer (London Rec. Soc., iv, 1968).

[6] R. Firth-Green, 'The early history of the Scriveners' Company and its so-called oaths', in *English Texts in Transition*, ed. S. Horobin and L. Mooney (York, 2014), pp. 1–20; Steer, *Scriveners' Company Common Paper*, pp. vii–xxiv, 49–50.

London and other towns and it needs no further elaboration here.[7] What set William Styfford (fl. 1430s–60s) and a few other scriveners, writers of the court hand and notaries public apart from their other colleagues in late medieval London was that they were also notaries imperial.[8] Both papal and imperial notaries were trained in Roman law and both appeared in England at roughly the same time, the second half of the thirteenth century. While the history of papal notaries, their training and their diplomatic skills are all well documented and much studied by later historians, the role of imperial notaries has been largely neglected. Unfortunately, as Patrick Zutshi has remarked, little is known about their appointment except that the Holy Roman Emperor had granted the right to certain counts palatine and their successors, the counts being imperial administrators and not rulers of the Rhine Palatinate. However, their activities in England were supposedly short-lived, since in 1320 Edward II forbade them from exercising their office. His reasons for so doing arose from the debate on whether the king was emperor in his own kingdom, as Philip IV of France had argued against Boniface VIII, to show that England, like France, was free of the empire. The difference between the two kingdoms was that while in France imperial notaries were replaced by royal notaries, in England they were not. 'After Edward II's enactment

[7] C. R. Cheney, *Notaries Public in England in the Thirteenth and Fourteenth Centuries* (Oxford, 1972); N. Ramsay, 'Scriveners and notaries as legal intermediaries in later medieval England', in *Enterprise and Individuals in Fifteenth-Century England*, ed. J. Kermode (Stroud, 1991), pp. 118–31; P. R. N. Zutshi, 'Notaries public in England in the fourteenth and fifteenth centuries', *Estudios sobre el Notariado Europeo (siglos xiv–xv)*, ed. P. Ostos and M. L. Pardo (Seville, 1997), pp. 93–107; A. F. Sutton, *The Mercery of London: Trade, Goods and People, 1130–1578* (Aldershot, 2005), pp. 179, 251–2; A. F. Sutton, 'Robert Bale, scrivener and chronicler of London', in *Regional Manuscript Studies, 1200–1700*, ed. A. S. G. Edwards (London, 2008), pp. 180–206; *The Book of Privileges of the Merchant Adventurers of England, 1296–1483*, ed. A. F. Sutton and L. Visser-Fuchs (Oxford, 2009), pp. 36, 104; M. Davies, '"Writyng, making and engrocyng": clerks, guilds and identity in late-medieval London', in *Medieval Merchants and Money: Essays in Honour of James L. Bolton*, ed. M. Allen and M. Davies (London, 2016), pp. 21–42; M. C. Erler, 'The Guildhall library, Robert Bale and the writing of London history', *Hist. Research*, lxxxix (2015), 176–86. For scriveners and their work in major provincial towns, see L. K. Bevan, 'Clerks and scriveners: legal literacy and access to justice in late medieval England' (unpublished University of Exeter PhD thesis, 2013). For some continental comparisons, see W. Prevenier, J. M. Murray and M. Oosterbuch, 'Les notaires publics dans les anciens Pays-Bas du xiiie au xvie siecle', in Ostos and Pardo, *Estudios sobre el Notariado Europeo*, pp. 53–72; W. Prevenier, J. M. Murray and M. Oosterbuch, *Notarial Instruments in Flanders between 1280 and 1452* (Brussels, 1995).

[8] Martin Seman and John Cosier in the late 14th century and William Brampton and John Chesham, *c.*1400 to the 1440s (H. Jenkinson, *The Later Court Hands in England from the Fifteenth to the Seventeenth Century* (Cambridge, 1927), pt. ii, plates I–IV; Steer, *Scriveners' Company Common Paper*, pp. 11, 12, 20, 21, 22, 165).

of 1320', Zutshi wrote, 'few notaries licensed only by imperial authority appear in English sources'.[9]

That is certainly true and, taking the point further, imperial notaries were few and far between in late medieval London, but they had a crucial role to play in international trade and banking, as will be seen. The notaries of Italy, south Germany and southern France have left behind vast collections of their *protocolla*, the books and rolls containing the original property deeds, marriage and dowry settlements and commercial contracts that were registered with them. Copies of the originals were then made from the registers to be kept by the parties involved or to be produced as evidence in court cases, properly certified by the notary's sign manual. The common law courts of England would have nothing of copies. The original deeds, with the clear impression of seal matrices attached, were the only evidence they would acknowledge. The continental notary also received a very different training from his English counterpart. Prevenier, Murray and Oosterboch assumed that the majority of the notaries active in the Low Countries at the end of the thirteenth century had studied in Italy and especially at the University of Bologna.[10] It seems unlikely that Styfford or any of the other imperial notaries in late medieval London went to Bologna or received any of their formal training at the business schools attached to the universities of Oxford and Cambridge, which in any case concentrated on the common law of England and not the Roman law of Europe. If Styfford received any training, then it can only have been from another imperial notary in England, in the same way as scriveners trained their apprentices.[11]

Who that might have been is a matter of speculation, but it is possible that he was the apprentice of John Chesham, who was appointed an imperial notary on 8 August 1416, coincidentally, or perhaps not, at the same time as the visit of Emperor Sigismund to London.[12] Chesham took the Scriveners' Company oath on 14 July 1417, not long after his appointment as a notary imperial; and if Styfford was his apprentice, then he must surely have had access to a series of training manuals, most notably that produced by the notarial school at Bologna, the *Summa Artis Notariae* of 1256, and possibly

[9] Cheney, *Notaries Public*, pp. 12–39; Zutshi, 'Notaries public in England', p. 97.

[10] Prevenier, Murray and Oosterbuch, 'Les notaires', pp. 60–3.

[11] A good account of an imperial notary training his apprentice can be found in T. O'Byrne, 'Notarial signs and scribal training in the fifteenth century: the case of James Yonge and Thomas Baghill', *Jour. Early Book Soc.*, xv (2012), 305–18.

[12] *Cal. Letter Bks. I, 1400–22*, p. 291; *The Great Chronicle of London*, ed. A. H. Thomas and I. D. Thornley (London, 1938), pp. 94–5; *Gesta Henrici Quinti*, ed. F. Taylor and J. S. Roskell (Oxford, 1975), pp. 129, 131, 133, 175, 179; C. T. Allmand, *Henry V* (London, 1992), pp. 104–9; for a detailed description of the visit, see N. Simms, 'The visit of King Sigismund to England, 1416', *Hungarian Stud. Rev.*, xvii (1990), 21–9.

the texts produced by Thomas Sampson and William Kingsmill, the London scrivener who moved to Oxford in about 1420 to teach business skills. Styfford himself did not take the Scriveners' oath until 20 April 1440. He described himself then as a citizen and writer of the court letter of the city of London and took the oath knowing that 'it had been instituted for the greater utility and repute … of the art'. He swore to hold and observe it with all his power, having corporately touched the sacred [Gospels] of the Evangelists, consenting above all to observe the new ordinances as much as it is in me. He wrote the oath with his own hand.[13]

The time difference of twenty-three years between the swearing of the two oaths is misleading, however. By 1436 both men were employed by Filippo Borromei and Partners of London and were paid 3s 4d a time to write protests to bills of exchange. Only an imperial notary could undertake such work, so by 1436 Styfford must have been admitted to their ranks, but how and by whom remains a mystery. Neither of them made a fortune from such work. Styfford's earnings from the Borromei were 16s 8d in 1436 and £1 13s 4d in 1437, mainly because he was paid 13s 4d for writing the testament of Peter Spidelin, a German merchant who was taken ill in London and died while being cared for by the staff of the Borromei bank in their house in St. Nicholas Lane.[14]

Styfford, then, was active as a scrivener and imperial notary from at least the mid 1430s to the early 1460s. There is no surviving body of his work, no Styfford *protocolla*, and what evidence we have comes mainly from Italian sources, from the Borromei archive and the transcripts of protests to bills of exchange made by Rawdon Brown and others for the first volume of his *Calendar of State Papers Venetian, 1202–1509*, published by the stationery office in 1864.[15] The first important document is the engrossed *protocollum* of the contract between Count Vitaliano I Borromeo (1385/91–1449) of the one part and Felice da Fagnano of Milan and Alessandro Palastrello of Piacenza on the other. The date of the contract in Milan was 12 March 1443 and of

---

[13] N. Orme, *Medieval Schools from Roman Britain to Renaissance England* (New Haven, Conn., and London, 2006), pp. 67–78, quotation at p. 71; Chesham's and Styfford's oaths can be seen in Jenkinson, *Later Court Hands in England*, pt. ii, plates III and IV.

[14] The ledgers of the Borromei banks in London for 1436 to 1439 and Bruges for 1438 are kept in the Borromeo-Arese family archive (Archivio Borromei dell'Isola Bella (ABIB)), libro maestro 7 (BLon) and libro maestro 8 (BBr) respectively. Styfford's accounts are BLon fos. 37.4, 45.2, 59.4; Chesham's are BLon fos. 32.1, 78.7, 150.7. A history of the banks and the folio numbering system are both explained on the Borromei Bank Research Project website <http://www.queenmaryhistoricalresearch.org/roundhouse/default.html> [accessed 10 Feb. 2019].

[15] These are to be found in TNA, PRO 31/14/189, 190, 191.

the copy in London 2 August 1443.[16] Its purpose was to establish a second Borromei bank in London after the apparent closure of the first branch in 1440–1, not because it had failed but because the original contract had come to an end and the profits had to be distributed among the partners. Most of the staff of the first bank, Giovanni and Niccolò Micheli and Alessandro Palastrello had remained in London. The *Views of the Hosts* show that they continued trading after 1441, although whether on their own account or for the bank is not clear.[17] In 1443 Count Vitaliano I decided to re-establish banks in Bruges, Barcelona and London, and there are draft contracts for all three banks in the Isola Bella archive, in Italian. The London partnership was to be managed by Vitaliano's brother-in-law, Felice da Fagnano, who had originally worked in Bruges. He was in Milan in 1443 and so knew the full terms of the London contract. Alessandro Palastrello of Piacenza had moved to London in 1438 and continued living there until at least 1456, when he was the Italian attacked by the young men of the Mercery whilst he was walking along Cheapside, setting off the anti-Italian riots of that year.[18]

It was because Palastrello was not in Milan for the making of the contract that a notarized copy was sent to London so that the new partner could be made fully aware of its terms and conditions. While its format may be familiar to ecclesiastical historians, since it is similar to *protocolla* drawn up by papal notaries, that will not be the case for medievalists who work on deeds, accounts and judicial records produced by the royal chancery or for private citizens, so it is worth looking at it in some detail. The original is in Latin and the English translation and punctuation here are this author's. The opening section is:

> In the Name of God Amen. By this present public instrument it will become apparent that in the year of the Incarnation of our Lord 1443, the sixth indiction, and the thirteenth year of the pontificate of the most Holy in Christ and our father and lord Eugenius, by divine providence Pope, in the presence of me, the notary and of the noble men Bernardo D'Alzate and Lodovico D'Alzate, both of Milan, especially summoned and requested as witness to this present,

---

[16] ABIB, Box File 1051, item (c).

[17] *The Views of the Hosts of Alien Merchants 1440–1444*, ed. H. Bradley (London Rec. Soc., xlvi, 2012), pp. 28–34.

[18] For the history of the banks see the Borromei Bank Research Project website at <http://www.queenmaryhistoricalresearch.org/roundhouse/default.html> [accessed 10 Feb. 2019]; P. C. Clarke, 'The commercial activities of Giovanni Marcanova di Giacomo', in *Cittidani Veneziani del Quattrocento: I due Giovanni Marcanova, il Mercante e L'umanista*, ed. E. Barile (Venice, 2006), pp. 247–373, at pp. 282–5, 357–64; J. L. Bolton, 'The city and the crown, 1456–61', *London Jour.*, xii (1986), 11–24, at pp. 12–4.

and the noble man Felice da Fagnano, son of a certain Messer Giacomo and Alessando Palastrello of Piacenza, in the house inhabited by me the notary underwritten situated in Lombard Street in the parish of St. Nicholas Acon, in the same place the said Felice presented a certain public instrument signed and made by Francesco de' Regius, son of a certain Messer Pietro, notary of the city of Milan, between the magnificent and powerful Lord Vitaliano Borromei born of a certain magnificent Lord Giacomo *of the city of Milan* (inter-lineated) of [the district of] Porta Vercellina, parish of St. Maria Pedonis of the one part and the said Felice in his own name and in the name and place and on behalf of the said Alessandro of the other part, of certain promises and agreements which will further appear in this instrument. And the said Felice asked and requested me, the public notary under written, to read out loud (*viva voce*) with a distinct voice to inform the said Alessandro and the aforesaid witnesses of the tenor of this instrument, word for word (*verbo ad verbum*) and it is as follows. In the Name of God Amen in the year from the Nativity of the same 1443, sixth indiction, Tuesday 12 March … [There follows the contract to establish a bank in London in the name of Felice da Fagnano and Alessandro Palastrello, with Count Vitaliano I Borromei as the senior partner.]

As Theresa O'Byrne has explained, notarized documents followed a strict formula for their opening lines, in which the date and the names of the parties concerned were listed, although the notary did not name himself until the eschatacol, the authenticating clause at the end of the *protocollum*. Here three date systems were used: the Incarnation of Our Lord, more commonly known in England as the Annunciation of the Blessed Virgin Mary, 25 March and the beginning of the New Year; the sixth indiction, a civil reckoning of time based on fifteen-year cycles which were computed from 312, the indiction of Constantine; and the year of the pontificate of Eugenius IV, who was elected to succeed Martin V on 4 March 1431. Then followed the list of those present: Fagnano, Palastrello and the two witnesses, Bernardo and Lodovico D'Alzate of Milan, then in London, and the notary himself, who revealed that his house was in Lombard Street in the parish of St. Nicholas of Acon. A map of the parish boundaries in 1856 shows that it must have been on the south side of Lombard Street, between Abchurch Lane to the west and St. Nicholas Lane to the east, where numbers 19–22 Lombard Street stood in that year.[19]

The original document had been brought from Milan by Felice da Fagnano. It was drawn up by another notary imperial, Francesco de' Regius from the district of Porta Vercillina (now Porta Magenta) and the parish

---

[19] The map can be found in *Collage: the London Picture Archive* <https://collage. cityoflondon.gov.uk> [accessed 10 Feb. 2019] Collage record 30713, Plan of the Parish of Saint Nicholas Acon's, Lombard Street, 1875.

of St. Maria Podone in central Milan, conveniently near to the Palazzo Borromeo. Styfford was now asked by Felice to read the lengthy contract out loud and this he presumably did, although whether in Italian or Latin is not specified. It is a long contract, it was August and one can only wonder if any of the four Italians there present dozed off. Apparently not, according to the concluding section, which again followed well-trodden formulae:

> The which public instrument having been read by me the public notary and heard and well understood by the said Alessandro, in the presence of me, the public notary underwritten, and the aforesaid Bernardo and Lodovico [D'Alzate], the said Alessandro, being neither forced nor compelled but of his own free and spontaneous will, as he has asserted, promises and has promised by this instrument to keep and to hold all those things promised by the said Felice in the name of the said Alessandro in the manner and form above written, and that at no time in the future to act against them or contradict them. And further, the said Alessandro concedes and promises and by this said instrument concedes and promises to keep, hold and observe all things contained in this instrument, according to the promises made in his name by Felice and made in this instrument, and they approve, praise, ratify and confirm all things contained in this instrument and by this present he approves, praises, ratifies and confirms in all things and for all things contained above, putting all fraud, deceit, collusion and evil purpose on his part behind him. And the said Felice and Alessandro have asked and required me, the notary public underwritten, to make one, two or more copies of the public instrument or instruments in exactly the same wording as above. This was enacted here in London in the house in which I the public notary underwritten live, as is said above, and in the presence of Bernardo and Lodovico, the witnesses specially summoned and invited.

The still unnamed imperial notary was asked to make or have made two or three copies of the document, and it must be one of these that was sent back to Milan to be stored in the Borromei archive. Then, finally, came the important clause that validated the whole document, the eschatocol:

> And I William Styfford, clerk, citizen of London, public notary by Imperial authority, because I was present at the above proceedings together with the witnesses, have put on this public instrument which was written elsewhere by another scribe and put into its present form by me, my singular and customary mark, as requested and required and as surety and witness to the premises. And it is apparent to me the above written notary that these words *civitatis mediolani* [of the city of Milan] have been inter-lineated between the third and fourth lines of this present document, counting from the top. The which things I the before written notary confirm.

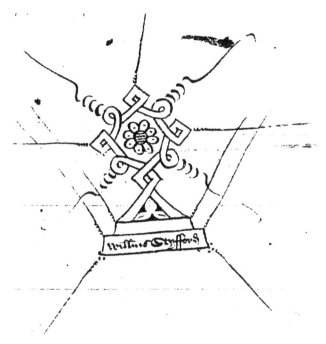

Figure 7.1. Sign manual of William Styfford, notary imperial from
the Archivio Borromei dell'Isola Bella, Box File 1051 (c).

Here Styfford at last identified himself, specified that the document had
actually been drawn up by another scribe but that he had put it into its
form, noted the interlineation between the third and fourth lines and put
his notary's mark (Figure 7.1).

Here we have a public notarial instrument which would have been only
too familiar to notaries and their clients in southern Europe, but better
known to papal notaries than to merchants in England. Much stress was
laid on the public duty of the attorney, something also evident in the oaths
scriveners swore on their admission to the Company. How much Styfford
was paid for his work we do not know, since the only surviving ledger for
the Borromei bank in London ends in 1439. What we do know, thanks
to Rawdon Brown's transcripts, is that Styfford was employed regularly as
an imperial notary by Venetian merchants in London in the 1440s, 1450s
and early 1460s to record that a bill of exchange had been protested and
returned to the original taker in Venice.[20]

---

[20] R. Brown had one of the best jobs in 19th-century Britain. Born in 1803, he arrived in
Venice in 1833 and lived there for the next 50 years until his death in 1883. For many years
he was paid an annual salary of £250 for collecting material on Anglo-Venetian relations.

A protested bill of exchange was a device used by Italian bankers to avoid the usury laws and make a profit from the imbalance between international exchange rates in southern and northern Europe.[21] By the fifteenth century the bill of exchange was a well-developed instrument that allowed a merchant to take up a series of loans repayable at various times and at reasonable interest rates. This was done through an exchange transaction in which there were usually four parties: the deliverer and taker in a town in one country; and the payor and payee in a different town in a different country. The taker in town one took up a loan in the local currency from the deliverer and wrote a bill of exchange on his agent or correspondent in the second town ordering him to pay the principal to a nominated recipient after a specified time (usance) in the local currency at an agreed exchange rate. On 10 November 1438 a bill of exchange from Venice was entered in the Borromei London ledger. It was for 400 Venetian ducats at an exchange rate of forty-five *sterlings* (pennies) per ducat and yielded £75 0s 0d *sterling*. The deliverer in Venice three months earlier was Cecco di Tommaso and Brothers, a Venetian banking company; the taker Carlo Querini of Venice; the payor in London Lorenzo da Marcanuovo, a well-known Venetian resident in London;[22] and the payee was the bank Filippo Borromei and Partners of London.

This may have been the transfer of liquid capital from Venice to London or money borrowed in Venice by Querini which he would eventually have to repay to the Tommasi. It could also have been the first part of a pre-arranged transaction on which the Tommasi made a handsome profit. Lorenzo da Marcanuovo could have refused to pay the bill, which would have resulted in a formal protest and the £75 0s 0d *sterling* would have been returned to Venice, this time at the lower exchange rate of 43 ⅚ *sterlings* per ducat, which would have yielded 441 ducats in Venice three months later, a not inconsiderable profit for the Tommasi.[23] When the two transactions were combined, with the same parties involved in each, then this was

His notes and transcripts were bequeathed to what was then the Public Record Office and is now The National Archives, which made them publicly available in 2012. They are a gold mine of information, including copies of 19 protests to bills of exchange, of which only 2 or 3 were eventually calendared in the *Calendar of State Papers relating to English Affairs in the Archives of Venice*, i. *1202–1509* (London, 1864).

[21] For a full discussion of how bills of exchange worked, see M. A. Denzel, 'The European bill of exchange: its development from the middle ages to 1914', in *Cashless Payments from the Antiquity to 1914*, ed. S. Chaudhuri and M. A. Denzel (Stuttgart, 2008), pp. 153–94.

[22] For Marcanuovo, see G. Nordio, 'Lorenzo Marcanova in Inghliterra, fattore dello zio Giovanni (1440–1444)', in Barile, *Cittidani veneziani del quattrocento*, pp. 377–93; Clarke, 'Commercial activities of Giovanni Marcanova', pp. 272–329.

[23] ABIB, BLon fos. 192.2a, 252.3d.

known as *cambium et recambium*, exchange and re-change, with the profit being made on the differential exchanges rates for the ducat against sterling and vice versa in southern and northern Europe.

The protest had to be made formally in the presence of an imperial notary and recorded by him in an equally formal manner, to be sent back to the taker of the original bill. This is, of course, where William Styfford became involved, being paid 3*s* 4*d* for his efforts, as we have already seen. The following is a typical example of a protest written by him, with the main body of the text being in Latin and the bill of exchange in Italian, using the Venetian dialect:

> 23 January 1443. Niccolò da Rabatta, factor of Jacomo Salviati and Partners, in my presence as a notary public and in the presence of the witnesses below written approached Giovanni da Ponte who was then present in my house in Lombard Street in the parish of St. Nicholas Acon and then, in the name of the Salviati above written, presented Giovanni with certain letters of payment for a certain exchange sent to Giovanni on behalf of Michele Zon [of Venice] and the same letters were publicly read out, the terms of the letter being these:

> + In the name of Jesus 8 November 1447 in Venice pay by this first [letter] of exchange after a month's sight of the same to ser Jacomo Salviati and Partners the value of six hundred ducats, that is to say 600, at 45 *sterlings* per ducat, received here [in Venice] when the letter was made from ser Michele Zondoneli. May God guard you, Michele Zon.

On the dorse of this letter was written:

> [To] ser Giovanni da Ponte in London. The which letters being presented and read, the said Niccolò admitted that he had already received £25 *sterling* on behalf of the Salviati from the said Giovanni and in response the said Giovanni said that he did not wish to pay the residue of the exchange [£87 10*s* 0*d sterling*]. Having heard this response and to solve the problem of the unpaid residue, Niccolò asked if there was anyone else in the house or outside the house who was willing to pay the residue of the exchange … No person or persons replied and so Niccolò made a protest and protested against the said Giovanni and Michele Zon, each of them, either of them or both of them … This was done here in London before witnesses especially called and sworn for the purposes, namely Bassiano de Rivargario of Venice and Federico de Nosorii of Florence and Francesco Cristiano, bill-broker, who certified to me the public notary that the exchange rate for the ducat on that day was 41 ⅚ths *sterlings*. And I William Styfford clerk, citizen of London, public notary imperial etc. etc.[24]

---

[24] TNA, PRO 31/14/189, item viii.

In its formality and its public nature this protest is much like the *protocollum* establishing the second Borromei bank in 1443. The proceedings quite possibly only took a few minutes and were relatively dignified, since they took place in Styfford's house. On other occasions Styfford, the witnesses and the bill-broker had to accompany the payee to the house of the payor and make the protest there. On 4 December 1453 he, Dardo and Donato Raimondo, Venetians, the witnesses, and Delzemetera, the bill-broker, with Andrea Graziani, Venetian, all went to the dwelling of Girolamo Badoer in the parish of St. Martin Outwich. There a bill of exchange for 200 ducats drawn at Venice on 4 September 1443 by Antoni d'Alberto of Brescia at usance (three months) in favour of Filippo Priuli and Andrea Graziani on Sebastiano and Girolamo Badoer, in London, at the exchange rate of 44½ *sterlings* per ducat, was read out to Girolamo. As it would probably have been cold in London in December 1453, we can only hope that the assembled company went into the house rather than standing out in the street to listen to the bill being read out loud. After he had heard it, Girolamo refused payment on behalf of himself and Sebastiano. Graziani then inquired whether anyone inside or outside would pay the bill; and the answer being 'No', he protested against the Badoers and the taker of the bill, Antonio d'Alberto. The bill-broker Delzemetera then certified to Styfford that the ducat was worth 39¹/3 *sterlings* in London on that day. Styfford would then have returned to his house on Lombard Street and either he or one of his employees would have drawn up the formal protest, as above, to be sent back to Venice.[25]

If these proceedings actually happened rather than being formally recorded, then they may have provided some innocent amusement for the bystanders or, perhaps, they confirmed their anti-Italian prejudices at such goings on. What they show us is that Styfford, as one of the few imperial notaries in London, had a steady source of income from writing protests for the Borromei, various Venetian and other Italian merchants. He must have known most of the Italian community in London and there are quite probably other protests and documents written by him yet to be discovered in private Florentine, Milanese, Venetian and Genoese archives. What he also kept was a day book, or more probably day books, with brief records of work done for Italian merchants.

In The National Archives there are two registers of debts, that is, of the contractual arrangements between creditors and debtors, including the terms and place of repayment, which could be abroad, at one of the great Brabantine fairs, for instance. One register, of the debts of Hanseatic

---

[25] *Calendar of State Papers Venetian*, i. 78–9.

and Low Countries merchants, was drawn up by John Thorpe, a London scrivener but not, as far as can be seen, an imperial notary. The other was kept by William Styfford and dealt exclusively with Italian merchants. Both date from 1457 to 1459 and they are linked to a series of proceedings in the exchequer court and recorded on the exchequer memoranda rolls for 1459–60. Various London merchants and provincial woolmen and clothiers were prosecuted for offering extended credit to aliens against the terms of the statutes of 8 and 9 Henry VI.[26] The contracts recorded in both books are a valuable source for English overseas trade and have been extensively analysed, first by Michael Postan and then, more recently, by Wendy Childs and Stuart Jenks.[27]

While it is fairly clear what these two registers *are*, we should also grasp what they *are not* and that is *protocolla*, notarial registers of original wills, contracts, conveyances and marriage settlements which then became public property. They were private property taken into public hands for a specific purpose, or even extracted from Styfford's and Thorpe's records so that the Lancastrian regime could punish suspected enemies, and most notably the Italians, through the courts.[28] Their very survival does, however, raise an interesting, if as yet unanswerable, question. Were Styfford and Thorpe unique, or did other scriveners, notaries public and notaries imperial keep registers or rolls of the various documents they drew up for their various clients, in rough form at least? It seems highly likely, but because they were private and not public records and remained the personal property of the compilers, as with other commercial records and, most frustratingly, mercantile accounts, they have not survived.

Ultimately, Styfford remains a shadowy figure. We do not know when he was born or to whom he was married. Styfford's will has not survived, assuming he made one, and when he died his daughter Elizabeth was left an orphan. On 29 November and 2 December 1466 respectively two bonds of £100 each were deposited in the city Chamber, the money to be paid to her when she reached her majority or married. The main subscribers were members of the Drapers' Company: John Brokford, John Hungerford and

---

[26] *PROME*, iv. 360–1, item 66 (8 Henry VI, 1429–30) and 377, item 31 (9 Henry VI, 1430–1).

[27] The registers are TNA, E 101/128/36 (Styfford) and E 101/128/37 (Thorpe) (M. M. Postan, 'Private financial instruments in medieval England', in *Medieval Trade and Finance* (Cambridge, 1973), pp. 29–54, at pp. 34–5 and n. 16; W. Childs, '"To oure losse and hindrance": English credit to alien merchants in the mid-fifteenth century', in Kermode, *Enterprise and Individuals*, pp. 69–98, at p. 70, for the statutes against credit; S. Jenks, 'Das Schreiberbuch des John Thorpe und der hansische Handel in London 1457/59', *Hansische Geschichtsblätter*, ci (1983), 67–114).

[28] Bolton, 'The city and the crown', pp. 15–21.

John Beauchamp to the first, with Richard Messynger, a goldsmith, and John Shugborough, William Burtone and William Holme to the second, with Thomas Risby, a brasier. Brokford (alias Wakely) and Hungerford acted with Thomas Urswyck, the recorder of the city, and others as feofees for John Jurdan, citizen and merchant of London, and Elizabeth his wife for property in Mynchon Lane, St. Dunstan in the East, in 1470. They were also involved together in a gift of goods and chattels in the mayor's court in the same year and with Richard Messynger, a prominent goldsmith and warden of the Company in 1463 and 1468. Brokford certainly knew Styfford since he appears in the latter's register of debts and was later prosecuted in the exchequer court for illegal credit transactions. By far the biggest fish in this group of drapers was John Beauchamp, however. His extensive dealings in the credit market have recently been investigated, and if Styfford worked for him and the other drapers they would have provided him with a steady source of income, which would help to explain why he had a house in such a prime position on Lombard Street.[29]

William Styfford had two important circles of clients, friends and acquaintances within the city, then. The first consisted of Italian merchants, the representatives of Italian merchant-banking partnerships based in London. The protests to the bills of exchange, the register of debts, some eighty-seven of them between 1457 and 1459, and the cases brought in the exchequer court in 1459–60, 110 in all, show that they included the managers of another Borromei bank in London, Alessandro Borromei and Partners of Venice, not Milan, and the factors or agents of the Bardi, Contarini, Doria, Giustiniani, Lomellini, with Homobone Gritti and Giovanni Walcomostrasso of Venice and Simone Nori of Florence, one of the managers of the Medici bank in London. Childs's work on Styfford's register shows that he wrote contracts of debt for a large portion of the Italian community in the city in the late 1450s and for their English clients, who were drawn from the leading members of the Drapers', Mercers' and Grocers' companies. His dealings with these men must have brought him a fair income, which may explain his relative wealth at his death.[30]

[29] *Cal. Letter Bks. L*, p. 69; *CPMR, 1458–1482*, pp. 66, 113, 149; E. Quinton, 'The drapers and the drapery trade of late medieval London' (unpublished University of London PhD thesis, 2001), p. 252 (for Brokford); Childs, '"To oure losse and hindrance"', p. 93; T. Reddaway and L. Walker, *The Early History of the Goldsmiths' Company 1327–1509* (London, 1975), p. 299; R. Goddard, *Credit and Trade in Later Medieval England, 1353–1532* (New York and London, 2016), pp. 70–9, esp. at p. 78.

[30] TNA, PRO 31/14/191; Childs, '"To oure losse and hindraunce"', pp. 75–86, 90–5; R. De Roover, *The Rise and Decline of the Medici Bank, 1397–1494* (New York, 1966), pp. 325–9; F. Guidi Bruscoli and J. Lutkin, 'Perception, identity and culture: the Italian communities in fifteenth-century London and Southampton revisited', in *Resident Aliens in Later Medieval*

The second, overlapping with the first since they sold the Italians cloth for export, consisted of members of the Drapers' Company and to these we can add a third, again overlapping with the other two, that of Robert Bale, scrivener and chronicler. Bale's circle has been intensively discussed by Anne Sutton, Mary Erler and others.[31] He was a man of considerable standing in London until the 1460s, when his well-known 'troubles' began and Styfford became involved in them. Bale had married Agnes, the niece of Thomas Haunsard, vintner, and fully expected that his wife would inherit her uncle's property. Haunsard, however, made a will which left his executors with considerable discretion as to the disposal of his goods and lands, and Agnes and Robert were more or less disinherited. Bale, dismayed by this turn in his fortunes, had little choice but to contest the will on behalf of his wife. Styfford acted as one of his witnesses as to what had actually happened at Haunsard's deathbed when the new will was made. Typically, Styfford's testimony ends with an eschatacol clause and his notarial mark, the only one of the six witness statements to be formally confirmed in this way. Friendship with Bale brought Styfford nothing but trouble, however. Bale was so short of money in 1456 that he sought a loan from William Lemyng, grocer. Lemyng required sureties and Bale eventually persuaded Styfford to provide a guarantee in the form of a bond for £100. Styfford seems to have doubted Bale's ability to repay the loan. He had had previous experience of a draper, John Claimond, defaulting on a bond of debt for £30, which suggests that Styfford, like other scriveners, may have been a moneylender.[32] In this case he demanded the deeds to Bale's property in the parish of St. Mary Magdalene, Southwark, as his surety. He was wise to be cautious. Bale defaulted on his loan to Lemyng and in Easter 1458 Styfford had to pay the £100 to Lemyng and his associates. At this point Styfford's friendship with Bale seems to have come to an abrupt end since he had him arrested and imprisoned.

As more names are added to Styfford's circle of friends and business associates, he becomes a less shadowy figure. He appears to have been a man

---

England, ed. W. M. Ormrod, N. McDonald and C. Taylor (Turnhout, 2017), pp. 89–104, at pp. 92–6; W. I. Haward, 'The financial transactions between the Lancastrian government and the merchants of the Staple from 1449 to 1461', in *Studies in English Trade in the Fifteenth Century*, ed. E. Power and M. M. Postan (London, 1933), pp. 293–320, at pp. 311–8.

[31] Sutton, 'Robert Bale'; Erler, 'Guildhall Library', pp. 179–80. I am grateful to Hannes Kleineke of the History of Parliament Trust for making his unpublished paper, 'The troubles of Robert Bale: the deathbed of Thomas Haunsard', available to me, citing TNA, E 135/7/36, item 6.

[32] LMA, CLA/024/02/004/307, 1455–7. The suggestion that scriveners may have been money-lenders is based on the frequency with which they appear in gifts of goods and chattels in the mayor's court. It is a subject in need of further investigation.

of some substance if he could pay £100 on Bale's behalf, even reluctantly. Yet his importance goes far beyond that of a scrivener or notary working for a number of Londoners and with links to the Drapers' Company. As Pamela Nightingale has argued, in the fourteenth century London became England's gateway port, where imports were landed and redistributed and exports were sent to destinations from the Baltic to the Mediterranean. Many factors went towards the making of a gateway city. It had to provide accommodation for all sorts, from the town houses of the great to the dwellings of the poor immigrants, both English and alien. There had to be good and effective government; courts for the rapid settlement of disputes; proper port facilities for the swift turn round of ships; good transport links with other parts of the country and in London's case especially with Southampton and Sandwich, its outports.[33] To these we should add the availability of notarial and scribal services staffed by scriveners who had command not only of Latin and English but also, when required, of French, Flemish, German and Italian. For the Italians, whose banking and commercial operations relied so heavily on the written word, it was vital that they had access to imperial notaries who could draw up *protocolla* and provide the essential authentication to make them acceptable in other countries and above all in Italy itself. William Styfford and his fellow notaries imperial were essential to the Italian trade and deserve far more attention than they hitherto have been given.

---

[33] P. Nightingale, 'The growth of London in the medieval English economy', in *Progress and Problems in Medieval England*, ed. R. Britnell and J. Hatcher (Cambridge, 1996), pp. 89–106; M. Kowaleski, *Local Markets and Regional Trade in Medieval Exeter* (Cambridge, 1995), pp. 179–21; O. Gelderblom, *Cities of Commerce: the Institutional Foundations of International Trade in the Low Countries, 1250–1650* (Princeton, N.J., 2013), pp. 2–15, 19–24.

8. Bankers and booksellers: evidence of the late fifteenth-century English book trade in the ledgers of the Bardi bank*

M. T. W. Payne

In late 1493 the Venetian bookseller Cyprian Reglia found himself based in Paris. He was about twenty-seven years of age and bore a distinctive scar on the flesh of his left palm, by the wrist. Among other things, Reglia was acting as the business associate of the London-based bookseller Peter Actors. Actors, a native of Savoy, had been appointed king's stationer in December 1485 and had outlets for his books in Oxford through his son Sebastian and his son-in-law John Hewtee.[1] Another relative, Anthony Actors, imported books into London in 1478.[2] The business was international for the nature of the book trade made this unavoidable. Although the printing press had been introduced into England by William Caxton in 1475 or 1476, very few had actually been set up by this date. Caxton himself had recently died and the only presses known to be operational in 1493 were those run by his successor Wynkyn de Worde and that recently established by Richard Pynson. A couple of other ventures

* I would like to express my profound gratitude to Francesco Guidi Bruscoli, who not only first brought the Bardi ledgers to my attention in a paper he gave at a conference in honour of James L. Bolton, but subsequently displayed unending patience and generosity in explaining the mechanics of the ledgers to me and in assisting me to decipher the Italian and its meaning. All errors in this understanding of course remain my own. I am also enormously grateful to the Bibliographical Society, a travel grant from which enabled me to travel to Florence to examine the ledgers.

[1] For Actors, see E. G. Duff, *A Century of the English Book Trade* (London, 1948), p. 1; P. Blayney, *The Stationers' Company and the Printers of London, 1501–1557* (2 vols., Cambridge, 2013), i. 111–12. For his importation of books from Paris in 1480 (from Pierre Levet) and 1483, see P. Needham, 'Continental printed books sold in Oxford, *c*.1480–3', in *Incunabula: Studies in Fifteenth-Century Printed Books Presented to Lotte Hellinga*, ed. M. Davies (London, 1999), pp. 243–70.

[2] A. Coates, 'The Latin trade in England and abroad', in *Companion to the Early Printed Book in Britain, 1476–1558*, ed. V. Gillespie and S. Powell (Woodbridge 2014), pp. 45–58, at p. 48.

M. T. W. Payne, 'Bankers and booksellers: evidence of the late fifteenth-century English book trade in the ledgers of the Bardi bank', in *Medieval Londoners: essays to mark the eightieth birthday of Caroline M. Barron*, ed. E. A. New and C. Steer (London, 2019), pp. 165–87. License: CC-BY-NC-ND 4.0.

into the domestic printing trade had come and gone, but as an industry it was yet to become firmly settled and by far the majority of printed books in circulation were to be imported from the Continent for some years to come.[3] In the 1490s Actors was the chief importer of printed books into England, as he had been in the late 1470s and early 1480s, although his royal warrant exempted him from customs duties.[4] The pay-off, as Peter Blayney argued, was presumably to import 'whatever books Henry [VII] wished'.[5] This involved not only foreign trading partners, but also family members established in helpful locations: Peter Actors's nephew John Actors, for example, worked out of Lyons.[6]

In December 1493, Actors was required to pay for what we must assume was a batch of books, which he had imported from Paris via Cyprian Reglia. The shipment must have been of a significant size for the outstanding bill was for £20.[7] Clearly Actors had no desire to travel to Paris to hand over the money to Reglia, so he made use of the sophisticated system for the transfer of money provided by the Italian bankers based around Lombard Street in London. In this instance he used his own bank, the Bardi, to transfer the funds, crediting his account on 18 December with the requisite cash. The bankers sent a bill of exchange to their agent in Paris, Manno Tannagli, and the sum was released to Reglia by the following 5 February. Tannagli wrote to the Bardi from Paris that he had released the money and Actors's account was duly debited with the equivalent sum of £20 sterling, at the exchange rate of 100 gold scudi. Reglia had presented himself to Tannagli to claim the money, with the added security against identity fraud noted in the bank's ledger, namely a description of the claimant's age and a distinguishing feature. The whole process was therefore completed in two months, without either party to the payment having to leave his own city.

Reglia's association with Actors, and England, clearly persisted. When Sebastian Actors, Peter's son, died in 1501 in Oxford, Reglia claimed for

---

[3] M. L. Ford, 'Importation of printed books into England and Scotland', in *The Cambridge History of the Book in Britain*, ed. L. Hellinga and J. Trapp (7 vols., Cambridge, 1999–2019), iii. *1400–1557*, 179–201; Blayney, *The Stationers' Company*, i. 47–8.

[4] 'Between 1478 and 1491 Actors imported more than 1,300 books valued in excess of £140' (C. P. Christianson, 'The rise of London's book trade', in Hellinga and Trapp, *Cambridge History of the Book in Britain*, iii. 128–47, at p. 137). See also P. Needham, 'The customs rolls as documents for the printed books trade in England', in Hellinga and Trapp, *Cambridge History of the Book in Britain*, iii. 148–63; Blayney, *The Stationers' Company*, i. 111–12.

[5] Blayney, *The Stationers' Company*, i. 111. In 1501 Actors was paid 14s for 5 printed books for the king (TNA, E 101/415/3, fo. 65).

[6] Florence, Archivio Guicciardini, Carte Bardi 12, fo. 127. See Appendix.

[7] Florence, Archivio Guicciardini, Carte Bardi 11, fo. 248.

money owing to him through his procurator John Aler.[8] Peter Actors claimed his son's binding tools through his son-in-law Hewtee. Reglia appears to have been based in Oxford from the late 1490s. In 1498 he had been involved in an action for debt at the court of common pleas brought by Bernard Dax, a brasier from London.[9] Dax claimed a debt of £18 from John Palewell, a vintner based outside the north gate of Oxford, with Reglia and John Walker, a bookseller also from Oxford, acting as sureties. Reglia himself is described as being a scholar of the university, although he is not listed in the standard guide to the students of Oxford.[10] The award of his BA and MA is not dated, but must be before 1502, from which date he is described in the University records as 'magister'. The case was remitted on the payment of 100s, but this and other instances suggest that Reglia was engaged in fairly large transactions and that he was well-travelled along traditional routes followed by the books he himself traded in: Venice, Paris, London and Oxford. By 1523 he was firmly back in Paris, as principal of the Collège des Lombards at the University of Paris.[11]

The system of which Actors and Reglia made use to transfer funds was firmly established by the 1490s.[12] The particular form of development of merchant banking stemmed from the Church's proscription of usury, that is, the lending of money at interest.[13] The growth of the banking sector reflects an Italian, and primarily Florentine, ingenuity with circumventing these laws. The preferred means of achieving this was through opportunities afforded by different currencies. To make international trade work, these currencies had to be exchanged, and rates of exchange were the tools by which profit could accrue. In order to facilitate this, there grew up around it the accompanying instruments by which this was achieved: bills of exchange and letters of credit.[14] This might enable an individual to save

---

[8] Oxford, Bodleian Library, Hyp/A/2 (Reg D), fo. 93v, calendared in W. Mitchell, *Registrum Cancellarii 1498–1506* (Oxford Hist. Soc., n.s., xxvii, 1980), pp. 95–7.

[9] TNA, CP 40/943; Mitchell, *Registrum Cancellarii*, p. 42.

[10] W Mitchell, *Epistolae Academicae, 1508–1596* (Oxford Hist. Soc., n.s., xxvi, 1980), p. 56; *BRUO (to AD 1500)*.

[11] O. Poullet, 'Les Voyages des frères Verrazane', *Quiquengrogne*, xxx (2002), 7–15.

[12] For the development of the Italian banking system, see R. de Roover, *The Rise and Decline of the Medici Bank, 1397–1494* (Cambridge, Mass., 1963); T. Parks, *Medici Money: Banking, Metaphysics, and Art in Fifteenth-Century Florence* (London, 2005); R. A. Goldthwaite, *The Economy of Renaissance Florence* (Baltimore, Md., 2009).

[13] Dante consigned usurers to the 7th circle of hell, along with sodomites (Parks, *Medici Money*, pp. 13–5).

[14] It should be noted that the Florentine bankers in London also provided a range of services, 'from credit to the transfer of money, and from the sale to the purchase of goods' (F. Guidi Bruscoli, 'London and its merchants in the Italian archives, 1380–1530', in *Medieval Merchants and Money: Essays in Honour of James L. Bolton*, ed. M. Allen and M. Davies

himself the danger of carrying money – by purchasing from his local bank, perhaps in London, a letter of credit, then travelling to his destination on the Continent and cashing in the letter on arrival in local currency. Such a process is evident among the entries in the Bardi ledgers when, for example, Michel Morin credited his account on 10 July 1495 with £16, to which sum he soon after added a further £6 1s 8d, the whole amount of £22 1s 8d being redeemed by 15 September by Morin himself in Paris.[15]

The same principle applied to the acquisition by merchants of bills of exchange in order to transfer money to foreign trading partners or clients. The letter or bill was bought in sterling and cashed in a specified currency, at a stated exchange rate, which allowed inevitably for the banker's profit. The interest was factored in but not technically charged. The bank made out the bill of exchange (in fact several copies were sent for reasons of security) and these copies were sent by them to the banker's agent at the destination. The banks ran their own courier system and fixed time-periods were usually allowed within which the bill had to be claimed, based on the length of time the journey supposedly took: London to Florence, ninety days; Florence to Bruges, sixty. Some entries in the ledgers, however, demonstrate that these guidelines could be flexible. As a result, the merchant had the security of transferring sums of money safely over long distances and the bankers made a profit without in theory stepping into the sinful realms of usury by charging interest. It also enabled the bankers, who were of course also merchants, to move sums of money between markets for their own benefit. Because profits were based on fluctuations and variations in exchange rates, medieval banking was necessarily a fundamentally international business.

From the fourteenth century onwards various, largely Florentine, families had cornered the market in the new banking systems and the huge fortunes of such hereditary empires as the Medici and the Borromei were built on these financial operations.[16] These were dynastic enterprises and the major families intermarried frequently. This meant that apparently rival firms often had complicated family connections. In addition, no individual firm, not even the Medici in their heyday, could have branches or agents in every

---

(London, 2016), pp. 113–35, at p. 122). This explains Actors's purchase from the Bardi of taffeta and other cloths on 6 June 1495.

[15] Florence, Archivio Guicciardini, Carte Bardi 12, fo. 38.

[16] For the Borromei, see, e.g., F. Guidi Bruscoli and J. L. Bolton, 'The Borromei bank research project', in *Money, Markets and Trade in Late Medieval Europe: Essays in Honour of John H. A. Munro*, ed. L. Armstrong, I. Elbl and M. M. Elbl (Leiden, 2006), pp. 460–88; J. L. Bolton, 'London merchants and the Borromei bank in the 1430s: the role of local credit networks', in *The Fifteenth Century X: Parliament, Personalities and Power: Papers Presented to Linda S. Clark*, ed. H. Kleineke (Woodbridge, 2011), pp. 53–73.

major market, so there was necessarily a great deal of co-operation between them: a merchant approaching a branch on Lombard Street who wished to transfer sums to Rome needed to know that his bill could be cashed there by the Medicis' correspondent. This might involve an arrangement with the Strozzi, who dominated business in that city.

The Bardi bank had been one of the major players in the fourteenth century, even described by the Florentine chronicler Giovanni Villani as one of the 'pillars of Christendom'.[17] Somewhat ironically, given the strictures against usury, the Church was one of the chief users of the banking system, since tithes and other financial levies needed to be regularly transferred from country of origin to Rome. The stress between the necessity of the system and moral condemnations of it is an ever-present factor in the later middle ages. However, the Bardi, along with the Peruzzi, went bankrupt in the late 1340s, primarily as a result of Edward III reneging on the huge loans they had advanced him to prosecute the Hundred Years' War.[18] Nonetheless, they did not go entirely out of business and by the early fifteenth century they had re-established operations sufficiently to reach into England once again. Various members of the family can be traced operating here from at least the 1420s. Giovanni di Agnolo di Zanobi de' Bardi had arrived in London by 1454; and in 1465 he and Gherardo Canigiani agreed to be the active partners in a short-term limited partnership set up by the powerful Piero de' Medici. By 1471 Giovanni de Bardi seems to have set up on his own, almost certainly in a sizeable property rented from the London draper William Brett, in or adjacent to Lombard Street, where agents of the other banks also congregated. But by the late 1470s Giovanni was spending increasing amounts of time back in Florence. At his death in 1488, the firm, known as the Heirs of Giovanni de' Bardi and Partners, was taken on by his nephew Agnolo di Bernardo de' Bardi. Agnolo also had another, legally separate, firm based in Florence, with the London firm dependent on the Florentine one. In the 1490s the manager of the London firm was Aldobrandino di Francesco Tannagli.[19] Aldobrandino's brother, Manno Tannagli, ran another company in Paris in partnership with Albizzo Del Bene and they

[17] On the Bardi see, e.g., F. Guidi Bruscoli, 'John Cabot and his Italian financiers', *Hist. Research*, lxxxv (2012), 372–93; Guidi Bruscoli, 'London and its merchants'.

[18] E.g., E. Hunt, 'A new look at the dealings of the Bardi and Peruzzi with Edward III', *Jour. Econ. Hist.*, i (1990), 149–62.

[19] Aldobrandino Tannagli appears regularly on the London customs rolls importing significant amounts of cloth, reflecting these merchant bankers' roles as importers of exotic and luxury goods; and in the exchequer accounts, supplying similar goods to the court (e.g. TNA, E 404/85). See also S. Gunn, 'Anglo-Florentine contacts in the age of Henry VIII: political and social contexts', in *The Anglo-Florentine Renaissance: Art for the Early Tudors*, ed. C. Sicca and L. Waldman (New Haven, Conn., and London, 2012), pp. 19–47.

represented the London Bardis' chief partner outside Italy. The London Bardi branch specialized in transfers to the Low Countries, Paris and Italy. Although the London firm was fairly profitable in the early 1490s, after 1496 this appears to have changed and Agnolo wound up the company in 1502. Many of those working with or for the company, including members of the Bardi family, set up their own firms thereafter.[20]

Although a significant number of the records of many Florentine banking houses have survived (the Arte del Cambio in Florence stipulated that all transactions had to be written down), relatively few of them relate to their operations outside Italy.[21] Not surprisingly, most of them stem from the activities of their head offices. However, two ledgers from the Bardi bank's London operations in the mid 1490s are to be found among the archives in the Palazzo Guicciardini in Florence.[22] The ledgers are consecutive and cover the period 1492 to 1494 and 1495 to 1498 respectively. They are the final ledgers, drawn up to reckon the accounts, and would have been accompanied by other preparatory account books (journals, cash books etc.), which would have recorded the same transactions at an earlier stage. The entries in the ledgers make reference to some of these other working volumes and the page numbers on which the related entries can be found (these procedural details have not been included in the summary in the appendix to this essay). The financial transactions of hundreds of merchants, priests, nobles and other individuals based or operating in London are recorded. In the main these relate to transfers of funds from London onto the Continent, very often via Manno Tannagli and Albizzo Del Bene's company in Paris, but also to the Low Countries, to Rome and elsewhere.

Among all the drapers and grocers, scholars and priests there are listed the accounts of six particular members of the book trade; five of them are styled *libraio*, or bookseller, and the other, Hans Coblencz, 'printer of books' ('*inpresatore di libri*').[23] Their names are given in Italian and sometimes it is clear that the bank clerk was unclear about how to record the curious sounding English – or German or French – words. So, for example, Peter Actors became Piero Attoris and Jean Huvin presumably lies behind the

[20] In early 16th-century Florence, the Bardi family forged close connections with the powerful Guicciardini family. This explains the survival of the ledgers among the Guicciardini family archives.

[21] For the survival of material relating to London and Bruges, see F. Guidi Bruscoli, 'Mercanti-banchieri fiorentini tra Londra e Bruges nel XV secolo', in *'Mercatura è arte': Uomini d'affari toscani in Europa e nel Mediterraneo tardomedievale*, ed. L. Tanzini and S. Tognett (Rome, 2012), pp. 11–44; and for London only in Guidi Bruscoli, 'London and its merchants', esp. pp. 115–6.

[22] Florence, Archivio Guicciardini, Carte Bardi 11 and 12.

[23] See, e.g., Carte Bardi 12, fo. 312.

rather garbled 'Giovanni Hwyn'. The entries under the respective accounts vary in length tremendously. In total the entries for the accounts of the six individuals in question amount to thirty-five items in the left hand (debit) side and forty-eight in the right hand (credit) side. However, the entries are completely dominated by the accounts of just two of these individuals: Peter Actors and Michel Morin. Their transactions comprise nineteen and fifty-six entries respectively (both debit and credit), over ninety per cent of the total. The other four individuals only conduct one transaction each, comprising one debit and one credit entry.

The entries themselves are usually vague about the precise purpose for the transfer of money. They give the name of the individuals to whom the funds are being transferred, but not the reason for the transferral. For example, in June 1495 Peter Actors sent £4 6s 8d to his nephew John Actors in Lyons (an example of Actors's familial network); throughout 1496 Actors made a sequence of payments to Jean Richard, the well-known bookseller based in Rouen; and, in his final entry, in May 1497, Actors transferred the relatively small sum of £1 12s 8d to a certain Giovanni Testodis in Lyons. These payments almost certainly all represent orders for books, but it is difficult to draw firm conclusions beyond this. A great many books were published in Lyons and Rouen in 1495. But the close association between Actors and Jean Richard in Rouen, presumably reflecting a steady supply of volumes into England, is significant, even if it is not possible to tie them to particular editions.[24]

In some instances we might start to draw more tentative conclusions about the precise bibliographical purpose of the payments. In late 1494 Godfrey Aste, a bookseller from the Brabant whose identity is uncertain, appears for the only time in the ledgers. On 1 December 1494 he transferred to Nicholas Lecomte, a bookseller then apparently in Paris (although the text is not entirely clear at this point), £6 10s, equivalent to 30 gold scudi. Lecomte had redeemed the money by late January 1495. On 24 November 1494 Lecomte had published Johannes de Garlandia's treatise on poetical metre, *Synonyma*, with its commentary by Galfridus Anglicus, printed for him by William Hopyl in Paris.[25] According to the colophon of that book,

---

[24] Richard published many books for the English market (using various printers, including Martin Morin), including a Sarum Breviary, 3 Nov. 1496 (*STC* 15802); books of hours (Use of Salisbury) in 1494 (*STC* 15879) and 1497 (*STC* 15885); a *Missale Saresberiense* on 4 Dec. 1497 (*STC* 16171); an edition of John Mirk's *Liber festivalis* in English on 22 June 1499 (*STC* 17966); and a *Manuale Saresberiense* in 1501 (*STC* 16139).

[25] *STC* 11608a.7. See *Catalogue of the Books Printed in the Fifteenth Century Now in the British Museum* (London, 1908–2007), pt. viii (France), p. 135 (hereafter *BMC*). It is possible that Aste was pre-ordering copies of Lecomte's own edition of the English sermon cycle,

Lecomte was then in London, based at St. Paul's churchyard, so either he was travelling back and forth between Paris and London, or the money was, in fact, destined for Hopyl as Lecomte's partner in the venture.

There are two other booksellers mentioned in the accounts who appear only once, neither of whose names provide completely certain identification. These are William Fox and, probably, Jean Huvin. In each of these instances their accounts seem to reflect occasions of them using the Bardi to move money which they themselves then collected; that is, as evidence of them travelling to and from the Continent. In the case of Huvin, this is particularly notable. In his entry Huvin credits his account on 20 June 1495 with £6 12s 6d (equivalent to 30 gold scudi), a sum which is then debited from his account on 27 February 1496, a full eight months later. The bill was exchanged for Huvin by Albizzo Del Bene, so this may be evidence of Huvin having been in London and travelling in early 1496 from there to Paris, rather than to Rouen, where he was normally based (although there are other instances of Del Bene cashing bills for Rouen). He must have been unknown to Del Bene, so we are given a physical description of him, along with his age at the time. This is significant not only for the details it gives us on Huvin's birth in c.1457 and for his notable physical features, but also because it seems to provide support for the suggestion that he was, for a short period, in a form of partnership with Jean Barbier and Julian Notary.[26] The argument centres on the printing of a copy of the *Questiones* attributed to Albertus Magnus by a new press near the church of St. Thomas the Apostle in London.[27] Although the printers are not named, the device on the colophon used a mercantile mark which contained three sets of initials. Two of these are identifiable from a later colophon as the printer Julian Notary and Jean Barbier (although the precise identification of Jean Barbier is uncertain). But the third, 'I H', has remained disputed. Duff first argued that Jean Huvin was the most likely candidate, but Peter Blayney has recently thrown doubt on this, arguing that the other leading candidate for the owner of the initials, Inghelbert Haghe, is just as plausible since he was at least known to have been in England in 1505 to 1507 and

John Mirk's *Liber Festivalis* (*STC* 17964), also printed by Wolfgang Hopyl, published on 26 Feb. 1495 (*BMC*, pt. viii, pp. 136–7). This was clearly intended for the English market but it seems more likely that the entry represented an order for copies of a book already printed. The *Synonyma* proved popular with English audiences, being reprinted by Pynson only two years later (*STC* 11609), then by de Worde in 1500 (*STC* 11610) and then in several more editions in the first decade of the 16th century.

[26] For this edition, see Blayney, *The Stationers' Company*, i. 63–7; *BMC*, pt. xi (England), p. 230.

[27] *STC*, p. 270.

1510. Alternatively, the initials might not be those of a printer or publisher at all, but could even be those of another merchant who funded the venture. 'If Huvin ever set foot in England', Blayney stated, 'the evidence is yet to be found'.[28] It is the entry in the Bardi ledgers which provides the requisite evidence.

The other single-entry bookseller is something of a conundrum. In the ledger for 1497 his name is given as 'Ghuglielmo Fox', a bookseller from Normandy residing (*dimorante*) in London. It is possible that this represents an Italian clerk's version of William Faques, who was later to become the king's printer for Henry VII and certainly was from Normandy.[29] Faques is only known to have been active as a printer in 1504 and 1505, some seven years later.[30] Presumably, to be given the role of king's printer, even at a date when this did not confer any particular exclusivity in printing, Faques must have had some significant experience in the book trade before 1504. This entry may provide evidence of Faques being active in London from as early as 1497 and apparently travelling to Paris, where he cashed in his own bill for £7 1s 8d. Alternatively, it may refer to someone else entirely. A stationer named William Fox is known to have been active at about this time and is to be found in court records from 1502.[31]

The only printer specified as such in the records is Hans de Coblencz, a German, recorded in his 1497 entry as a resident of Paris.[32] He is, indeed, generally known to have been resident there, but as the London customs accounts show, he was certainly receiving shipments into England between 1502 and 1508, when his name is entered on the rolls.[33] The Bardi ledger seems to demonstrate that prior to the spring of 1497 he had also travelled to England, at which point he returned to Paris, moving some £30 3s 4d (or 140 scudi) to be collected by himself in June of that year.[34] The timing of Hans de Coblencz's travels and the movement of his funds link to the most evident examples of the production and circulation of particular editions, for on the same day that Coblencz cashed in his own bill for over £30, he also received a bill for £6 from Michel Morin, the individual with by far

---

[28] Blayney, *The Stationers' Company*, i. 65.

[29] Blayney, *The Stationers' Company*, i. 71–3; Duff, *Century of the English Book Trade*, p. 54. In one of his colophons Faques describes himself as 'Guilliermum faques normanum'.

[30] Faques is recorded as an importer of paper in March 1503 (TNA, E 122/80/2). There is some slight evidence for an association with England back to 1495 (Blayney, *The Stationers' Company*, i. 72).

[31] Blayney, *The Stationers' Company*, i. 88 and 156.

[32] For Coblencz, see P. Renouard, *Imprimeurs Parisiens* (Paris, 1898), p. 75.

[33] Christianson, 'The rise of London's book trade', p. 141.

[34] Apparently confirming the suggestion that Coblencz, like Jean Richard, 'may have spent more time in England than has been realised' (Blayney, *The Stationers' Company*, i. 93).

the highest number of entries in the ledgers.[35] Morin's entries represent two thirds of the overall total relating to the book trade and are spread over three separate pages.

Morin himself, then aged about thirty, appears to have travelled from London to Paris on several occasions (which is not surprising, given that he is generally thought to have been Paris-based), in both the spring and autumn of 1495 and again in spring 1497, transferring for his own use the very large sums of £43, £22 and £43 respectively. Although he clearly relied heavily on the Bardi, he was initially unknown enough to require the requisite identity check, giving us the colourful additional information that he seems to have suffered from a slightly deformed little finger, which he could not properly extend.

Throughout 1495 to 1497 Morin made regular payments to the well-known Parisian bookseller Jean Petit, as well as to Hans Coblencz in Paris. While many of these payments doubtless represent the purchase of miscellaneous stock already printed, some of the entries surely cover payments for the production of two well-known works. On 11 April 1497 Pierre Levet printed in Paris an edition of Alexander Carpentarius's *Destructorium vitiorum*, a best-selling treatise of invective and didacticism on contemporary morals by an obscure early fifteenth-century English writer.[36] This edition was aimed squarely at the English market. The colophon informs us that it was printed by Levet for himself, Hans de Coblencz and for Michel Morin. The Bardi ledgers suggest that, if it is this publication which is covered and not another unknown volume, Morin did not deal with Levet but only with Coblencz and that Jean Petit was also, possibly, involved in the venture. The sums he was being paid by Morin were recorded under the same days as Coblencz. The latter's presence in England until June 1497 may, therefore, be at least partially explained. And Morin's journey to Paris, cashing in his large amount of over £30 on the same day that Coblencz received his £6 from Morin, can also be explained by this joint venture (although not the finer details of the business arrangements). Earlier and subsequent transfers of sums by Morin to Coblencz may represent other instalments of the same process. If so, this demonstrates the significant outlay required to fund an extensive print run, as well as further evidence for the commissioning of books for the English market by merchants based in England but using continental printers.

---

[35] Shipments of books into London in 1503 and 1506 by Michel Morin may well be in association with Coblencz, suggesting a long-standing partnership between these two (Christianson, 'The rise of London's book trade', p. 141).

[36] Incunabula Short Title Catalogue <https://data.cerl.org/istc/ia00394000> [accessed 9 July 2019]. See *BMC*, pt. viii, p. 103.

In autumn 1496 Morin transferred the equivalent of 60 scudi, in a number of instalments, to a certain 'Awry' or Arigho Charim, a German printer active in Paris, with further payments culminating in 100 gold scudi in May 1497.[37] While it is not entirely clear who this represents, it may well be an Italian clerk's attempt to make sense of a name given to him by Morin, a Frenchman, in England, referring to a German: Ulrich Gering, one of the three co-partners who had founded the first press in France at the Sorbonne more than twenty years before.[38]

The money paid by Morin to Ulrich Gering on 3 May 1498 (100 scudi, equating to £21 2s) may represent part-payment, probably the closing payment, for the printing and delivery of a well-known Sarum missal produced by Ulrich Gering and Berthold Rembolt for Wynkyn de Worde, Michel Morin and Pierre Levet on 2 January 1497.[39] Whether the previous payments by Morin to Gering, of £13 in September 1496 and £26 in June 1497, represent part of the same long-running venture, it is not possible to be sure. If they do, this would represent a total investment by Morin, probably along with or on behalf of de Worde, of £60 or 280 scudi.

While the entries in the accounts of booksellers and printers clearly provide the most immediate evidence of the workings of the continental book trade at the end of the fifteenth century, there are other entries in the ledgers which also throw some light on this. The humanist Thomas Linacre, scholar and physician and friend of Erasmus, More, Colet and Grocyn, is believed to have spent almost all of the 1490s in Italy, from 1487 in Florence studying Greek under Politian and Demetrius Chalcondylas, then in Rome, before moving to Venice and Padua in the north and taking a degree in medicine from Padua in 1496.[40] There he fell into the circle of Aldus Manutius and his efforts to promote the study of Greek. Linacre is not known to have returned to England until he reappeared in London in the summer of 1499. It is therefore surprising to find an account for him in the ledgers of the London Bardi branch.[41] In it he is described as a *studiente inghilese*. His account records that on 21 June 1493, for a sum of 13s 4d (probably representing shipping expenses), Linacre had arranged through

---

[37] It is curious that we do not see transfers of money to his relative Martin Morin, a printer based in Rouen. Perhaps these were effected by a different means. For Martin Morin, see *BMC*, pt. viii, pp. 394–8.

[38] See *BMC*, pt. viii, pp. 20–31.

[39] *STC* 16169.

[40] For Linacre and his books, see V. Nutton, 'Linacre, Thomas (c. 1460–1524), humanist scholar and physician', in *ODNB* <https://doi.org/10.1093/ref:odnb/16667> [accessed 2 Feb. 2019]; and J. Trapp, *Erasmus, Colet and More: Early Tudor Humanists and Their Books* (London, 1991), pp. 96–100.

[41] Florence, Archivio Guicciardini, Carte Bardi 11, fo. 83.

the Bardi for the delivery of his box of books (*sua chassetta di libri*), which was sent by Manno Tannagli from Paris to Oxford via London. He had made the payment to the London branch of the Bardi from Oxford via an unnamed English priest. The costs of delivery were settled that autumn and the books had been delivered by the end of October. Like others mentioned in the ledgers, Linacre's travels to and from the Continent may have been more frequent than usually recognized.

The Bardi ledgers provide a wealth of evidence of the book trade at the end of the fifteenth century. They add another layer to our understanding of how this circulation of books operated and the reliance on the sophisticated Italian banking system for their importation and sale. But they also offer a demonstration of the sheer variety of merchants at work in London at the time. At first sight, the growth of the trade in printed books through London appears to have been almost exclusively in the hands of foreigners: importers and dealers active in London from the Low Countries, France and Germany, using the banking facilities of Italians based around Lombard Street. However, one must be cautious. Native London merchants who were involved in the trade may be obscured from view by their broader descriptors (draper, grocer etc.). William Caxton was, after all, a mercer and would very probably have been listed as such if he had featured in the ledgers. The general lack of detail within the entries confounds other attempts to pinpoint those involved. The majority of liturgical books, for example, seem to have been imported by grocers, and the financial transactions for such imports may well lie anonymously behind other entries in the ledgers.[42] In addition, the ledgers provide an insight into only part of the mercantile chain which took a book from printer to bookshelf. As alien merchants, these importers could only sell on their wares in London wholesale; only freemen of the city were allowed to sell retail. The books imported by Morin and Actors and others would have required local booksellers to sell individually to customers. Nonetheless, for an understanding of the mechanism by which an increased volume of printed books began to arrive in England through London, and for the individuals involved in the trade, the Bardi ledgers clearly provide invaluable insights.

---

[42] Blayney, *The Stationers' Company*, i. 96. Another example may be provided by the draper William Wilcocks. He is known to have supported the publication in London of two books by John Lettou as early as 1480–1. Little is known of his other roles in the book trade. Wilcocks features in the Bardi ledgers and it is not impossible that some of his transactions relate not only to cloths.

Appendix

The following entries are summaries of all the entries in the ledgers specified as those of booksellers (*libraio*) based in London and making use of the Italian branch of the Bardi also based in London. They are not intended to be complete diplomatic transcriptions. For reasons of clarity and space, it seemed best to summarize the content of each entry in as concise a way as possible, leaving out, for example, cross-references contained in the entries to other financial volumes which do not survive. The emphasis has throughout been on their importance to the history of the book trade, rather than to banking practice.

The entries in the ledgers are double entry, with amounts debited from the account on the left hand side and those credited to it on the right. The double page openings are numbered, rather than foliated (recto and verso), and this numbering has been retained.

Peter Actors, bookseller of Savoy (Florence, Archivio Guicciardini, Carte Bardi 11)

Opening 248

20 February 1493: debited £20 to the value of 100 gold scudi. Manno Tanagli wrote from Paris by a letter of the 5th that he had paid this by the bill of exchange to Master Cyprian Reglia.

23 August 1494: debited £5 4s 2d to the value of 25 gold scudi. Mannelli wrote from Lyons to say that he had paid the sum on the Bardi's instructions to [Gladro?] Robinson, a Frenchman.

Peter Actors, bookseller of Savoy (Florence, Archivio Guicciardini, Carte Bardi 12)

Opening 127

5 June 1495: account debited £4 6s 8d to the value of 20 gold scudi. Mannelli wrote from Lyons that he had paid this on our order to John Actors of Savoy.
6 June 1495: account debited £12. A sale of 53½ verges of taffeta was made to him at 4s 6d per verge. Time to pay: within six months for the first half to be paid on six December, 6 more months for the second half, on 6 June 1496. The full amount would be £12 0s 9d, but the Bardi settled for £12.

15 September 1495: debited £16 8s to the value of 75 gold scudi of Pisa. Del Bene wrote from Paris that he had paid this by the bill of exchange to Jean Richard of Rouen.

27 July 1496: debited £21 12s 2d to the value of 100 gold scudi of Pisa. Del Bene wrote from Paris that he had paid this sum by the bill of exchange to Jean Richard of Rouen.

27 July 1496: debited £10 16s 8d to the value of 50 gold scudi of Pisa. Del Bene wrote from Paris that he had paid this sum to Jean Richard of Rouen.

26 May 1497: debited £1 12s 8d to the value of […] gold scudi of Pisa. Giovanni Mannelli wrote from Lyons that he had paid this sum by the bill of exchange to Giovanni Testodis.

Peter Actors, bookseller of Savoy (Florence, Archivio Guicciardini, Carte Bardi 11)

Opening 248

18 December 1492: credited his account £20.

The Bardi drew up a bill of exchange for 100 gold scudi to be paid to Master Cyprian Reglia a Venetian in Paris, who was said to be about 27 years old with a scar on the flesh of his left hand near to his arm. They wrote to Manno Tanagli in Paris.

6 November 1493: credited his account £5 4*s* 2*d* to the value of 25 gold scudi. It was paid in some days before by him at Lyons.

Peter Actors, bookseller of Savoy (Florence, Archivio Guicciardini, Carte Bardi 12)

Opening 127

6 June 1495: account credited £4 6*s* 8*d* to the value of 20 scudi. To be paid to John Actors of his nephew in Lyons.

21 July 1495: credited £16 8*s* to the value of 75 gold scudi to be paid at Paris on the 6th day after sight to Jean Richard of Rouen bookseller.

15 December 1495: credited £5 as part of the bond.

6 February 1496: credited £1 as a part of the bond of £6.

20 June 1496: credited £3 as part of the bond for £6 which was payable on the 6th.

25 June 1495: credited £21 12*s* 2*d*.

Drawn from him to the value of 100 gold scudi to pay at Paris on the 6th day on view of a letter.

23 July 1496: credited £3 for the rest of the bond of £6.

6 August 1496: credited £10 16*s* 8*d*.

30 May 1497: credited £1 12*s* 8*d*.

Sum drawn on the first of the same month from the account up to 8 gold scudi to be paid at Lyons to John Testidis of Savoy, who was said to be about 32 years old with two small marks in the middle finger of his left hand, and then to John Charmaill of Lyons.

Michel Morin of Normandy (Florence, Archivio Guicciardini, Carte Bardi 12)

Opening 38

3 April 1495: debited £43 6*s* 8*d* to the value of 200 gold scudi. Albizzo Del Bene wrote from Paris that he had paid this and received the quittance from Manno Tanagli.

27 July 1495: account debited £11 0*s* 10*d* to the value of 50 gold scudi. Del Bene wrote from Paris by a letter of the 12th of the said month that he had paid by this the bill of exchange to Hans Coblencz, a German.

27 July 1495: account debited £3 6*s* 3*d* to the value of 15 gold scudi. Del Bene wrote that he had paid the sum to Jean Petit.

15 September 1495: debited £22 1*s* 8*d* to the value of 100 gold scudi. Del Bene wrote from Paris that he had settled this.

15 September 1495: account debited £4 8*s* 4*d* to the value of 20 gold scudi. Del Bene wrote from Paris that he had paid this sum on instruction to Jean Charboner.

28 December 1495: account debited £32 10*s* to the value of 150 gold scudi. Del Bene wrote from Paris by a letter of the 12th of the said month that he paid this sum to Hans Coblencz

13 February 1496: account debited £5 8*s* 4*d* to the value of 25 gold scudi. Del Bene wrote from Paris by a letter of the 25 January that he had paid this sum to Jean Petit, bookseller.

13 February 1496: account debited £5 8*s* 4*d* to the value of 25 gold scudi. Del Bene wrote from Paris that he paid this sum to Hans Coblencz, a German.

Opening 197

20 June 1496: debited £39 to the value of 180 gold scudi of Pisa. Del Bene wrote from Paris that he had paid it by the bill of exchange.

19 September 1496: debited £13 to the value of 60 gold scudi of Pisa. Del Bene wrote from Paris that he had paid it by the bill of exchange to 'awry charim' [Ulrich Gering?], a German.

Michel Morin of Normandy (Florence, Archivio Guicciardini, Carte Bardi 12)

Opening 38

25 March 1495: credited his account £43 6s 8d ['transferred as a debit to the red book marked 'V' fol.232'].

2 June 1495: account credited £14 7s 1d.

A sum drawn to the value of 50 gold scudi to pay at Paris to Hans Coblencz, a German, bookseller. Del Bene wrote on the 6th past that he had settled it.

Another bill of exchange was drawn to the value of 15 scudi to pay in Paris to Jean Petit, bookseller.

10 July 1495: account credited £16. A bill of exchange was drawn to the value of 100 gold scudi to pay to him. He was said to be about 30 years old with the little finger on his left hand bent so that he could not extend it. Settlement was to be six days after sight of the bill.

To this was added £6 1s 8d which he was to have on the 8th day.

30 July 1495: account credited £5, to be paid to Jean Charboner in Lyons.

12 October 1495: £4 received from Jean Charboner, a priest from Normandy. A 'biglia' (receipt?) was given.

10 November 1495: account credited £25, as a part of the £32 10s to the value of 150 gold scudi which was to be paid by a bill of exchange to Hans Coblencz, a German in Paris. The remaining £7 10s Morin promised to pay within 4 days.

12 November 1495: account credited £5.

28 November 1495: account credited £4.

1 December 1495: account credited £8.

50 gold scudi: of which 25 is to be paid in Paris to Hans Coblencz, and 25 scudi to Jean Petit, a Frenchman to which should be added £2 16s 8d.

Account credited £2 16s 8d.

Opening 197

27 February 1496: account credited £2 16s 8d by Bernardo Giachi.

16 May 1496: credited £26.

This £26 was part of a total of £37 to the value of 180 gold scudi to be paid to him at Paris. He was said to be about 31 years old with the little finger of the left hand a little deformed so that he could not extend it.

7 January 1497: debited £10 16s 8d to the value of 50 gold scudi of Pisa. Del Bene wrote from Paris that he had paid it by the bill of exchange.

7 January 1497: debited £26 to the value of 120 gold scudi of Pisa. Del Bene wrote from Paris that he had paid it to 'arigo charin' [Ulrich Gering?], a German, by the bill of exchange.

7 January 1497 debited £5 8s 4d to the value of 25 gold scudi of Pisa. Del Bene wrote from Paris that he had paid it by the bill of exchange to Jean Petit, bookseller.

22 February 1497: debited £10 16s 8d to the value of 50 gold scudi of Pisa. Del Bene wrote from Paris that he had paid it by the bill of exchange to Hans Coblencz, a German.

22 February 1497: debited £32 10s to the value of 40 gold scudi of Pisa. Albizzo Del Bene wrote from Paris that he had paid it by the bill of exchange.

Opening 312

28 June 1497: debited £6 10s 0d to the value of 30 gold scudi. Del Bene wrote from Paris by a letter of the 18th last that he had paid this sum by bill of exchange to Hans Coblencz, a German.

28 June 1497: debited £10 16s 8d to the value of 50 gold scudi. Del Bene wrote from Paris by the same letter that he had paid this sum by bill of exchange to Jean Petit, bookseller.

18 August 1497: debited £43 6s 8d to the value of 200 gold scudi. Del Bene wrote from Paris to say that he had paid this on the 28th past by bill of exchange.

The remaining £2 he promised to pay within two days at the Bardi office.

1 June 1496: credited £2, from his servant John. The money was brought in cash by Bernardo Giachi for the remainder of the above exchange.

5 August 1496: credited £12 to the value of 60 gold scudi to be paid at Paris to 'awry charim' [Ulrich Gering?], a German, printer of books.

The remaining £1 he promised to pay within four days.

30 August 1496: credited £1.

3 October 1496: credited £35. That part to the value of 120 gold scudi to be paid at Paris to 'awry charim' [Ulrich Gering?], German, a printer of books, and that to the value of 50 gold scudi to be paid at Paris to Hans Coblencz, printer of books

The remaining £1 16s 8d he promised to pay within 8 days.

7 November 1496: credited £13 5s.

£1 16s 8d outstanding on the total of £5 8s 4d to the value of 25 gold scudi credited on the 7th past; this was drawn from the account to be paid at Paris to Jean Petit, bookseller; the portion to the value of 50 gold scudi to be paid at Paris to Hans Coblencz printer of books.

The remaining £4 16s 8d was outstanding.

23 November 1496: credited £4 16s 8d.

5 December 1496: credited £21 13s 4d, to the value of 150 gold scudi, to be paid to him by Del Bene within 4 days. The remaining £10 16s 8d was outstanding.

5 April 1497: credited £10 16s 8d.

Opening 312

18 April 1497: credited £6 to the value of 30 gold scudi of Pisa to be paid in Paris to Hans Coblencz, a German, printer of books. And £10 6s 8d to the value of 50 gold scudi of Pisa to be paid in Paris to Jean Petit bookseller.

18 May 1497: credited £11 6s 8d.

13 June 1497: credited £18 16s 4d.

17 June 1497: credited £2.

All to the value of 200 gold scudi of Pisa to be paid to him at Paris.

To this was added £22 10s 0d.

30 April 1498: debited £42 10s to the value of 200 gold scudi. Albizzo del Bene wrote from Paris by a letter of the 3rd instant that he had paid it by the bill of exchange.

3 May 1498: debited £21 2s 0d to the value of 100 gold scudi. Del Bene wrote from Paris by a letter of the 22nd past that he had paid by bill of exchange to 'arigho Warin' [Ulrich Gering?], a German bookseller.

3 May 1498: debited £8 13s 4d to the value of 40 gold scudi of Pisa. Del Bene wrote from Paris by the same letter that he had paid this sum by bill of exchange to Hans Coblencz.

3 May 1498: debited £8 13s 4d to the value of 40 gold scudi. Del Bene wrote from Paris by the same letter that he had paid this sum by bill of exchange to Jean Petit, bookseller.

Hans Coblencz, a German printer of books living in Paris (Florence, Archivio Guicciardini, Carte Bardi 12)

Opening 312

28 June 1497: debited £30 3s 4d to the value of 140 gold scudi. Del Bene wrote from Paris by a letter of the 19th instant that he had paid it by the bill of exchange.

Godfrey Aste of Brabant, bookseller (Florence, Archivio Guicciardini, Carte Bardi 12)

Opening 177

13 February 1495: debited £6 10s to the value of 30 gold scudi. Del Bene wrote from Paris by a letter of the 25th last that he had paid it by the bill of exchange.

2 September 1497: credited £10.

23 September 1497: credited £12.

9 October 1497: credited 10s.

21 November 1497: credited £22 11s.

17 February 1498: credited £35 16s 8d.

£15 16s 8d for a 'biglia' (receipt?) concerning such sum: it was the remainder of 180 scudi for which he was given bills of exchange to Paris in three instalments until 21 November plus £20 of a new letter.

27 February 1498: credited £2 10s

By this and by £20 outstanding to the value of 200 gold scudi of Pisa to be paid at Paris to him.

There was £20 outstanding

18 May 1498 account credited £11.

30 June 1498: account credited £9.

Hans Coblencz, a German printer of books living in Paris (Florence, Archivio Guicciardini, Carte Bardi 12)

Opening 312

18 April 1497: account credited £30 3s 4d, to the value of 40 gold scudi of Pisa to be paid to him in Paris by Del Bene.

Godfrey Aste of Brabant, bookseller (Florence, Archivio Guicciardini, Carte Bardi 12)

Opening 177

1 December 1494: credited £6 10s to the value of 30 gold scudi to be paid to Nicholas Lecomte, bookseller, in [...]. Settlement date 6 days after sight.

'Giovanni Hwyn' [Jean Huvin] of Rouen, bookseller (Florence, Archivio Guicciardini, Carte Bardi 12)

Opening 186

27 February 1496: debited £6 12*s* 6*d* to the value of 30 gold scudi. Del Bene wrote from Paris by a letter of 16th last that he had paid this by the bill of exchange.

William Fox [William Faques?], of Normandy, bookseller living in London (Florence, Archivio Guicciardini, Carte Bardi 12)

Opening 383

3 May 1498: debited £7 1*s* 8*d* to the value of 34 gold scudi. Del Bene wrote from Paris by a letter of 23rd

'Giovanni Hwyn' [Jean Huvin] of Rouen, bookseller (Florence, Archivio Guicciardini, Carte Bardi 12)

Opening 186

20 June 1495: credited £6 12*s* 6*d*. To be drawn on a bill of exchange to the value of 30 gold scudi to be paid to him. He was said to be about 38 years old with a mole on the second finger of the left hand, next to the big finger on the inside. Settlement date 6 days after sight of the bill.

William Fox [William Faques?], of Normandy, bookseller living in London (Florence, Archivio Guicciardini, Carte Bardi 12)

Opening 383

8 December 1497: credited £7 1*s* 8*d*. To be drawn from the account to the value of 34 gold scudi to be paid to him at Paris. He was said to be about 35 years old with a mark on the thumbnail of one hand.

9. Nicholas Alwyn, mayor of London: a man of two loyalties, London and Spalding*

Anne F. Sutton

Nicholas Alwyn[1] was a mercer and merchant adventurer who achieved the mayoralty of London at the age of sixty-four in 1499. The elaborate month's mind he ordered in his home town of Spalding (Lincs.) and his benefactions, which favoured the close-knit area of Spalding, Cowbit, Pinchbeck, Moulton and Weston[2] in his lifetime and in his remarkable testament of 1505,[3] were enough to ensure him a place in local memory for at least a generation. His house in Spalding – later called Ayscoughfee Hall – was built for his relaxation and for his heirs. After much alteration, it is now the local museum and has elevated him to the status of local legend. A recitation of his real career and a disposal of the legends are secondary purposes of this chapter; its most important purpose is to bring to life this immigrant Londoner who, despite his success in the capital city, remained a man of the Fens.

---

* I am most grateful for Lincolnshire details from Nicholas Bennett; for advice about peasants and manorial accounts from Chris Briggs; for Surrey details from Graham Dawson; for copies of wills from Christian Steer; and for a tour of churches round Spalding from Shaun Tyas; and also to the Spalding Gentlemen's Society (hereafter SGS) and its librarian for their courtesy and permission to consult their manuscripts.

[1] His name is spelled here in the way consistently used in his will and city of London sources, rather than the affectation of Aldwyn adopted in Spalding certainly by the time of John Grundy, who drew a plan of the town in 1732, now in the care of the SGS.

[2] Bound by their communal dykes, intercommoning and long traditions of co-operation over maintenance of the fens and subject to one main manorial court, that of the priory of Spalding (H. E. Hallam, *Settlement and Society: a Study of the Early Agrarian History of South Lincolnshire* (Cambridge, 1965), pp. 24–7, 215–23). For Hallam's assertion that the area was economically depressed in Alwyn's lifetime, see H. E. Hallam, 'The agrarian economy of South Lincolnshire in the mid-fifteenth century', *Nottingham Medieval Stud.*, xi (1967), 86–95.

[3] This testament is referred to frequently throughout this article (TNA, PROB 11/15, fos. 9–12); it should not be confused with his will.

Origins, trade and the creation of a fortune, 1436–1506

Nicholas was born in Spalding to Richard and Margaret Alwyn, probably in 1436.[4] The emphasis on Cowbit in his testament may suggest they were of that hamlet or had strong ties there.[5] They were not among the villein (*nativi*) tenants of Spalding priory, which held two of the three manors of Spalding, and have not been found among the tenants of the third manor there held by Crowland abbey, of which two contemporary accounts survive.[6] His parents can be assumed to have been a prosperous couple of the town of Spalding, its harbour sharing in the trade of the east coast. They had enough wealth to apprentice him in 1452 (aged about sixteen) to John Brodesworth, a mercer of London and merchant adventurer.[7] Brodesworth appears to have been a maverick, for he had bought entry to the Mercers, owned property in Essex and Yorkshire, was regularly fined by his new company and took a great many apprentices (at least sixteen). He was in debt by the late 1440s, when he was declared to have no shop in the city and even arrested and sent to the Tower of London. He recovered, however, and continued to take apprentices, such as Alwyn in 1452. This erratic career may suggest that the Alwyns had limited funds and could not afford the high premium demanded by a more eminent and respected mercer, or that they had a business connection with Brodesworth through the port of Spalding – but, as has been said, the background of the family has not been discovered. Brodesworth failed or died, leaving no will, probably in the later 1450s.[8] Alwyn was transferred to

---

[4] Alwyn's testament provides the names of his parents, their tombstone and his chantry in Spalding parish church. The determined local legend which made Richard 'Aldwyn' a stapler and the first builder of Ascoughfee hall (*c*.1420–*c*.1450) was publicized but not initiated by Richard Gough in *Britannia, or a Chorographical Description of the Flourishing Kingdoms of England, Scotland and Ireland by William Camden*, enlarged by R. Gough (3 vols., London, 1789), ii. 289. No confirmation of this has been found.

[5] Cowbit chapel (a dependency of Spalding priory) appeared several times in his will: his gift of £10; 20*s* to its Trinity guild; its priests were to attend his month mind; it received 2 torches after the exequies; its poor shared in gowns and money with Spalding (see n. 110).

[6] A John 'Haldyn' paid rent on 2 acres of meadow in 1478–9 to Crowland abbey in the area (Lincoln Archives Office (hereafter LAO), 6 Anc 5/1, m. 1). No Alwyns have been found in SGS, Myntling Register of Spalding Priory, which recorded pedigrees of the priory's *nativi*. Neither SGS, Wrest Park Cartulary (for Crowland abbey) nor Cambridge University Library, Additional MS. 4400, survey made for Crowland, *c*.1476–7, refers to them.

[7] For the minutiae of trade, administration and career structure of the Mercers' and the Merchant Adventurers' Companies, see A. F. Sutton, *The Mercery of London: Trade, Goods and People 1130–1578* (Aldershot, 2005). Dates of admittances to the Mercers before 1464 are derived from the author's notes from the Mercers' Company of London (hereafter MC), wardens' accounts, 1348, 1390–1463 (hereafter WA) and the register of members.

[8] Brodesworth (also Brod, Brodeworth, Brodiseworth, Brodysworth) can be found between 1431 and 1446 trading in linen, worsted, woollen cloth, some scarlet and madder in

finish his apprenticeship with the eminently respectable Richard Rich of Ironmonger Lane. He was admitted to the Company in 1463,[9] after completing a ten-year apprenticeship which demanded several years abroad learning the trade of mercer and merchant adventurer (the overseas company which had its headquarters in the Low Countries and was dominated by the London Mercers); he learnt to sell English cloth at the Brabant fairs and buy the finest linens. He had to master French and Dutch, with some Latin for account keeping. Alwyn's recorded trade overseas started in 1456–7 and he continued to appear in the customs accounts, exporting English cloth, importing linen and general merceries, until 1502.[10] He was not in the wool trade of Calais: neither Brodesworth nor Richard Rich was a stapler and Alwyn could not learn that trade from them. It is clear that Alwyn only added the wool trade to his business in the late 1470s, probably as a result of the interests of his son-in-law, Henry, a member of the prestigious and wealthy Cantelowe family.[11] He was included in the pardon of 4 May 1480 as both a mercer and stapler (implying a trade in wool a little earlier); and he appears frequently to have traded in wool with Cantelowe until Henry's death in 1491 and thereafter he continued to trade in wool until at least 1502.[12] He was never one of the high-

---

the surviving London customs accounts. There is no sign of him as a stapler in the London wool accounts. He paid to enter the livery of the Mercers 1435–7 (MC, WA 1435–6 and 1436–7, fos. 123v, 124). In 1436 he was found to have land assessed at £16 (S. L. Thrupp, *The Merchant Class of Medieval London* (Ann Arbor, Mich., 1948), p. 379; *CPMR 1437–57*, p. 114). Of his apprentices, Alwyn, Nicholas Hagar, Richard Pope and Nicholas Glover had to be transferred to new masters.

[9] MC, WA 1463, and register of members. For the Rich Family, see A. F. Sutton, *Wives and Widows of Medieval London* (Donington, 2016), pp. 124–5 and *passim*; their wills do not refer to Alwyn.

[10] E.g. TNA, E 122/194/11, petty custom, Mich. 1461–20 May 1462 (35 cloths, m. 10d); E 122/194/16, tonnage and poundage 2 Feb.–Mich. 1463 (paper, painted glass, linen, brushes, mm. 2–4d); E 122/194/15, petty custom Mich. 1463–27 Jan. 1464 (10 cloths, m. 7d); E 122/128/15, Sandwich customs accounts 1474–5 (17 May 1475, gold thread, buckram and brigandine nails); E 122/194/23, petty customs Mich. 1477–Mich. 1478 (117 cloths, mm. 8d, 9, 12–12d, 15d); *The Overseas Trade of London: Exchequer Customs Accounts 1480–1*, ed. H. S. Cobb (London Rec. Soc., xxvii, 1990), petty custom Mich. 1480–Mich. 1481 (115 cloths), nos. 309, 452, 465, 498, 571; E 122/129/13, Sandwich customs account Mich. 1486–Mich. 1487 (linen, lawn, cotton, sheets and laces of thread, 5 Nov., 23 July); E 122/78/9, petty custom 1490–1 (43 cloths, mm. 9d, 11d); *CPR 1494–1509*, pp. 282–4, pardon to adventurers, 16 June 1502.

[11] This contradicts the Spalding legend which makes him and his father staplers (and knights). Alwyn was not in the 1472 list of staplers (TNA, SC 1/57/111). I am indebted to a new transcript of this damaged manuscript given to me by Alan Rogers and David Grummitt.

[12] *CPR 1476–85*, p. 244, Pardon, 4 May 1480 (alias Halewyne, Alewyne); and see Sutton, *Mercery*, pp. 312–3. He appears in the following accounts: 1480–1, in *Overseas Trade of London*, nos. 600–2 (no individual amounts given); TNA, E 122/78/2, Wool Customs accounts, 19 June–27 Sept. 1483 (with Henry Cantelowe); E 122/78/5, Mich. 1487–Mich. 1488 (over 81

flyers, but he made his fortune.

In 1463 Alwyn had been accorded the status of a shop-keeper, the same year as his admittance to the Mercers' Company, which meant his capital had been assessed as £100. This was the first step up the hierarchy and suggests he had indulged in personal trade as an apprentice (as does his appearance in customs accounts before 1463), an activity which was forbidden without the permission of his master – or alternatively that he now had family money behind him.[13] Ambition marks his entire career: apart from the formalities of admission in the wardens' accounts, the first reference to him was a fine of 6s 8d for his uncourteous language to the wardens in the accounting year of 1463–4. From 1466 to his death he indentured regular apprentices, some of whom came from his home county or town (see below).[14] His business ability and languages meant that he was chosen to advise on the arguments to be presented by the Adventurers appointed to the embassy negotiating about the ban on English cloth imposed by the duke of Burgundy, the lord of the Low Countries, in 1468.[15] Almost ten years later he was appointed to assess the wealth of his fellow mercers for a benevolence for Edward IV before his invasion of France, but he failed to record his own liability and had to be entered later among those worth £10 a year or having £100 worth of goods. At this time he was living in the central ward of Cheap, but not yet in his final house (see below). Despite his peccadillo over the tax assessment, he was involved in the choice of men to ride to meet Edward IV on his return from France and the purchase of livery cloth for the occasion.[16] He was increasingly on committees, deputed to discuss the payment of the king's customs; to control the worsted men of Norwich who were intruding on the mercers' trade in worsted goods in London; to prevent young men of the Company attending fairs and selling their

---

sacks and 15,600 fells with Henry Cantelowe); E 122/78/8, Mich. 1489–Mich. 1490 (with Henry Cantelowe; account damaged); E 122/78/10, Mich. 1490–Mich.1491 (over 34 sacks); E 122/79/3, Mich. 1491–Mich. 1492 (over 11 sacks and nearly 6,000 fells); E 122/73/4, Mich. 1493–Mich. 1494; E 122/79/9, Mich. 1501–Mich. 1502 (800 fells).

[13] Sutton, *Mercery*, pp. 210–11.

[14] No dates for apprentices entering their service are known after the end of the wardens' accounts in 1464 and the only source is MC, register of members: after a ten-year apprenticeship the following men were admitted to the Company as Alwyn's past apprentices: 1476 Thomas Blenche; 1481 Henry Brooke; 1483 Robert Jackson; 1489 Richard Jones; 1491 Richard Alwyn [his son]; 1495 Michael English; 1497 John Knight; 1509 Hugh Smith and Nicholas Tickhill; 1512 William Butler and Robert Smith; 1525 John Fayrey and William Tales. For the Smiths see below.

[15] *Acts of Court of the Mercers' Company 1454–1527*, ed. L. Lyell and F. D. Watney (Cambridge, 1936) (hereafter *AC*), pp. 61–2. The date of his elevation to the livery is unknown.

[16] *AC*, pp. 7, 8–9, 80, 88, 91; Sutton, *Mercery*, pp. 190–2.

goods outside the city; and to advise on the reform of the English currency in relation to those circulating across the Channel.[17] He was one of many mercers fined in 1479–80 for their dishonesty over the king's customs and took part in the lengthy negotiations with Edward IV over the heavy fine that was the consequence.[18]

In 1481 he was a warden, third of the four, so he had missed the lowest rank of renterwarden; the master was Robert Tate, of the wealthy stapler family. This was a significant career point for Alwyn.[19] Prestigious tasks continued: he was involved in the Adventurers' restraint of trade, aimed in particular at the fair towns of Brabant in 1483: his apprentice, Richard Jones, and another of Henry Cantelowe infringed the terms of the restraint in order to make a handsome profit, probably with their masters' connivance, and one of the Adventurers' ambassadors, Hugh Clopton, did the same. They all had to face proceedings before the Mercers.[20] He represented the Mercers among the Adventurers at a diet in Calais in 1486, took part in the formulation of answers to complaints against London mercers by merchants of Bristol, and in 1487–8, when he was the second warden of the Mercers (Hugh Clopton being master), he represented them again when they were harangued by the chancellor over their trade with the Low Countries. Alwyn was master of the Mercers in 1495 to 1496 and he was now an alderman, the office of master usually being held by an alderman. From 1488, however, his profile in Mercer and Adventurer matters was becoming less pronounced, although he appears to have remained involved in negotiations over the injuries endured by Adventurers in Calais when Henry VII forced them to conduct their trade through that town: as he was one of the mercers who was both an adventurer and a stapler, he had certain advantages.[21] Easier matters in which he was concerned were the assessment of the possibilities of Crosby hall for Mercer assemblies – he might have considered whether its hall would be necessary for his own mayoral feast – and the arrangements to welcome the mercer Hugh Clopton, absent in his home town of Stratford-

---

[17] *AC*, pp. 92, 100.

[18] *CPR 1476–85*, p. 244 (specified as a stapler for the first time, see above); Sutton, *Mercery*, pp. 312–3.

[19] *AC*, p. 285; Sutton, *Mercery*, p. 556 (list of wardens).

[20] *AC*, pp. 157, 161–2, 163–4ff.; *The Book of Privileges of the Merchant Adventurers, 1296–1483*, ed. A. F. Sutton and L. Visser-Fuchs (London and Oxford, 2009), pp. 18–28 (misbehaviour, at pp. 25–8).

[21] *AC*, pp. 294–5, 300, 198–9 (the pages of the *AC* are not always in chronological sequence); Sutton, *Mercery*, ch. 11, for Henry VII's fear of merchant adventurers conspiring with his rebels in the Low Countries, which led him to hinder their trade, e.g., by forcing them to leave the Low Countries and trade through Calais, much disliked by both adventurers and staplers.

upon-Avon (Warwickshire), to take up his position as mayor of London in 1491.[22]

Alwyn undoubtedly had his eye on the highest civic office, but his city career had been late in starting. He was a common councilman by the late 1470s, but it took him a long while to advance beyond this. In February 1481 he had been elected for Cordwainer Street ward (where his last great house was located, in St. Mary le Bow churchyard) to manage the collection of the benevolence of 5,000 marks granted to Edward IV for the war against the Scots and appoint the ward collectors; and in 1482 and 1483 he was one of the two commoners elected city auditors during the mayoralties of Sir William Heryot and Sir Edmund Shaa.[23] In 1491 he represented the city in parliament, served as sheriff from 1494 to 1495 and from July 1496 was elected alderman, first for Coleman Street ward and then for Bassishaw. The election as alderman gave him the opportunity to acquire arms: *argent, a fess engrailed azure, between three lions rampant sable*. In 1499 he was elected mayor at the age of sixty-four, the high point of his London career.[24]

He took his oath in the Guildhall on 28 October 1499[25] and on the following day travelled by water to Westminster to take his oath before the barons of the exchequer, accompanied by all the livery companies in their barges, that of the Mercers taking pride of place with minstrelsy, trumpets and banners flying. He returned to his mayoral feast and in the evening he went to St. Paul's to pray at the tomb of the parents of St. Thomas Becket and returned home by torchlight – was he to transfer something of this impressive ceremony to his own parents' grave?[26] All mayors needed a large house for their mayoral festivities and duties throughout the year, but especially for their mayoral feast. It is likely Alwyn was able to hold this in his great house in St. Mary le Bow parish. Since 1483 he had been busy buying (a process finalized by the time of his mayoralty[27]) a substantial property

[22] *AC*, pp. 213, 220–1.

[23] *Cal. Letter Bks. L*, pp. 175–6, 195, 210. These appointments allow us to suppose he was on the common council by the end of the 1470s.

[24] A. B. Beaven, *The Aldermen of the City of London* (2 vols., London, 1908 and 1913), i. 273 (MP); ii. 19. It is significant that Beaven accords him no knighthood. On the arms, see E. H. Gooch, *A History of Spalding* (Spalding, 1940), p. 250.

[25] He left £73 6s 8d for a 'hankyng of tapecery' to serve for the high dais in the Guildhall, or other things to serve in the same hall.

[26] C. M. Barron, *London in the Later Middle Ages: Government and the People 1200–1500* (Oxford, 2004), pp. 152–4.

[27] His feoffees in 1483 were his two sons-in-law, Henry Cantelowe and William Heryot junior, and John Haw, the lawyer. Haw quitclaimed his interest in the property in 1502 (Cantelowe and Heryot were dead). Alwyn's last feoffees were John Pickton (see below), Richard Golofer (once his fellow apprentice) and William Carkeke, his all-important

on the cemetery of that church, once owned by the famous mercer family of William Coventry (d. 1406) and his sons, in the ward of Cordwainer Street. The house had the essential large hall over twenty feet wide (length not known) with a dais for a high table, a parlour and entry and a chapel.[28] His year as mayor saw no great event: it was rumoured that Katherine of Aragon would be arriving for her marriage to the prince of Wales and the city planned for her reception, but this was delayed for another year and this delay probably ensured that Alwyn did not attract a knighthood, a fact not aided by the death of the king's son, Edmund, whose requiem he and the aldermen attended.[29]

It was his parish church of St. Mary le Bow where Alwyn chose to be buried: in the choir, at his executors' discretion, under the 'sepulcre that John Worsip did make', with a marble stone over his grave (40s to be divided between the parson and the churchwardens). He made many carefully costed depositions for his funeral, which would have had the additional panoply laid on by the city and his company for a past mayor.[30] He, unusually, wanted four priests to carry his body to burial, the livery men of his company 'to go by them' (20d to each of the eight) – the Mercers' Company was to have a 'jewel' (£13 6s 8d).[31] There were to be twenty-four torches of 20 lbs wax at both his burial and month's mind (total cost £6 13s 4d), and John Ash, waxchandler (who was also an overseer of his testament and so may be presumed a friend), was to make an 'honest hearse' and find all the wax and workmanship for 10 marks. The twenty-four bearers at both

---

scrivener friend (D. Keene and V. Harding, *Historical Gazetteer of London before the Great Fire*, i. *Cheapside* (Cambridge, 1987), 104/11, p. 245).

[28] His testament provides a basic description (TNA, PROB 11/15, fo. 10r–v): *In the hall*: a long table for the 'high deyes' of 6 'verges' long by 1 'verge' wide [fo. 10v], with a chair and 7 high joined stools and 2 trestles. Also 2 side tables with 4 trestles and 2 long forms with the benches and a standing cupboard. *In the entry before the parlour*: a laver with 3 spouts. *In the parlour*: 2 tables and 4 trestles with 2 forms and a dozen joined stools and a standing cupboard. *Buttery*: all the shelves with 'almery to the same', bins. *The Great Chamber*: a standing bed with boards, a long table and 2 trestles, a cupboard. *Chapel*: an altar of alabaster of the Passion of Our Lord, with desks belonging to the chapel. *Compter*: a compter board with all the shelves and aumbreys belonging. All the standing beds in each chamber. *Outside the Kitchen*: a cistern. Another cistern in *the coming in*. *The Yard*: 2 cisterns ('sestrons'). *Stable*: a coop for poultry.

[29] R. R. Sharpe, *London and the Kingdom* (3 vols., London, 1894–5) i. 334–5. Angel Don was involved in the 1499 preparations (Sutton, *Wives*, p. 206).

[30] Testament, see n. 3. Cf. the funeral of Thomas Bradbury (although he died in office as mayor) (Sutton, *Wives*, pp. 307–9).

[31] He remembered the Company's under-beadle, the master, fellows, clerks and poor men of Whittington College and almshouse, as well as St. Thomas of Acre (£6 13s 4d for repairs), where lay the Mercers' hall, master, brethren and children of the choir.

ceremonies were to have 4*d* each time (total 16*s*) and a black gown and hood made from black 'lining' (total £6 13*s* 4*d*). Most important were the distributions of 12*d* each to 3,000 poor of London (£150), with £4 for the labour of distribution; and a further 1*d* each to 6,000 poor at his month's mind, when the distributors were to receive a total of 20*s* for their work and 'for the place that the dole shal be made'. The preacher of the sermon at his month's mind was to be Simon Foderby, newly a doctor of theology and parson of St. Peter's Cornhill since 1503 (10*s*).[32] Alwyn valued him, perhaps as a fellow Lincolnshireman, and left him an additional bequest of a pair of coral beads of ten *aves* with two square paternosters of silver gilt. It was essential to have his name remembered before the higher ranks of the city who assembled at the sermons at St. Paul's Cross and the Easter sermons at St. Mary's hospital Bishopsgate (40*s* 4*d* to each priest). In St. Mary le Bow, apart from the month's mind, there were to be further services to care for his soul and carry his name before the parishioners: a daily *Dirige* and mass of requiem by note by ten priests and two clerks (each to receive 10*s*), with two tapers of 4lbs burning at his grave during divine service for a month (40*s*), and the sexton was to have 3*s* 4*d* for their lighting and quenching. After the formal exequies were over, he provided for the parish priest to pray for his soul from the pulpit every Sunday for twenty years (total 40*s*); for a ten-year chantry at the altar of St. Nicholas (at 10 marks per annum and a vestment of red worsted with all its apparel, which he had lately had made); and, third, a further twenty-year obit for the souls of himself, 'my late wif' and children, with priest, clerk, bells, bread and payments to the poor (13*s* 4*d* yearly). Finally, the steeple of St. Mary le Bow was to have 100 marks for its making and repair and for no other matter. The only other city church to be mentioned was St. Magnus, when the north side was taken down to widen the street (£6 13*s* 4*d*).

His London 'great place', mayoralty and funeral displayed his achievements to all. Alwyn had, however, achieved the mayoralty and aldermanry comparatively late, and a reason for this can be suggested: an alderman had to be worth £1,000 in moveable goods before his nomination could be accepted, for it was a laborious and expensive office, requiring leisure away from business, and he had had the heavy expense of providing for adult children.[33] The cost of property acquired in the 1480s in the city and in his home town, where he was also building – for his own pleasure and for his family – may have been another reason.

---

[32] Simon Foderby alias Grene, from Helpringham, Lincs., canon of Lincoln from 1509, rector of St. Peter's from 1503 to his death; known for his learning; died 1536, buried Lincoln Cathedral (*BRUO (to A.D. 1500)*, ii. 702–3).

[33] Cf. Richard Rich (Sutton, *Wives*, pp. 65–6, 124–5).

Alwyn's family and London circle

Alwyn married twice, and of the children who survived to adulthood, his eldest son and two daughters seem to have been generously provided for. His first marriage, to Joan,[34] took place soon after his emergence from apprenticeship, and his first surviving son, Richard, was born about 1465 (Figure 9.1). Richard was apprenticed to Nicholas himself and was admitted to the Mercers in 1491 at the usual age of twenty-six. Richard traded briefly as an adventurer in cloth in 1490–1 and as a stapler from 1489–90 and 1491–2.[35] He married Margaret Thomas, sister of the mercer John Thomas,[36] and had a son, born in 1495 and called Nicholas.[37] Richard can be assumed to have died soon after.

Alwyn never names his daughters and the name of only one has been discovered despite their good marriages, undoubtedly supported by large dowries. Margaret married Henry, a younger son of Sir William Cantelowe, one of the richest and best known of mercer families.[38] Alwyn's bequest to an Ellen Pypyn, once living with William Cantelowe (6s 8d), his bequest to repair a road near Dunstable (Bedfordshire) (the Cantelowe's home area) and his taking of John Fayrey of Dunstable as his apprentice[39] all suggest affection

[34] No surname has been discovered for her; the sole reference to her Christian name is in Alwyn's husting will.

[35] TNA, E 122/78/9, Mich. 1490–Mich. 1491 (60 cloths, mm. 7d, 11d); E 122/78/8, wool accounts 1489–90 (over 18 sacks, account damaged); E 122/79/3, 1491–2 (over 6,000 fells). He may have traded before admittance to his company; the dates in the Mercers' register cannot always be taken too precisely.

[36] John Thomas, mercer, left his deceased sister's son, Nicholas Alwyn, a dozen silver spoons with 'knoppes' in 1506 (TNA, PROB 11/15, fo. 114v).

[37] Aged 11 in 1506 at the death of his grandfather (*Calendar of Inquisitions Post Mortem of the Reign of Henry VII* (3 vols., London, 1898–1959), iii, no. 1135).

[38] Sir William Cantelowe had been mayor in 1461 (d. 1464). Henry married three times (his first wife, Elizabeth, had left no issue alive) and he referred to neither of his dead wives in his will. His third wife, Joan, widow of Thomas Fabian and Stephen Gibson, both mercers, brought with her 2 Fabian children and 6 Gibson children to join Henry's 2 children by Margaret Alwyn. Henry died in Dec. 1490 aged 43 and his widow Joan was executor with Nicholas Alwyn and William Heryot. The children's portions were left to the care of their grandfather and William Heryot (TNA, PROB 11/8, fos. 210v–13). Henry's widow Joan died in 1492 and her executors were the same as her husband's (TNA, PROB 11/ 9, fos. 105v–1077v) (Sutton, *Wives*, pp. 79–82 and nn. 40–52). Henry left his brother-in-law Richard Alwyn, stapler, £20 and his wife 40s (fo. 212); and Margaret, wife of William Heryot, £3 6s 8d; he referred to his 'place' at Tooting and made bequests to Tooting and Streatham (fo. 211v); and his priest William 'Jely' for his exhibition at Cambridge (fo. 211v). Alwyn acted as Henry's feoffee for property in Bedfordshire, the county where the Cantelowes originated (*A Descriptive Catalogue of Ancient Deeds*, ed. H. C. Maxwell Lyte (6 vols., London, 1890–1915), vi. C5099).

[39] On Fayrey, see Sutton, *Wives*, pp. 208 n. 145, 209 n. 149.

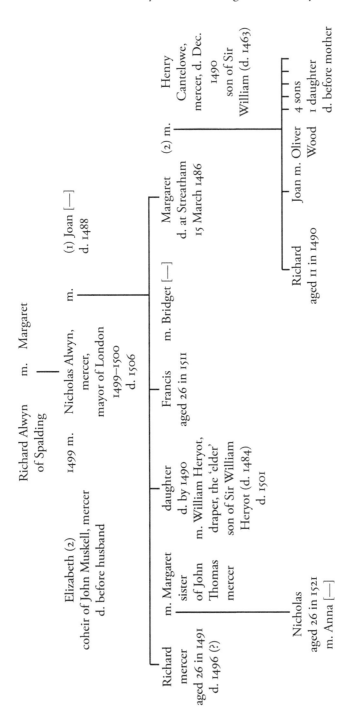

Figure 9.1. Alwyn family tree (A. F. Sutton)

for the whole family and its concerns, as does his personal relationship with Thomas Cantelowe (see below). Margaret Alwyn-Cantelowe died young on 5 March 1486 and was buried at Streatham (Surrey) under a brass showing her with five sons and two daughters and recording the names of her father and husband in an epitaph-prayer to the Virgin Mary. Henry Cantelowe's own country place was at nearby Tooting – and her father was to leave bequests in his testament to repair the church's nave, to provide candles to burn on her grave during Easter and for the repair of the roads between Streatham and Tooting Beck and Croydon.[40] The Cantelowe marriage produced Richard, who was left a gold ring by Alwyn, and Joan, who was left a primer by her grandfather, by which time she was already married to Oliver Wood and had a daughter of her own, who was left a jewelled *Agnus Dei* by her grandfather.[41] Richard Cantelowe and Joan Wood were to be the heirs to Alwyn's estate after the death of his direct male heirs; in the event there was to be nothing to inherit. The Cantelowes' fortune was, however, to survive to the next generation and was a highly complex estate, including the inheritances of children in the care of Henry Cantelowe's last wife Joan (d. 1493): two step-children from her first husband, Thomas Fabian, and her own six by her second husband, Stephen Gibson.[42] Alwyn served as executor of Henry and of his widow, Joan, and was one of the sureties for Henry's children's estate in October 1494 with his old associate John Pikton,[43] John Mille, mercer, and William Heryot, draper, for over £590.[44] Alwyn's other

---

[40] M. Stephenson, *A List of Monumental Brasses in Surrey* (new edn., Bath, 1970), pp. 492–3. It is worth noting that the church of Blechingley, Surrey, benefited from a vestment embroidered with flowers and his mark because his apprentice Nicholas Tickhill came from there.

[41] For a pedigree of 2 generations of Woods, including Oliver and his 5 brothers (and sister, wife of Sir Robert Tate, mayor of London 1488–9), children of Richard Wood, mayor of Coventry (1454, 1467) and Margaret, whose 2nd husband was Sir William Taillour, mayor of London 1468–9, and who died in 1483 (her considerable wealth made her a valuable associate and mother), see A. F. Sutton, *A Merchant Family of Coventry, London and Calais: the Tates c.1450–1515* (London, 1998), esp. p. 6.

[42] William Ilam, mercer, died 1493 and left 6s 8d to William Porter, servant of 'master Alwyn', and the same to Nicholas Tickhill, apprentice of Alwyn; to Alwyn he left all the money 'my masters' Thomas Fabian and Henry Cantelowe and Joan Cantelowe (their widow) left to him under their testaments (TNA, PROB 11/9, fo. 186).

[43] John Pikton, mercer, came from Dursbury; his marriage to the twice-widowed Margaret (born Dey, see n. 58) financed his rise to adventurer-status and wardenship of the Mercers; he died in 1505 (TNA, PROB 11/14, fos. 229v–30; Sutton, *Wives*, pp. 62, 63, 76, 92).

[44] *Cal. Letter Bks. L*, pp. 303–4, n. 1: on 13 July 1497 Oliver Wood received Joan's estate as her husband. The inquisition *post mortem* of Henry Cantelowe, Dec. 1490, shows Alwyn and Heryot among his feoffees and that Richard was 11 at his father's death (*CIPM HVII*, i., no. 629). Alwyn was careful to demand in his testament acquittances from all the children of the persons to whom he had acted as executor.

daughter (name unknown) had married this William Heryot II, draper, the elder of two sons, both called William, of Sir William Heryot, draper, whose trade stretched from Iceland to Italy, who had been entertained by Edward IV himself and who died in 1484.[45] Alwyn's daughter was dead by 1490 and her husband had married again to a Margaret (surname unknown); he had a daughter (unnamed) who was left £6 13s 4d by Alwyn, but she was probably her father's illegitimate daughter, Elizabeth. William Heryot died in 1501, leaving his widow, Margaret, to be his executrix with Nicholas Alwyn his 'lovyng fader in lawe'.[46]

Alwyn had another son: Francis, born in 1485, perhaps the last in a sequence of children born to Joan, who died in 1488.[47] He was apprenticed to the mercer Richard Berne by his father in 1501. Meanwhile, Alwyn decided belatedly to enlarge his family after the death of his eldest son and two daughters and married his last wife in March 1500, while he was mayor. She was Elizabeth, one of the two surviving daughters and heiresses of John Mustell, mercer. She also died before Alwyn, possibly in childbirth.[48]

When, in early 1505, he composed the will (dated 22 February 1505) concerning his lands, which was to be proved in the husting court (not to be confused with his long testament), Nicholas Alwyn had a choice between two male heirs and grandchildren by his daughter Margaret Cantelowe. He provided for his grandson (by his eldest son Richard) and his own son, Francis, while minors, from the rent of his properties and £400 (and any surpluses) was to be divided between them when of age. He chose to ignore strict male primogeniture and to leave all his landed property, save one block, to his youngest son, Francis.[49] Francis, at the age of twenty-six, would receive four messuages in St. Mary le Bow and two in the parish of St. Mary Magdalen Milk Street, the rents to be collected by

[45] The sequence of daughters, both unnamed, is taken from the depositions in Alwyn's testament and will. Sir William Heryot died in 1484; Sir William's widow, Joan, is mentioned with her fellow executors and son William Heryot (*CPR 1494–1509*, pp. 27–8). William Heryot II or 'the elder' continued his father's trade; for death of his Alwyn wife before 1490, see n. 38.

[46] William Heryot, II (TNA, PROB 11/12, fos. 84–85v).

[47] *The Bede Roll of the Fraternity of St Nicholas*, ed. N. W. and V. A. James (London Rec. Soc., xxxix, 2004): Nicholas and Joan were admitted in 1485 (nos. 262–3); her death was recorded in 1488 and his in 1506 (nos. 293, 454).

[48] Alwyn married Elizabeth in March 1500 (*Cal. Letter Bks. L*, p. 245 and n.). Mustell's will is at TNA, PROB 11/7, fos. 144–5. For Mustell, see Sutton, *Wives*, pp. 206, 232–3.

[49] *Calendar of Wills Proved and Enrolled in the Court of Husting 1258–1688*, ed. R. R. Sharpe (2 vols., London, 1889–90), ii. 625–6. The calendar reads ambiguously and has omissions, so the original has been checked. It is not clear why this will was only brought into court in 1518 by Alderman Robert Aldernes and John Wilford, scrivener; it was annotated as examined by Nicholas Rutland, clerk.

the executors, who would provide for Francis's keeping and save any surplus for him (or Nicholas if Francis should die).[50] Further remainders went to Joan Wood and then to Richard Cantelowe, her brother. In default of all heirs, the St. Mary le Bow property was to be added to the endowment of the Coventry chantry in the parish church and the names of Nicholas and his wife Joan were to join those prayed for there, while the messuages in St. Mary Magdalen were to go to the Mercers' Company to ensure that the livery of the company attend the services of the chantry. His property in Spalding was to be occupied by his executors for one year and then the issues were to support Francis, who was to inherit, with remainder to Nicholas; if there were no heirs it was to be sold to benefit the poor of Spalding and Cowbit and to repair local roads and bridges. Nicholas was to receive the nine messuages and ten gardens on Bermondsey Street in St. Olave's Southwark, held from the abbot of Bermondsey, the income to support Nicholas until he was twenty-six; the remainders went to Francis, Joan Wood and Richard Cantelowe and in default of heirs were to be sold to benefit several standard charities in London, Spalding and Cowbit. Alwyn also had an interest in a 'great newe place in Milkestrete' once belonging to Henry Cantelowe and entailed on Richard, his son, with remainder to his sister, Joan Wood, and thereafter to Thomas Cantelowe, son of Sir William Cantelowe and brother of Henry. Alwyn had been granted his interest by Thomas Cantelowe and now Alwyn wished that this interest should benefit his own grandson, Nicholas, if the Cantelowe heirs failed. Last, but not least, was a bequest of a messuage and garden in St. Giles Cripplegate to Alice Hedge, identifiable as his housekeeper.

Nicholas's wishes concerning his lands were not repeated in detail in his long testament of 2 October 1505, with its long codicil of 18 January 1506 (eleven days before he died on 29 January), proved at Lambeth on 11 February 1506, but they were endorsed. This has to be stated, for the inquisition *post mortem* of 11 June 1506 into his estate, as presented by four feoffees (not the executors of the Lambeth testament), reversed the two male heirs and declared the inheritance should pass by strict rules of primogeniture to the grandson, Nicholas, then aged eleven, when he was twenty-six. Francis received the remainder, followed by Joan Cantelowe-Wood and her brother Richard Cantelowe and in default of heirs the properties were to be sold to benefit charities in London and Spalding.[51] In the event, the wishes of Nicholas Alwyn, as presented in his husting court

---

[50] The first year's issues went to the executors who occupied all his property.

[51] His feoffees in the inquisition *post mortem* were John Hawe, Thomas Rich, William Jeffrey and John Gare (all living). The inquisition is dated 11 June 1506 (*CIPM Henry VII*, iii, no. 1135, recording his death as 29 Jan. 1506).

will – its contents clearly known despite its late passage through that court – prevailed. Francis became formally of age in 1511 and received £200 and half of all the profits accrued by Alwyn's executors from their management of the estate since his death, plus the major part of the property. Francis's good fortune apparently went to his head. By 1513–6 he owed £140 to Philip Meredith, mercer of London, and another £20 to two mercers of Norwich, Hamund Lynstead and Alderman Robert James. He managed to avoid arrest but an inquest into his property was held[52] and he had to extricate himself with letters of protection of July 1515 and March 1516.[53] He can be found listed as an adventurer in January 1516, so it can be assumed he survived these problems.[54] In 1518, when he was referring to himself as a gentleman and was apparently married to a woman called Bridget (surname unknown), Francis divided the property in St. Mary le Bow and sold three messuages along Bow Lane to John Sedley, an auditor of the exchequer, to pay off part of a debt, the rest to be paid back from the rent of Francis's great place in the churchyard, which he and his wife then granted to feoffees to hold to their use. By 1522, the great place where Nicholas Alwyn had held his mayoralty was in the hands of John Gostwyke and William Carkeke junior and both Francis and his nephew (now aged twenty-six) were called to warrant the transaction.[55] The only satisfactory element in this sorry story was that the great place in St. Mary le Bow was acquired by William Carkeke, the scrivener son of the scrivener who had been a long-term friend of the elder Nicholas and writer of his testament and will. The property in Southwark, left by Nicholas Alwyn to his grandson and namesake, was also sold, conveyed by him and his wife, Anna, to a Francis Lovell in 1522.[56] No further details have been found about the careers of Francis or the younger Nicholas. It cannot be doubted that the Spalding property was also disposed of between 1511 and 1522 by Francis. As will be seen, this date fits well with the few facts known from the Spalding end.

Alwyn's associations and property in both London and Spalding were recorded in his elaborate testament and can be recreated – his disastrous evaluation of his male heir did not extend to his appreciation of friends

---

[52] TNA, C 131/101/7, C 131/107/4.

[53] Protection as a member of the retinue of Sir Richard Wingfield, deputy of Calais (*Letters and Papers, Foreign and Domestic, Henry VIII, 1509–30*, ed. J. S. Brewer (4 vols., London, 1864–1920), ii. 744, 1651.

[54] List of Jan. 1516 (*AC*, p. 433).

[55] Keene and Harding, *Historical Gazetteer of London*, 104/11, pp. 245–6, 247; also see n. 27.

[56] By a collusive recovery to Richard Heigham and Robert Spring, presumably Lovell's trustees (TNA, CP 40/1036), £334. This detail has been kindly supplied by Graham Dawson.

and associates. To take London first. His earliest acquaintances as a young immigrant from the Fens would have been his fellow apprentices in the somewhat fraught household of John Brodesworth. Richard Golofer can be picked out: both he and Alwyn had to be transferred to new masters; both traded before formally admitted to the Mercers; both reached a personal evaluation of £100 in 1475; and both achieved a wardenship of the Mercers within a year of each other. Alwyn included Golofer among his feoffees for his main dwelling in the city and took Nicholas Golofer as his godson (to whom he left a bequest of 6s 8d).[57] Alwyn undoubtedly developed loyalties: he stood surety with three other mercers for the estate of the two sons of John Dey, a cutler of St. Laurence Old Jewry, in 1475, and the tie was sufficient for him to leave forty poor men of the Cutlers' Company 12d each.[58] But other tasks were routine and there is no suggestion of closer ties than civic rank: he was a feoffee for Sir Henry Colet (who acted in the same capacity for him)[59] and helped to set up obits for the goldsmith Sir Edmund Shaa and for Thomas Wyndout and Thomas Northland, both aldermen and mercers.[60] He made a notable gift to Alderman Roger Acherley, draper, whose son was his godson: his horse litter 'complete' and his best purse of black velvet 'pyrled' with gold with double rings of silver-gilt that he wore when he was mayor, items which prove friendship but also suggest the infirmity of age.[61]

Many men and women received black cloth so that they might walk in his funeral procession, attend his exequies, see him into the ground and eat and drink afterwards at his great house at both funeral and month's mind (total cost £133 6s 8d); and surely these were regarded with friendship by the testator? Among them was Peter Waterbearer, who presumably kept the several cisterns in his great place full, so there was gratitude, too. The total cost of the cloth was to be 100 marks and it was to be suited to the rank of each recipient. There were no aldermen or civic officials in Alwyn's list of sixty-two persons (apart from those receiving gifts) – they would

[57] He outlived Alwyn and died in 1517 (Sutton, *Mercery*, pp. 533–4, 558). For Alwyn's feoffees, see n. 27.

[58] *Cal. Letter Bks. L*, p. 143. Margaret, daughter of John Dey cutler, married John Pikton mercer, who was one of his executors (d. 1475) (TNA, PROB 11/6, fos. 154–155v). His widow, Margaret Dey, died in 1494 with 5 living children and leading mercers as her executors (TNA, PROB 11/10, fos. 82v–83). See above for Pikton.

[59] *CIPM Henry VII*, iii, nos. 52, 57, 61.

[60] Obits for Sir Edmund and Hugh Shaa at St. Thomas of Acre (Keene and Harding, *Hist. Gazetteer London*, 145/17, p. 185); *CWH*, ii. 611 (Wyndout and Northland)).

[61] Roger Acherley's will (written 1515) shows links to John Warner (see below) and refers to a Mrs. 'Alwey' (TNA, PROB 11/21, fo. 103r–v); declared intestate in 1524 because of the lapse of time.

have automatically been expected to attend the funeral and month's mind of a past mayor. The sixty-two included all his household and family (the Cantelowes and Henry Cantelowe's step-sons John, Thomas, William and Stephen Gibson) and Mrs. Wood, who must be assumed to be Alwyn's granddaughter. The wives of many of the men were listed with their husbands and also many wives with no husbands, all presumably widows.[62] His leading overseers were William Paver, a lawyer who was to give long service as common clerk of London between 1511 and 1533;[63] Richard Berne, a mercer, to whom he had entrusted his son Francis as apprentice; and John Ash, waxchandler.[64] Each of them was to have £10 for his labours and was accompanied by his wife. Most important was William Carkeke, the local scrivener who had made his wills and drawn up his deeds over the years, 'for especial love that I owe unto hym' – his fees and reward of £26 13s 4d were to be paid promptly. No doubt of long acquaintance and use were William Melborne, still chamberlain of the city at this date (£10), whose wife, 'Mrs. Chamberlain', received another £10; and his servant, Maud of the Isle, 6s 8d.[65] Monetary rewards also went, along with the black cloth, to Mr. John Rede, notary of the diocese of Lincoln and procurator of the court of Arches (£3 6s 8d).[66] Londoners who had probably originated in Spalding were Thomas Maison and his wife[67] and Margaret Swan, possibly a relative of the merchant adventurer and skinner, Richard Swan, born in Spalding and long dead, who had acted as a feoffee for Alwyn's property in Spalding.[68] Also given cloth and expected to attend were the several young men he had

[62] Wives of William Bereman, Henry Worley, Gray of Richmond, Richard Hawkyns draper, Richard Hawkyns leatherseller [sic], Symond Pratt – none immediately identifiable. Do these reoccur later in the will as Mercy Gray (£3 6s 8d), Agnes Pratt, once wife of Thomas Hardy (£3 6s 8d) and Helen Hawkins (£3 6s 8d)?

[63] For Paver, see J. Baker, The Men of Court 1440–1550: a Prosopography of the Inns of Court and Chancery and the Courts of Law (Selden Soc., supp. ser., xviii, 2 vols., London, 2012), p. 1208; he committed suicide.

[64] On Berne: his will refers to wives, Margaret and Marion (his widow); parish of St. Magnus (see Alwyn's gift above); property in Bedfordshire; no references to Alwyn; he died in 1525 (TNA, PROB 11/21, fos. 309v–310v). See Bedfordshire Wills Proved in the Prerogative Court of Canterbury 1383–1548, ed. M. McGregor (Bedfordshire Hist. Rec. Soc., lviii, Bedford, 1979), no. 100, pp. 125–7. Ash: no will survives for him.

[65] Melborne/Milbourne/Mylborne, a painter who transferred to the Drapers' Company; chamberlain 1492–1505 (not re-elected 1506), d. 1511, pace Beaven, The Coronation of Richard III, ed. A. F. Sutton and P. W. Hammond (Gloucester, 1983), pp. 372–3.

[66] For Rede, see A. F. Sutton and L. Visser-Fuchs, 'VeRus celluy je suis (True I am): a study of John Russell, bishop of Lincoln and chancellor of England for Richard III', Ricardian, xxvii (2017), 1–75, at p. 44 and n. 58.

[67] See also n. 99 for John Maison.

[68] See n. 98 for Swan.

supported at Cambridge: William Jely/Joly, previously supported by Henry Cantelowe; a Christopher Joly (26s 8d yearly for five years); and a Thomas Joly (£13 6s 8d over five years).[69] Richard Wall, a fellow of Catherine Hall, Cambridge (26s 8d), who was similarly expected to attend, may have been connected to these young men. Alwyn's godchildren were recipients of 6s 8d each, but not expected to attend.[70]

Female servants were as conspicuous in his testament as his apprentices: Margaret with one hand (6s 8d); Margaret Deill (£6 13s 4d and a hoop of silver-gilt); Alice Sharp, possibly wife of John Sharp, another of his servants (£3 6s 8d and a flat hoop of base gold enamelled). Alice Hedge occupied the most conspicuous but unspecified position in his household, probably housekeeper in the largest sense.[71] He left her a property in St. Giles Cripplegate, as well as the option of managing his house in Spalding until the heir was of age and £50 for her personal use (she also benefited under remainders if they fell in). She was expected to attend all his exequies. The level of his trust was explicit in his charge to her of £40 to be dispensed in halfpenny bread to poor prisoners at the eight prisons of London and Westminster; she received the 'advantage' of this task for her labour, which he reckoned as 1d in each shilling. In his codicil, he left her a ring of fine gold with a ruby and a pointed diamond; a cupboard with an 'almery' and a 'rennyng tille theryn, my lawe bedde that I am wont to lye upon with the canope, the coverlit of tapestry of the iij kynges of Coleyn', with all things belonging; a goblet of silver with cover half-gilt, weight 10 oz 'swaged'; 'also the hanging beam in my chamber' with five candlesticks, an old square silver salt weight 9 oz and three silver spoons with round knops, weight 3 oz. It may be significant that although the London friaries were expected to attend his funeral (20s each), it was female religious houses which were singled out with sums, directed to both the head of the house and to the nuns: Stratford-at-Bow, Clerkenwell, the Minories, Kilburn, Halliwell, St. Helen's Bishopsgate and Heigham, as well as the sisters of St. Bartholomew's and St. Thomas's hospitals. He also remembered one hundred poor maidens with two pewter quart pots each for their marriages (£10).

In the codicil of his testament he noticed special relationships. All his relatives received an item of jewellery. Francis received his great hoop ring of base gold set with a diamond and a ruby 'that I was wont to were'.

---

[69] For Christopher and William Joly (but no Thomas), see *BRUC*, p. 332. Alwyn specified that remainders should benefit university education.

[70] Nicholas Golofer, Nicholas Statham, Nicholas Jones, Nicholas Acherley, Nicholas Brown and the daughter of William Haddon, shearman, 20s. On Wall, see *BRUC*, p. 611.

[71] Not identified. She is also mentioned as the mother of 'William Hossy' in Alwyn's testament.

The Woods were favoured: Oliver Wood received his crimson gown lined with damask and three yards of black velvet; his wife Joan a primer on parchment with silver clasps covered with black damask; and their daughter (unnamed) an *Agnus Dei* of gold with a ruby and three orient pearls with spangles pendant. Joan's brother Richard Cantelowe received a gold ring braided or wreathed; and his wife a ring of base gold with a seal therein like a strawberry. Outside the family circle, the mercer Edward Crosfield and his wife Joan received not only £6 13s 4d each, but a gold ring with a sapphire for her and a gold ring with a counterfeit diamond for their daughter Margaret. The wife of Eustace Knyll, a well-established mercer and adventurer, was given Alwyn's ring of fine gold with a table diamond. John Gare, girdler and his long-term feoffee, received a broad, coarse girdle of red damask with harness and bars of silver gilt and his wife Joan £20. Robert Jones, gentleman, was left £6 13s 4d and his wife Alice was given a pair of coral beads with four silver-gilt gauds and another £6 13s 4d; the Joneses were perhaps the parents of his apprentice Richard Jones.

If his apprentices are considered generally, it has to be concluded that he ran a household where loyalty to the master was easy, natural and rewarded. His many apprentices, called 'servants' if they were now in his service, are readily identifiable from the Mercers' records (see above). Many were involved in the work of his testament, funeral and month's mind in London and Spalding, headed by the senior Nicholas Tickhill and Hugh Smith, down to William Tales, who was barely indentured[72] – unfortunately few of them have left wills. Chief among them was his main executor, Michael English, his faithful servant, 'whom I have ever founde true'.[73] It was English who shouldered most of the burden after his main colleague, Angel Don, died: he had the care of the £400 which was to go to the two heirs

---

[72] Nicholas Tickhill came from Blechingley, Surrey (as Alwyn tells us) but neither he nor Hugh Smith left surviving wills. Tales was admitted to the Mercers in 1515 and no will survives. Both Smith and Tales were to be made free of the Staple at Alwyn's cost. Tickhill was well rewarded: a ring of base gold set with an amethyst, a standing nut of 180 z., a pair of leg harness, a pair of vambraces and a 'bycocket', which suggest he was of soldierly leanings.

[73] Michael English, mercer, married first a daughter of Thomas Wood, goldsmith and alderman, a contemporary of Nicholas Alwyn (not of the Coventry Wood family) (T. F. Reddaway and L. E. M. Walker, *The Early History of the Goldsmiths' Company 1327–1509* (London, 1975), pp. 315–6). English's will of 1537 refers to his wife Anne and her brother, James Wylford; Anne and his eldest son, James, were executors and his overseer was James Wylford; he left 10 children. His will also refers to his being bound to Anne Don, widow of Angel Don, and to William Bretton, executors of Angel, in £200 in case of trouble over the will of Nicholas Alwyn for a 7-year period ending in 1513; and that he had still not received the obligation back; he refers his executors to the 'box of my quittances for my said Master Alwyns business' (TNA, PROB 11/27, fos. 193v–194; proved 30 Jan. 1539).

(with no surety expected); he oversaw the disposal of Alwyn's wool at Calais with Tickhill and Smith; he and his wife Margaret attended the funeral in black gowns; she received Alwyn's great hoop of gold; and he attended the month's mind in Spalding. He was rewarded with £100, a sum which he certainly earned, and Alwyn's wagon.

Alwyn's other executor was Angel Don, a grocer who had married into a family with Lincolnshire origins. Angel Don's mother, Mistress Bretton, may have been the initial connection here. Angel was the son of John Don, mayor of Southampton, and his wife Agnes, who remarried the London ironmonger William Bretton (d. 1485). His mother's remarriage took Angel to London, and her career as a stapler after her second husband's death took him into that trade; he married Anne, daughter of John Sparrow, a grocer of London and Lincolnshire, and there was an active Sparrow family in Spalding known to Alwyn (see below). These were some of the connections that drew Angel and Alwyn together, quite apart from their civic roles. Alwyn's respect and affection for Mrs. Bretton took the form of black cloth and a gold sovereign; Angel's wife had another sovereign.[74] The grocer connection can be extended: John Warner, past armourer, grocer and alderman (since 1503), was left a black gown, with his wife, and 'a house for a saddle of light tawney velvet and the harness belonging sett with gilt bolyons'.[75] Did the grocer link in fact go back to Alwyn's earliest days in London as a raw sixteen-year-old in 1452? Had he been pointed towards Robert Gayton, grocer of London, who had come from Spalding and prospered and who might welcome a boy from the Fens?

Alwyn's friends in Spalding and the early history of Ayscoughfee Hall

Nicholas Alwyn's love for and commitment to Spalding are witnessed by his testament. His London success made him an impressive example for those who had remained at home. He planned an elaborate funeral and remembrance in London, but he was equally determined that his month's mind at Spalding would have pious fireworks which involved everyone he knew there and benefited every poor person in the district, so that his name would be carried throughout the hundred of Elloe.

For modern Spalding, Alwyn's most interesting act was to acquire a large property on the River Welland near the parish church and to build a large house, now known as Ayscoughfee Hall. This was facilitated by his close

---

[74] Sutton, *Wives*, esp. pp. 180, 202 n., 206–9; minor mistakes will be found in the notes there regarding Alwyn's children.

[75] William Warner died in 1511 (TNA, PROB 11/16, fos. 297v–298). For his family ties to Roger Acherley see above.

connection to the Gayton family, a fact underlined by his inclusion of Master Robert Gayton in the obit of his parents and himself in the parish church. The Gaytons have not proved easy to trace or interrelate as no wills survive for them and they seem to have had a predilection for variants of Reynold and Reginald.[76] A tentative pedigree has been devised, using the descent of their property and known dates as guides (Figure 9.2).

A Robert Gayton became a grocer of London in 1424–8.[77] It was usual for a younger son to be so apprenticed, leaving the elder son at home to inherit, but the unpredictability of survival might bring the inheritance to the former apprentice in due course. It is known this Robert had a brother, 'Reynold' (the elder?), and that both were alive in 1468 and well known among the leaders of the Spalding community.[78] Robert's reliability is suggested by regular gifts of goods and chattels to him and his engagement as a feoffee for the eminent John Welles, grocer, alongside Sir John Fastolf and Sir William Estfeld.[79] He and his wife Isabel were permitted in 1445–6 to have a private altar and choose their own confessor.[80] His career progressed steadily and probably included a regular trade in Italian raw materials for the cloth industry, until he became a warden of the Grocers in 1458, when he stood surety for Genoese merchants with many other Londoners, including the future mayor, William Heryot, in 1459.[81] In 1461 he was living in Dowgate ward, but he had property in the more central area of St. Mary le Bow,[82] where Nicholas Alwyn was to become prominent; in the same year he made

---

[76] No useful Gaytons/Geytons can be found in *BRUO* or *BRUC*. A Thomas and a William Gayton had been apprenticed mercers in 1435, but no subsequent careers have been found for them. A Robert Gayton was a conspicuous acquirer of properties at Shillington (Beds.), an estate of Ramsey abbey, 1414–5, but no further connection can be made (*The Liber Gersumarum of Ramsey Abbey: a Calendar and Index of BL, Harley MS. 445*, ed. E. Brezette DeWindt (Toronto, 1976), nos. 1286–4234 *passim*; with grateful thanks to A. DeWindt for her advice.

[77] London, Guildhall Library, Grocers' Company, Register of Admissions, 19th century index, MS. 11592A under 1428 and 1432, noted as warden 1444 and 1457; the original register (MS. 11592) starts in 1484.

[78] 6 July 1468 a gift of goods and chattels from Thomas Hoby of Spalding, yeoman, to John Davison, master of the hanaper, Robert Gayton, and Reynold Gayton, his brother, and their executors, etc. Witnesses: John Terald, William Mayson, Robert Smith, John Fell and John Carter (*CCR 1468–76*, no. 103). Teralds/Torolds and Maisons rented land from Crowland in the area (CUL, Additional MS. 4400, fos. 54, 56). See nn. 105, 106.

[79] *CCR 1435–41*, pp. 48, 226, 231.

[80] *Calendar of Papal Registers: Papal Letters*, viii, *1427–47*, ed. J. A. Twemlow (London, 1909), p. 305.

[81] *CPMR 1413–37*, pp. 250–1 (goods from Bolognese merchant, 1430); *CPMR 1437–57*, pp. 95, 173; *CCR 1454–61*, p. 333 (surety).

[82] *Cal. Letter Bks. K*, p. 397; *CCR 1454–61*, pp. 393–4.

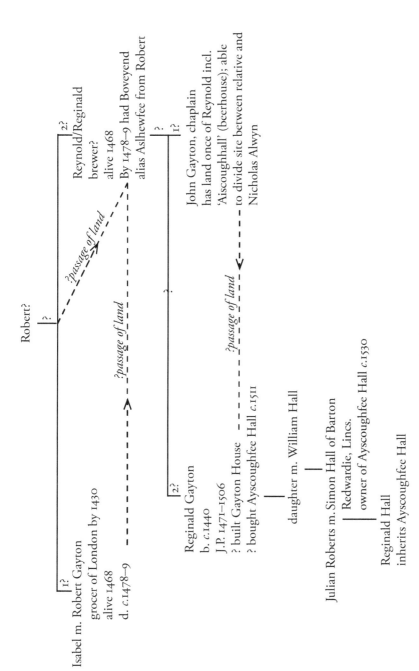

Figure 9.2. Gayton family tree (A. F. Sutton)

two gifts of his goods and chattels, purpose unknown. He was alive in 1468 and involved with his brother and other men of Spalding.[83] He died in the 1470s and certainly before 1478.[84]

The date of death of Robert Gayton, grocer of London, is suggested by a surviving account by John Clony, member of a local family, given black cloth to attend his month's mind by Alwyn and lessor of land from Crowland abbey.[85] Clony was collector of rents and farmer of Spalding, Gosberton, Pickall and Pinchbeck for the abbot of Crowland. His account, covering the year from Michaelmas 1478 to Michaelmas 1479,[86] provides a key reference to the site that Nicholas Alwyn was to buy: '*feod' Boueyend alias Aslhewfee nuper in tenura hered' Nicholi Steynton, modo in manibus <Roberti; deleted> Reginaldi Geyton hoc anno – xij d.*' [the fee[87] Boueyend alias Aslhewfee late in the tenure of the heir(s) of Nicholas Steynton, now in the hands of <Robert> Reginald Geyton, this year – 12*d*]. Gayton's fullp. or no.? amount owed is recorded at the end of the account, '*Sup*': *Reginaldu' Gayton – iiij li. iij s. ob*'. The Steynton family has not been identified.[88]

---

[83] *CPMR 1458–82*, pp. 1, 158; *CPR 1467–77*, p. 80; see also n. 78 above.

[84] Among the many puzzles about this family is the existence of another Robert Gayton in London, who is only known because he joined the Fraternity of the Parish Clerks in London in 1480 and was recorded as dead by them in 1507 under the title 'Master' Robert Gayton. He was therefore not the grocer (born *c*.1400) and is unlikely to have been the 'master' in Alwyn's obit as he survived Alwyn by at least a year (*Bede Roll of the Fraternity of St. Nicholas*, nos. 217, 467).

[85] John Clony himself held several blocks of *nativi* land (CUL, Add. MS. 4400, fos. 55, 56); a William Clony paid an increment rent for a place of land *cum lez poles*, 4*d*, which implies *nativus* status *temp*. Henry VI (SGS, Wrest Park Cartulary, fo. 205v). Old 'Clone's wife' and John 'Clone' junior both received black cloth from Alwyn. The family appears to have been *nativi* in origin (E. D. Jones, 'The Spalding priory merchet evidence from the 1250s to the 1470s', *Jour. Med. Stud.*, xxiv (1998), 155–75, at p. 161, n. 46, for a 'Cluny' in the early 1300s), but the family is not among the Myntling pedigrees (there is a Cony family, fo. 67v).

[86] LAO, 6 Anc 5/1, mm. 1r, 2r; the author is indebted to Hallam, 'Agrarian economy', p. 86 for the reference to this account. Few account or court rolls exist for Crowland abbey in this period (F. M. Page, *The Estates of Crowland Abbey* (Cambridge, 1934), pp. 1–8, esp. at p. 3).

[87] The term 'fee' has created problems for commentators and is best translated as 'property' or 'free tenure'. There is no reason to assume this was ever a knightly 'fee', as asserted by Gooch, who tried to link it to the Askew/Ascough family (Gooch, *Spalding*, pp. 251–2) and developed by R. Davies, *Ascoughfee Hall: the Early History* (Spalding, 2012), pp. 29–32. The ambitious presentation of it as a knightly fee could have started in the time of the Gaytons and Alwyns and was sufficiently well known by the 1530s for it to be included as a fee held by Crowland in the *Valor Ecclesiasticus*, ed. J. Caley and J. Hunter (6 vols., London, 1810–34), iv. 86: '*feod' de Askehughe pro terra in Spaldyng, xijd*'. The alternative name of Boveyend is an all-important splash of cold water on any assertion of knightly status.

[88] The alternative name of Boveyend and the previous owners called Steynton have not been located by the present author. Another place is accorded its own name of 'Collys' just

The Gaytons also included a John Gayton, chaplain, recorded in a 1470s survey of Crowland abbey's *libere tenentes* and *native tenentes/terrae* in Pinchbeck, Spalding, Cowbit and 'Pykale':[89]

Johanne Gayton, capellano, pro feodo de Browne,[90] nuper in tenura Reynold[i] Gayton iacenti in pynchebek et Spaldyng in diversis parcellis, quarum parcellarum principalis placea illius feodi, vocata Aiscoughhall, nuper existens a Berehouse, que quidem Berehowse iacet iuxta aquam de Weland ex parte occidentali et iuxta newgate ex parte orientali et iuxta tenementum domini prioris et conventus de Spaldyng ex parte australi, et reddit per annum – vij s. vij d.[91]

[John Gayton chaplain, for the fee *de Browne* late in tenure of Reynold Gayton lying in Pinchbeck and Spalding in divers parcels, of which parcels the principal place of this fee is called 'Aiscoughhall', lately being a 'Berehowse', which said beer house lies next to the water of the Welland on the west part and next to Newgate on the east part, and next to a tenement of the lord prior and convent of Spalding on the south part, and pays by the year – 7s 7d]

John Gayton also held a messuage in Holbeach from Crowland abbey in 1476.[92] It is likely that John the chaplain was an intermediary owner and one who would not have heirs of his body and might therefore be willing to divide his large property among relatives or sell part to a wealthy purchaser.[93] No commentator has emphasized the sheer size of the property, of which only one part was a great brew house (called Aiscoughhall in the survey, replacing the misleading 'fee' with the catch-all 'hall') and which abutted on the parish church and a tenement to the south owned by the

---

before the entry for Boveyend in this account; and a garden place called 'Dormo'pyte' is another not far from the abbot's court house on the Spalding side of the Welland (CUL, Add. MS. 4400, fo. 57r–v). It was increasingly common for a family to confer a name on their house once they had collected enough parcels together (see, e.g., the discussion of the Custs below).

[89] CUL, Add. MS. 4400, fos. 53–9. This survey is not dated and is inserted within a longer survey of Edward I's time. It can be compared to a rental of Holbeach of 16 Edward IV, fos. 82–8, another insertion (and see n. 92). The lack of overlap of names between this survey and the Clony account of 1478–9 is worrying.

[90] Bruen = to brew; also breu, browe; ppl. browen, bronw, bru(w)en [O.E. breowan; breaw, bruwon; browen], in *Middle English Dictionary*. Bre-ern (n) brow(h)ern (OE breaw-ern] = brewhouse, brewery (*MED*).

[91] CUL, Add. MS. 4400, fo. 54.

[92] The property in Holbeach from Crowland in 1476: John 'Geyton' a messuage lying between land of John Fisher on east, a small way and land of Thomas Kydale and Richard Welby on west and its north abutting on Washgat (CUL, Add. MS. 4400, fo. 85).

[93] Hallam was inclined to make John the son of Reginald (Hallam, 'Agrarian economy', p. 86 n. 2), but that may make things far too complicated, given the uncertain date of the survey.

prior of Spalding. Of this large site, several people could have been tenants, and subtenants, of Crowland abbey, including the Steyntons and Gaytons.[94]

In the 1470s it is unlikely Nicholas Alwyn had sufficient resources to think of buying property in his home town. The lawyer Reginald Gayton, however, was at the very beginning of his career in Lincolnshire.[95] He had received a legal education and can be found as a justice of the peace on the quorum for Holland from 1471. He was to continue to be appointed to commissions until and including that of 1506; he also undertook other useful local legal tasks.[96] He was to succeed to part of John Gayton's very large property, west and south of the church, and to build his own Gayton House of brick (or enlarge that of John the chaplain) at some date after 1480.[97]

On 13 May 1489 Alwyn was rich enough to acquire sufficient of this large property on which to build and create a spacious surround of orchards and gardens: John, son of Thomas Toft of Spalding, conveyed to Nicholas Alwyn and Henry Cantelowe, merchants of staple, Sir Henry Colet, William Heryot draper, Richard Swan skinner,[98] John Maison grocer[99] and

---

[94] A comparison with John Grundy's map of the messuages near the church of Spalding shows the extent of the rest of the property between the church and the river and the triangular site extending up the Welland. Davies shows ancient walls revealed by excavation, not yet explained (*Ayscoughfee Hall*, pp. 2, 6).

[95] Reginald has in the past been assumed to have been the son of Robert the grocer and Isabel Gayton (e.g., R. Purslove, *History of Ayscoughfee Hall* (South Holland Museum Service, Oct. 1994), pp. 2–3). However, no source is cited. Making Robert the grocer the father of the lawyer Reginald creates too many unanswered questions over the property.

[96] Baker, *Men of Court*, i. 741 and see n. 107.

[97] Gayton House, later called Holyrood House, was studied at the time of its demolition by T. W. Townsend, 'Holyrood House Spalding', a typescript of 1959 (I am grateful to the Spalding Gentlemen's Society for sight of this typescript). He dated the oldest part of the house to *c*.1500; the inclusion of elements of widely different dates taken from a supposed guildhall he ascribed to alterations carried out by Sir William Rigden (d. 1610) (pp. 6–8); and found the use of the word 'guildhall' to be late (p. 10). This 'guildhall' is misleadingly assumed to be the original part of Gayton House in the 1480s, with further confusions about Cowbit chapel (D. L. Roberts, 'Ayscoughfee Hall: the building of a great merchant's house', *Lincolnshire Hist. Archaeol.*, x (1975), 37–47, at p. 39, citing Townsend). Photographs of Holyrood House can be found in Davies, *Ayscoughfee Hall*, pp. 27–8.

[98] Richard Swan came from Spalding and had property there (Sutton and Hammond, *Coronation of Richard III*, pp. 402–3).

[99] John Maison, grocer of London, was certainly of Spalding with property there; he died in 1498 providing for souls who included John Lambe, grocer of London, and his wife Emma (once of Spalding and whose executor he was) in St. Pancras church, London, in his will (TNA, PROB 11/11, fo. 208). Emma Lambe died in 1473 and left land in Spalding (TNA, PROB 11/6, fos. 96v–98). A John Mayson had been a tenant in Spalding holding from Crowland abbey, before 1476 (CUL, Add. MS. 4400, fo. 54v.; see also n. 78).

Thomas Blenche,[100] all citizens of London, 'a site of land with edifices upon it between the vicarage and Newgate Street, Spalding' (now Love Lane). The sole grantor, John Toft, was, or was to become, the vicar of Pinchbeck. Of Alwyn's feoffees, both Swan and Maison had land and connections in Spalding, while the role of his sons-in-law and the useful weight of Colet, recently mayor of London, are self-evident. The witnesses were all described as men of Spalding: Robert Scarborough,[101] William Hode, Philip 'Sparowgh',[102] Robert Smith[103] and William Raynoldson. Scarborough was a chaplain of Spalding parish church and therefore a monk of the priory. Both Hode[104] and Robert Smith were to be remembered in Alwyn's will, along with John Toft (by then vicar of Pinchbeck). Alwyn made certain the transaction was recorded on the close roll of chancery.[105] Unfortunately invisible are the processes whereby Alwyn reached this point, the network of previous conveyances and agreements and the consent of the abbot of Crowland, as well as the good will of the prior of Spalding and the chaplains and churchwardens of the adjacent parish church.

The little evidence that survives for his place or house comes from Alwyn's will – he did not give it a name or call it great. Like Gayton House, it was built of the fashionable brick. He left £5 to Whitehead of Stanground for carrying his timber to Spalding; and as Stanground is near Peterborough and on the Welland it may have travelled down river. Important craftsmen

---

[100] Blenche was one of Alwyn's first apprentices, admitted 1476 and in 1495 nominated but not elected silkweigher (*AC*, p. 241); he was probably dead before Alwyn.

[101] Scarborough was a chaplain of the church in 1500 (M. Brassington, P. Case and R. Seal, *The Parish of St. Mary and St. Nicholas Spalding: the History of a Fenland Parish* (Spalding, rev. edn., 1997), p. 57; another chaplain of that date was John Sparrow. Reynaldson has not been identified).

[102] The Sparrows were relatives of Angel Don, one of Alwyn's executors (see above). In Spalding they were well-to-do tenants of Crowland abbey and probably of Spalding priory, taking leading roles in disputes and local affairs with the Teralds/Torolds, such as the fight with the men of Deeping finally adjudicated by Bishop Alnwick *c.*1450 (T. Allen, *The History of the County of Lincoln* (2 vols. in 1, Lincoln, 1833–4), ii. 286; J. Mackman, '"To theire grete hurte and finall destruction": Lord Welles's attacks on Spalding and Pinchbeck, 1449–50', in *Foundations of Medieval Scholarship: Records Edited in Honour of David Crook*, ed. P. Brand and S. Cunningham (York, 2008), pp. 183–95, at pp. 184, 187, 189).

[103] Robert Smith and his wife attended Alwyn's month's mind in Spalding. Robert Smith 'the elder' received £3 6*s* 8*d* and it seems probable that both Robert and Hugh Smith, apprentices and servants of Alwyn who benefited under remainders of his will, were the elder Robert's sons. Robert Smith, apprentice, received a bequest of £10, while Hugh had considerable responsibilities under the testament and was an overseer (and received £6 13*s* 4*d*, a broken ring of gold enamelled, bed and bedding).

[104] His ancestors were *nativi* (see below).

[105] *CCR 1485–1500*, no. 659.

involved may be: Stephen of 'Tangham', a carpenter, left £5, and Bunting, a carpenter, late of Needham Market, Suffolk. Alwyn gave £5 to be spent on the latter's soul by the advice of Bunting's son, who was now abbot of Bury St. Edmunds. It is self-evident that Alwyn would have re-used any timber already in the buildings on site: the great brewery, for example, may have had a sizeable roof.[106] Once established there, he had 'hustilments in my place' which were included in the bequest of the place to his son Francis (but not detailed), and Alwyn's care for it was shown by his wish that his trusted Alice Hedge should take charge of the house, if she would, until the heir was twenty-six, a possible total of sixteen years if Nicholas proved to be the survivor. She or another custodian was to have 20s a year to undertake repairs. If both boys died, the money from the sale of the property was to benefit the poor of Spalding and London.

Francis's improvident career leads to the supposition that he sold the Spalding house, probably on his inheritance in 1511 or soon after and during the lifetime of Reginald Gayton, justice of the peace for Holland. We have no date of death nor will for Reginald, only his last appointment as a justice in 1506[107] – as a lawyer, he might well have had the money to add Alwyn's place to his estate in the last years of his life. It is known that Reginald married and left a daughter who married William Hall of Nottinghamshire. Their son, Simon Hall of Burton Pedwardine, Lincolnshire, held Ayscoughfee Hall around 1530 and in due course it passed to Simon's son, Reginald Hall.[108]

Ignorant of this future, Alwyn's elaborate testament recreated his Spalding community in 1505–6. It is an area where few account rolls, no parish registers and few wills (Spalding priory held probate rights over its manors) survive. Although Crowland held a substantial manor which included part of the town and all the property relating to this article, the great priory

---

[106] The dendrochronology of 34 wood samples in 2003 suggested a date of 1450 (Davies, *Ayscoughfee Hall*, p. 13). The existence of previous buildings on site confuses any attempt to identify any part which Alwyn built. Roberts was happy to place the surviving roof timbers architecturally in the late 15th and early 16th centuries ('Ayscoughfee Hall', pp. 38–9).

[107] Apprentice at law retained by duchy of Lancaster 1498–9 or later; deputy steward of Long Sutton, Lincs., for the duchy, 1489–92 or later (Baker, *Men of Court*, i. 741). The 1490s saw him on commissions and a feoffee of Sir William Hussey, the chief justice (*CIPM Henry VII*, i, nos. 1166, 1209; and *Feet of Fines of the Tudor Period [Yorks]: Part 1: 1486–1571*, ed. F. Collins (Yorkshire Archaeol. and Topograph. Assoc. Rec. Series, 2 vols., Leeds, 1887), ii. 17 (Trinity Term 18 Henry VII, 1503)). In 1490, along with the abbot of Crowland, he and William Paynell, another local lawyer of Fishtoft (Lincs.) and his fellow justice, were detailed to see that the annuity of £40 was paid to the abbess of Syon by the prior of Spalding (*CCR 1485–1500*, no. 491; Baker, *Men of Court*, ii. 1212, for Paynell).

[108] A. R. Maddison, *Lincolnshire Pedigrees* (Harleian Soc. l–lii, lv, 4 vols., London, 1902–6), ii, Hall family, pp. 444–5.

controlled the larger part of Spalding, Moulton, Weston,[109] Pinchbeck, Cowbit and the hamlet of Pickall (Pykhale); held the dominant manorial court and the advowsons of the parish churches of Spalding, Pinchbeck, Moulton and Weston; and oversaw Cowbit, the chapel and cemetery of which were consecrated by the bishop for the ease of the inhabitants on 28 April 1486.[110] By the time he died Alwyn was already a notable benefactor, including local projects of which he was proud: to repair the new bridge on the highway 'that I made' between Spalding and Pinchbeck, £3 6s 8d; to repair the bridge through the park towards Pinchbeck 'that I made', £3 6s 8d; to repair Pinchbeck bridge, £3 6s 8d; and 20s to repair Peterborough bridge. A bequest of £100 was to repair the roads between Spalding and London. The church was to have its rood-loft gilded and garnished, or other ornaments, at discretion, £30. The cornice still bore the arms of Alwyn, the Mercers and the Staple in the early nineteenth century and he may have contributed to the north porch and certainly to some of the glazing.[111] Its guilds of the Trinity and St. John received £3 6s 8d and 40s respectively and

---

[109] Alwyn paid the vicars of Moulton and Weston (unnamed) for *Dirige* and mass (20s), with 6 assistant chaplains each (who were to receive 12d each); and the poor of each place received £16 13s 4d (4d each). W. E. Foster, 'On the history of All Saints' church, Moulton', *Associated Architectural Societies Reports and Papers*, xx (1889–90), 248–63: the vicar of Moulton at the time of his death was William Bonde (1498–?). G. A. Poole, 'On the churches of SS. Mary and Nicholas, Spalding and Weston St. Mary, and chapel of St. Nicholas Wykeham', *AASRP*, i (1850–51), 347–60: Poole notes the north porch and the adjacent additions as *c*.1480 (p. 352 and plan opposite p. 353). For Spalding church's status under the priory, see *Visitations of Religious Houses in the Diocese of Lincoln: iii: Records of Visitations held by William Alnwick, Bishop of Lincoln, A.D. 1436 to A.D. 1449*, pt. 2, ed. A. H. Thompson (Lincoln Rec. Soc., xxi, 1929), p. 342, n.

[110] Bishop Russell carried this ceremony out in person while making an extended stay at Crowland abbey from 16 Apr. (LAO, Russell's Register, fos. 74v–84). Gough printed the details precisely: the bishop's certification of 11 May 1486 stated 'that year 13 days before' – i.e., 28 Apr. 1486 – he had consecrated Cowbit chapel and cemetery, granting sacramentals to be performed there for the inhabitants of Cowbit and 'Pykhall' because of the bad roads etc.; the priory had consented to this (endorsed '*composito inter Cubyt et nos pro capella de Cubyt*' (*Britannia*, ii. 240)). Gough went on to note that the Alwyn's arms were in the east window. Gooch's attempt to link this event to a consecration of the chapel in Ayscoughfee Hall does not bear examination (*Ayscoughfee Hall*, p. 250), but was repeated in Purslove, *History of Ayscoughfee Hall*, p. 1; and Davies, *Ascoughfee Hall*, p. 28.

[111] The carved oak cornice of the screen had in its centre carvings identifiable as the arms of the Mercers' Company and the wool bags of the Staple (Allen, *History of the County of Lincoln*, i. 289). Alwyn's arms and glass asking for prayers for Sir William 'Hariot' stapler and draper were recorded in *Lincolnshire Church Notes made by Gervase Holles, A.D. 1634 to A.D. 1642*, ed. R. E. G. Cole (Lincoln Rec. Soc., i, Lincoln, 1911), p. 168; the text relating to Heryot is likely to be connected to Alwyn. For the north porch see Allen, *History of the County of Lincoln*, i. 287; and Poole, 'On the churches of SS. Mary and Nicholas', p. 352 and n. 109 above.

the Trinity guild of Cowbit, 20s. Spalding priory's cloister was given £5 for repairs.

In his role as public benefactor Alwyn intended to be seen off in magnificent style and he might have expected to have the local gentry at his month's mind. The knightly class was above him, but the Custs, a hard-working peasant family of this area which had projected members into London, had a mercer connection contemporary to Alwyn and had begun to refer to their own house as the Cross with Hand at Pinchbeck,[112] might have been invited. More pretentious (at least in the minds of their descendants) were the Welbys of Moulton, who also had London connections, held the local offices of bailiff or steward (and even sheriff) and leased extensive property from the monks of Crowland; or the Pinchbecks and Bellers of Pinchbeck.[113] Some of these certainly knew Alwyn or were known to Reginald Gayton. To take one example, it is surely revealing that the Welbys of Moulton, always a village apart as it was not dominated by a grange of the priory, were not in this particular Londoner's will, they did not receive black cloth and were not expected to be at his exequies. Only one scion of an ancient family, who was fast establishing himself among the local gentry at this time, was given black cloth: Master Ogle, who can be identified as Richard Ogle, father of his more famous namesake, the future steward of Crowland abbey.[114] The only other name of consequence dropped by Alwyn was that of the Master Gayton who was to share his chantry's prayers. It can be suggested that Alwyn had not, by the time of his death, forged strong ties to the more important local men. To judge by his support of bridges and the parish church, he regarded himself more as a useful parishioner, one whose financial success could improve local amenities, but one not too far advanced above the status of his parents buried under the flagstones of the church.

His special acquaintances in Spalding were defined by his gifts of black cloth, headed by Mrs Gayton – there is no male Gayton in the list and it may

---

[112] *The Records of the Cust Family of Pinchbeck, Stamford and Belton in Lincolnshire 1479–1700*, compiled by Lady Elizabeth Cust (London, 1898), p. 12: Stephen Titchmarsh mercer had John Cust as his apprentice and acted as executor of Christina Cust in 1454.

[113] Richard Welby of Moulton had executors who included William Dunthorn, common clerk of London in 1482; his property 'Valentines' in Moulton went to his brother Thomas and the family had lands in Holbeach, Fleet and Wynthorp ('Lincolnshire wills proved in the prerogative court of Canterbury 1471–1490', ed. C. W. Foster, *AASRP*, xli (1935), 179–218, at pp. 216–8). Welbys occur in CUL, Add. 4400. See Maddison, *Pedigrees* for the Bellers, Pinchbeck and Welby; and E. Green, 'The knightly family of Pynchebek of Pinchbeck, Lincoln', *Lincolnshire Notes and Queries*, i (1888), 173–7.

[114] For Moulton, see Hallam, *Settlement*, pp. 207–9; and Maddison, *Pedigrees*, p. 730, for Ogle.

be suggested she was the wife of Reginald Gayton. Officials and neighbours included the Clonys, old and young, rent collectors of Crowland abbey, and 'Adlard Trowthe', who had served as the abbey's clerk of courts.[115] Men who had done him a service can be identified as William Hode (a gown and £3 6s 8d) and Robert Smith, along with John Toft, vicar of Pinchbeck, who both received cloth and gifts. No chaplain of Spalding is identifiable by name, although 'Sir' John Byrde may be one. John Harrison of Moulton and his wife received cloth and Harrison an extra 20s. Harrison and William Hode (Hode witnessed the conveyance to Alwyn of his Spalding property) are the only men in Alwyn's will whose families can be found recorded as *nativi* of Spalding priory in the late 1470s – they may be assumed to have been free by 1506 or the classification had been dropped.[116] Unidentifiable persons receiving black cloth were James Dalton, John Taverner, Nicholas Idom, William Pecoke, Richard Romford and his wife (they also received £3 6s 8d) and Parsle's wife (20s). A John Rous, Aylward's wife of Weston, and Alice, wife of John Burre the elder, all received 6s 8d. Each of the four parish clerks received 6s 8d.

Alwyn died on 29 January 1506. A month later his elaborate month's mind was to take place in Spalding, nearly 100 miles from London.[117] It is a display of piety remarkable for its cost and the sixteen Londoners whom he subsidized to attend. His two executors, his overseers (William Paver and Richard Berne), each accompanied by a servant, his apprentices, headed by Nicholas Tickhill and Hugh Smith, John Fayrey, down to the youngest of them, William Tales, just sixteen, his housekeeper Alice Hedge, his chaplain William Joly, an unidentified John Meryell and his cook, John Haydon. They were to provide their own horses, but he paid for their meat, drink and horsemeat there and back (£33 6s 8d) with another £20, presumably for

---

[115] For Clonys, see above. Richard Trought/Trouth held land from Crowland in the 1470s (CUL, Add. MS. 4400, fos. 54, 57v). Athelard Trough, 'once clerk of our courts', appeared in a document concerning the office of pittancer of Crowland abbey, 4 Nov. 1483 (SGS, Wrest Park Cartulary, fo. 47r–v).

[116] SGS, Myntling register, compiled in the late 1470s: for Hode, alias Oxherde family of three generations, see fo. 62v, supported by references in Myntlyng's Kalendar of past court rolls, fos. 51, 56–7, 60–2. Harrison, alias Illary of Moulton (associated with the Welbys of Moulton), 4 generations, of which the last had no names (fo. 61 and Kalendar, fos. 57, 58, 60–2), with dates as late as 6 Edward IV [1466–7]; and all the entries about Harrisons from 36 Henry VI [1457–8] onwards concern absence without licence. The Harrisons/Illarys and Hode/Oxherds took their oaths to their lord and were absent without leave (31–2 Henry VI [1452–4] to 14 Edward IV [1474–5] fos. 260v–267).

[117] Allen, *History of the County of Lincoln*, i. 277, with an illustration of Spalding church and Ayscoughfee Hall behind a wall across the Welland and ships visible at the quay to the north.

the overall expenses. It was not necessarily an easy a journey in February – many of the roads threaded their way through fens and along causeways over many bridges. Both the parish church and the priory were to perform the month's mind on the same day: the bellman of the town was to call for prayers (20s), the bells of the church were to ring (5s) and those of the priory (5s). Twelve priests of Spalding and nearby Cowbit chapel (if there were twelve) were to attend (12d each), the four parish clerks and sexton (8d each) – and all seventeen received an additional 2s each. The twenty-four monks of the priory received 6s 8d each, the two clerks 12d and the prior 20s to say mass. His hearse – empty of his body, already buried in London – was to have fourteen torches of 20 lbs (at a cost of 8s 4d each) and the bearers were to be found 'of the xl men of my lyverey' (4d each). The torches were to end up on the eight altars of the parish church (which he could name), of Cowbit and the priory.[118] Gowns made from three yards of northern tawny, at 16d the yard, were given to forty poor men and women of Spalding and Cowbit and 3,000 men, women, children and servants, rich and poor, of the same places were to have 12d each, any surplus going to the poorest (total £150). Poor clerks of Spalding were to have 6s 8d.

Remembrance continued past the month's mind in Spalding, as in St. Mary le Bow. The financial complexities were to be handled by his servants and past apprentices, Hugh Smith and Nicholas Tickhill, who were to hold £240 raised from the sale of Alwyn's wools at Calais. First, there was to be a twenty-year obit for the souls of himself and his parents, 'our' children and Master Gayton (at 13s 4d per annum). Second, for the same twenty years, every Sunday a priest in his surplice with twenty-eight poor men and women between matins and mass were to say *De Profundis* with versicle and orisons at the gravestone of his parents. Those who could not were to say an *ave*, the paternoster and creed; and one of the men was to say openly, 'God have mercy on the souls of Richard Alwyn and Margaret his wife, of Nicholas their son, Robert Gayton and all Christians' and the rest were to say 'Amen'. Each person of the thirty present was to receive 1d (total expense 6s 8d each Sunday). At Cowbit and Pickall a priest and nine poor persons were to pray for the same souls each Sunday and receive 1d each (10d a week). Last, there was to be a priest to sing at the altar of St. John in the parish church of Spalding for the same souls for ten years (8 marks per annum) and have the use of the red worsted vestments from the altar 'in my house' at Spalding. The altar of Our Lady at the North Door in the

---

[118] The high altar (2), altars of St. John, Corpus Christi, Holy Trinity, St. Thomas, St. Helen, St. George and the altar of Our Lady of the North Door (1 each); both Cowbit chapel and the priory's high altar 2 each.

market place of Spalding – presumably of the priory and accessible by the townspeople – was to receive his vestment of white damask 'brawdered' with flowers, on which his mark was to be set.

Nicholas Alwyn's real memorial is his remarkable testament, flamboyant but modest. He had not collected an estate to support his heir in idleness: he expected him to work at his trade and make money, as he himself had done. The London house and the country house in the Fens were to be the background of a London business and a relaxation among a prosperous, independent-spirited country community where he and his parents had been respected. His wealth, acquired elsewhere, allowed him to repay the community of his birth with bridges, ornaments for the church, aid and clothing for the poor. It seems probable that he expected his heir to continue his chantry at the end of the twenty years. In contrast, his son Francis was calling himself 'gentleman' in the 1520s, accrued the debts of a gentleman and apparently sold his father's place at Spalding as easily as he did that in London. Francis's carelessness highlights his father's careful lists of his friends that bring his personality into focus within two different communities. The wider circles of his three trades (mercer, adventurer and stapler) Alwyn ignored. The Spalding connection seems to have been the more permanent attachment, with the gravestone of his parents, a solid object which gave him identity. Alwyn's great position as mayor over the year when the fifteenth century became the sixteenth did not, apparently, overawe him. He created his own new house in Spalding – his London house had been created by earlier generations – and he created it within a community still ruled by the manorial courts of a prior and an abbot, very unlike the self-governing world of London. Spalding men and women had, however, long traditions of standing up to their lord, making themselves heard, fighting the sea and the waters of the rivers and fighting all those who intruded upon their rights.[119] A discussion of the merits of London versus Spalding and the Fens, over wine and before a fire, could have voted either way in either of Alwyn's houses.

---

[119] Compare Hallam, *Settlement*, pp. 198–203, 207–9, 213, 215–6, 218–22 on the period before 1348; and J. Thirsk, *Fenland Farming in the Sixteenth Century* (Leicester, 1953), who both emphasize the prosperity of the Spalding area, the commercial spirit and harbour of the town of Spalding, which recorded tolls on a wide array of goods.

III. Londoners remembered

10. Charity and the city: London Bridge, c.1176–1275

John A. McEwan

The rebuilding of London Bridge in stone in the period c.1176–1209 was a major undertaking, similar in scale to building 'a large castle or cathedral in terms of costs, manpower and materials required'.[1] When completed, the new bridge not only proved an important amenity for the people of London, allowing them to pass with greater ease over the River Thames and bringing more trade to their city, but also posed political challenges. Londoners invested significant resources in building the bridge, but keeping it in working order required constant maintenance.[2] Who would pay for repairs and ensure they were carried out? By studying the men who took charge of the bridge in the years between c.1176 and 1275, the shifting balance of power between the various groups that had an interest in the bridge can be traced and through this the growth of the authority of the civic government over the city of London and its people.

The rebuilding of London Bridge in stone was a significant bridge building project, but within its regional context it was not unique. In England and France in the twelfth century a number of bridges were built, or rebuilt, in stone and these projects were organized in a variety of ways.[3]

---

[1] The precise dates when the bridge was under construction are difficult to determine and work may well have proceeded intermittently over many years, perhaps one arch at a time. The end result was a bridge 276 metres long formed of 19 piers supporting 19 stone arches. The southern abutment has been investigated by modern archaeologists. They date it, on the basis of timbers used as piles and sillbeams, to 1189 or 1190. The abutment was a timber and rubble structure faced with masonry. The height of the original abutment could not be determined, but there was surviving masonry up to 2.99 metres high and it consisted of 'Purbeck marble, Kentish ragstone from the Maidstone area, and quartz-rich sandstone and a shelly limestone of uncertain source' (B. Watson, T. Brigham, and T. Dyson, *London Bridge: 2000 Years of a River Crossing* (London, 2001), pp. 85, 89–92 and 125; see also G. Milne, *The Port of Medieval London* (Stroud, 2003), ch.7).

[2] V. Harding and L. Wright, 'Introduction', in *London Bridge: Selected Accounts and Rentals, 1381–1538*, ed. V. Harding and L. Wright (London Rec. Soc., xxxi, 1995), pp. vii–xxix, at pp. xxi–xxiv.

[3] The building of the stone bridge at Avignon was reportedly instigated, in the late 12th century, by a boy who miraculously threw an enormous stone into the river to form the

J. A. McEwan, 'Charity and the city: London Bridge, c.1176–1275', in *Medieval Londoners: essays to mark the eightieth birthday of Caroline M. Barron*, ed. E. A. New and C. Steer (London, 2019), pp. 223–44. License: CC-BY-NC-ND 4.0.

People considered the building and maintaining of bridges a Christian work and could treat them as charitable enterprises.[4] Kings could also support bridge-building through the imposition of taxes and other customary duties.[5] In London the stone bridge replaced an earlier bridge which was once supported by a customary duty.[6] Therefore, in the late twelfth century the Londoners could look for inspiration and models for the finance and governance of the stone bridge to charitable bridge-building projects and to their own experiences with royal administration.

There is little evidence, it is important to note, to suggest that London's own civic government could make a substantial contribution to the administration of London Bridge in the twelfth century.[7] Nonetheless, by the later thirteenth century the city had assumed an important role. A sign of this development is a reference in 1275 to the civic government holding an election to appoint men to take charge of the bridge.[8] Therefore, between c.1176 and 1275 the city's role in the administration of the bridge had changed, but when did this change happen and what do the timing and circumstances of the change reveal about the development of the government's relationship with the people of the city? The bridge's records offer evidence that previous scholars have not fully taken into account.

The bridge's archives preserve property records that name men who acted on behalf of the bridge from the late twelfth century onwards (Table 10.1). Gwyn Williams, in his study of thirteenth- and fourteenth-century

---

foundation of the first pier (M. N. Boyer, 'The bridgebuilding brotherhoods', *Speculum*, xxxix (1964), 635–50, at p. 638).

[4] *Ancient Laws and Institutes of England*, ed. B. Thorpe (2 vols., London, 1840), ii. 283; D. Harrison, *The Bridges of Medieval England: Transport and Society, 400–1800* (Oxford, 2004), p. 194.

[5] Rochester Bridge in Kent offers a well-documented example from this period of a system of customary duties divided among a series of estates to support a bridge (N. P. Brooks, 'Rochester Bridge, AD 42–1381', in *Traffic and Politics: the Construction and Management of Rochester Bridge, AD 43–1993*, ed. N. Yates and J. M. Gibson (Woodbridge, 1994), pp. 1–35, at pp. 16–20; see also Harrison, *Bridges of Medieval England*, pp. 186–90).

[6] Exceptions from these duties offer some evidence for their existence. For example, King William II granted the canons of St. Paul's the right of holding their lands free from any obligation, in the form of gelds or work, to the 'castle of London, and for the wall and the bridge and the bailey and cart-work' (*Early Charters of the Cathedral Church of St Paul, London*, ed. M. Gibbs (Camden Soc., 3rd. ser., lviii, 1939), no. 13).

[7] D. Keene, 'London Bridge and the identity of the medieval city', *Trans. London and Middlesex Archaeol. Soc.*, li (2000), 143–56, at p. 148; see also Harding and Wright, *London Bridge*, p. ix. For an overview of the state of the governance of London in this period, see C. N. L. Brooke and G. Keir, *London, 800–1216: the Shaping of a City* (London, 1975); S. Reynolds, 'The rulers of London in the twelfth century', *History*, lvii (1972), 337–55.

[8] LMA, CLA/023/CP/01/003, m. 5.

London, demonstrated that the history of the government could fruitfully be approached through the personal histories of the leading men in the community.[9] Using similar methods, this chapter will trace the history of the bridge by establishing the sequence of men involved in its direction and considering their backgrounds, interests and affiliations. Some men were only associated with the bridge organization briefly, but others were involved for many years and it is these long-established men whose biographies are particularly revealing of the changing relationship between the bridge and the civic government.

In the late sixteenth century John Stow asserted that the rebuilding of the bridge in stone was a project initiated by Peter of Colechurch, a 'priest and chaplaine'.[10] Peter's existence is well attested in contemporary records and his seals show that he identified himself as a priest while acting on behalf of the bridge.[11] Stow suggested that one of Peter's first achievements was the establishment of a bridge chapel, and once it was completed 'many charitable men gaue lands, tenements, or summes of money towards maintenance thereof', which surviving records verify.[12] Other aspects of Stow's account are more difficult to confirm. Stow credited the king, a cardinal and the archbishop of Canterbury with offering important financial support. Moreover, Peter of Colechurch died before the bridge was finished and Stow suggested that 'worthy Marchants of London, Serle Mercer, William Almaine, and Benedict Botewrite' then completed the work.[13] Thus, Stow shared credit for the construction of the bridge between the crown, the Church and the leading men of London, but he contended that even before the project was completed, responsibility for the direction of the bridge had passed to several leading Londoners. However, Stow's reference to Serlo, William and Benedict, who participated in the affairs of the bridge in the 1220s and 1230s (Table 10.1), well after the death of Peter of Colechurch, suggests that Stow may not have appreciated the full sequence of events.

Building on the work of previous generations of historians, modern scholars have offered a number of interpretations of the events of the late twelfth and early thirteenth centuries.[14] Derek Keene noted that 'the

---

[9] G. A. Williams, *Medieval London: From Commune to Capital* (London, 1963).

[10] *A Survey of London by John Stow*, ed. C. L. Kingsford (2 vols., Oxford, 1908), i. 22–3.

[11] LMA, CLA/007/EM/02/F/023; J. A. McEwan, *Seals in Medieval London, 1050–1300: a Catalogue* (London Rec. Soc., Extra Series, i, 2016), nos. 170, 172.

[12] For a donation from Henry son of Ailwin, London's 1st mayor, see LMA, CLA/007/EM/02/B/094; Watson, *London Bridge*, pp. 119–21.

[13] Stow, *Survey of London*, i. 23.

[14] Compare the views of modern historians with those of the mid 20th century: M. B. Honeybourne, 'The pre-Norman bridge of London', in *Studies in London History Presented*

bridge project and its estate originated in a period when the institutional expression of the citizens' collective authority was at an early stage' and that consequently, he argued, 'the enterprise became an independent trust rather than an integral element of civic administration'.[15] If, as an 'independent trust', it was not an 'element of civic administration', what form did the 'trust' take? Christopher Brooke emphasized that the leading figure in the bridge project was Peter 'vicar of St. Mary Colechurch', but added that Londoners were involved through 'a series of confraternities and guilds' whose members then raised money 'as a pious and charitable work'.[16] As Brooke suggested, the way in which the bridge project was organized in its early years was probably indebted to charitable models, in keeping with the existing tradition in England of treating the building of bridges as an act of piety.[17] Indeed, on the Continent at this time, and particularly in the south of France, charitable organizations were busy building bridges, so there were contemporary parallels.[18] The bridge was probably established as a charitable and 'independent trust', but acknowledging this leaves historians of the thirteenth century to establish when the bridge was brought under the authority of the civic government.

Chronicles, judicial materials and royal records offer evidence on the governance of the bridge in the early to mid thirteenth centuries, but the most important sources are documents preserved in the archives of the bridge itself.[19] These records are largely concerned with property because, from an early date, the bridge acquired land that served as an endowment. Indeed, some of the earliest properties were located on the bridge itself. In 1202 the crown proposed that buildings should be placed on the bridge to provide rents.[20] In 1212 a fire swept through Southwark and onto the bridge, reaching as far as the centrally located bridge chapel, which suggests that the bridge was lined with houses and shops by this date.[21] When in 1244 royal justices asked the Londoners by what warrant they had built

---

to *Philip Edmund Jones*, ed. A. E. J. Hollaender and W. Kellaway (London, 1969), pp. 17–39, at p. 30; Williams, *Medieval London*, p. 86.

[15] Keene, 'London Bridge', p. 148; see also Harding and Wright, *London Bridge*, p. ix.

[16] Brooke and Keir, *London, 800–1216*, p. 110.

[17] Thorpe, *Ancient Laws and Institutes*, ii. 283; Harrison, *Bridges of Medieval England*, p. 194.

[18] M. N. Boyer, *Medieval French Bridges: a History* (Cambridge, Mass., 1976), ch. 3.

[19] Watson, *London Bridge*, pp. 119–20.

[20] *Rotuli Litterarum Patentium in Turri Londinensi Asservati 1201–1216*, ed. T. D. Hardy (London, 1835), p. 9.

[21] M. Brett, 'The annals of Bermondsey, Southwark and Merton', in *Church and City, 1000–1500: Essays in Honour of Christopher Brooke*, ed. D. Abulafia, M. Franklin and M. Rubin (Cambridge, 1992), pp. 279–310, at pp. 305–6.

on the bridge, they responded that the structures had been erected by the wardens and brethren of the bridge with the alms of the people of London. They asserted that the structures represented an improvement to the fabric because they allowed people to move across the causeway 'securely and boldly' and helped to fund the maintenance of the bridge.[22] Properties on the bridge were part of the original nucleus of the bridge's endowment, but the bridge also acquired lands in other parts of London, Southwark and in the surrounding region. The bridge kept records relating to its properties, particularly the deeds documenting their acquisition, and those records can identify men who acted on behalf of the bridge organization.

When Peter of Colechurch died in 1205, he was buried in the bridge chapel.[23] Stow suggested that, following Peter of Colechurch's death, a group of 'merchants' from London took charge of the project, but contemporary records indicate that these were men who could personify the bridge's charitable status (Table 10.1). King John intervened in the appointment of Peter's successor and directed that a royal almoner, known as brother Wace, and a 'law-worthy man' of London, selected in consultation with the mayor of London, should be granted responsibility for the bridge.[24] Brother Wace took charge of the administration of the bridge's endowment[25] and although the identity of Wace's colleague, if indeed one was appointed, is obscure, it is clear that in subsequent years the practice of having two or more men share responsibility for administering the bridge became conventional. Brother Wace's immediate successors seem to have been either chaplains or members of the bridge's own brotherhood. Richard of Muntfichet, in a document dated 1212–4, handed over a mill to 'London Bridge and the brethren'.[26] These men are difficult to identify, but a deed dated 1213 tersely remarked that 'Martin and Geoffrey' entered into an understanding with Henry de Arches and Margaret his wife concerning land in the parish of All Hallows Barking.[27] The absence of second names suggests that they were members of the brotherhood rather than merchants of London. Thus, responsibility for the bridge probably did not shift directly from Peter of

---

[22] *The London Eyre of 1244*, ed. H. M. Chew and M. Weinbaum (London Rec. Soc., vi, 1970), no. 344.

[23] Brett, 'Annals of Bermondsey', pp. 302, 305.

[24] *Rotuli Litterarum Clausarum in Turri Londinensi Asservati*, ed. T. D. Hardy (2 vols., London, 1833–44), i. 49; Hardy, *Rotuli Litterarum Patentium*, p. 58. Williams described the mayor in this period as 'the personifications of the city' and 'by his oath a delegate of the king' (Williams, *Medieval London*, p. 29).

[25] *Chartulary of the Hospital of St. Thomas the Martyr, Southwark, 1213 to 1525*, ed. L. Drucker (London, 1932), no. 233.

[26] LMA, CLA/007/EM/04/001/394/474.

[27] LMA, CLA/007/EM/04/001/160/141.

Colechurch to 'worthy Marchants of London' but first came to rest in the hands of the 'brotherhood' that had taken shape during Peter's lifetime and was devoted to serving the bridge.

The brotherhood admitted both men and women. Three mid thirteenth-century agreements recording the reception of married couples into the brotherhood survive.[28] Each couple made a payment to the bridge, which suggests that the agreements were corrodies.[29] In 1255–6 the brethren admitted Thomas Iuvene and Isabel his wife.[30] They were to receive a servant, living space within the 'enclosure' (*clausus*) and an allowance of one mark a year for clothing; and they agreed to be 'faithful, honest and reverent' as is customary among 'religious men'. In return, they donated funds to the bridge which were used to purchase rents. In 1250–1 John, son of Matthew and his wife Juliana, joined the brotherhood on similar terms.[31] They received a chamber within the 'enclosure', a servant and 1 mark for their clothing; and they were asked to be faithful, honest and reverent to the wardens and the brethren. In 1277 Henry 'in-the-lane' and Isabel his wife gave 100 marks to the bridge and in return, for the term of their lives, they received two chambers and a solar located in the 'enclosure'.[32] Furthermore, each day they were also provided with food and drink in the same proportions as were given to two chaplains. Although these couples may not have been typical of the brotherhood's membership, all three agreements point to the existence of a collection of houses where the brothers and sisters lived in a communal fashion.

Some of the brothers may have been men who could take an active role in managing the bridge's estates. In 1280 Martin the chaplain, John the clerk and the bridge wardens granted John of Brokele, bridge brother, lands owned by the bridge in Lewisham and Greenwich 'for his sustenance'. A detailed agreement was drawn up that listed the value of the estate and an inventory of the contents.[33] The inventory included a variety of tools and farm implements as well as geese, hens, three horses and six oxen. There were also a mill and seventy-six acres of land sown with corn, rye, oats, peas, vetch, beans and barley. The agreement stipulated that John of Brokele had

---

[28] LMA, CLA/007/EM/02/A/039 and CLA/007/EM/02/A/051; *Munimenta Gildhallæ Londoniensis: Liber Albus, Liber Custumarum, et Liber Horn*, ed. H. T. Riley (3 vols., London, 1859–62), iii. 449–53.

[29] B. F. Harvey, *Living and Dying in England, 1100–1540: the Monastic Experience* (Oxford, 1993), pp. 181–4 and ch. 6.

[30] LMA, CLA/007/EM/02/A/039. Thomas may have had a connection to the cloth trade (*The London Eyre of 1276*, ed. M. Weinbaum (London Rec. Soc. xii, 1976), no. 70).

[31] LMA, CLA/007/EM/02/A/051.

[32] Riley, *Munimenta Gildhallæ*, iii. 449–53.

[33] LMA, CLA/007/EM/02/G/028 and CLA/007/EM/02/G/037.

to pay to the bridge 50s a year in rent, but he failed as an estate manager and in June 1297–8 he was asked to return custody of the estate.[34] At that time it was noted that brother John was not only behind in his rent payments, but that stock and implements had disappeared and he had failed adequately to maintain the mill, woods, hedges and houses. The same day, another bridge brother, John of Lewisham, was sworn as the new 'baillif' of the estate.[35] Although some brothers may have managed estates, perhaps they were not all suited to this work.

A more common role for bridge brothers was to participate in fundraising. In 1253, for instance, the brethren of the bridge were granted protection for 'their messengers, collecting alms for the maintenance of themselves and the bridge'.[36] Their success in soliciting donations is underlined by the dedication clauses of the thirteenth-century deeds. Between 1228 and c.1238, for example, Matilda and her husband Alexander Palmer confirmed a gift to the bridge in a deed that noted the gift was for 'God and the blessed Thomas the Martyr and London Bridge and the Brothers and Sisters there serving God'.[37] In 1235–36, the executors of Roger le Duc gave 21s 8d of rent from property on the bridge to the work of London Bridge and the 'brothers of the same Bridge' for the benefit of Roger's soul.[38] In 1237–8 Albin son of Alan noted that he had paid 1 mark of silver to the 'brothers and sisters' of the bridge.[39] In 1271 William Blund of Lewisham and Berta his wife confirmed land to the 'brothers and sisters of the Bridge House of London'; and brother John was recorded as giving William and Berta 13s 2d.[40] Many of the dedication clauses in the early thirteenth-century deeds emphasized the religious and charitable character of the bridge, acknowledging God, the bridge's patron saint Thomas Becket and the prominence of the bridge brothers and sisters. These dedication clauses demonstrate that members of the bridge brotherhood played an important public role by representing the organization to the Londoners.

Another focal point of the bridge organization was the bridge chapel, where Peter of Colechurch was apparently buried, for it served as a centre for both the religious life of the bridge and the administration of the endowment. When Martin, son of Robert Dun, gave 'God and the blessed Thomas the Martyr and London Bridge' a gift of 10d of rent in c.1235, the

---

[34] LMA, CLA/007/EM/02/A/046 and CLA/007/EM/02/C/033.
[35] Riley, *Munimenta Gildhallæ*, ii. 95.
[36] *CPR 1247–58*, p. 213.
[37] LMA, CLA/007/EM/02/A/006.
[38] LMA, CLA/007/EM/04/001/233/244.
[39] LMA, CLA/007/EM/02/A/026.
[40] LMA, CLA/007/EM/02/F/032.

deed specified that the rent was to be paid on the altar of the Blessed Thomas 'on London Bridge'.[41] In return for prayers in the bridge chapel, in 1244–8 John Everard released the bridge from an obligation.[42] The chapel was also used as a venue for the confirmation of agreements well into the fourteenth century.[43] At least two chaplains regularly served in the chapel: Godefrid and Simon were mentioned in 1220–1; William of Hereford and Godard in *c.*1240–56; and Godard and Richard in the mid thirteenth century.[44] In the later thirteenth century records mentioned the chaplains James of St. Magnus, Martin and William Wrethernghey, who all participated in managing the bridge's properties (Table 10.1). Throughout the thirteenth century the chapel was an important place for the administration of the bridge's endowment. Moreover, it had an important complement of staff, which included several chaplains, some of whom contributed to the administration of the endowment. Peter of Colechurch's legacy included not only the bridge and an endowment to support its maintenance, but also an organization. This organization was composed of men and women who, as chaplains or members of a brotherhood, could personify the bridge's charitable status. They lived in a communal fashion in a complex of buildings on the south bank of the Thames, in Southwark, near the bridgehead. They raised funds for the bridge but they also contributed to the administration of its endowment.

Early in the reign of Henry III the organization was augmented by a pair of laymen who formed an additional layer of authority within the bridge organization. In 1220–1 Henry of St. Albans and Robert of Winchester, 'proctors of London Bridge', and Arnald the chaplain made a grant confirmed with the 'consent' of the 'brethren'.[45] As such records suggest, the laymen did not take over from the chaplains and brothers their role in administering the endowment, but rather shared it with them.[46] This is underlined by cases in which the lay bridge officials appeared in records of exchanges not as parties but rather as witnesses. For example, in *c.*1225

---

[41] LMA, CLA/007/EM/02/B/041.

[42] LMA, CLA/007/EM/02/B/049.

[43] LMA, CLA/007/EM/02/A/029.

[44] LMA, CLA/007/EM/02/A/003; CLA/007/EM/02/A/015; and CLA/007/EM/02/F/010.

[45] LMA, CLA/007/EM/04/001/387/465.

[46] The men involved in the direction of the bridge were known by a variety of titles, including 'proctor' (*procurator*) and 'warden' (*custos*). The situation at the hospital of St. Giles was similar and Honeybourne argued that 'until 1299' the head was 'normally called "master", although "proctor", "warden", and "keeper" ... terms so far as can be judged of equivalent meaning, [were] also used' (M. B. Honeybourne, 'The Hospital of St. Giles-in-the-Fields, Holborn', in *The Victoria History of the County of Middlesex*, i. ed. J. S. Cockburn, H. P. F. King and K. G. T. McDonnell (Oxford, 1969), p. 208, n. 16).

Warin de Wadessele made a grant to 'God, the blessed Thomas the martyr, and London Bridge' and the witnesses included Serlo the Mercer, 'warden' of the bridge.[47] While his title indicates that he was present in an official capacity, Serlo's role as a witness rather than a party to the agreement suggests that he was there to offer support and oversight but had not supplanted the chaplains and brethren as sole administrator of the bridge.

More than thirty men are known to have contributed to the administration of the bridge's endowment during the thirteenth century, including members of the brotherhood, chaplains and laymen (Table 10.1). In the 1220s and 1230s perhaps the most important laymen were Henry de St. Albans, Serlo the Mercer and Michael Tovy. They always worked in partnership with other men, but their sequential terms of office and contrasting careers offer an indication of how the organization changed during their terms of office.

Henry of St. Albans's origins are obscure, but he was a member of the civic community. Henry had property in the parish of St. Martin Vintry.[48] He had a son named William and his daughter Margery married John Viel (sheriff, 1218–20).[49] Henry and Serlo served together as sheriffs of London in 1206–7 and then both pursued mercantile careers. In 1207 Henry was one of several Londoners who sold wine to the crown.[50] In subsequent years references in royal records show that he was involved in shipping and the trade in wine and wool.[51] Through this work he developed a close relationship with the crown, which led to his appointment in 1222 as keeper of the exchange of London. This was an important royal financial office, which he retained until 1226.[52] In these years he also participated in a number of transactions on behalf of the bridge and frequently appeared in witness lists of bridge deeds, where he was consistently assigned a place of precedence.[53]

[47] LMA, CLA/007/EM/02/B/011; see also LMA, CLA/007/EM/02/A/041.

[48] *Cartulary of St. Bartholomew's Hospital Founded 1123: a Calendar*, ed. N. J. M. Kerling (London, 1973), no. 843.

[49] Hardy, *Rotuli Litterarum Clausarum*, i. 517; *CPR 1225–32*, p. 133; *Curia Regis Rolls*, ed. C. T. Flower and P. Brand (19 vols., London, 1922–), xvi, no. 1790; Drucker, *Chartulary of the Hospital of St. Thomas*, nos. 161, 449.

[50] Hardy, *Rotuli Litterarum Clausarum*, i. 88.

[51] *CPR 1216–25*, pp. 466, 467; Hardy, *Rotuli Litterarum Clausarum*, i. 119, 128, 187, 189, 227.

[52] Hardy, *Rotuli Litterarum Clausarum*, i. 526; ii. 128; T. F. Tout, *Chapters in the Administrative History of Mediaeval England; the Wardrobe, the Chamber, and the Small Seals* (6 vols., Manchester, 1920–33), i. 236.

[53] LMA, CLA/007/EM/02/A/003; CLA/007/EM/02/A/023; CLA/007/EM/02/A/042; CLA/007/EM/02/B/044; CLA/007/EM/02/B/082; CLA/007/EM/02/B/093; CLA/007/EM/02/C/001; CLA/007/EM/02/C/015; CLA/007/EM/02/F/007; CLA/007/EM/04/001/203/187; CLA/007/EM/04/001/386/462; CLA/007/EM/04/001/387/465; CLA/007/EM/04/001/393/473; CLA/007/EM/04/003/17/21.

He then disappeared from the witness lists of transactions involving the bridge but he remained active in London through the 1230s.[54] Henry's career illustrates the complex affiliations of prominent Londoners in the early thirteenth century. He served as a sheriff and his daughter was married to another sheriff, but Henry pursued connections with King John and his son and successor, Henry III. As keeper of the exchange he was accountable to the crown and thus a royal officer, but he also offered financial services to the crown and can be glimpsed acting on the king's behalf in more informal capacities in other periods. How he became involved in the bridge organization is obscure, but his simultaneous service in the royal exchange and the bridge suggests that within the bridge organization he may have acted as an informal representative of the king.

Serlo the Mercer has been described as the 'archetype of the late twelfth-century mercer who made good'.[55] He is first mentioned in charters dated (through internal evidence) between c.1190 and c.1200.[56] He was then known as Serlo son of Hugh of Kent and he owned a large block of property, described in the records as his 'fee', in the parish of St. Martin Outwich, which lay in the north-east section of the city. He served with Henry of St. Albans as sheriff of London in 1206. Like Henry, Serlo was involved in mercantile activity. In 1215 King John's barons revolted and took control of London.[57] Caught in the midst of this conflict, the Londoners decided they needed new leadership and Serlo the Mercer became mayor.[58] Serving as mayor at this point involved keeping peace in the city, but it also posed financial challenges, as the Londoners had made a substantial loan to the French prince, Louis, who had attempted to oust King John, and Serlo, along with Henry of St. Albans, played a role in organizing Louis's repayment.[59] When the immediate crisis passed Serlo stepped down as mayor, but he was reappointed in 1217 and served until 1222. Matthew Paris would later describe him, albeit in connection with a crisis in 1222, as a '*vir prudens et pacificus*' [a prudent and peaceable man].[60] However, like Henry of St. Albans, there is little evidence that he served as an alderman,

---

[54] *The Cartulary of Holy Trinity Aldgate*, ed. G. A. J. Hodgett (London Rec. Soc., vii, 1971), no. 1018; *CCR 1227–31*, p. 358; Hodgett, *Cartulary of Holy Trinity Aldgate*, no. 618; Flower and Brand, *Curia Regis Rolls*, xv, nos. 788, 1807.

[55] A. F. Sutton, *The Mercery of London: Trade, Goods and People, 1130–1578* (Aldershot, 2016), pp. 11–3.

[56] *Westminster Abbey Charters, 1066–c.1214*, ed. E. Mason (London, 1988), nos. 374–6.

[57] J. C. Holt, *Magna Carta* (2nd edn., Cambridge, 1992), pp. 263, 490–1.

[58] *Chronicles of the Mayors and Sheriffs of London*, ed. H. T. Riley (London, 1863), p. 4.

[59] Chew and Weinbaum, *Eyre of 1244*, nos. 195, 316.

[60] *Matthæi Parisiensis, Monarchi Sancti Albani: Chronica Majora*, ed. H. R. Luard (Rolls Ser., lvii, 7 vols., London, 1872–83), iii. 72.

so he, too, may not have been fully integrated into the close-knit group of men who dominated local government in the city. During his second term as mayor he witnessed a substantial number of transactions involving the bridge, which suggests that he worked with Henry of St. Albans to oversee the affairs of the bridge.[61] When Serlo resigned from the mayoralty, he then took a more formal role within the bridge organization which lasted until the mid 1230s and involved offering oversight and contributing to administration.[62] Henry of St. Albans and Serlo the Mercer might seem to have had contrasting careers, as one focused on service to the crown and the other to the civic community, but their work on the bridge suggests that the bridge organization remained an area of co-operation between the city and the king.[63] However, Henry was followed by Serlo and Serlo then served with the bridge organization for many years, which suggests that it was the civic community that was more determined to influence the affairs of the bridge in the 1220s and 1230s.

After Serlo's departure, Michael Tovy assumed his role in the bridge organization.[64] Tovy's origins are difficult to establish, but he had interests in Kent which suggest ties to that region.[65] In London he was known as a goldsmith but he was also involved in the wine trade and perhaps offered financial services.[66] Tovy certainly had an exceptional career in civic politics. He served for a term as sheriff in 1240–1, not long after he acquired an aldermanry, and in 1244 he was appointed mayor.[67] Arnold son of Thedmar suggested that he was a populist and that he courted controversy by attempting to push through the re-election of Nicholas Bat to a second

[61] LMA, CLA/007/EM/02/A/003; CLA/007/EM/02/A/023; CLA/007/EM/02/A/078; CLA/007/EM/02/B/093; CLA/007/EM/02/C/001; CLA/007/EM/04/001/242/263; CLA/007/EM/04/003/35v/140.

[62] LMA, CLA/007/EM/04/001/238/253.

[63] J. A. McEwan, 'Les Londoniens fournisseurs de la cour royale au XIIIe siecle', in *Paris, Ville de Cour*, ed. B. Bove, M. Gaude-Ferragu and C. Michon (Paris, 2017), pp. 185–94, at p. 194.

[64] Michael Tovy, the mayor and bridge official, needs to be distinguished from his son, Michael Tovy 'the younger' (Weinbaum, *Eyre of 1276*, nos. 146, 296; LMA, CLC/313/L/H/001/MS25121/1436).

[65] *CPR 1247–58*, p. 4; *Calendar of Kent Feet of Fines to the End of Henry III's Reign*, ed. I. J. Churchill, R. Griffin and F. W. Hardman, Kent Archaeol. Soc., xv (Ashford, 1956), p. 260.

[66] LMA, CLC/313/L/H/001/MS25121/134; CLC/313/L/H/001/MS25121/1418; *Calendar of the Liberate Rolls Preserved in the Public Record Office* (6 vols., London, 1916–64), iv. 167 and 456.

[67] A. B. Beaven, *The Aldermen of the City of London, Temp: Henry III–1908* (2 vols., London, 1908), i. 372; J. A. McEwan, 'The aldermen of London, c.1200–80: Alfred Beaven revisited', *Trans. London and Middlesex Archaeol. Soc.*, lxii (2011), 177–203, at p. 193.

consecutive term in the office of sheriff in 1245.[68] Tovy's proposal aroused resistance from some of the aldermen, but they were unable to block his motion because of his popular support.[69] The crown intervened and not only forced the removal of Nicholas Bat from office but also insisted that Tovy be replaced as mayor. A few years later Tovy was reappointed mayor and he served two more terms, from 1247 to 1249. Throughout these years Tovy was also active within the bridge organization, where he both offered oversight and participated in administration. For example, among the records from the year 1248–9 a deed refers to a quitclaim granted to the 'master and brethren' of London Bridge which Tovy witnessed as mayor.[70] Another shows that William of Welcomestowe and Margaret his wife confirmed some land to 'London Bridge, and the brothers and proctors' and the witnesses to the exchange included Michael Tovy as mayor.[71] However, another record notes that Imbert, prior of Bermondsey, granted land to Michael Tovy, 'warden of London Bridge', for the upkeep of the bridge.[72] The mid thirteenth-century records suggest that Michael Tovy had a hand in managing the endowment, even as he continued to support and oversee the chaplains and brethren administering the bridge's assets.

The participation of Henry of St. Albans, Serlo the Mercer and Michael Tovy in the governance of the bridge testifies to the increasing role of lay Londoners within the organization. Henry of St. Albans and Serlo the Mercer, while contemporaries, chose different paths of advancement. Henry was valued by the crown for his financial and administrative abilities and was associated with the bridge while he served in a royal office. Serlo had considerable influence in the civic community, although he does not seem to have served as alderman; and he proved, through several terms as mayor, that he could work with the crown. Serlo's formal involvement in the affairs of the bridge started shortly after he left civic politics. Michael Tovy, by contrast, was probably a young man when he first appeared as a bridge official. Tovy possessed considerable civic political ambition and during his association with the bridge he scaled the rungs of the civic political ladder, serving as sheriff, alderman and mayor. That Tovy, as mayor, combined posts in both organizations might be taken as evidence that the bridge had been formally brought under the authority of the civic government, but rather it points in the opposite direction, as it is difficult to imagine Tovy submitting

---

[68] C. M. Barron, *London in the Later Middle Ages: Government and People, 1200–1500* (Oxford, 2004), pp. 311–4.

[69] Riley, *Chronicles of the Mayors and Sheriffs of London*, p. 12.

[70] LMA, CLA/007/EM/02/B/092.

[71] LMA, CLA/007/EM/04/001/143/122; see also CLA/007/EM/04/001/236/249.

[72] LMA, CLA/007/EM/04/001/236-237/250.

to an audit administered by either the crown or the civic government (see below). Tovy's career thus shows that, by the mid thirteenth century, the leading men of London were interested in directing the administration of the bridge's endowment, but it also shows they did not yet have the capacity to do this through agents, who could be appointed by the civic government and then held accountable by the government.

Before examining the events of the third quarter of the thirteenth century, it is useful to touch on the history of the leper hospital of St. Giles in the Fields, Holborn, as it helps to establish the political context in which charitable organizations in the city operated. The hospital was founded by Queen Matilda (d. 1118), wife of Henry I, but in the following years the hospital received significant new donations from Londoners that increased the endowment. Londoners were keen to ensure that the hospital was well funded, but also well administered. Like the bridge, the hospital was a twelfth-century foundation and around the time of Magna Carta, as with the bridge organization, there is evidence that leading members of London's mercantile community were becoming involved in the governance of the hospital. For example, a deed from this era noted that the proctor of the hospital, William de Cokefield, together with the 'brothers and sisters' of the hospital, acted with the 'consent' of Thomas de Haverhill and William Hardel, 'wardens' of the hospital.[73] Both 'wardens' were important and influential men in civic politics: Thomas de Haverhill was, at about this time, serving as an alderman in the civic government, and William Hardel served briefly as mayor, following Serlo the Mercer. In the mid thirteenth century a number of mayors of London participated in the oversight of the administration of the hospital's endowment.[74] However, as in the case of the bridge the participation of men who also served as mayors did not mean that the hospital had become a department of the civic government. When, in the later thirteenth century, it became politically important to define more clearly the respective spheres of authority of the king and the civic government, they fought over the selection of lay Londoners as 'wardens' of the hospital and the king prevailed.[75] In the fourteenth century the civic authorities continued to put forward their version of events, arguing that the hospital had been founded by a Londoner who provided that 'two persons of the City, elected by the mayor and aldermen, should be wardens ... to see that the issues of the said lands, tenements, and rents were properly

---

[73] Saint Bartholomew's Hospital Archives, London, HC/1/192.

[74] *Cartularium Monasterii Sancti Johannis Baptiste de Colecestria*, ed. S. A. Moore (2 vols., London, 1897), ii. 299; Kerling, *Cartulary of St. Bartholomew's Hospital*, no. 593; BL, Harley MS. 4015, fos. 118v, 136.

[75] Honeybourne, 'The hospital of St. Giles-in-the-Fields', pp. 206–10.

expended for the benefit of the said lepers'.[76] The fourteenth-century civic authorities' claims about the origins of the hospital were ill-founded, but they are important because they show that by the fourteenth century the civic government wanted to exercise oversight of the hospital through a pair of elected wardens and the king denied them this privilege. The case of the leper hospital shows that in the later thirteenth century the crown regarded oversight of charitable organization in the city as a privilege which it was not prepared to concede unquestioningly to the civic government. The dispute in the late thirteenth century between the civic authorities and the crown over the appointment of wardens for the bridge was thus not an isolated conflict but part of a broader struggle to define the scope of the civic government's authority in the city.

The dispute between the king and the civic government over the appointment of wardens of London Bridge broke out in earnest in the 1260s. Following Michael Tovy's retirement, Godard the chaplain took the leading role in administering its endowment. Godard was active in the bridge organization during Tovy's tenure of office; and when Tovy left, Godard began conducting transactions on behalf of the bridge, with oversight from lay wardens.[77] However, following the rebellion of 1263–5 the Londoners submitted to the king.[78] As part of a campaign to assert his authority over the city, Henry III handed the bridge to Queen Eleanor. The queen then placed the bridge in the custody of the hospital of St. Katherine by the Tower, whose masters she appointed.[79] The hospital of St. Katherine was instructed to hold the wardenship of the bridge and 'apply the rents, tenements and other things belonging thereto within and without the city to the repair of the bridge'.[80] In practice, the hospital ensured that the bridge was operated by men who would obey the queen, such as Thomas Chelke, the master of St. Katherine's hospital, and William son of Richard, who was a notable royalist.[81] By 1271 they had been succeeded by Stephen of Fulborn and James of St. Magnus. Stephen was Thomas's successor as master of St. Katherine's hospital, but he also held many other positions,

---

[76] *Cal. Letter Bks. G*, pp. 27–8.

[77] LMA, CLA/007/EM/02/B/027; CLA/007/EM/02/B/072; CLA/007/EM/02/F/010; CLA/007/EM/04/003/29v/94.

[78] J. A. McEwan, 'Civic government in troubled times: London *c*.1263–1270', in *Baronial Reform and Revolution in England 1258–1267*, ed. A. Jobson (Woodbridge, 2016), pp. 125–38, at p. 130.

[79] C. Jamison, *The History of the Royal Hospital of St. Katherine by the Tower* (London, 1952), pp. 17–9.

[80] *CPR 1258–66*, p. 507.

[81] McEwan, 'Civic government', pp. 134–5.

including by 1273 bishop of Waterford and by 1274 treasurer of Ireland.[82] In contrast to Stephen, James of St. Magnus's first loyalty was probably to the bridge organization.[83] As he had considerably less standing than Stephen, he may have had the day-to-day responsibility for administering the bridge. However, Margaret Howell has argued that in financial affairs Eleanor proved that she was determined to obtain as much income as possible and 'condoned ruthless exploitation of estates in her wardship'.[84] Indeed, under her direction the bridge was operated in a way which suited her rather than the Londoners.

Setting responsibility for the bridge in the hands of a hospital only cloaked the queen's authority over the bridge. When the bridge officials came to terms with the representatives of the church of St. Peter of Ghent, the deed noted that in the event of a dispute the issue would be settled in the presence of Queen Eleanor or other 'worthy men'.[85] An agreement of 1271 notes that Stephen of Fulborn acted on the 'command' of the queen.[86] The same year, James of St. Magnus 'and the masters and brothers' of the bridge acted with the consent of the queen in assigning a shop in the parish of St. Magnus the Martyr to Robert Lambyn.[87] The treatment of the chantry of Richard Cook perhaps illustrates the type of transactions that were conducted during the queen's oversight of the bridge. The will of Cook, proved in the hustings court on 2 May 1269, provided that houses in the parish of Colechurch would be transferred to the bridge to support a chantry in the bridge chapel.[88] Queen Eleanor, however, soon sold the property to the Friars of the Sack in return for 60 marks and made them responsible for the chantry in a transaction described as being conducted with the 'assent and will of the Friar Stephen of Fulborn … and the rest of the brethren' of the Bridge House.[89] The Friars of the Sack in turn transferred the properties to Robert FitzWalter, the lord of Baynard's Castle.[90] All these transactions benefited

[82] LMA, CLA/007/EM/02/F/004; J. A. Watt, 'English law and the Irish Church: the reign of Edward I', in *Medieval Studies Presented to Aubrey Gwynn, S.J.*, ed. J. A. Watt, J. B. Morrall and F. X. Martin (Dublin, 1961), pp. 133–67, at p. 143, n. 41; H. G. Richardson and G. O. Sayles, *The Administration of Ireland, 1172–1377* (Dublin, 1964), p. 81.

[83] LMA, CLA/007/EM/02/F/016.

[84] M. Howell, *Eleanor of Provence: Queenship in Thirteenth-Century England* (Oxford, 1998), pp. 274–5.

[85] LMA, CLA/007/EM/02/A/061.

[86] LMA, CLA/007/EM/02/C/014.

[87] LMA, CLA/007/EM/02/F/045.

[88] LMA, LMA, CLA/023/DW/01/004 (3).

[89] *Cal. Letter Bks. C*, pp. 61–2.

[90] C. Starr, 'Fitzwalter family (per. c.1200–c.1500), nobility', in *ODNB* <https://doi.org/10.1093/ref:odnb/54522> [accessed 2 Feb. 2019].

the participants at the expense of the long-term interests of the bridge by diminishing the resources supporting Richard Cook's chantry.[91] Had the queen, through her agents, ensured that the bridge was well maintained, then perhaps the Londoners would have tolerated her administration. Instead, the bridge's fabric was neglected, which generated discontent.

Arnold son of Thedmar captured the tenor of public opinion when he remarked in his chronicle that the officials appointed by the queen 'collected all issues of the rents and lands of the said bridge, converting the same to I know not what uses, but expending nothing whatever upon the repairs of the said bridge'.[92] In 1274–5 the crown gave local juries the means to comment on local government and they complained about how the bridge was managed.[93] Maintenance work was not being carried out, leaving the structure in an increasingly precarious state. If a section of the bridge had collapsed, it would have had to be reconstructed, which would not only have been expensive and inconvenient for the Londoners but would have broken a key link in the transport network and disrupted the economy of the entire region. The queen, through her appointees, had exploited the bridge's endowment for almost a decade, but by 1275 the crown probably judged that it was financially risky and politically costly to continue. An entry in the husting rolls recorded that in May 1275 the king 'restored the bridge' to the city 'at the instance and by the diligent persistence of mayor Gregory of Rokesle'.[94] However, the king did not hand control over the bridge back to the bridge brothers and the chaplains but rather to the civic government, which was determined that for the foreseeable future it would directly administer the bridge's endowment.

The civic government used the opportunity offered by the 'restoration' to assert its own authority over the bridge. Perhaps this was partly motivated by a desire to make it more difficult for the king to interfere in the affairs

---

[91] After the queen returned control of the bridge to the Londoners, the bridge officials struggled to secure the return of the houses in Colechurch. In 1302–3 Robert FitzWalter agreed to return the property provided he was released from the obligation of securing a chaplain to celebrate mass on behalf of Richard Cook (LMA, CLA/007/EM/04/001/413/497; CLA/007/EM/02/C/037).

[92] Riley, *Chronicles of the Mayors and Sheriffs*, p. 147.

[93] *Rotuli Hundredorum Temp. Hen. III. et Edw. I.*, ed. W. Illingworth (2 vols., London, 1812–8), i: (Aldersgate), pp. 414, 429; (Aldgate), pp. 420, 426; (Bassingshaw), p. 403; (Bread Street), p. 428; (Broad Street), p. 410; (Candlewick), pp. 420–1, 430; (Cheap), p. 406; (Colemanstreet), p. 412; (Cornhill) pp. 408, 427; (Dowgate), p. 422; (Queenhithe), p. 419; (Tower), pp. 405, 427. As some of the ward returns have been lost, the opinions of all the ward juries are not fully represented in the records and discontent may have been even more widespread.

[94] LMA, CLA/023/CP/01/003, m.5.

of the bridge in the future, but it also helped to restore the reputation of the bridge organization in the eyes of the civic community. People wanted to know the bridge would be well-administered, but they also wanted a say in the process, so the civic government organized an election, involving representatives from the wards, to appoint bridge wardens accountable to the civic government. Gregory of Rokesle himself, who was then serving as mayor, together with the alderman of Langbourn ward, Nicholas of Winchester, were the first bridge wardens following the 'restoration' (Table 10.1). However, at the end of their term of office the king asked them to submit to an audit. Gregory argued that if he submitted to an audit, even if it was only with regard to his actions as a bridge official, it risked undermining his authority as mayor.[95] Gregory and Nicholas were then succeeded by men who did not already hold important civic offices. The decline in the standing of the bridge wardens may have been partly due to the threat of audits, which discouraged the city's leading men from serving in the office, but it is also important to note that between 1285 and 1298 the governance of the city was directed not by its own mayor, but rather by a royal warden appointed by the king.[96] Consequently, towards the end of the century the bridge was dependent on the civic government, but the civic government was directed by a royal appointee. These appointees were, perhaps, not interested in allowing men who already held important posts in the civic government to accumulate further power. Nonetheless, following the restoration of the bridge the civic government gained more authority over the bridge, even if the civic government itself remained vulnerable to royal interference.

Although the civic government changed how the bridge organization was directed and handled funds, it also worked, with some encouragement from the crown, to restore the bridge's finances. The civic government found the bridge new sources of revenue. In February 1282 the crown granted Rokesle, as the mayor of London, permission 'to associate with himself two or three discreet and lawful citizens of London' and collect tolls at the bridge for its repair 'until the next Parliament after Easter'.[97] In July 1282 the grant was renewed for a further three years.[98] By 1282 surviving enrolments of debts preserved in the city's records indicate that the civic authorities were

---

[95] *CPR 1281–1292*, p. 10; J. A. McEwan, 'The politics of financial accountability: auditing the chamberlain in London c.1298–1349', in *Hiérarchie des pouvoirs: délégation de pouvoir et responsabilité des administrateurs dans l'Antiquité et au Moyen Âge*, ed. A. Bérenger and F. Lachaud (Metz, 2012), pp. 253–69, at p. 259, n. 27.

[96] McEwan, 'Politics of financial accountability', p. 257.

[97] *CPR 1281–1292*, p. 10.

[98] *CPR 1281–1292*, p. 30.

encouraging the parties to these agreements to direct penalties payable for breaches of contract to the bridge.[99] A more significant addition to the revenue of the bridge were the proceeds from the operation of the stocks market.[100] The market had only recently been created as part of an attempt to reorganize trading in the city and it was intended to provide a covered location for the buying and selling of fish. During the mayoralty of Henry le Waleys the civic authorities decided that the substantial rents paid by the fishmongers for the use of the market should be devoted to the bridge.[101] All these sources of revenue were important, but the financial foundations of the organization remained the endowment and charitable donations, which the chaplains and brethren continued to collect. In January 1281 the crown granted its protection to 'the keepers of London Bridge, or their messengers', who were 'collecting alms throughout the realm for the repair of the bridge which has fallen into a ruinous state'.[102] In 1297 William son of Henry Boydin gave 'London Bridge and the brothers of that place and their successors' one penny of rent 'in perpetual alms'.[103] Studies of donations recorded in the husting wills suggest that a high-water mark of the popularity of the bridge as a recipient of donations was reached in the early fourteenth century. Harry Miskimin found that in the first decade of the century almost eighty per cent of wills enrolled in the husting court offered donations to the bridge.[104] Nonetheless, the bridge was now firmly under the oversight of the civic government. References to agreements reached between grantors and a bridge chaplain at the 'instance' of the bridge wardens imply that real authority in the organization now rested firmly in the hands of the civic government's representatives. John son of John Jukel, for example, confirmed land to Martin the chaplain and the brethren of the bridge at the 'instance' of Thomas Cros and Edmund Horn, wardens of the bridge.[105] In 1287 William, son of William le Hwyte of Lewisham, at the 'instance' of the bridge wardens, likewise transferred a rent to Martin the chaplain.[106] Although the nature of the bridge organization may have been clear to Londoners, to outsiders it still seemed to be a charitable enterprise. In 1295 the abbot of St. John's Colchester was collecting a tax on the Church

---

[99] *Cal. Letter Bks. A*, pp. 51–3, 56.

[100] Watson, *London Bridge*, p. 123.

[101] LMA, CLA/007/EM/02/F/049.

[102] *CPR 1281–1292*, p. 422.

[103] LMA, CLA/007/EM/02/F/059.

[104] H. A. Miskimin, 'The legacies of London: 1259–1330', in *The Medieval City: Essays in Honor of Robert S. Lopez*, ed. H. Miskimin, D. Herlihy and A. L. Ludovitch (New Haven, Conn., 1978), pp. 209–27, at pp. 222–3.

[105] LMA, CLA/007/EM/02/B/010.

[106] LMA, CLA/007/EM/02/B/042.

granted in aid of the Holy Land and he asserted that London Bridge should contribute.[107] However, the bridge wardens successfully argued that it should not contribute on the grounds that they were laymen. By 1295 the bridge organization still had features of a charitable trust but its finances were firmly under the control of laymen appointed by the civic government.

Peter of Colechurch's legacy included both the bridge itself and an organization devoted to its maintenance, and change in that organization during the thirteenth century can be traced through its leadership. In the early years of the thirteenth century, lay participation in the governance of the bridge proved compatible with the bridge's charitable mission and its independent status. Leading Londoners such as Henry of St. Albans, Serlo the Mercer and Michael Tovy offered oversight and advice, but they also had a hand in managing the endowment. However, these men were not appointed by the civic government, which at this point in its history was itself still in the process of consolidating its own position as the principal civic political institution. Then the bridge, because of its importance to the civic community and its valuable endowment, was, in the mid thirteenth century, dragged into the struggle between the crown and civic government for authority in London. In 1265 the crown took control of the bridge, but it proved unable to operate the bridge in the long term, so in 1275 it gave the bridge to the city, which then incorporated it into the framework of the civic government. Remarkably, the assertion of civic control over the bridge did not erase its charitable status. What had been two distinct organizations with contrasting approaches to organizing the people of London towards common goals were brought together. As its relationship with London Bridge demonstrates, by the end of the thirteenth century the city of London, as an institution of government, had grown dramatically in power, influence and complexity. Londoners became willing to permit the civic government to take responsibility not only for such things as operating courts, organizing the watch and collecting taxes, which were its traditional roles, but also for overseeing the administration of an endowment that provided the Londoners with an amenity that improved their lives and remembered past benefactors.

---

[107] LMA, CLA/007/EM/02/C/028, CLA/007/EM/04/001/413–14/498; see also H. S. Deighton, 'Clerical taxation by consent, 1279–1301', *Eng. Hist. Rev.*, lxviii (1953), 161–92, at pp. 171–5.

Table 10.1. Men involved in the administration of London Bridge, *c.*1176–1300

Name	Date	First datable reference	Last datable reference
Peter of Colechurch	1176–1205	M. Brett, 'The Annals of Bermondsey, Southwark and Merton', in *Church and City 1000–1500: Essays in Honour of Christopher Brooke*, ed. D. Abulafia, M. Franklin and M. Rubin (Cambridge, 1992), p. 302	M. Brett, 'The Annals of Bermondsey, Southwark and Merton', p. 305
Brother Wace	1205	*Rotuli Litterarum Clausarum in Turri Londinensi Asservati*, ed. T. D. Hardy (2 vols., London, 1833–44), i. 49; *Rotuli Litterarum Patentium in Turri Londinensi Asservati: Anno 1201 ad Anno 1216*, ed. T. D. Hardy (London, 1835), p. 58	n/a
Martin	1213	LMA, CLA/007/EM/04/001/160/141	n/a
Geoffrey	1213	LMA, CLA/007/EM/04/001/160/141	n/a
Robert of Winchester	1220–1	LMA, CLA/007/EM/02/A/003	n/a
Henry of St. Albans	1220–1 to 1222–7	LMA, CLA/007/EM/02/A/003	LMA, CLA/007/EM/04/003/17–17v/21
William Aleman	1222–7 to 1236–7	LMA, CLA/007/EM/04/003/17/21	LMA, CLA/007/EM/04/003/22v–23/48
Arnald the Chaplain	*c.*1220–1	LMA, CLA/007/EM/04/001/387/465	n/a

Name	Date	First datable reference	Last datable reference
Roger le Duc	1222–5	LMA, CLA/007/ EM/02/B/011	n/a
Serlo the Mercer	1222–5 to 1237/8	LMA, CLA/007/ EM/02/B/011	LMA, CLA/007/ EM/02/A/73
Benedict the Shipwright	1232	*CPR 1225–1232*, p. 501	n/a
John Bulloc	1232	*CPR 1225–1232*, p. 501	n/a
Robert the Chaplain	1237–8	LMA, CLA/007/ EM/02/A/73	n/a
Michael Tovy	1240–55/6	LMA, CLA/007/ EM/02/B/064	LMA, CLA/007/ EM/02/B/039
Robert of Basing	1249–51	LMA, CLA/007/ EM/02/F/046	LMA, CLA/007/ EM/02/F/006
Stephen of Ostergate	1255–6	LMA, CLA/007/ EM/02/A/039	n/a
Godard the Chaplain	1258/61– 1263/4	LMA, CLA/007/ EM/04/001/593/607	LMA, CLA/007/ EM/02/A/022
Robert of Cornhill	1263–4	LMA, CLA/007/ EM/02/A/022	n/a
Thomas Chelke	1269–71	LMA, CLA/007/ EM/02/F/002	n/a
William son of Richard	1269–71	LMA, CLA/007/ EM/02/A/061	n/a
Brother John	1271	LMA, CLA/007/ EM/02/F/032	n/a
Stephen of Fulborn	1271–74/5	LMA, CLA/007/ EM/02/C/014	LMA, CLA/007/ EM/02/F/004
James of St. Magnus	1271–3	LMA, CLA/007/ EM/02/F/045	LMA, CLA/007/ EM/04/001/ 408 /489
Gregory de Rokesle	1275–80	LMA, CLA/023/ CP/01/003, m.5	LMA, CLA/007/ EM/02/G/028
Nicholas of Winchester	1275–80	LMA, CLA/023/ CP/01/003, m.5	LMA, CLA/007/ EM/02/G/028
John the clerk	1280–1297/8	LMA, CLA/007/ EM/02/G/028	LMA, CLA/007/ EM/02/A/046

Name	Date	First datable reference	Last datable reference
Martin the chaplain	1280–87	LMA, CLA/007/EM/02/G/028	CLA/007/EM/02/B/042
Richard Knotte	1283–4	LMA, CLA/007/EM/02/F/042 and CLA/007/EM/02/F/003	n/a
Thomas Cros	1283/4–1294/5	LMA, CLA/007/EM/02/F/042 and CLA/007/EM/02/F/003	LMA, CLA/007/EM/04/001/391/470
Edmund Horn	1287–1294/5	LMA, CLA/007/EM/02/B/042	LMA, CLA/007/EM/04/001/391/470
William Wrethernghey	1298	*Munimenta Gildhallæ Londoniensis*, ii. 94–5	
William Jordan	1298	*Munimenta Gildhallæ Londoniensis*, ii. 94–5	
John le Bernere	1298	*Munimenta Gildhallæ Londoniensis*, ii. 94–5	
Thomas Romeyn	1298	*Munimenta Gildhallæ Londoniensis*, ii. 94–5	

11. John Reynewell and St. Botolph Billingsgate*

Stephen Freeth and John Schofield

Introduction: a notable medieval burial

Caroline Barron has always been interested in the aldermen and mayors of the city of London, as witnessed by her work on Richard Whittington.[1] This chapter presents some recent discoveries about a mayor of the generation just after Whittington: John Reynewell (Reynwell, Raynewell and other variant spellings), mayor in 1426–7. We study a burial in the parish church of St. Botolph Billingsgate in Thames Street, for which the combined archaeological and documentary evidence suggests it was Reynewell. The interior of the church also now begins to come to light, joining other London parish churches which can be reconstructed by archaeological and documentary evidence, another of the honorand's interests.[2]

In 1982 the Museum of London excavated a large site next to Billingsgate market in Lower Thames Street in the city of London; this included part of the parish church of St. Botolph Billingsgate (Figure 11.1), destroyed in the Great Fire of 1666. Sixty-six skeletons were recorded in the portion of the church which fell inside the archaeological excavation. Of these, six seem to be of the fifteenth century and the rest of the first half of the seventeenth century. A double brick grave in a fifteenth-century extension of the church

* This chapter draws on material in the publication of the Billingsgate excavation: J. Schofield, L. Blackmore and J. Pearce, with T. Dyson, *London's Waterfront 1100–1666: Excavations in Thames Street, London, 1974–84* (Oxford, 2018). We are very grateful to the editors of the present volume for comments on the drafts of this paper.

[1] C. M. Barron, 'Richard Whittington: the man behind the myth', in *Studies in London History Presented to Philip Edmund Jones*, ed. A. E. J. Hollaender and W. Kellaway (London, 1969), pp. 197–248.

[2] E.g., in the vicinity of St. Botolph's, St. Andrew Hubbard (*The Church Records of St. Andrew Hubbard Eastcheap c.1450–c.1570*, ed. C. Burgess (London Rec. Soc., xxxiv, 1999)) and St. Mary at Hill (*The Medieval Records of a London City Church (St. Mary at Hill) A.D. 1420–1559*, ed. H. Littlehales (Early English Text Soc., o.s., cxxv and cxxviii, 1904–5)). For an archaeological and documentary survey of 61 of the London churches, see J. Schofield, 'Saxon and medieval parish churches in the City of London: a review', *Trans. London and Middlesex Archaeol. Soc.*, xlv (1994), 23–145.

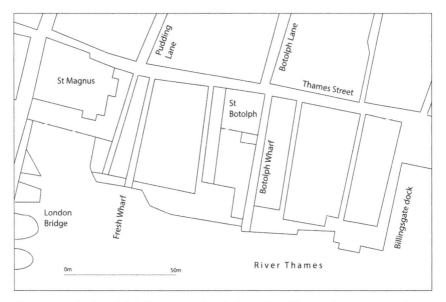

Figure 11.1. St. Botolph Billingsgate church (centre) in Thames Street in 1520, from the British Historic Towns Atlas volume for London (1989) (drawn by J. Schofield). The small projection at the south-east corner is the vestry added in the 1450s.

building to the south contained two skeletons. They are known by the numbers given to them by the excavators. Skeleton [783] was of a man in his sixties (Figure 11.2). He lay above a female skeleton [937] which had an estimated age of 36–45 years.

Osteological analysis has been undertaken by Jelena Bekvalac of the Museum of London.[3] Skeleton [783] had several pathological conditions: first, he had a possible well-healed fracture in his left fibula. Second, in his thoracic vertebrae there was evidence of Diffuse Idiopathic Skeletal Hyperostosis (DISH), which causes fusion of the vertebrae. DISH is linked to a high-protein diet and a well-off lifestyle, especially in older men; it is found in skeletons from the Roman period onwards. Third, his right hand showed evidence of osteoarthritis, which was also found in his cervical (neck) vertebrae. Small impressions on the bone within one of his eye sockets suggested *cribra orbitalia*, which has been proposed to be an indicator of iron-deficiency anaemia. Many of his teeth had been lost with the socket spaces remodelled, indicating they had been lost long before he died. The few teeth remaining had mineralized plaque (calculus), decay (caries) and

---

[3] J. Bekvalac, 'Analysis of the human skeletal remains from St. Botolph Billingsgate', in Schofield et al., *London's Waterfront*, pp. 386–407.

Figure 11.2. Double brick tomb in St. Botolph's containing a man and a woman (beneath his skeleton) (Museum of London Archaeology; scale 0.5m).

periodontal disease. Whoever he was, he was suffering the aches of old age. The skeletal remains of the younger woman [937] did not reveal any observable pathological changes, but a number of her teeth were affected by decay (caries) and mineralized plaque (calculus).

This man may be John Reynewell (d. 1445) himself, in the lower brick part of a grave or tomb within the church extension which he had sponsored. The brick part would have been below floor level. The substantial substructure implies a stone monument above, with either a brass or a pair of effigies on it, but no evidence has survived (a brass is probably more likely). The monument would have faced an altar in the east wall and a window above, but no evidence of either remains. The identity of the woman remains a mystery (as does their double occupancy of half the brick grave, with the other half being empty, which is probably the result of the removal of a lead coffin). Reynewell had a daughter, Frideswida, but she became a nun at the Minories, so was presumably buried there. The woman buried at St. Botolph's may be Reynewell's wife, whose name is unknown.

But other candidates for the identity of the skeleton should also be considered. Here analysis is limited by the excavation being only of the south part of the church. The double brick grave was the only trace of a substantial monument found. John Stow described how the church 'hath had many fayre monuments therein, now defaced and gone … al destroyed by bad and greedy men of spoyle'; he had found records of burials here of a dozen worthy citizens, though he does not mention tombs (naturally, in the circumstances). Besides the Reynewell(s), restricting the possibilities to the fifteenth century, Stow mentioned the burials of Nicholas James, sheriff (d. 1423); William Reynewell, John's father (d. 1404); Stephen Forster, mayor 1454 (d. 1458) and the rebuilder of Ludgate, and his wife Agnes; and William Bacon, sheriff in 1480.[4] One of these, Stephen Forster, might seem appropriate because his wife Agnes, according to Stow, was buried with him. But here Stow was in error. Agnes Forster, in her will of 1484, desired to be buried in St. Stephen Walbrook.[5] Her burial there is noted in the will of her eldest son John, who died in 1488; he wished to be buried near her.[6] Nor is this likely to be the burial of Reynewell's own father, William, and his wife

---

[4] *A Survey of London by John Stow*, ed. C. L. Kingsford (2 vols., Oxford, 1908), i. 207–8. All have short biographies in S. Thrupp, *The Merchant Class of Medieval London* (Ann Arbor, Mich., 1948), pp. 322–64.

[5] TNA, PROB 11/7, fos. 65–6.

[6] TNA, PROB 11/12, fos. 157v–158. John Forster's will is dated 31 May 1488 and he is likely to have died soon after. However, it was not proved until 4 March 1500/1. The note of probate explains that the executors had refused to act. We are grateful to Jane Williams for this information.

Isabel. The burial is clearly within the church extension, which is dated by the documents and stratigraphy to the first half or middle of the fifteenth century, and William Reynewell died in 1404. William Bacon, haberdasher (d. 1492), might be a candidate, but then we would have to explain why he is occupying a place of distinction in the middle of the aisle floor.

St. Botolph Billingsgate church in the middle ages

The south part of the site of St. Botolph's occupied the north-west corner of the excavation of 1982, in the open space west of the Billingsgate fish market building of 1875, between Lower Thames Street and the River Thames. From a combination of the excavation findings and documentary evidence (wills, churchwardens' accounts and vestry minutes from the fourteenth to seventeenth centuries), a proposed development plan of the church is given (Figure 11.3). The documentary history provides the stages of growth. The church is first mentioned around 1140, but most of the twelfth-century building lay outside the excavation, beneath the pavement of present Lower Thames Street. St. Botolph's expanded to the south in the middle of the fifteenth century through a grant to the parish by John Reynewell, mayor 1426–7, administered through his trustees by 1456 at the latest. Reynewell's gift was an existing stone building a few metres to the south, which was then incorporated into the body of the church, the space between becoming a new aisle. This, originally separate, building stood on a vault, which was subsequently let out by the parish as part of the storage facilities on Botolph Wharf, certainly from the final years of the sixteenth century and possibly before.

Most of the new aisle was within the excavation and it contained fragments of a tiled floor; a double brick grave of the mid fifteenth century was located centrally towards the east end of the space. The east wall was of flint and chalk chequerwork (Figure 11.4). It had later been covered with plaster (hence keying marks on the chalk blocks), perhaps before the Reformation. Various pieces of window tracery and other carved stone discovered during the excavation in 1982 (numbering over 600) are currently in store and may be analysed in the future. One further decorative element, recovered during the widespread clearance for construction in 1984, is a stone corbel in the form of an angel bearing a shield (Figures 11.5(a) and 11.5(b)). This is now in Welby near Grantham, Lincolnshire. The carving is of exceptional quality. The corbel dates from the fifteenth century, perhaps c.1450–75 from the treatment of the angel's hair. The angel is dressed in an alb and the shield appears to show a merchant's mark, denoting the donor. The mark is similar to fifteenth-century merchants' marks on brasses in Dunstable (Bedfordshire), Cirencester (Gloucestershire) and Chipping Norton

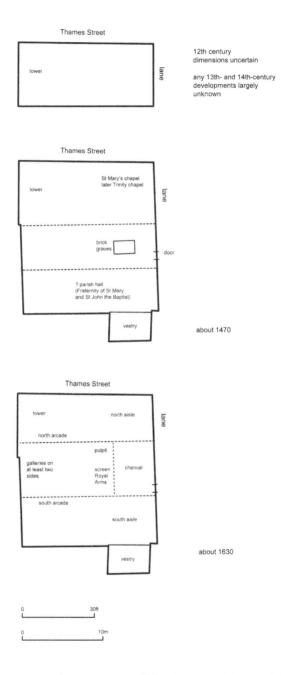

Figure 11.3. The main stages of development of St. Botolph Billingsgate church (drawn by J. Schofield).

Figure 11.4. The chequerwork internal facing of the east wall of the new aisle, looking east, as excavated in 1982 (Museum of London Archaeology; scale 1m).

(Oxfordshire);[7] if it does incorporate the letter 'R', as suggested, this might indicate Reynewell. As the corbel was recovered from a landfill site in Essex to which earth from the Billingsgate site was being trucked (this was in 1983–4; protective legislation for such things would follow in 1990), we can only say it came from the Thames waterfront near St. Botolph's.

In his panorama of about 1540, Wyngaerde shows the church with two separately roofed aisles, with a prominent tower at the west end of the northern one (Figure 11.6). The southern of the two roofs must therefore have been above the extension. The precise way Reynewell's originally separate building was incorporated into the church is not known and there are no clear documentary references to its use. The vaulted undercroft forming its lower storey was always a separate feature, entered only from the lane. The floor above, the main floor of the building, did not survive to be recorded. There was probably some form of access from the church. Though there is no direct evidence, we propose on the basis of its much higher floor level (about 3 ft. 3 in. above the adjacent aisle) that the main room of this now-incorporated stone building became some kind of

[7] F. A. Girling, *English Merchants' Marks: a Field Survey of Marks Made by Merchants and Tradesmen in England between 1400 and 1700* (Oxford, 1964), pp. 40–1.

Figure 11.5(a). Angel corbel recovered from a landfill site in Essex in 1984 (photograph © G. de la Bédoyère).

Figure 11.5(b). Close-up of the merchant's mark on it and one suggestion about its form (photograph © G. de la Bédoyère; suggested mark, S. Freeth and J. Schofield).

parish space, a long hall (or succession of rooms) equivalent in area to the undercroft beneath. There is no information on whether the building had, or then acquired, further rooms above. The parish had a fraternity which obtained a royal licence in 1371.[8] The only London analogy for which there is graphic evidence is the hall of the Fraternity of the Trinity at St. Botolph Aldersgate, established by 1389, possibly in 1377.[9] This was a first-floor hall in a timber-framed range which belonged to the fraternity, a short distance from the church in Aldersgate; its site is now covered by the roundabout at the junction of Aldersgate and London Wall highways.[10] It is similar in size. Overall, however, even with this increase, St. Botolph remained a small church in comparison with others in the immediate neighbourhood, such as St. Michael Crooked Lane, St. Magnus and All Hallows the Great.[11]

We can reconstruct many aspects of the interior of the church, and some of its building history, from the late fourteenth century to 1666. We arrange these as a short tour of the interior, but not dealing with the post-Reformation changes, which are described in the recently published account.[12] In the chancel there was an image of Our Lady on the south side of the high altar (John Park, 1413)[13] and an image of St. Botolph on the north side (Thomas de Snowdylonde, 1361;[14] Richard Segrym,

---

[8] This was the Fraternity of St. Mary, founded in 1361 in St. Mary's chapel by the will of Thomas de Snowdylonde, the rector. Both will and royal licence were copied into the St. Botolph's parish cartulary (LMA, P69/BOT3/D/001/MS00059, fos. 15v–16 and 13v–14). See also C. M. Barron, 'The parish fraternities of medieval London' [1985], repr. in *Medieval London: Collected Papers of Caroline M Barron*, ed. M. Carlin and J. T. Rosenthal (Kalamazoo, Mich., 2017), pp. 135–63, at p. 142.

[9] *Parish Fraternity Register: Fraternity of the Holy Trinity and SS. Fabian and Sebastian in the Parish of St. Botolph without Aldersgate*, ed. P. Basing (London Rec. Soc., xviii, 1982), pp. xvii–xix.

[10] *The London Surveys of Ralph Treswell*, ed. J. Schofield (London Topographical Soc., cxxxv, London, 1987), pp. 36–7. Internal views of the hall with the redrawn Treswell plan are in J. Schofield, *Medieval London Houses* (rev. edn., London, 2003), figs. 118a–b, 129, 188.

[11] Plans of these and other churches in 1667 are given by J. Leake in his 'Exact Survey' of the city (BL, Additional MS. 5415.1.E); the plans of St. Botolph and 6 nearby churches are redrawn in Schofield et al., *London's Waterfront*, fig. 235.

[12] Pre-Reformation, our chief sources are over 100 wills of parishioners dating between 1313 and 1558. For a detailed list, see S. Freeth, 'Wills mentioning the fabric, ornaments, fraternities, chantries or earlier burials in the church or cemetery of St. Botolph Billingsgate to 1558', in Schofield et al., *London's Waterfront*, pp. 407–13. For the post-Reformation changes see Schofield et al., *London's Waterfront*, pp. 235–51.

[13] LMA, DL/AL/C/002/MS09051/001, fo. 283v.

[14] The will was copied into the St. Botolph's parish cartulary (LMA, P69/BOT3/D/001/MS00059, fos. 15v–16). It was also proved in the hustings court (LMA, CLA/023/DW/01/088 (84), calendared in *Calendar of Wills Proved and Enrolled in the Court of Husting, London, A.D. 1258–A.D. 1688*, ed. R. R. Sharpe (2 vols., London, 1888–9), ii. *A.D. 1358–A.D. 1688*, p. 22, where the image of St. Botolph is wrongly stated to be on the south side of the high altar).

Figure 11.6. The waterfront immediately downstream of London Bridge
*c.*1540, by Anthonis van Wyngaerde (Ashmolean Museum; detail from
WA1950.206.7, © Ashmolean Museum, University of Oxford). On the
right the church of St. Botolph is named and given prominence.

1495).[15] The chancel appears generally to have been reserved for clergy burials,
as was often the case. Snowdylonde was the rector; Segrym was a chaplain
or curate.[16] William Symmes, 1439, left 10 marks 'to paint the Sepulchre
ordained by him' (*ad pictand' sepulcrum eiusdem ecclesie sancti Both'i per me
nuper ordinat' & non in alio usu, x marc*).[17] Such Easter sepulchres, for the
host and crucifix between Good Friday and Easter morning, were frequently
made of wood but here might have been of stone.[18]

There was a canopy over the high altar. The maintenance instructions
for the canopy are written into the parish cartulary, where it is stated

---

[15] LMA, DL/C/B/004/MS09171/008, fos. 85v–86.

[16] The only known request for lay burial in the chancel was by Thomas Marmeon esquire
'of Thurlbe' (Thirlby, Lincolnshire) (1517). One of the witnesses to his will was Edward
Marmyon, a chaplain or curate of St. Botolph's, whose own will (leaving no instructions
about his burial) was proved in the prerogative court of Canterbury in 1541 (TNA, PROB
11/28, fos. 243r–v).

[17] TNA, PROB 11/3, fos. 199v–200, at fo. 200.

[18] E. Duffy, *The Stripping of the Altars: Traditional Religion in England c.1400–c.1580* (2nd
edn., London, 2005), pp. 29–37.

to have been given by William Laurence in 1472.[19] Richard Rawlyn had left 40s for a canopy for the high altar in 1471; perhaps this was merely a contribution.[20] As for more portable items, John Witteneye, chaplain, 1406, bequeathed his best vestment of blue embroidered silk, his best silver chalice, a missal and portable breviary and a book of divinity (*vestimentum suum optimum de serico blodio & brouderizato et suam optimam calicem argenti unum missale & unum portiphorium ac unum librum divinitatis ibidem in dei servicio imperpetuum permansur'*).[21] Richard Awbrey, 1474, left 40s towards a suit of vestments.[22] Richard Johnson, priest, 1487, left a 'processionary' (that is, a processional, a book containing litanies, hymns etc. to be used in religious processions).[23] Nicholas Alday, 1518, left money for two copes of red damask to be made, 'with Tonnes and Burres' [barrels and flowers?] like the suit of copes at St. Clement's Sandwich.[24]

In the nave William Reynewell, 1404, father of John Reynewell, left 6s 8d 'to the light of the Holy Cross on the High Beam' (*lumini sancte Crucis super altam trabem*).[25] John Colyn, 1405, left 3s 4d 'to maintain the light on the beam' (*ad sustentacionem luminis trabe in dicta ecclesia*).[26] Geoffrey Maughfeld, 1407, left a candle weighing 20 lbs 'for the light on the high beam' (*lumini super altam trabem in predicta ecclesia sancti Botulphi*).[27] Roger Wade, 1408, left four candles 'to maintain the light on the beam before the Cross' (*ad sustentacionem luminis trab' coram cruce*).[28] Nicholas James, 1434, asked to be buried where his children lay, before the *pulpitum* [chancel step].[29] Richard Rawlyn, 1471, already mentioned, asked to be buried in the nave of the church, before the crucifix.[30] William Bullee, 1518, asked to be buried 'afore the Rood in the body of the church'.[31] Henry Rigby, 1521, asked to be buried 'within the midst of the church', that is, in the nave aisle.[32]

---

[19] LMA, P69/BOT3/D/001/MS00059, fo. 46v.

[20] TNA, PROB 11/6, fos. 28–29, at fo. 28v.

[21] LMA, DL/AL/C/002/MS09051/001, fo. 159v.

[22] TNA, PROB 11/6, fos. 130v–131v, at fo. 130v.

[23] LMA, DL/C/B/004/MS09171/007, fo. 66v.

[24] TNA, PROB 11/19, fos. 78v–79.

[25] TNA, PROB 11/2A, fos. 36–37v, at fo. 36.

[26] LMA, DL/C/B/004/MS09171/002, fo. 71.

[27] LMA, DL/C/B/004/MS09171/002, fos. 104–5, at fo. 104v.

[28] LMA, DL/C/B/004/MS09171/002, fo. 125.

[29] TNA, PROB 11/3, fos. 138v–141, at fo. 139. We are grateful to Christopher Wilson for explaining this term.

[30] TNA, PROB 11/6, fos. 28–9, at fo. 28.

[31] TNA, PROB 11/19, fo. 42.

[32] LMA, DL/C/B/004/MS09171/009, fo. 179v.

It is possible that the church had a tower at the west end from the beginning. References from the fifteenth century imply a tower. John Knotte, 1448, asked to be buried *infra porticum*, where his wife lay; presumably within the entrance lobby of the church, probably under the tower (there was no projecting porch). He also left 20s to paint and make a new door for the church in the best manner possible (*versus picturam & fabricacionem ostii dicte ecclesie sancti Botulphi, ita quod conetur meliori modo quo poterit*).[33] Thomas Crofton, 1439, requested ringing of bells at his funeral;[34] the same John Knotte, 1448, as above, asked that bells not be rung. Both imply that the '4 great bells' listed in the inventory of church goods of 1552, or some of them, were already installed in the tower. Thomas Langeforde, 1517, asked to be buried at the church door, 'under the holy water stock'. Again, this was probably under the tower.[35]

The most prominent chapel, as in many parish churches, was dedicated to the Virgin. Oliver de Kent, 1323, left an annual quitrent of 40d for a perpetual light in honour of Our Lady and All Saints.[36] Thomas de Snowdylonde, the rector, 1361, already mentioned, left 60s to the fabric of St. Mary's chapel, together with a missal, a consecrated chalice, a white vestment, a *Legenda Sanctorum* and a cup 'neither gilt nor consecrated' (*fabric' capelle beate marie eiusdem ecclesie sancti Botulphi lxs. unum missale unum calicem consecratum unum vestimentum album consecratum unam legendam sanctorum et unum calicem non deoratum nec consecratum*).[37] He also established a perpetual chantry there, for his own soul and for the welfare of the Fraternity of St. Mary in the same chapel. However, he asked to be buried on the north side of the high altar. This may suggest that St. Mary's chapel was at this early date on the north side of the church, perhaps against the northern buttress of the chancel arch. (The extension of the church building to the south was still far in the future.) Andrew Pykeman, 1391, also set up a perpetual chantry in St. Mary's chapel. His will mentions a *candelabrum* for feast days.[38] Geoffrey Maughfeld, 1407, already mentioned, left a second candle weighing 20 lbs 'to the light of the Fraternity of the Blessed Virgin Mary'

[33] LMA, DL/C/B/004/MS09171/004, fo. 227. Knotte described himself as 'citizen and tailor'. His bequests included 100s to the Tailors and £4 to persuade a fellow tailor, Thomas Davy, to act as his executor. No doubt these are the same individuals that were masters of the Tailors in 1427 (Knotte) and 1436 (Davy).

[34] LMA, CLC/L/VA/G/001A/MS15364, Vintners' Company Wills Book, fo. 32.

[35] TNA, PROB 11/18, fo. 219.

[36] LMA, CLA/023/DW/01/051 (108).

[37] LMA, CLA/023/DW/01/088 (84) and in the St. Botolph's parish cartulary (LMA, P69/BOT3/D/001/MS00059, fos. 15v–16).

[38] LMA, CLA/023/DW/01/119 (71); and TNA, PROB 11/1, fos. 62–3. An extract is in the St. Botolph's parish cartulary (LMA, P69/BOT3/D/001/MS00059, fo. 11r–v).

(*lumini fraternitatis beate marie*).[39] Robert Muston, 1420, left 4 marks for ornaments for St. Mary's altar.[40]

However, references to St. Mary's altar now cease. From 1439 there are references to a Fraternity of Our Lady and St. John the Baptist;[41] and from 1465 we hear of a new altar, of Our Lady and St. John the Baptist.[42] This, we suggest, was within the new extension to the south. The will of William Laurence, 1477, makes it clear that there were now three altars: the high altar, the altar of Our Lady and St. John the Baptist and 'the altar in the north aisle'.[43] This third altar was perhaps the former St. Mary's altar. On 23 January 1542/3 William Lucar, priest, was appointed to the perpetual chantry of Thomas Snowdylonde, established in St. Mary's chapel in 1361, almost 200 years earlier. Lucar was appointed jointly by the churchwardens and the wardens of the Fraternity of the Virgin Mary and St. John the Baptist, who together were the 'true patrons' (*veri patroni*) of the chantry. The new altar and new fraternity were thus the reincarnation of the former altar, chapel and fraternity of St. Mary.[44]

The former St. Mary's altar appears to have been rededicated later to the Trinity. Robert Atkinson, 1531, asked to be buried 'by the Trinity altar, under Our Lady of Pity';[45] William Stoderd, 1537, likewise asked for burial 'before the picture of Our Lady of Pity in the Trinity chapel on the north side of the church'.[46] These are the only references to this statue, which was probably relatively new.[47] William Bodley, 1540, asked for burial 'under the door as they [*sic*] go into the Trinity chapel where my father and my mother and Elizabeth my wife lie on the left hand of my father's tomb'.[48] This suggests some sort of partition or screen. References to the altar and Fraternity of Our Lady and St. John the Baptist include the following. Agnes Clerke, 1466, left a vestment and altar cloth to the Fraternity of the Blessed Virgin Mary and St. John the Baptist, worth £3 each.[49] John Payn,

---

[39] LMA, DL/C/B/004/MS09171/002, fos. 104–5, at fo. 104v.

[40] TNA, PROB 11/2B, fos. 160v–161, at fo. 160v.

[41] The earliest reference is in the will of William Symmes, 1439 (TNA, PROB 11/3, fos. 199v–200, at fo. 200).

[42] The earliest reference is in the will of Alice Abraham, 1465 (LMA, DL/C/B/004/MS09171/005, fos. 374v–375, at fo. 374v).

[43] TNA, PROB 11/6, fos. 208v–210v, at fo. 209.

[44] LMA, DL/A/A/006/MS09531/012/001, part 1, fo. 142v.

[45] TNA, PROB 11/24, fo. 84.

[46] TNA, PROB 11/27, fos. 17r–v, at fo. 17.

[47] The original spelling of Stoderd's will, which is in English, has 'pycture'. We are grateful to Christopher Wilson for pointing out that at this date a 'picture' was almost always three-dimensional, i.e., a statue, not a painting or hanging.

[48] TNA, PROB 11/28, fo. 132v.

[49] LMA, DL/C/B/004/MS09171/005, fo. 381v.

1466, and John Paris, 1485, both mentioned a roll of benefactors or bede roll of the fraternity.[50] William Laurence, 1477, left £13 6s 8d for two vestments with apparels, to be used for his five-year chantry at the altar of Our Lady and St. John and then to pass to the fraternity at the end of the five years for the fraternity's priest at the altar of Our Lady and St. John.[51] Sir John Yong, 1482, left to the chapel of Our Lady his best mass book, his best chasuble with the alb belonging to it, two silver-gilt cruets and his best paxbread (osculatory), garnished with stones.[52] Joan Chicheley, 1521, left a diaper tablecloth to be divided between the high altar and Our Lady's altar. The latter could have been either an altar of Our Lady of Pity in the Trinity chapel on the north side, or that of Our Lady and St. John the Baptist in the new south aisle.[53]

Unusually, the parish cartulary mentions two elaborate late fifteenth-century ornaments in the church: a canopy, already mentioned, and an automaton of St. George and the dragon.[54] These must have been expensive and a source of pride. The entries in the cartulary comprise the maintenance instructions for both items, not full descriptions. The canopy was given by William Lawrence ('lawrauns'), apparently in 1472. It was for the blessed sacrament to hang in above the high altar. The canopy was suspended on a chain and was lifted up and down by a rope. Wires bore 'imagery' and 'threads' spread out the cloth.[55] The statue of St. George on a beam, set up on St. Botolph's day in 1474, showed him in armour, on horseback, with a dragon, a castle, a maiden and a king and queen. The maiden and king and queen were 'turned' by a line fed through two spindles in the castle towers. St. George and the horse were turned by a crank in the castle floor.

Both had been made by William Parnell of Ipswich, Suffolk, his son John and his apprentice William Baker. William Parnell was an expert in statues and engines for pageants, responsible for this aspect of the annual celebrations in Ipswich of the guild of Corpus Christi. He was also called upon in July 1467 to provide decorations, heraldry, statues etc. for the visit of Queen Elizabeth Woodville to Norwich. He and his son were almost

---

[50] John Payn: LMA, P69/BOT3/D/001/MS00059, St. Botolph's parish cartulary fos. 26v–28v; John Paris: TNA, PROB 11/7, fos. 151–152v.

[51] TNA, PROB 11/6, fos. 208v–210v, at fo. 209.

[52] TNA, PROB 11/7, fos. 29–31.

[53] LMA, DL/C/B/004/MS09171/009, fo. 193v.

[54] LMA, P69/BOT3/D/001/MS00059, fos. 46v–47. This automaton was not unique in the city. There was another at St. Mary Woolnoth, also a St. George (H. B. Walters, *London Churches at the Reformation, with an Account of their Contents* (London, 1939), p. 468).

[55] A rare surviving example of a canopy, or rather its wooden core, from the late 15th or early 16th century survives at Dennington, Suffolk, and in recent years has been brought back into use.

certainly responsible for some of the medieval carving that survives in churches in East Anglia, for which no written records survive.[56]

There was no room for a churchyard. In consequence, at the end of the fourteenth century the parish acquired a small detached churchyard on the north side of Thames Street, east of Botolph Lane. This was consecrated in 1393. It still survives as an open space called One Tree Park in the forecourt of an office block.[57] However, as in most parishes, wealthy parishioners often sought burial in the church itself, as we know from Stow.[58] It is possible that among the several hundred pieces of carved stone from the church recovered in 1982 are fragments of altars and tombs.

The rich fittings of the church were still fresh in the memory in 1552, when they were listed as having been sold.[59] They included at least ten copes, twenty-one banners and three streamers; three and a half hundredweight of latten (brass plate) 'taken out of the gravestones';[60] 'a tabernacle that did hang over the altar'; 'a large painted cloth that was wont to hang before the Rood'; 'a valance of buckram about the Sepulchre'; 'the table [retable] over the high altar'; 'a hanging of cloth of gold for the Trinity altar'; and a total of 508 sq. ft of 'old glass'. The church still possessed much else, including more

---

[56] We are grateful to the late John Blatchly of Ipswich for information about William Parnell; and to Phil Butterworth for early access to his essay with E. Williamson, 'The Mechanycalle "Ymage off Seynt Iorge" at St. Botolph's, Billingsgate, 1474', in *Medieval Theatre Performance: Actors, Dancers, Automata and their Audiences*, ed. by P. Butterworth and K. Normington (Woodbridge, 2017), pp. 215–38. This includes transcripts of the texts in the cartulary about both the St. George and the canopy. A transcript of the text about the St. George, with a brief commentary, is also in *Ecclesiastical London*, ed. M. C. Erler (Records of Early English Drama, Toronto, 2008), pp. 292–3.

[57] The licence in mortmain dated 7 Aug. 1392 is copied into the parish cartulary (LMA, P69/BOT3/D/001/MS00059, fo. 5v). So is the record of consecration on 13 March 1392/3, at fo. 6v. The inquisition *ad quod damnum* is TNA, C 143/418/3. See also J. Colson, 'Local communities in fifteenth-century London: craft, parish and neighbourhood' (unpublished University of London PhD thesis, 2011), pp. 205–6.

[58] Stow, *Survey of London*, i. 207–8.

[59] TNA, E 117/4/57, inventory of church goods of St. Botolph Billingsgate.

[60] Two fragments of monumental brasses from St. Botolph's may still exist: (1) a brass shield of *c*.1500, bearing the pre-1512 arms of the Fishmongers' Company, was discovered on the Billingsgate foreshore in 1982 and remains in private hands (Schofield et al., *London's Waterfront*, p. 206). The shield is 5.2 in. tall, a size appropriate to a monumental brass. It also bears a single, central rivet-hole, the normal method of fixing such shields to gravestones; (2) a tiny fragment of a brass inscription in Latin was likewise discovered at Billingsgate by a mudlark in 1984 and donated to the Museum of London (Museum reference 84.304). Scarcely 2.7 in. in any dimension, this bears the words *uxor e[ius]* [*his wife*]. It can be dated to around the second quarter of the 15th century. Its pristine condition suggests that it came from a raised tomb. Stephen Freeth is most grateful to John Clark, formerly of the museum, and to Hazel Forsyth of the museum for access to this fragment.

copes, three hearse cloths (one for servants), a 'pair of organs', two bibles, a *Paraphrases*, four 'great bells' and a *sanctus* bell.

The parishioners of St. Botolph Billingsgate

St. Botolph's in the middle ages was a wealthy parish, with wealthy parishioners. In 1428 its yearly value, £32, was one of the highest in the city.[61] In the late fifteenth century John Benyngton, being sued in chancery by John Mottram, clerk, about the non-return of an antiphoner, claimed that St. Botolph's parish had bought it for £14 10s.[62] This was a huge sum, enough to pay a chantry priest for over two years. Wills of wealthy parishioners are numerous. Nicholas James, ironmonger, 1434, left money for a 'Majesty' (a representation probably of Mary or Jesus, enthroned in glory) for Cromer, Norfolk, for new pews at Croydon and for a new east window in St. Olave Southwark;[63] Stephen Forster, 1458, left 1,000 marks to each of his two sons and 500 marks to his daughter;[64] Richard Rawlyn, grocer, 1471, left £300 to his son and £200 to each of his two daughters;[65] William Laurence, grocer, 1477, left to a kinswoman his one-third share of the crayer (coasting vessel) the Martin of London and asked that his household (his servants and dependants) be kept together for one year to make it easier for them all to find new jobs.[66]

The wills also hint at trade links to other towns. Ralph Double, fishmonger, 1392, who died at New Shoreham, left money to the parish church and priory there;[67] Thomas Bronyng, fishmonger, 1418, forgave debts in [New] Romney in Kent;[68] Peter Welles, pewterer, 1450, left £20 for a chalice for St. Mary's, Faversham;[69] William Canynges, son of the great William Canynges

---

[61] *Cal. Letter Bks. K*, p. 71. Those city churches with higher yearly values than St. Botolph's were, in descending order: St. Sepulchre (£65); St. Bride (£47 13s 4d); St. Lawrence Jewry, St. Magnus, St. Michael Cornhill and St. Vedast (£40 each); All Hallows Bread Street (£36 13s 4d); and St. Dunstan in the East (£33 6s 8d). The yearly values of the parishes contiguous to St. Botolph's were as follows, from west to east: St. Magnus (£40); St. Margaret New Fish Street (£20); St. George Botolph Lane (£8); and St. Mary at Hill (£25 6s 8d).

[62] TNA, C 1/51/253–5, of either 1475–80 or 1483–5. The antiphoner appears eventually to have been bequeathed to St. Mary at Hill in 1491–2 in return for an obit. See the churchwardens' accounts of St. Mary at Hill (LMA, P69/MRY4/B/005/MS01239/001/001, fo. 93v); and Colson, 'Local communities', p. 197.

[63] TNA, PROB 11/3, fos. 138v–141, at fos. 139, 139v, 141.

[64] TNA, PROB 11/4, fos. 110–111v, at fos. 110v–111.

[65] TNA, PROB 11/6, fos. 28–9, at fo. 28v.

[66] TNA, PROB 11/6, fos. 208v–110, at fo. 210.

[67] TNA, PROB 11/1, fos. 42–3, at fo. 42.

[68] TNA, PROB 11/2B, fos. 103–4, at fo. 103v.

[69] TNA, PROB 11/1, fos. 89r–v, at fo. 89.

of Bristol, died at the house of Stephen Forster, fishmonger and former mayor, in 1458;[70] Forster himself came originally from Somerset[71] and, dying in the same year, appointed William Canynges senior as an overseer of his own will;[72] Thomas Yogge, vintner, 1509, left 300 quarters of salt for a new rood loft in St. Andrew's, Plymouth;[73] and Nicholas Alday, grocer, 1518, already mentioned, not only left money for 'two copes of red damask' to be made for St. Botolph's, like the suit of copes at St. Clement's Sandwich, but forgave Mr. Wingfield of Sandwich the eleven yards of chamlet that he owed. The Aldays were a wealthy Sandwich family.[74]

Some parishioners possessed books. For example John Witteneye, chaplain, 1406, left a book called *Esse* to the master of the school at St. Dunstan in the East.[75] Richard Bodley, grocer, 1491, left all his English books (*omnes libros meos anglicos*), frustratingly unnamed, to his son; his beautiful (finest?) psalter (*meum pulchrum psalterum*) to his daughter Isabella; and his primer to his daughter Emma.[76] He was from the same family as the founder of the Bodleian Library in Oxford and was warden of the Grocers' Company in 1488–9. From their inscriptions, two or possibly three of his books survive as Cambridge, Corpus Christi MS. 142 (Nicholas Love's *Life of Christ* and a Life of St. Katherine); and Edinburgh University Library MS. 39 (a very fine London-made book of hours).[77] The *Life of Christ* was a 'canonical' text of the fifteenth century of which more than twenty copies survive in libraries.[78] The book of hours, according to a catalogue of the Edinburgh University library manuscripts, shows 'English illumination of the early part of the 15th century at its best'. It contains eleven historiated initials; that for the office of the dead shows mourners and two priests around a coffin draped with a hearse-cloth and surrounded by candles, with

---

[70] TNA, PROB 11/4, fo. 103v.

[71] See the biography of his widow Agnes (C. Barron, 'Forster [Foster], Agnes (d. 1484), wealthy widow and prison reformer', in *ODNB* <https://doi.org/10.1093/ref:odnb/54439> [accessed 30 Aug. 2016]).

[72] TNA, PROB 11/4, fos. 110–111v, at fo. 111.

[73] TNA, PROB 11/16, fos. 147v–148, at fo. 147v.

[74] TNA, PROB 11/19 fos. 78v–79, at fo. 79. For Sandwich, see H. Clarke et al., *Sandwich: 'the completest medieval town in England': a Study of the Town and Port from its Origins to 1600* (Oxford, 2010), p. 139.

[75] LMA, DL/AL/C/002/MS09051/001, fo. 159v.

[76] TNA, PROB 11/9, fos. 5v–6, at fo. 6.

[77] A. F. Sutton, 'Lady Joan Bradbury (d 1530)', in *Medieval London Widows, 1300–1500*, ed. C. M. Barron and A. F. Sutton (London, 1994), pp. 209–38, at p. 212.

[78] M. Sargent, 'What do the numbers mean? A textual critic's observations on some patterns of Middle English manuscript transmission', in *Design and Distribution of Late Medieval Manuscripts in England*, ed. M. Connolly and L. R. Mooney (York, 2008), pp. 205–42.

other clergy in the background (Figure 11.7).[79] Edward Marmyon, 'clerk and parson' of St. Botolph's, 1541, left to the parish priest of St. Botolph's, William Ruffurth, his 'great book called *Distructionum Viciorum*', perhaps a garbled rendering of Alexander Carpenter's *Destructorium Vitiorum*.[80] Clearly some of the more prominent parishioners were well-read.

John Reynewell

One of St. Botolph's wealthiest parishioners, a great benefactor of both parish and city, was John Reynewell (*c*.1380–1445), alderman from 1416 to 1445, sheriff in 1411–2 and mayor of London 1426–7. He was a major city figure, perhaps even more so than other mayors because of his benefactions to the city. The surviving records are frustratingly incomplete, but we can build some picture of the man and his life.[81] He was a member of the Fishmongers' Company (though sometimes given as an ironmonger),[82] the son of William Reynewell, a member of the Ironmongers' Company and an alderman 1397–1403, and his first wife, Isabel. John had two younger brothers, William and Thomas, and two sisters, Cristina and Joan. William Reynewell the father was buried in St. Botolph's in 1404, next to Isabel.[83]

John Reynewell was auditor of London in 1409–11, 1414, 1417 and 1419 and a member of parliament for the city in 1410, 1415, 1433 and from 1445 until his death. In December 1407 he was one of four commissioners appointed for levying in the city the tenth and half a tenth granted in the last parliament and for returning the money into the exchequer. In December 1433, along with the city's three other MPs in the last parliament and the bishop of London, he was, by royal letters patent, appointed a commissioner to apportion the sum granted for the relief of the tenth granted by parliament to the king among the poorer wards of the city. Gregory's *Chronicle* refers to him as 'the good mayor of the city of London' and mentions that in 1428 parliament agreed that he should be mayor of the Staple of Calais for the three following years.[84] During Reynewell's London mayoralty in 1426–7

---

[79] C. R. Borland, *A Descriptive Catalogue of the Western Medieval Manuscripts in Edinburgh University Library* (Edinburgh, 1916), pp. 63–4.

[80] TNA, PROB 11/28, fos. 243r–v, at fo. 243v.

[81] We are most grateful to Clive Burgess for making available his unpublished notes on Reynewell and in particular for the reference to the Navy Records Society.

[82] E.g., in 1433 (*Cal. Letter Bks. K*, p. 166).

[83] See Thrupp, *Merchant Class*, p. 363; and the will of William Reynewell senior (TNA, PROB 11/2A, fos. 36–37v).

[84] J. C. Wedgwood, *History of Parliament: Biographies of Members of the Commons House 1439–1509* (2 vols., London, 1936–8), i. 715; *Cal. Letter Bks. I*, p. 61; *Cal. Letter Bks. K*, p. 177; *The Historical Collections of a Citizen of London in the Fifteenth Century*, ed. J. Gairdner (Camden Soc. n.s., xvii, 1876), pp. 161, 164.

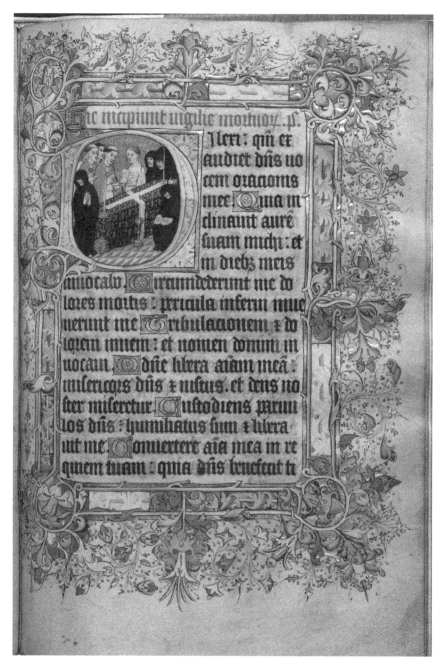

Figure 11.7. Edinburgh University Library MS. 39, a book of hours which once probably belonged to Richard Bodley: miniature on fo. 70r from the office of the dead (courtesy of Edinburgh University Library Special Collections).

the north gateway of the drawbridge on London Bridge began to be rebuilt: according to John Stow, Reynewell laid one of the first corner stones, the other three being laid by the sheriffs and bridgemasters, and on each one the name *Ihesus* was engraved or written.[85] The gate is shown by Wyngaerde around 1540.

Reynewell was rich. In March 1417/18 he was one of the citizens who advanced money for the king's expedition abroad, he himself lending £20. In the 1436 lay subsidy roll, his lands in London and Warwickshire were assessed at £120 per annum, one of the highest figures recorded either for a private individual or for an institution. For comparison, we may note the Mercers and Goldsmiths at £70 yearly each and the nunnery of St. Helen Bishopsgate at £133 per annum.[86] We have glimpses of how he made his money. First, there was overseas trade, largely in wool. In 1408 he and his partner Drew Barentyn (mayor 1398–9 and 1408–9) were exporting wool, hides and wool fells through London and Chichester for the Calais Staple.[87] In 1412 they and others were involved in a disastrous expedition to export wool and other merchandise worth a total of £24,000 to the Mediterranean. The ships and goods were seized at Genoa and the factors thrown into gaol.[88] On 7 July 1435, after he had ceased to be mayor of the Staple of Calais, Reynewell was awarded £1,000 at arbitration in what must have been a most bitter dispute with the Staple, giving the then mayor of the Staple his receipt.[89] In 1437 Reynewell was shipping wheat and beans from Norfolk and Lincolnshire to London, to victual the city.[90]

There was also privateering (bordering on piracy), ship repair and naval stores. In 1413 or 1414 a ship belonging to Reynewell and others captured at sea the Santa Clara, a Castilian ship carrying goods for two merchants, Juan Martinez (John Martyns) and Agostino Lomelino (Augustine Lomelyn), who were covered by a safe-conduct. The captors had to return the royal Castilian standards, some armour and weapons and the ship's dog.[91] In 1416

---

[85] Stow, *Survey of London*, i. 25.

[86] *Cal. Letter Bks. I*, pp. 202–3; Thrupp, *Merchant Class*, p. 383, quoting the lay subsidy roll (TNA, E 179/238/90).

[87] *CPR 1405–1408*, p. 469.

[88] *CPR 1408–1413*, pp. 461–2; *CPR 1413–1416*, p. 90. See also *The Navy of the Lancastrian Kings: Accounts and Inventories of William Soper, Keeper of the King's Ships, 1422–1427*, ed. S. Rose Navy Records Society, cxxiii, London, 1982), pp. 9, 241–2.

[89] *CCR 1429–35*, p. 360. We are grateful to Jane Williams for this reference. One of the arbitrators on Reynewell's behalf was Stephen Forster, mayor of London in 1454–5. For Forster. see J. Williams, 'A late-medieval family and its archive: the Forsters of London, c.1440–c.1550' (unpublished University of London PhD thesis, 2011).

[90] *CPR 1436–1441*, p. 99.

[91] *CPR 1413–1416*, p. 192; *CCR 1413–1419*, pp. 166–7; Rose, *Navy of the Lancastrian Kings*, pp. 19–20 and 241–2.

Reynewell sold to William Soper, a merchant at Southampton who was also the clerk of the king's ships, various materials for a new *ballinger* for the duke of Bedford's expedition for the relief of Harfleur, as follows: 1 cwt, 1 quarter, 2 lbs of fine oakum (*fyn ocom*) at 10s 1½d, and 294 ells of canvas for a sail at £9 11s 5d. In about 1417 Reynewell sold twenty-two ships' masts to Soper to repair various vessels. All these stores were bought from Reynewell in London for transport to Southampton.[92]

Near the end of his life Reynewell owned freehold property in the city in the parishes of St. Botolph Billingsgate, St. Mary at Hill, All Hallows the Great and St. Andrew Cornhill and leasehold property in St. Mary at Hill and All Hallows the Great. He also possessed property in Calais. Now, by deeds of 6 May and 19 June 1441, he conveyed all of this property, including the leaseholds, to trustees.[93] The trustees were William Cumbes, William Abraham, John Roskyn, John Colston, John Gyffard and William Stafford.[94] Reynewell then, by his will dated 18 September 1443, asked his trustees to convey all this property to the city for charitable purposes. The city must have possessed a copy of this will, but it seems never to have been proved and enrolled in the hustings court or elsewhere and its text appears to be lost. Fortunately much of it, including Reynewell's charitable intentions, was recited along with the two trust deeds of 1441 and the details of his London leaseholds in a will made by the last surviving trustee, William Stafford, on 25 October 1458. This tells us that trustees Cumbes, Roskyn, Colston and Gyffard had soon died, so that Abraham and Stafford became possessed (*seisiti fuimus et possessionati*) of all the property. Abraham, on 5 October 1458, then released his entire interest to Stafford. Now Stafford devised to the city corporation all of Reynewell's London properties, including the leaseholds, to hold for the charitable purposes specified by Reynewell in his will of 1443. There was one small last-minute adjustment.

---

[92] Fragmentary naval accounts, part of National Maritime Museum, Greenwich, MS. 4102. See Rose, *Navy of the Lancastrian Kings*, pp. 212, 226. A *ballinger* was a vessel of 30–120 tons, propelled by oars and/or sails, for 'swift reconnaissance, the rapid conveying of important messages or passengers, and piracy'.

[93] 6 May 1441: Plea and Memoranda Roll A68 (LMA, CLA/024/01/02/69), fo. 6, calendared in *CPMR 1437–1457*, p. 165; 19 June 1441 (LMA, CLA/023/DW/01/169 (46)). These deeds include Reynewell's property in Calais. They do not specifically mention the London leaseholds, but later documents show that these were included.

[94] Cumbes was a fellow fishmonger and an alderman from 1437 to 1452. Abraham was sheriff in 1447 and several times master of the Vintners' Company. Colston was later one of the administrators of Reynewell's estate after his death. Stafford, another vintner, was a benefactor of the Vintners' Company and feoffee of two company estates (A. Crawford, *History of the Vintners' Company* (London, 1977), pp. 202, 281). Roskyn and Gyffard remain unidentified. For a brief biography of Cumbes, see Thrupp, *Merchant Class*, pp. 334–5. For Abraham's will, proved in 1462, see LMA, DL/C/B/004/MS09171/005, fo. 326v.

Stafford had recently come into possession from the city corporation of a stone house (*domus petrina*), which he planned separately to give to St. Botolph Billingsgate church to serve as a vestry, in memory of Reynewell. This had an annual value of 20*s*. The terms of Reynewell's bequest were therefore altered so that the city corporation could take 20*s* per annum in compensation from Reynewell's London estate. Stafford's will of 25 October 1458 is recorded in the hustings and elsewhere.[95]

Two points are worth noting here. First, Stafford's will of 25 October 1458 concerned itself solely with Reynewell's London property. Its recitals of the trust deeds of 1441 omit the references in those deeds to the Calais property. Its recital of Reynewell's will of 1443 also omits any mention of Calais. The Calais property must have been conveyed to the city by another document, now lost to us. Second, the trust deeds of 1441 and the will of 1443 described the city properties as being Reynewell's entire London portfolio, but on 20 July 1443, after he had conveyed his main estate to trustees, Reynewell conveyed a *domus* on the south side of the church of St. Botolph Billingsgate which he had acquired in 1409 to a different but overlapping set of trustees for other purposes, as will be described shortly.

By the 1560s the city's 'Reynwell Estate', with two other similar estates (Philipot and Carpenter), formed three separate, short accounts appended to the city chamber's general account. Reynewell's was the most substantial, with a rental in the 1580s of just over £125. By the 1630s these three separate accounts had been merged into the general account, but the totals of each rental were still clearly identified. The properties comprising each estate also continued to be listed separately in the rentals until 1784. Thereafter they were merged into the topographical headings of the general rental and their origin was no longer indicated.[96]

Reynewell's properties in All Hallows the Great and in Calais are of particular interest. The All Hallows property comprised a 'great house', the former house of John of Northampton, mayor 1381–3, in Windgoose Lane ('Wendegaynelane' in Reynewell's will). This included a dyehouse and a

---

[95] LMA, CLA/023/DW/01/207 (31) (proved and enrolled March 1477/8). A virtually complete text of the will is also in the St. Botolph's parish cartulary (LMA, P69/BOT3/D/001/MS00059, fos. 23–5). Stafford's will of 25 Oct. 1458 is crucial to understanding Reynewell's generosity to the city and parish, but is very long and very complex. Fortunately, the Latin text is printed in full on pages 22–7 of appendix C of C. P. Cooper's *Report* of 1837 on Rymer's *Foedera*, from a 15th-century certified copy preserved in the archives of Hamburg. Cooper's report, left unpublished at the time, was eventually printed by the Public Record Office in 1869. Appendix C is available online at <http://dbooks.bodleian.ox.ac.uk/books/PDFs/300078953.pdf> [accessed 14 Feb. 2019].

[96] *Chamber Accounts of the Sixteenth Century*, ed. B. R. Masters (London Rec. Soc., xx, 1984), pp. xxvi–xxvii.

wine cellar and was where Reynewell actually lived. The freehold site was augmented with leasehold ground, held from Elsing spital under an eighty-year lease at £7 per annum commencing in 1427. In 1475 the freehold site was granted in perpetuity by authority of the king in parliament to the Hanseatic merchants to be part of the Steelyard, in return for an annual rent of £70 3s 4d. (The leasehold site was similarly conveyed, by arrangement with Elsing spital.) In the 1580s this former freehold of Reynewell's was the largest item in the city's rental of the 'Reynwell Estate'. An unusual result of the king's grant is that many deeds of this and adjoining sites are (or were) preserved in cartulary books and other records in Germany.[97] Reynewell's property in Calais was the former earl of Hereford's inn. In 1430 it was in the king's hands and when he granted it to Reynewell it was 'ruinous'. *Letter Book O* records that in 20 Henry VIII (1528–9) the city sent two representatives to Calais to look after the Reynewell property.[98]

It is puzzling that Reynewell devised these properties to the city by his will since he is known to have died intestate. On 9 November 1446 the two administrators of his estate were discharged by the archbishop of Canterbury, as noted in his register.[99] It seems, therefore, that Reynewell's will of 1443, with its stipulation that his trustees should convey his trust property to the city, took effect automatically at his death in 1445, apparently without formal probate or enrolment.[100] The entry in the archbishop's register merely indicated that Reynewell had made no will soon before he died. William Stafford's will of 25 October 1458, which finally conveyed Reynewell's London property to the city, therefore fulfilled his duty under Reynewell's will.

---

[97] C. L. Kingsford, 'Historical notes on mediaeval London houses', *London Topographical Record*, xi (1917), 28–81, at pp. 55–6, 'Northampton Inn'; J. M. Lappenberg, *Urkundliche Geschichte des Hansischen Stahlhofes zu London* (2 vols., Hamburg, 1851), i. 68–72 and 'Urkunden' [Documents], nos. 43–4, 86, 105, 127, 150. Document no. 105 is another copy of Stafford's will of Oct. 1458.

[98] *CPR 1429–36*, p. 54; *Letter Book O* (now LMA, COL/AD/01/014), fo. 84. For a recent account of Calais, the centre of the principal English export in the middle ages, raw wool, see S. Rose, *Calais: an English Town in France, 1347–1558* (Woodbridge, 2008).

[99] Lambeth Palace Library, Stafford's register, fo. 144, 9 Nov. 1446: '*Nono die mensis Novembr' Anno domini et loco predictis Johannes Colston et Johannes Newerk administratores bonorum Johannis Reynewell dum vixit Civis et Aldermanni Civitatis London' nuper ab intestato decedentis acquietati sive dimissi fuerunt ab officio*' (on 9 Nov. in the year and place aforesaid [1446, Lambeth] John Colston and John Newerk, administrators of the goods of John Reynewell [who] while he lived [was] a citizen and alderman of the city of London, lately dying intestate, were discharged from their office).

[100] Wills took effect on death; until then they had no force (G. Jacob, *A New Law Dictionary* (9th edn., London, 1772), under 'Will').

Stafford's will, in turn, will have come into force at his death in late 1466 or early 1467. This, too, seems not to have required formal probate at the time, for probate and enrolment in the hustings only took place almost twenty years later, in March 1477/8, as already mentioned. Informal arrangements nevertheless seem to have allowed the city to administer Reynewell's city property while Stafford was still alive. In February 1463/4 Reynewell's former 'great house' in All Hallows the Great was occupied by an elderly alderman, John Walden, as tenant of the city.[101] The city also had control of Reynewell's Calais property. On 5 October 1447 it leased it to alderman William Coumbes [*sic*] for thirty years at 6 marks per annum 'in recognition of his services in the execution of the will of the said John Reynwelle, who devised property in the city of London and said town of Calais to the use of the commonalty of the said city'.[102]

Reynewell's known benefactions to the city can be summarized as follows. He asked his trustees, as soon as possible after his death (*tam cicius quo melius fieri posset post suum decessum*), to convey his London property to the city in perpetuity. The income, after all expenses of maintenance and the payment of 40 marks yearly to Reynewell's son William and his legitimate heirs and annual pensions for life to his sister Cristina (10 marks) and daughter Frideswide, a minoress near the Tower (26s 8d), was to fund the following charitable purposes. The first group were personal matters. There was to be 12 marks each year for a chaplain to celebrate (*divina celebraturum*) every day forever in the charnel chapel in the cemetery of St. Paul's Cathedral for the souls of Henry Barton, late alderman, and Joan his wife; 40s to the chamberlain of the cathedral to celebrate, *per notam*, every year on 1 September *Placebo* and *Dirige*, with a mass of requiem on the morrow, for Reynewell's own soul and for the souls of his parents William and Isabel, forever; 13s 4d to the churchwardens of St. Botolph Billingsgate at Easter for an annual obit for the soul of John Reynewell and the other souls aforesaid, *per notam*, on Friday in Pentecost week, with solemn ringing of bells, *Placebo* and *Dirige* and mass of requiem on the morrow and other appropriate ceremonies, forever; 13s 4d to each of the churchwardens of All Hallows the Great and St. Andrew Cornhill for the same purpose; and every Sunday the rector of each of these three churches devoutly to commend to God by name the souls of John Reynewell and his parents William and Isabel.

The second group was for city institutions and officials. There was to be £32 to Billingsgate ward, £28 to Dowgate ward and £6 to Aldgate ward to

---

[101] *Cal. Letter Bks. L*, p. 44.
[102] *Cal. Letter Bks. K*, p. 322.

relieve the inhabitants every time that a fifteenth (that is, tax) should be granted by Parliament to the king and *pro rata* for fractions of a fifteenth, forever; £10 per annum to the exchequer to exonerate the annual fee due from the city's sheriffs for the fee farm of Southwark, to free all Englishmen coming there or passing through from tolls and other payments hitherto levied by the sheriffs, forever; £8 each year to the sheriffs in lieu of tolls at the great gate of London Bridge or at the drawbridge, forever; both the last above to apply to Englishmen and not to aliens from overseas (*sint personarum indigenarum et nullarum personarum alienigenarum*); 20*s* to the mayor, 6*s* 8*d* to the city recorder and 13*s* 8*d* to the chamberlain, every year, for their trouble taken to carry out the above; 6*s* 8*d* per annum to the aldermen of the three wards to see everything performed faithfully; and 3*s* 4*d* each year to each of the two keepers of the Bridge, forever. Any surplus after these payments was to be divided into two equal portions, one to install a granary in the city with wheat for relief in times of need; and the other to cleanse the 'shelpes' [sandbanks] and other obstructions of the River Thames, as done in Prussia and other places overseas.

Reynewell's trusts were taken seriously. In 1533 the wording in his will concerning the relief of the three wards from fifteenths was translated into English, written out on parchment and displayed openly in Guildhall for all to see.[103] Unfortunately, in 1539 the mayor failed to read this and several inhabitants of Dowgate ward spent a day and a night imprisoned in the Tower after he noticed £8 unpaid from a past fifteenth. The prisoners did not give in, declaring that they would 'stick to the will of Master Reynewell … that the ward of Dowgate shall pay none money for no fifteen, except there be above three fifteenths in one year'. As the London memoranda records, 'By the help of God they paid none. Deo Gracias'.[104]

Reynewell was not only a great benefactor to the city, but to the church of St. Botolph Billingsgate as well. Through trustees he gave it a house (*domus*, which may have been a warehouse, not a dwelling house), formerly part of Botolph Wharf, a long-established landing place for goods and persons. This *domus* lay south of and parallel to St. Botolph's church, which we now know from the archaeological record to have included at this time some empty ground between the actual church building and the *domus*. (The rest of the wharf lay south and east of the *domus*.) This allowed the church to be extended to the south across this empty ground so as to incorporate the *domus* into the church, the former empty ground forming a new aisle. Conveyances from 1409 onwards record how Reynewell acquired the *domus*

[103] Sharpe, *Calendar of Wills*, ii. 576, n. 2.
[104] Stow, *Survey of London*, ii. 310.

from the city and granted it to trustees on 20 July 1443.[105] By 1456 William Stafford was the last remaining trustee and by his will dated 20 August in that year he devised to the rector and wardens of St. Botolph the land, now part of the church and on its south side, which had once included a *domus*, part of Botolph Wharf (*illa terra mea sive solus iam parcella ecclesie sancti Botulphi … situat' in parte australi eiusdem que olim erat quedam domus que fuit parcella kaii sive wharvi vocat' Botulphiswharf*). This he (and others who had since quitclaimed the property to him) had acquired from the late John Reynewell. The gift was intended for the enlargement of the church and in memory of Reynewell, the testator and the co-feoffees.[106] All of these arrangements were explained and confirmed by archaeology in 1982.[107]

The brick grave which we suggest was Reynewell's lay in the new aisle. We see no difficulty in Reynewell being buried there in 1445, even though Stafford did not devise the *domus* to the church until his will of 1456 and remained alive until 1466 or 1467. The phrasing of Stafford's will suggests that the *domus* was long gone; the church already owned the site of the new aisle; and we see Reynewell's conveyance to trustees in 1443 as evidence that he intended the *domus* to be given to the church. Building works may well have started immediately.[108]

In a second will, drawn up on 25 October 1458, with which we are already familiar, Stafford noted his possession of a stone house (*domus petrina*), of an annual value of 20s, on the south side of St. Botolph's church, which had been granted to him and his heirs by Geoffrey Boleyn, mayor 1457–8, and which Stafford wished to bequeath to the rector and wardens as a vestry (*tanquam vestibulum*) in memory of John Reynewell. The mayor and commonalty were now given 20s yearly from Reynewell's estate in recompense.[109] In yet another will, written on 30 December 1458, Stafford bequeathed to the church of St. Botolph for use as a vestry the stone house with stone vault and stone walls under the house, which he held by grant of Boleyn and the commonalty. This house, adjoining the church to the

---

[105] St. Botolph's parish cartulary (LMA, P69/BOT3/D/001/MS00059, fos. 11v–12, 14–15). The trustees were William Abraham vintner, John Walden grocer, William Stafford vintner, Thomas Crofton chaplain and John Bydeford clerk and their heirs. For full details of the conveyances, see Schofield et al., *London's Waterfront*, pp. 187–8. The documentary research was by T. Dyson in the 1970s and 1980s.

[106] LMA, CLA/023/DW/01/211 (1), proved and enrolled 19 March 1480/1.

[107] Schofield et al., *London's Waterfront*, pp. 188–99.

[108] This parallels how some livery companies had the use of their halls through trustees long before they acquired legal ownership. For example, the Tailors are believed to have been using their hall through trustees from at least 1347, but did not own it until 1392 (M. Davies and A. Saunders, *History of the Merchant Taylors' Company* (London, 2004), p. 14).

[109] LMA, CLA/023/DW/01/207 (31), proved and enrolled 2 March 1477/8.

north and the city's land to the south and west, measured 16 ft in length from east to west and 12 ft in width from north to south.[110] Stafford's wills of October and December 1458 specifying a vestry had been anticipated by the appointment of five members of common council on 10 May 1455 to determine whether there would be any loss to the city in a grant to the church of St. Botolph of a certain parcel of the common soil on the east side of the church for enlarging the vestry.[111] The findings of this enquiry are not recorded but the outcome was evidently the grant to Stafford by Mayor Boleyn and the commonalty in return for an annual payment of 20s.

These various wills of Stafford were made in proper form, commencing with *In dei nomine amen* and finishing with the appointment of executors, though omitting instructions for burial. What is extraordinary is that they were *all* proved and enrolled in the hustings (but not, it seems, in a church court), albeit over ten years after his death in 1466 or 1467 and in seemingly random order. The opening phrasing of each will also made it clear that it only dealt with a part of Stafford's estate.[112] Normally, any will was revoked automatically by a later one and any later additions had to be in the form of a codicil. Wills were not supposed to be made in instalments.[113] Whether these multiple wills were unique to Stafford, a peculiarity of the city or merely something which is made apparent by the city's extensive surviving records is unclear. More research is needed.

The merchant's mark seen on the angel corbel is so far unidentified. We know from Stafford's seal on yet another will, his fourth that is known to us, dated 24 December 1463, that he was armigerous.[114] He will surely have

---

[110] LMA, CLA/023/DW/01/210 (15), proved and enrolled 9 Oct. 1480.

[111] LMA, COL/CC/01/01/005, journal of the court of common council, fo. 241v.

[112] For example, Stafford made his will of 1456 'for the disposition of that property of mine now parcel of the church of St. Botolph Billingsgate' (*ad disposicionem illius terre mee iam parcelle ecclesie sancti Botulphi iuxta Billyngesgate*).

[113] See Jacob, *Law Dictionary*, under 'Will'. We are most grateful to Christopher Whittick for his help with the legal-history aspects of Stafford's wills. The hustings officials may also have had concerns. Stafford's wills of 20 Aug. 1456 and 30 Dec. 1458, proved and enrolled comparatively close together in March 1481 and Oct. 1480, are introduced with statements that they were proved 'as to the clauses relating to a lay fee' (*quoad articulos laicum feodum tangen*), perhaps to imply that they formed part of a fictitious single, and longer, original will by Stafford.

[114] This will devised property in Botolph Lane to St. Paul's cathedral. Uniquely, it survives as an original deed sealed with Stafford's seal (St. Paul's Cathedral Archives, LMA, CLC/313/P/008/MS25271/068) as well as a hustings enrolment (CLA/023/DW/01/200 (13), proved and enrolled 16 July 1470). Stafford left two more wills. On 22 May 1466, near the end of his life, he gave instructions for burial along with various bequests of cash and moveable goods. This was proved in the normal way in the commissary court of London in June 1467 (LMA, DL/C/B/004/MS09171/006, fo. 45v). A sixth will, dated the previous day,

wanted his coat of arms to be displayed in the church and not his merchant mark. The same could be said for Reynewell if he, too, was armigerous, as many mayors and aldermen were.[115] But merchants in high civic office often used both forms of identification, a mark and a coat of arms.[116]

According to John Stow, Reynewell, described as a fishmonger, died in 1445 and was buried in St. Botolph Billingsgate. Stow recorded an epitaph, though since the monument had almost certainly disappeared by the end of the sixteenth century it is unlikely that he saw it in the church:

> Citizens of London, call to your remembrance,
> The famous Iohn Rainwell, sometime your Maior,
> Of the Staple of Callis, so was his chance.
> Here lieth now his Corps, his soule bright and faire,
> Is taken to heavens blisse, thereof is no dispaire.
> His acts beare witness, by matters of record,
> How charitable he was, and of what accord,
> No man hath beene so beneficiall as hee,
> Unto this cities in giving so liberally
> Great substance of livelode, wherfore now agre
> To pray unto God that reynethe eternally
> His soule to embrace and take to his mercy.
> He died in October the xxiij
> Of the reigne of the noble sixt Henry.[117]

This inscription is notable for its length, but was not exceptional in London. Stow recorded two other, slightly later, fifteenth-century epitaphs in English on monuments, of John and Margaret Shirley of 1456 in the church of the hospital of St. Bartholomew's Smithfield and of John Shrow of 1487 in St. Michael Crooked Lane.[118] However, Reynewell's inscription is unusual in

---

21 May 1466, gave land to the Vintners. This is recorded in the Vintners' Company Wills Book (LMA, CLC/L/VA/G/001A/MS15364), but not in the hustings or a church court. For further details of all of Stafford's wills and transcripts and translations of the Latin texts of the devises to St. Botolph Billingsgate, see Schofield et al., *London's Waterfront*, pp. 407–13.

[115] J. Goodall, 'The use of armorial bearings by London aldermen in the middle ages', *Trans. London and Middlesex Archaeol. Soc.*, n.s., xx (1959), 17–21.

[116] This caveat is provided by Elizabeth New. See also E. A. New, 'Representation and identity in medieval London: the evidence of seals', in *London and the Kingdom: Essays in Honour of Caroline M. Barron*, ed. M. Davies and A. Prescott (Harlaxton Medieval Studies, n.s., xvi, Donington, 2008), pp. 246–58.

[117] Stow, *Survey of London*, i. 207; the last five lines are omitted in Stow's published text but are in his manuscript draft (now BL, Harley MS. 538) and were supplied by C. L. Kingsford in his notes (*Survey of London*, ii. 309).

[118] Stow, *Survey of London*, ii. 23 and i. 222 respectively.

giving only the month in which he died and not the exact date of death. It may have been a later replacement.

John Reynewell died intestate, as noted above. But he left much documentation, even if some of it is a little obscure. The documents are now matched by an archaeological discovery. In conclusion, we suggest that skeleton [783] was possibly John Reynewell, mayor in 1426–7, and we have described what is known about this important but hitherto little-recognized civic leader of the years immediately after Richard Whittington. Further, whoever the excavated couple were, they lay in a parish church which was internally as rich as any other in the city of London in the medieval period. We hope this chapter has shown how the documentary and archaeological records of the medieval city are both, in their own ways, exceptionally rich and should be researched together.

12. The testament of Joan FitzLewes: a source for the history of the abbey of Franciscan nuns without Aldgate*

Julian Luxford

This chapter selectively analyses a testament (to be called a 'will' for the sake of convenience) made by a widow named Joan FitzLewes in December 1511. Joan was a friend of the abbey of Franciscan nuns outside Aldgate (that is, the Minories) and intended to become a nun herself.[1] Thus, her will represents a form of ritual oblation, a shedding of worldly affairs and persona as a precondition of taking the habit. It foreshadowed worldly rather than bodily death: in this regard it is exceptional.[2] The fact that it survives in its original form, signed and sealed, heightens one's sense of its significance for its maker. This is an important point to emphasize. To ignore its status as an object and use it only for what its text communicates, which is the normal lot of medieval wills, would be a shame and also rather short-sighted in light of the developing scholarly tendency to treat the physical substance of documentation as data.[3] Regarded simply as a record of things planned and done, the will is shorter and less remarkable than many others of its time. Its main textual interest lies in what it reveals of the Minories: all fresh information, as it happens, for Joan's will has managed to dodge scholarship

* I am very grateful to Clive Burgess for reading a draft of this chapter and offering numerous helpful suggestions; and to Christian Steer for references, advice and encouragement. I cheerfully acknowledge the usefulness to this chapter of the unpublished work by Martha Carlin and Catherine Paxton cited below.

[1] FitzLewes may be spelled FitzLowes in the sources; Lewes is an alternative spelling, though not, to my knowledge, in relation to Joan.

[2] It is sometimes assumed that propertied laypeople who became monks or nuns made wills as a preliminary step, but the process was unnecessary and evidence is rare. Another example is a will made by Dorothy Slight in 1535 (TNA, PROB 11/25, fo. 226), discussed by V. Bainbridge, 'Syon abbey: women and learning c.1415–1600', in *Syon Abbey and Its Books: Reading, Writing and Religion, c.1400–1700*, ed. E. A. Jones and A. Walsham (Woodbridge, 2010), pp. 82–103, at p. 85.

[3] A tendency that proceeds largely from M. T. Clanchy's extraordinary book *From Memory to Written Record: England 1066–1307* (3rd edn., Chichester, 2013).

J. Luxford, 'The testament of Joan FitzLewes: a source for the history of the abbey of Franciscan nuns without Aldgate', in *Medieval Londoners: essays to mark the eightieth birthday of Caroline M. Barron*, ed. E. A. New and C. Steer (London, 2019), pp. 275–95. License: CC-BY-NC-ND 4.0.

on the abbey until now. Yet the unusual circumstances of its composition and its rough-edged materiality combine with what it says to make a claim on the attention of those who study late medieval London. If this is true of Caroline Barron, at least, then the choice of a subject involving several of the areas that have nourished and profited by her work will, it is hoped, seem less forced than it could.

Joan FitzLewes's will is in The National Archives, filed by itself as a land revenue deed (Figure 12.1).[4] This means that it is not among the bulk of surviving documentation to do with the abbey, which is largely comprised of conventual leases (filed as exchequer documents) and scattered references in late medieval probate registers and court rolls.[5] Perhaps its classification explains why it has been overlooked in the past: it is not, anyway, obvious how a document of this type, which does not mention real property, should be classified. The text, written in English, is a little over 1,000 words long and occupies one side of a single, unindented sheet of parchment 12.5 in. high by 18.5 in. wide. This sheet was originally folded into six for archiving and there is an endorsement stating what the document is and who witnessed the ritual of signing and sealing that activated it. The document's formality is marked by an elaborate penwork initial at the beginning; larger and bolder lettering at the start of many of its clauses; the signature of the testatrix; the name plus *signetum manuale* of the scrivener (one John Worsopp); and the impression of a seal in red wax which hangs from a parchment tag.[6] This impression is damaged and was not very clear to begin with, as some sort of rough-weave fabric was pressed onto it when the wax was still pliable. As a result, the seal's inscription is illegible, although a cross at its centre is clear enough.

The endorsement makes it plain that Joan impressed a seal in her own right. Indeed, it was normal for testators both to sign their wills and to seal them as a double insurance against impropriety. Although relatively few original wills of this type seem to exist, a clause that mentions signing and sealing occurs in many probate copies.[7] There is a typical specimen

---

[4] TNA, LR 15/2.

[5] An important, underworked seam of documents is TNA, E 303/9/181–203.

[6] Worsopp (d. 1538) was evidently a preferred scrivener of the nuns. He signed another document of the abbey (TNA, E 303/9/201; made 1514) and his name also appears on the parchment seal-tag of Joan's will, made of an earlier, cut-up document. Elizabeth New has told me he was an active member of the Jesus guild in St. Paul's Cathedral during the 2nd and 3rd decades of the 16th century. His own will is TNA, PROB 11/27, fos. 177v–178.

[7] E.g., TNA, PROB 11/8, fos. 144v–146v (will of John Alfegh; made 1489); PROB 11/12, fos. 105v–106 (will of Sir Thomas Bryan; made 1500); PROB 11/12/, fos. 106r–v (will of Roger Reyff; made 1500); PROB 11/21, fos. 168–169v (will of Sir Robert Wotton; made 1523); PROB 11/27, fos. 177v–178 (will of John Worsopp; made 1538). That few original

Figure 12.1. London, TNA, LR 15/2. The testament of Joan FitzLewes. Reproduced by permission of The National Archives.

in the will of Sir Robert Rede, a chief justice of the common pleas (d. 1519): 'In witnesse wherof to this my testament I haue putt my sealle and subscribed my name with myne owne hande'.[8] Margaret, Lady Hungerford (d. 1478), for whom three original wills survive, went one better than this by having the bishop of Salisbury sign and seal her second and third wills, 'forasmuch as my seal and subscription is not to meny men knowen'.[9] While supernumerary insurance of this sort was unnecessary (and presumably unavailable) to Joan FitzLewes, its use by Margaret illustrates with special clarity the importance of manifest personal intervention (extending to the exercise of social leverage) to the forensic validity of a will. As on a charter, the phenomenal evidence of such intervention supplied the ultimate validation of the text.

Understandably, scholars are not accustomed to thinking about this because they routinely deal with depersonalized transcripts which encourage the view that a will is only as useful as what it says. This has caused, or at least nurtured, the roundly unjustified notion that medieval wills are too formulaic in structure and content to reveal anything much of personal identity and misleading to the point of deceit.[10] In the case of Joan's will, as must originally have been the case with many others, nothing militates more directly against this than the signature at the bottom (Figure 12.2). Joan's signature – 'Jone Fyzlowyes' in a careful but unkempt hand that

---

wills survive was noted by M. L. Zell, 'Fifteenth- and sixteenth-century wills as historical sources', *Archives*, lxii (1979), 67–74, at p. 67, n. 1. Probably, however, very little inquiry has been made for them: they are not a commonly recognized class of document.

[8]　TNA, PROB 11/19, fos. 97–100, at fo. 98v.

[9]　M. A. Hicks, 'The piety of Margaret, Lady Hungerford (d. 1478)', *Jour. Eccles. Hist.*, xxxviii (1987), 19–38, at p. 22.

[10]　This notion arose partly as a corrective to a too-enthusiastic embrace of wills as autobiography, epitomized by W. K. Jordan's now sneered-at statement that wills are 'mirrors of men's souls' (W. K. Jordan, *Philanthropy in England 1480–1630: a Study of the Changing Pattern of English Social Aspirations* (London, 1959), p. 16). This statement is often cited dismissively: see, e.g., C. Marsh, 'In the name of God? Will-making and faith in early modern England', in *The Records of the Nation*, ed. G. H. Martin and P. Spufford (Woodbridge, 1990), pp. 215–49, at p. 215; A. D. Brown, *Popular Piety in Late Medieval England: the Diocese of Salisbury 1250–1550* (Oxford, 1995), p. 21; R. Marks, *Image and Devotion in Late Medieval England* (Stroud, 2004), p. 8. More generally, it was a reaction to a common, uncritical assumption that wills provide comprehensive summaries of testators' property and intentions, a scholarly blind spot noted by Clive Burgess, 'Late medieval wills and pious convention: testamentary evidence reconsidered', in *Profit, Piety and Possessions in Later Medieval England*, ed. M. Hicks (Gloucester, 1990), pp. 14–33. Caroline Barron for one has demonstrated how tractable a will can be when approached as an object of study in its own right (C. M. Barron, 'The will as autobiography: the case of Thomas Salter, priest, died November 1558', in *Recording Medieval Lives*, ed. J. Boffey and V. Davis (Harlaxton Medieval Studies, n.s., xvii, Donington, 2009), pp. 141–81).

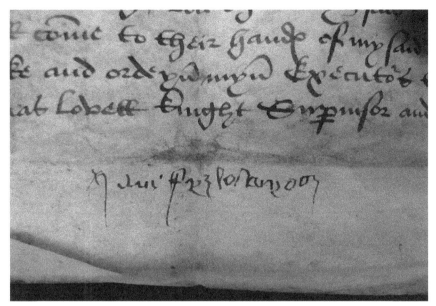

Figure 12.2. Detail of Figure 12.1, showing Joan FitzLewes's signature.

implies something like lack of writing practice, arthritis or simply a cold day – places an effective emphasis on her personal investment in the will's provisions. Here, through the still-manifest proxy of her own hand, is the 'I' who floats in the voice of the text: 'I woll', 'I make', 'I bought', 'I yeve', 'I owe', 'I know', 'I entend', 'I bequeth', 'I was'.[11] The signature also invites one to think about the circumstances of the will's ratification, which involved, as the endorsement says, the application of seal and signature under the eyes of nine men, followed by a little ceremony when the signatories and their witnesses handed the document over to the nuns. These formalities were presumably important and affecting to Joan. To say this is not, of course, to claim that the signature can reveal anything the text does not, but rather that it has the ability to sensitize a receptive mind to the personal circumstances and context of the will's making in a way potentially fruitful to study of the document. Comparison of Joan's autograph with the inert-looking copies of testators' signatures sometimes included in probate transcripts provides the best support for this claim.[12]

---

[11] A thoughtful review of the forensic and symbolic status of signatures on medieval documents is B. Fraenkel, *La signature: genèse d'un signe* (Paris, 1994). In the context of this chapter, see particularly pp. 17–25, 98–112.

[12] For a probate copy of a signature, see TNA, PROB 11/17, fos. 56–57v (will of William Maryner of 1512).

As it happens, the will is easily the fullest source of information we have about Joan. It contains the only clear indications of her character and ambitions. But other sources are important for understanding her attachment to the Minories and it is worth glancing at these before turning to the will and its contents. It would be possible to build up a more detailed picture of her life before 1511 than the one that follows, but as the focus of this chapter is on Joan as an aspiring nun rather than a laywoman with husband, children and other responsibilities, the following remarks will be confined to an economical sketch.

Joan was born into the FitzSimond family in 1452 or 1453. At an inquisition held on the death of her father Robert in 1474 or 1475 her age was given as twenty-two. The FitzSimond seat was the manor of Mocking Hall at Barling in south-east Essex, but her inheritance included two manors in each of Norfolk and Oxfordshire plus the moiety of another in Northamptonshire.[13] She acquired the surname with which she signed her will from Philip FitzLewes (d. 1492), whom she married in or after 1483.[14] The FitzLewes family, though a recent creation, were highly prosperous and also had their seat in southern Essex.[15] Joan had been a bride twice before she married Philip: to Robert Tymperley and Henry Wentworth.[16] Tymperley was named as her husband in the inquisition mentioned above and another document named both him and Joan as vendors of a messuage and garden in Fenchurch Street, London, in 1476.[17] He probably died soon after, as Henry Wentworth, the second husband, died in 1483.[18] Joan was also a mother. Through her will she asked that one of her two intended monuments display 'my name and whose doughter that I was, my husbonds names and the names of my children'. As two of her executors were called

[13] F. Blomefield and C. Parkin, *An Essay Towards a Topographical History of the County of Norfolk* (2nd edn., 11 vols., 1805–10), ix. 100.

[14] H. L. Elliot, 'Fitz Lewes, of West Horndon, and the brasses at Ingrave', *Trans. Essex Archaeol. Soc.*, n.s., vi (1898), 28–59, at p. 38; J. C. Wedgwood, *History of Parliament: Biographies of Members of the Commons House 1439–1509* (2 vols., London, 1936–8), i. 539 (on Richard FitzLewes); C. Paxton, 'The nunneries of London and its environs in the later middle ages' (unpublished University of Oxford DPhil thesis, 1992), p. 24.

[15] For the basis and extent of FitzLewes prosperity, see A. D. Carr, 'Sir Lewis John, a medieval London Welshman', *Bull. Board of Celtic Stud.*, xxii (1967), 260–70.

[16] Her husbands are named in a will of William Maryner (d. 1512), with whom Joan collaborated to arrange commemoration (discussed below) (LMA, CLA/023/DW/01/236 (14)). I thank Christian Steer for sending me images of all the documents from this archive cited in this essay.

[17] Society of Antiquaries of London, SAL/MS/650/35.

[18] See <http://www.oxford-shakespeare.com/Probate/PROB_11-12-265.pdf> (p. 2), compiled as part of the Oxford authorship project: <http://www.oxford-shakespeare.com/documents.html> [both accessed 28 Aug. 2018].

Thomas Tymperley and Robert Wentworth, it might be assumed that they were sons rather than relations by marriage. However, the Thomas in question is probably the same man who served as a rent-collector for the abbey in the period 1514–6 and his father was named John, not Robert.[19] And Joan's only known child by her second husband was named Nicholas, rather than Robert, Wentworth. This Nicholas Wentworth was the only child named in Joan's will, suggesting that the other child or children to be commemorated on her monument predeceased her.[20]

By her marriage to Philip FitzLewes Joan entered a family with close links to the Minories. A nun named Alice FitzLewes was abbess between 1494 and 1501 (the precise duration of her leadership is unknown), shortly before which Philip was acting as the abbey's steward (he is documented in the post between 1487 and 1490).[21] The steward was the senior lay officer in a Franciscan nunnery.[22] This coincidence and the fact that FitzLewes is a distinctive name imply that Alice and Philip belonged to the same family. Indeed, Alice may have been Philip's niece. It is known that Philip had a niece who was a nun at the Minories; he also had a granddaughter who was professed there.[23] As steward, Philip was entitled to reside within the abbey. There were houses for the lay officials on the north side of the precinct, away from the nuns' cloister, one of which Philip was renting in 1487/8 for £2 per annum.[24] It is impossible to say how long or often he resided there, for he had other important offices which took him elsewhere.[25] The point to emphasize here is that if one assumes that Joan lived with him, as it is reasonable to do, then her experience of this solemn and feminine environment was a probable catalyst for her decision to become a nun. Other

[19] A. F. C. Bourdillon, *The Order of Minoresses in England* (Manchester, 1926), p. 35; M. Carlin, 'Historical gazetteer of London before the Great Fire. St. Botolph Aldgate: Minories, East Side; the abbey of St. Clare; Holy Trinity Minories' (unpublished typescript, University of London, Institute of Historical Research, 1987), p. 4.

[20] Nicholas is also the only child named in the anniversary Joan arranged through William Maryner (see n. 16 above).

[21] Paxton, 'The nunneries of London and its environs', p. 25 and n. 58; Carlin, 'Historical gazetteer of London', p. 4; *The Religious Houses of London and Middlesex*, ed. C. M. Barron and M. Davies (London, 2007), p. 148 (Alice as abbess); Paxton, 'The nunneries of London and its environs', pp. 24, 87 (Philip as steward).

[22] The office of steward has been characterized as 'practically a sinecure' and typically invested in someone capable of influence on the nuns' behalf (Bourdillon, *Order of Minoresses*, p. 33 (quotation); also E. Power, *Medieval English Nunneries c.1275–1535* (Cambridge, 1922), pp. 146–7).

[23] Paxton, 'The nunneries of London and its environs', pp. 24, 25.

[24] Carlin, 'Historical gazetteer of London', pp. 31, 32, 34, 35. In 1539 there were two stewards, each paid £2 13s 4d (Bourdillon, *Order of Minoresses*, p. 33).

[25] See Wedgwood, *Biographies of the Members of the Commons*, i. 539, for these roles.

influences were no doubt active. For example, she had an independent link to the abbey by virtue of the fact that a great-niece of hers, Anne Tyrell of Beeches in Essex, was a nun there.[26] Her religious kinswomen set her an example and she probably envied them their status. It is easy to see why, under such circumstances, she decided to have Christ for her fourth spouse and the title 'Dame' used in her will may suggest that she became a vowess after Philip FitzLewes died.[27]

If Joan's decision is intelligible, its chronology is unclear before 1509. In theory she was free to become a nun after Philip died in 1492, but she evidently preferred to wait. While it is likely that she maintained an active interest in the abbey during the intervening years, there is little evidence for this. Joan may have resided in the precinct for much of this period, or visited the abbey only occasionally. However, by 1509, when she was in her late fifties, she was making preparations for entering the order by arranging anniversaries for herself and those she was obliged to help. This, of course, was something she could not do once professed. She set up two anniversaries, to be observed 'solempny by note' in the abbey church, respectively on 26 March and 26 November.[28] Additionally, she funded a light in the monastery and another in a parish church near the FitzLewes' seat at Barling. In each case, she channelled the means to pay the nuns through a London citizen named William Maryner (d. 1512). Maryner made several deeds and at least two wills, one of them entirely devoted to the commemoration of Joan and her family. The prayers and pittances it specified were to be funded out of the rents and property she had granted him.[29] Conceivably, this expedient was intended to ensure maintenance of the anniversaries in the period after Joan had relinquished control over her affairs to the abbess. It certainly created a paper trail.[30] Perhaps she felt obliged to ensure the spiritual succour of her family. In any case, her own will places no commemorative obligations on her executors.

This brings us to the content of Joan's will. As far as is known, it is the last significant piece of evidence about her.[31] There is nothing particularly

---

[26] Paxton, 'The nunneries of London and its environs', p. 25.

[27] I am grateful to Clive Burgess for advocating this possibility.

[28] Paxton, 'Historical gazetteer of London', pp. 25, 127, 138–9; see also the documents cited in n. 30 below.

[29] LMA, CLA/023/DW/01/236 (14) (dated 20 Jan. 1512). John Worsopp wrote the original will from which this copy was taken. Maryner's other will (TNA, PROB 11/17, fos. 56–7; dated 31 March 1512) does not mention Joan or the Minories.

[30] TNA, LR 14/299; LR 14/550; LMA, CLA/023/DW/01/236 (64) (dated 17 Aug. 1509: a copy of TNA, LR 14/550); CLA/023/DW/01/236 (32) (dated 26 Nov. 1511, only 11 days before Joan made her will).

[31] She is mentioned in a deed made on 4 June 1520 by her son Nicholas Wentworth as

unusual about the structure of the text. After a preamble mentioning Joan's third husband and father come instructions about burial, a tomb and a second monument. Then there is a reckoning of what she was owed by three debtors, totalling £108, and, at greatest length, the things she wanted done with this money. Among these were gifts to named individuals for specified purposes, including annuities payable to her four executors during her lifetime, an arrangement which emphasizes the fact that her will was made in anticipation of imminent social rather than bodily death. Any residue was to be put into the hands of the abbess for building works. If the text's structure is conventional, however, the content, as conditioned by Joan's intention to become a nun, is not. Thus, she commissioned no prayers or masses for her soul or those of her family and friends and disposed of no real property. Neither did she dispose of any personal effects, although like any woman of her social quality she presumably had her share, of which the 'litill englissh booke like a prymer' left to her by a nephew, John Tyrell of Beeches (d. 1493), was a representative.[32] Appropriately, she placed much at the discretion of the abbess. Nearly everything she asked for was to be funded out of the debts owing to her. The real and movable property she owned by inheritance and marriage is invisible and must have been disposed of by separate preliminary arrangements. Perhaps, like her friend William Maryner, she made more than one will.[33]

A detailed picture of the will's contents can be had from the transcription at the end of this chapter. What follows is a selective account, starting with the initial clauses after the preamble. Here Joan directed that she be buried in the choir of the abbey church 'by the ffete of the excellent Princess Elizabeth, late duches of Norffolk, under the awter of our blessed Lady'; and outlined the monuments she wanted set up in the church to commemorate herself and others.[34] These monuments were evidently important to her, for the directions in respect of them occupy about one sixth of the whole text and they are the only things in her will whose funding did not rely on repayment of debt. She wanted two monuments, one a 'marbyll' stone' over her grave 'with an image of a nonne in laten' and four shields of her

---

olim et perantea uxor Henrici Wentworth (LMA, CLA/023/DW/01/236 (93)). The deed calls Wentworth her heir. As Joan became a nun, this may not prove her dead.

[32] TNA, PROB 11/10, fos. 146–7, at fo. 146 (noticed in Paxton, 'The nunneries of London and its environs', p. 25).

[33] Again, I thank Clive Burgess for advice on this point. Such a will would have contained details of real property, personal effects and a wider range of beneficiaries (e.g., servants).

[34] It is unclear why Joan referred to Elizabeth Talbot as 'princess'. It could have been out of simple respect, or due to the representation of a ducal coronet on Elizabeth's tomb, or because of some confusion by Joan of Elizabeth with her daughter Anne Mowbray, who was married to one of Edward IV's sons and also buried in the Minories (see below).

arms; the other, destined for the nave, of two components, a latten plate in the wall with her name and those of her parents, husbands and children inscribed on it and a stone in the pavement beneath with her arms on it. This stone was to be 'a ffote & more in length'.

The request for two monuments is curious and each one is unusual in its way, at least in relation to surviving evidence. England can show very few surviving brasses and incised slabs to nuns and what there is gives little basis for reimagining Joan's effigy.[35] Further, it is impossible to know whether the heraldry was to represent only the FitzLewes and FitzSimond families, or to include Tymperley and Wentworth as well.[36] Margaret FitzLewes (d. 1466), a sister of Joan's third husband, had a brass with four different shields, apparently to signify her three marriages (this survives at Ingrave in Essex).[37] It appears that the commemorative inscription that would ordinarily have appeared on the gravestone was in this case transposed to the nave, where the abbey's servants and visitors could read it. If so, then this may have been because biographical information conveyed through words, as opposed to the symbolism of heraldry, was deemed to compromise a Franciscan nun's anonymity too frankly. Certainly, an image of a nun accompanied by statements of her individuality would have embodied an unedifying (if not unparalleled) contradiction, particularly in the enclosure of the choir. As for the nave memorial, the coupling of a slab in the pavement with a wall-mounted inscription was evidently a way of alerting readers that Joan was actually buried in the church, if not directly at their feet. The stone slab was a diminutive gravestone by proxy. If not, then it is difficult to guess its purpose. Wall-mounted memorials, or memorial windows, were and are usually considered in relation to tombs covering or adjacent to actual graves: the will of Robert Fabyan (d. 1511) includes a contemporary London example of such juxtaposition.[38] Many existed independently of tombs, of course, but not demonstrably in the sort of combination Joan wanted.[39]

---

[35] M. Norris, *Monumental Brasses: the Memorials* (2 vols., London, 1977), i. 63, 88, 147, 169; ii, figs. 85, 173, 199; J. Page-Phillips, *Palimpsests: the Backs of Monumental Brasses* (2 vols., London, 1980), i. 47; ii, pl. 40; F. A. Greenhill, *Incised Effigial Slabs: a Study of Engraved Stone Memorials in Latin Christendom, c.1100–c.1700* (2 vols., London, 1976), i. 103–4.

[36] FitzSymond bore *Gules, 3 escutcheons Argent*; FitzLewes bore *Sable, a chevron between 3 trefoils slipped Argent*.

[37] Elliot, 'Fitz Lewes, of West Horndon', pp. 39–43 and pl. 1.

[38] See, e.g., D. Brine, *Pious Memories: the Wall-Mounted Memorial in the Burgundian Netherlands* (Leiden, 2015), p. 25 and *passim*; *Testamenta Vetusta: Being Illustrations from Wills of Manners, Customs, etc.*, ed. N. H. Nicolas (2 vols., London, 1826), ii. 510 (Fabyan).

[39] Cf. J. Bertram, *Icon and Epigraphy: the Meaning of European Brasses and Slabs* (2 vols., [n.p.], 2015), i. 321. Two lost Oxfordshire monuments which included nothing but brass shields, called 'curious' by Bertram (i. 196), were possibly relics of the sort of pairing discussed here.

However, this probably reflects only a loss of evidence. Joan's grasp of the advantages of such a monument was probably based on her acquaintance with other examples, quite possibly in the nave at the Minories.

The complete eradication of the church above ground level means that the setting of both monuments is impossible to reconstruct accurately. Indeed, it is hardly worth speculating about the nave at all. A pre-Reformation list of fourteen people of aristocratic blood buried in the Minories indicates that Edmund de la Pole, eighth earl of Suffolk (executed 1513), and his wife Margaret (d. 1515) were buried in the nave.[40] It states that they were buried 'in the church', as opposed to the choir or chapter house, which are the other two locations it specifies. There were also some requests in wills for burial in the church, as opposed to the choir, as well as at least one for burial in the 'churchyard'.[41] But this gives no real imaginative purchase and it only seems safe to say that the nave was commonly used for lay burials and, if so, that it probably had its share of sepulchral monuments. The list is more helpful with respect to the choir. Seven of the names in it were located either at the high altar or in the choir generally. Of these, the heart of the abbey's founder, Edmund of Lancaster (d. 1296), and the body of Margaret, countess of Shrewsbury (d. 1467), were respectively located at the north and south ends of the high altar. As the east end of the church (like the nave) lacked aisles, this suggests burials either up against or recessed into walls. Of the others, Isabel, a daughter of Thomas of Woodstock, duke of Gloucester, was located in the middle of the choir: she had been a nun in the late fourteenth century and is documented as abbess between 1413 and 1424.[42] The burials of three others – Agnes, countess of Pembroke (d. 1368); Anne Mowbray, the child duchess of Norfolk and York (d. 1481); and Anne's mother Elizabeth Talbot, duchess of Norfolk (d. 1506) – were assigned to the 'quere', while the latest, of Mary Reading (d. 1531), was in the 'closse quere'. The word 'closse' here indicates a customary, gendered division of

[40] BL, Lansdowne MS. 205, fo. 19: printed (with redundant folio number) in E. M. Tomlinson, *A History of the Minories, London* (London, 1907), pp. 68–9. On internal evidence, the list was made between 1515 and 1531. A final entry about Mary Reading (d. 1531) was added in a different and apparently later hand. The list is assumed to have been compiled from inscriptions on monuments in situ (B. Watson and W. White, 'Anne Mowbray: a 15th-century child burial from the abbey of St. Clare, in the London borough of Tower Hamlets', *Trans. London and Middlesex Archaeol. Soc.*, lxvii (2016), 227–60, at p. 231) but this may be wrong: e.g., a martyrology or oral report may underlie it.

[41] E.g., Tomlinson, *History of the Minories*, p. 75; Carlin, 'Historical gazetteer of London', p. 16; *Testamenta Eboracensia or Wills Registered at York*, iv, ed. J. Raine (Surtees Soc., liii, Durham, 1869), *p.* 233; TNA, PROB 11/2B, fo. 127v (will of Elizabeth Kyriell of 1419 mentions two burials); PROB 11/15, fos. 273–4 (will of Laurence Harris of 1508).

[42] See Carlin, 'Historical gazetteer of London', for documentary references to Isabel (p. 8).

the presbyteries of Franciscan nuns' churches according to which the nuns were separated during the *opus Dei* from the resident friars who served them as priests.[43]

The specification about the closed choir in this one instance might lead to an assumption that the burials assigned by the list's compiler simply to the choir were located in the friars' division of the presbytery. This would extend to Joan FitzLewes, who, as noted, requested burial 'by the ffete' of Elizabeth Talbot. However, testamentary evidence shows otherwise and also helps to clarify Joan's intentions. In her will Elizabeth Talbot asked to be buried not just in the choir, as the list states, but 'in the nonnes quere'. Presumably she achieved what she wanted. Elizabeth also specified that her grave be 'nyghe unto' that of one Anne Montgomery (d. 1498).[44] This Anne Montgomery, widow of Sir John Montgomery (executed 1462), was sister-in-law of John Clopton (as such, she is represented in the stained glass of Long Melford church (Suffolk)).[45] Mary Tyrell, a niece of hers, was a nun at the abbey.[46] Elizabeth Talbot's sister-in-law Jane, the widow of Sir Humphrey Talbot (d. 1505), also requested burial 'within the inner choer' and 'nyghe the place and sepulture where the body of maistres Anne Mon[t]gomery [...] restith'. Like Joan FitzLewes, she wanted a flat tombstone laid on her grave, but with 'the picture of a dede corse in his wynding shete', plus the heraldry of her husband and herself and inscriptions soliciting prayers for both of them.[47] Jane's own tomb was cited in the will of Joyce Lee (d. 1507), one of whose daughters was a nun of the abbey. Joyce wished to lie 'in the wheer [*sic*] ... also nygh to the buriall of my lady Talbott as convenyently may be'.[48]

This pleasingly reciprocal evidence helps one to appreciate Joan's thinking. It indicates a mausoleum defined by aristocratic and gentry women buried

---

[43] Carlin, 'Historical gazetteer of London', p. 15. According to the will of Laurence Harris, there were five friars at the Minories in 1508 (TNA, PROB 11/15, fos. 273–4, at fo. 273v).

[44] TNA, PROB 11/15, fos. 196v–197. Her will is printed in J. Ashdown-Hill, 'Norfolk requiem: the passing of the house of Mowbray', *Ricardian*, xii (2001), 198–217, at pp. 212–5.

[45] Anne was of the Darcy family. No will can be found for her. The image at Long Melford is now in the seventh window on the north side of the nave. (An image of Elizabeth Talbot is in the first window.) On the Long Melford image, see A. Eavis, '"*Urbs in rure*": a metropolitan elite at Holy Trinity, Long Melford, Suffolk', in *The Urban Church in Late Medieval England: Essays in Honour of Clive Burgess*, ed. D. Harry and C. Steer (Harlaxton Medieval Studies, n.s., xxix, Donington, 2019), pp. 82–106.

[46] Paxton, 'The nunneries of London and its environs', p. 23.

[47] TNA, PROB 11/14, fos. 302v–303.

[48] TNA, PROB 11/15, fos. 173v–174. P. Tudor-Craig stated that Joyce 'took the veil' at the Minories herself (*Richard III* (London, 1973), p. 53), but there is no apparent evidence that she was a nun and her will was made and proved within a month.

independently of men in a way that, effectively, conformed to the ideal of female religious enclosure. In this sense, the centrally located burial of the abbess Isabel of Woodstock was emblematic.[49] These women's links to the abbey during life, which included the professed status of relatives and periods of personal residence within its walls (Elizabeth Talbot lived at the Minories, on and off, for twenty years or more), inevitably brought them into contact with one another. This in turn suggests why they may have wanted burial together in the same part of the church, in a sort of 'sorority of death'.[50] A blunter way of putting the matter is that a shared desire for burial as close as possible to the abbey's high altar created the effect of a largely female mausoleum and that this may have encouraged further women to seek burial there.

Beyond observing that the high altar and its associated burials lay towards the east end of the church, it is difficult to pinpoint the location of Joan's tomb.[51] Even its position relative to other graves is indistinct. If Joan's request for burial at Elizabeth Talbot's feet had been an expression of devotion, then one might imagine two contiguous monuments, but there is little to show that these women were friends. More obviously, and like her peers, Joan cited an existing tomb in order to make her preferred area of burial as clear as possible.[52] 'Area' is a better word to use here than 'site', for none of the sources mentioned above gives the modern historian a positive sense of place. The locational expressions relating to burial found in medieval wills and other documents (for example, '*juxta*', '*coram*', '*sub*', '*super*', '*in medio*' and their vernacular equivalents) are routinely ambiguous unless fixed by material evidence and there is no such evidence for the Minories.[53] A request to be buried east (that is, 'at the feet') of someone else

[49] Assuming she was buried in the nuns' division of the choir.

[50] On their residence and contact, see, e.g., Ashdown-Hill, 'Norfolk requiem', pp. 209–11; W. E. Hampton, 'The ladies of the Minories', in *Richard III: Crown and People*, ed. J. Petre (Gloucester, 1985), pp. 195–202, at pp. 197–201.

[51] That the friars' division of the choir lay west of that of the nuns is shown by Jane Talbot's request for burial in the 'inner choir', which certainly pertained to the nuns. The church was about 130 ft long internally (Carlin, 'Historical gazetteer of London', gives a total length including the walls of 141 ft (p. 14)) and there is no obvious reason to suppose that much space was reserved between the high altar and the eastern wall.

[52] This effectively substitutes a utilitarian consideration for the attractive idea (for which, see Tudor-Craig, *Richard III*, p. 53; and Hampton, 'The ladies of the Minories', p. 98) that Anne Montgomery and Elizabeth Talbot were considered charismatic and that this is why their graves were cited in other women's wills. However, this idea should not be dismissed entirely.

[53] The only known dimension germane to this chapter is that the generality of the choir (friars' and nuns') extended west by at least 58 ft. The grave of Anne Mowbray (Elizabeth Talbot's daughter), which the early 16th-century list locates in the choir, was found by

need not imply immediate proximity or even axial orientation. Joan's other stipulation, 'under the awter of our blessed Lady', is no more precise. It is hardly likely that a grave was burrowed in beneath the high altar; and if it was, then her monument with its image and heraldry cannot have rested directly over it, as her will required. In this context, 'under' was almost certainly supposed to mean 'in front of', as its Latin equivalent '*sub*' often did.[54] At most, the phrasing shows that Elizabeth Talbot's grave, Joan's tomb and the high altar existed near one another in an uninterrupted (but possibly meandering) west-east sequence.

At this point, it is worth briefly restating the basis for thinking that Joan's tomb lay before the high altar. Simply put, the high altar in an abbey dedicated to the Virgin Mary will have carried the same dedication and this is the dedication stated in Joan's will. We know this altar was in the nuns' division of the choir because Elizabeth Talbot asked for burial in that division and Joan requested a grave near hers. It makes sense to think that the high altar occupied the nuns' enclosure, that is, the 'inner choir' of Jane Talbot's will. A devil's advocate might propose that the nuns' choir contained a secondary altar dedicated to the Virgin, but there is no reason to believe it did. The only whiff of evidence for a distinct Lady altar arises from the mention of the burial of Henry le Waleys in 1302 in a chapel dedicated to the Virgin, but if this chapel was different from the abbey church, then there is anyway no basis for thinking that the nuns' choir stood in it.[55] Martha Carlin associated both the Henry le Waleys Lady chapel and a 'parisshe chapell' mentioned in a will of 1508 with the collateral structure that lay on the north side of the abbey church and became the parish church of Holy Trinity after the Reformation.[56] This is the most likely interpretation of the evidence.

Joan's burial in a location of prestige equal to or greater than that of the founder and numerous women of greater social quality, where priests trod and the nuns in choir constantly bent their attention, was at least remarkable. It was perhaps the more remarkable for a nun and, what is more, one represented on her tomb as a nun. While nuns could normally expect

---

archaeologists at that distance from the east end of the church (Carlin, 'Historical gazetteer of London', pp. 14, 17; Watson and White, 'Anne Mowbray', pp. 232–6).

[54] Just as '*super*' often has the sense of 'behind' (or, in churches, 'east of').

[55] *Calendar of Wills Proved and Enrolled in the Court of Husting, London, A.D. 1258–A.D. 1688*, ed. R. R. Sharpe (2 vols., 1889–90), ii. 96–7; *Lateinische Schriftquellen zur Kunst in England, Wales und Schottland vom Jahre 901 bis zum Jahre 1307*, ed. O. Lehmann-Brockhaus (5 vols., Munich, 1955–60), ii. 222 (no. 2965).

[56] Carlin, 'Historical gazetteer of London', p. 18; TNA, PROB 11/15, fos. 273–4, at fo. 273v (quotation).

burial outside the church, Joan sought a grave better situated than that of any abbess. Her ability to obtain it was very probably due to a combination of material gifts and goodwill built up through long association. The same combination of gifts and friendship may account for the nuns' willingness to admit her at the age of about sixty. According to the Rule for Franciscan nuns, whose surviving English witness is a fifteenth-century manuscript that probably belonged to the abbey, 'None woman schal be resseyuyd, woche for age … be nat couenable & suffisaunt for to kepe þe maner of life'.[57] Whatever her physical state in 1511, adoption of someone of Joan's maturity represented a financial risk against which any religious institution would require insurance. At least part of this insurance came in the form of a profession fee sufficient to cover the cost of basic maintenance for several years. Thus, by her will, Joan assigned £13 6s 8d to the abbess for her profession. Although little comparative evidence survives, there is reason to think this reflected a standard fee that was required regardless of age. Joan also bequeathed £13 6s 8d 'towards the buyldyng of the cloyster of the said Abbey'; the two sums add up to £26 13s 4d, which is precisely what Henry VIII paid for the profession of the much younger Elizabeth de la Pole in 1510.[58]

This bequest to the cloister was echoed twice at the end of the will, where Joan stated that any financial residue and any legacy unpayable by reason of the intended beneficiary's death should be given to the abbess 'towards the byldyng & making of the forsayd cloyster'. The cloister and its building are thus mentioned thrice. Taken together, this suggests that the abbey's cloister was indeed being renovated or rebuilt in the years around 1511. Of course, 'cloister' can be a synonym for 'monastery' and 'making' and 'building', singly or in combination, for the routine upkeep of buildings. However, the iteration in this case invites a literal reading, especially in light of the fact that Joan used a different expression in leaving money to the Grey Friars of London ('I yeve & bequeth unto the reparacion of the church and howse of the Greyffryers' etc.). If this surmise is acceptable, then the references are the only known documentary evidence for work on the abbey's cloister

---

[57] *A Fifteenth-Century Courtesy Book and Two Fifteenth-Century Franciscan Rules*, ed. R. W. Chambers and W. W. Seton (Early English Text Soc., o.s., cxlviii, 1914), p. 83. The manuscript is now Oxford, Bodleian Library, MS. Bodley 585, fos 48–104.

[58] The list of aristocratic burials mentions Elizabeth's burial in the abbey, but not in a specific place, implying a grave in the nuns' cemetery rather than the church. She was probably dead by 1515 (G. E. Cokayne, *The Complete Peerage of England, Scotland, Ireland, Great Britain* (8 vols., London, 1887–98), vii. 307, n. g). For other known profession fees, including Elizabeth de la Pole's, see Bourdillon, *Order of Minoresses*, p. 38; Carlin, 'Historical gazetteer of London', p. 6.

in any period. More gifts towards building are recorded after a fire caused extensive damage to the precinct in 1518, but the cloister at the heart of the complex is apparently not mentioned again.[59]

The will's other clauses have little immediate bearing on Joan's religious vocation. She left money to eleven individuals, including four women. One of these, Beatrice Lewes, was probably an affine, although there is no mention of a relationship. Joan left £3 6s 8d 'to [her] professing', but whether Beatrice was destined for the Minories or some other nunnery is not revealed. Another, Florence Parker, called 'cosyn', was to have 40s upon her marriage. These consecutive bequests made a pair that, whether by accident or design, expressed the two possible sorts of marriage. Three creditors were reimbursed: a woman named Julyan Manfeld was given £6 13s 4d of insurance against her failure to inherit; and two men, Oliver and William Manfeld, were given £3 6s 8d each for a 'stok', a word which usually referred to a tree-trunk or a receptacle of some sort, but probably meant something else here (Manfeld was a gentry family).[60] Joan left £13 6s 8d in the safekeeping of the abbess for the use of her son, Nicholas Wentworth, when he required it, a clause which evokes both the minutiae of the abbatial brief in general and the detailed arrangements and relationships which teem beneath the surface of this particular document. At the end she ordained as her executors the aforementioned Thomas Tymperley and Robert Wentworth, William Mordaunt and Roger Eton and named Sir Thomas Lovell as their overseer. It was, perhaps, germane to her choice that Lovell was a great benefactor to another London nunnery, the Augustinian priory of Holywell at Shoreditch, where he was buried in 1524.[61]

The fact that performance of almost all the actions specified in the will was dependent on the collection of debt may seem to place the satisfaction of Joan's wishes in doubt. This doubt cannot be entirely removed, but the three debtors were probably good for the money. For one thing, the will expresses confidence that they would pay up on request. There is no conditional phrasing: at the end it is stated that the executors should pay the beneficiaries out of the debts as they were received, with no allowance made for default. It seems unlikely that Joan would have staked something as important as her profession fee upon a doubtful source of income. The names of the debtors also inspire optimism. Sir Richard Lewes (d. 1528) and

---

[59] For the fire and subsequent gifts, see Bourdillon, *Order of Minoresses*, pp. 47 and n. 2, 65, 73; Carlin, 'Historical gazetteer of London', pp. 4, 22, 23. The cloister's site has been traced (Carlin, 'Historical gazetteer of London', p. 25).

[60] William Manfeld is called 'gentilman' (and one Thomas Manfeld '*armigero*') in LMA, CLA/023/DW/01/236 (32).

[61] *A Survey of London by John Stow*, ed. C. L. Kingsford (2 vols., Oxford, 1908), ii. 73.

Sir Roger Wentworth (d. 1539), who between them owed almost all of the money, were relatives by marriage.[62] With the third debtor, John Osborne, who evidently owned or had a stake in Joan's ancestral manor of Mocking Hall in 1511, they belonged to the coterie of southern Essex gentry from which Joan herself sprang. This does not prove them reliable, but it seems a better indication of reliability than might have been had from debtors outside Joan's circle. For his part, Richard Lewes was one of those helping Joan to put her affairs in order as late as November 1511.[63]

These comments lead to a general (and concluding) caveat about the use of medieval wills as evidence. It is axiomatic that, by itself, no prescriptive document can demonstrate the effects it was intended to have. Corroborative evidence is required and for Joan FitzLewes this is in short supply. It is conceivable that she never became a nun, that her monuments were never made and that nothing else was achieved by her will. In light of this, it is perhaps best not to attempt a summary of what the will tells us about the Minories for, just possibly, it is deceptive. Yet if one cares about economy of hypothesis, one will be comfortable in assuming that most or all of its requests were met. Joan was wealthy and prudent and she planned things out in advance. The abbey was stable and of good character at the time and Joan was familiar to its residents. No material evidence can be expected of a site so thoroughly destroyed as the Minories and no further documentation expected for a woman who surrendered herself to religious enclosure. The 'plague of pestilence' that struck the abbey in 1515, killing twenty-seven nuns, deepened the silence of the period.[64] From the historian's point of view, Joan FitzLewes disappears behind the records into what the poet called 'the darkness of the darkness forever'.[65] What remains of her is a voice of ink on parchment at the bottom of which is a small waxen symbol and a scratchy signature from which her hand will never quite be absent.

---

[62] On these men, see Wedgwood, *Biographies of the Members of the Commons*, i. 334, 935.
[63] LMA, CLA/023/DW/01/236 (32).
[64] Stow, *Survey of London*, i. 126 (quotation).
[65] As imagined by Captain Cat in Dylan Thomas's play *Under Milk Wood* (D. Thomas, *Under Milk Wood* (London, 1968), p. 71). See also n. 31.

Appendix

The testament of Joan FitzLewes dated 7 December 1511

This testament is held by The National Archives at Kew, filed by itself as a land revenue deed (LR 15/2). There is no date of probate and there is no trace of the registered will in the courts of London, Lambeth or Canterbury. In the transcription which follows paragraph numbers have been inserted for ease of reference.[66]

1. **In the name of God amen**, the vij[th] day of the moneth of December in the yere of our lord God M[l]CCCCCxj and in the thurde yere of the reigne of Kyng Henry the viij[th]. **I, Dame** Johane ffitzlewes, widow, late the wife of Philipp ffitzlewes and doughtor and heire of Robert ffitz Simond late of Barlyng in the countie of Essex, squyer, being in good helth and hole of mynde (laude and praysyng be unto almighty God) make, ordeyn and dispose this my present testament in manner and forme ensuing, that is to wite:

2. **ffurst** I yeve and and bequeth my soule unto almighty Iesu my maker and redemer and to our blessed Lady the Virgyn Seint Mary and to all the holy company of heven, and my body to be buried within the quere of the churche of the abbey of the Myneres without Algate of London by the ffete of the excellent princes Elizabeth, late duches of Norffolk, under the awter of our blessed Lady in the same quere.

3. **And I** woll that myn executors underwritten prouide for a marbyll stone to be leid ouer me with an image of a nonne in laten and iiij scochons of myn armes thereon. **And** without, in the body of the church of the same monastery, upon the walle there, **I woll** that my said executors cause a plate of laten to be sett with a scripture to be writen theron of my name and whose doughter that I was, my husbonds names and the names of my children. And under the same scripture, on the grounde, a stone of a ffote & more in length to be leid with myn armes theron as by the discrecion of my said executors shalbe thought most best to be done.

4. **And** where as Sir Richard Lewes, knight, is indetted & oweth unto me by ij obligacions xx[li] sterling; **Item** Sir Roger Wentworth by my obligacions lxxx[li] sterling, **And** John Osborne of Moking Hall by

---

[66] Contractions have been expanded, capitalization and punctuation modernized and parentheses inserted in two places. Interlineation is indicated by '\/'. The bold headings are those of the scribe.

obligacion viij^{li} sterling, **Which** said somes of money I woll shalbe distributed and disposed in manner and forme folowing, that is to say:

5.   **Where** as I entend by the sufferaunce of God to be professed nonne within the said abbey & place, **I yeve** and bequeth unto the abbes of the same place for my profession thereto be had xiij^{li} vj^s viij^d. **Item** I yeve & bequeth unto the same abbes towards the buyldyng of the cloyster of the said abbey xiij^{li} vj^s viij^d. **Item** I yeve & bequeth unto the reparacion of the church and howse of the Greyffryers of London vj^{li} xii^{js} iiij^d.

6.   **Item** I yeve and bequeth unto Iulyan Manfeld if she fortune nott to be heire of her faders londs vj^{li} xiij^s iiij^d. **Item** I yeve & bequeth unto Cuthberd Harryson xl^s to be deliuered unto him in the ffest of Pentecost next coming after the date of this my present testament. **Item** I yeve & bequeth unto sir John Walker xx^s to be deliuered unto him at the said ffest of Pentecost. **Item** I yeve & bequeth unto William Manfeld for a stok to occupye iij^{li} vj^s vij^d. **Item** I yeve & bequeth unto Olivere Manfeld for a stok to occupye iij^{li} vj^s viij^d.[67] **Item** I yeve to the professing of Beatrice Lewes iij^{li} vj^s viij^d. **Item** I yeve & bequeth unto my cosyn ffloraunce Parker, the doughter of maister Parker of Norffolk, xls, to be deliuered unto her the tyme of her marriage. **Item** I yeve & bequeth unto sir Richard that I bought the horse of, in recompense for the same, xiij^s iiij^d. **Also** I woll that my said executors of the forsaid somes of money content & pay unto Syr William Walgrave, knight, for money that I owe unto hym, to be paid at the forsaid ffest of Pentecost, cvj^{li} [or vj^{li}] xiij^s iiij^d.[68] **Item** to mastres Rochestre late the wif of Henry Baker, for money due unto her in the ffest of Seint Mighell Tharchaungell next coming after the date herof vj^{li} xiij^s iiij^d.

---

[67] Despite the difference of a penny, the same sum was presumably intended for both men.

[68] The character preceding 'vj' can only be read as 'c' and is redundant if not part of the sum. If it is redundant, then one wonders at the carelessness of it (compare the suggestion of scribal error in n. 67 above). However, the sums Joan was owed came to only £108, which would not have been enough to cover such a large debt plus her other bequests.

When Waldgrave (d. 1528), a Suffolk man, made his will, he left 20s to the Minoresses for an obit (TNA, PROB 11/22, fos. 227–8). This indicates a special interest and an avenue of connection to Joan, because all his other religious bequests were local.

7. **Item** I yeve & bequeth to myn executors for ther labour and besynes in the executing of this my present Testament & last wyll, that is to say, to William Mordaunt, gentilman, yerly during my naturall lyf xxs. **Item** to Roger Eton, gentilman, yerly during my said lyf naturall, xiij^s iiij^d. **Item** to Robert Wentworth, gentilman, yerly during my said naturall lif x^s. **And** to Thomas Tymperley yerly during my said lif naturall x^s.

8. **And I woll** that my said executors of the forsaid somes of money, at such tyme as they haue resseyved them, deliuer into the hands of my said lady abbes to the use of Nicholas Wentworth my sonne xiij^{li} vj^s viij^d, which I woll shalbe deliuered unto hym as he shall haue need therof. And the residue of all the said sommes of money \this my wyll performed/ I woll shalbe deliuered into the hands of my said lady abbes to content such detts as shalbe demanded and axed for me of right, if any such be (as I know none), and to be employed & disposed in byldyng & making of the forsaid cloyster.

9. **Provided** alwey that if any of the forsaid parties \to whome/ my bequest is made fortune to decesse during my lyff natural, than I wyll that the said legacyes & bequests by me afor graunted to any persone so diyng shall hoolly remayn during my said lyff unto the forsaid abbes towards the byldyng & making of the forsayd cloyster.

10. **And I** woll that myn said executors be not charged to pay any of my forsaid legacyes & bequests but of such somes of money as shall come to their hands of my said detts, and as my said detts unto them shalbe content & paid.

11. **And of** this my present testament I make and ordeyn myn executors the forsaid William Mordaunt, Roger Eton, Robert Wentworth and Thomas Tymperlay, and Sir Thomas Lovell,[69] knight, superuisor and ouerseer of the same. **Yoven** the day and yere abouesaid.

Jone Fyzlowyes   J. Worsopp

[On the dorse, in a somewhat different hand but almost certainly by the same scribe.]

This present testament was sealed, subscribed and deliuered by the wythynnamed dame Johane ffitzlewes the day and yere withinwriten, in the

---

[69] Lovell, along with Richard FitzLewes, Cuthbert Harrison, John Walker (called '*capellanus*') and William Manfeld are also cited in the agreement with William Maryner which Joan sealed on 26 Nov. 1511 (LMA, CLA/023/DW/01/236 (32)). See n. 30 above.

presence of William Mordaunt, Roger Eton, Gentilmen, John Worsopp, notary, Robert Wentworth, Thomas Tymperley, William Mansfeld, Olyvere Manfeld, John Osborne of Mokynghall and John Higham.

13. Souls of benefactors at Grey Friars church, London*

Christian Steer

John Barre alias Markeby, citizen and skinner of London, died on 20 July 1439. He was buried in the south aisle of the city's Franciscan church, where his grave was marked by a tomb slab and an inscription recording his name, craft and date of death. His was one of 682 monuments recorded in the register of the Grey Friars of London.[1] Markeby's will, sealed only twelve days before his death, left a quitrent of 5 marks to the rector of St. John Walbrook and the wardens of the Skinners' Fraternity of the Assumption of Our Lady, to endow a chaplain to celebrate at the altar of the Virgin Mary in the parish church of St. John's. But it was at Grey Friars church, where Markeby was buried, that an anniversary service, his annual obit, was to be celebrated in perpetuity, with *Placebo* and *Dirige* followed by requiem mass the next morning.[2] It was not unusual for a memorial service to be held by the grave, and studies of medieval London and elsewhere have demonstrated the importance of this relationship.[3] But the role of the friaries in the commemoration of the dead, through the provision of anniversary and chantry services, has largely remained in the shadows.[4]

---

* I thank Nick Holder, Stephanie Hovland and Paul Simpson for their help in the preparation of this chapter. In the discussion which follows 'Grey Friars' has been adopted to describe the building and the term 'Greyfriars' to describe the brothers of the order.

[1] C. L. Kingsford, *The Grey Friars of London* (Aberdeen, 1915), p. 126.

[2] LMA, CLA/023/DW/01/167 (59) and TNA, PROB 11/3, fos. 200–202v.

[3] E.g. C. Steer, 'A community of the dead in late medieval London', *Medieval Prosopography: Special Issue 'Those who worked, those who fought, and those who prayed. In honor of Joel T. Rosenthal'*, xxxii (2018), 181–94, at pp. 190–1; C. Burgess, 'Obligations and strategy: managing memory in the later medieval parish', *Transactions of the Monumental Brass Soc.*, xviii (2012), 289–310, at pp. 300–1; N. Saul, *English Church Monuments in the Middle Ages: History and Representation* (Oxford, 2009), pp. 120–9; J. M. Luxford, 'The collegiate church as mausoleum', in *The Late Medieval English College and its Context*, ed. C. Burgess and M. Heale (Woodbridge, 2008), pp. 110–39, at pp. 115–6; E. Duffy, *The Stripping of the Altars: Traditional Religion in England 1400–1580* (London, 1992), pp. 327–30.

[4] N. Holder, *The Friaries of Medieval London: From Foundation to Dissolution* (Woodbridge, 2017), pp. 293–304; J. Röhrkasten, *The Mendicant Houses of Medieval London*

The written evidence for burial at the Grey Friars by Newgate has revealed a necropolis of almost 1,000 graves in the church, its four chapels, the cloister and in the cemetery, and yet we know little on intercession by the friars.[5] Chantries and obits celebrated by the mendicant orders came to an abrupt end in 1538 and were long gone by the time of the 1548 inspection by Edward VI's chantry commissioners. There are no chantry certificates and we are largely reliant on testamentary instructions. Some 220 wills, proved between 1258 and 1538, have been examined, which has revealed the popularity of gift-giving and benefaction to the city Grey Friars.[6] The purpose of this chapter is twofold; to consider how those buried in the Franciscan church chose to be commemorated by anniversaries and chantries there; and to shed further light on the importance of this order with medieval Londoners. The surviving wills represent citizens of London who enjoyed the freedom of the city and those without citizenship, together with transitory residents, such as aliens from overseas and 'foreigns', that is, those from elsewhere in England who died while in the city. The latter, transient group were Londoners by abode rather than by freedom. Collectively, the instructions they made for their commemorations in their wills suggest how all types of Londoner chose to be remembered by the city's Franciscans. These instructions will be considered alongside a chantry agreement – the only one known to have survived – between William Cantelowe and John Kyry, warden of Grey Friars, which was ratified in 1460 on behalf of Thomas Gloucester (d. 1447) and his wife Anne. It is rare for such agreements to survive, and for the first time a translation is provided in the appendix to this chapter.[7] Testamentary evidence has been used to reveal the identities of those who set up anniversary and chantry

---

1221–1539 (Münster, 2004), pp. 459–70. For celebrations in other Franciscan churches in late medieval England, see, e.g., M. Robson, 'The commemoration of the living and the dead at the Friars Minor of Cambridge', in *Commemoration in Medieval Cambridge*, ed. J. S. Lee and C. Steer (Woodbridge, 2018), pp. 34–51.

[5] Kingsford, *Grey Friars of London*, *passim*. On the funerary monuments of Londoners in Grey Friars church, see C. Steer, 'The order of St. Francis in medieval London: urban benefactors and their tombs', in *Saints and Cults in Medieval England: Proceedings of the 2015 Harlaxton Symposium*, ed. S. Powell (Harlaxton Medieval Studies, n.s., xxvii, Donington, 2017), pp. 172–98.

[6] The 220 surviving wills were enrolled in the hustings, commissary and archdeaconry courts of London, the Prerogative Court of Canterbury and the archbishop's court at Lambeth.

[7] Only five others are known. For Austin Friars, see TNA, LR 14/488 (chantry agreement of Philip Bernard, vintner, 1418); LR 14/87 (chantry agreement of William, marquess Berkeley, 1491); LR 14/129 (chantry agreement of William Calley, draper, 1509); and LR 14/91 (chantry agreement of Nicholas Gerard, clothman of Wycombe, 1515). For Crutched Friars, see Chester Record Office DCG–x–132 (chantry agreement of Sir John Skevington, merchant tailor, 1516).

services at Grey Friars church. This evidence, when taken alongside the remarkable chantry agreement set up by William Cantelowe, sheds new light on the construction of memory and the ways in which the Franciscan friars cared for the souls of their benefactors in late medieval London.

Londoners and the Grey Friars

In the autumn of 1224 four Franciscan brothers, Richard of Ingworth, Richard of Devon, Henry of Treviso and Melioratus, arrived in the city of London.[8] They stayed briefly with the Dominican brothers in Holborn before moving to a house given to them by a city sheriff, John Travers, in Cornhill. These poor men of Christ were welcomed by Londoners with open arms, and a year later the Franciscans established their London convent near Newgate in a property provided for them by John Iwyn, a mercer, who himself later joined their order. The aldermanic class were particularly supportive of the Franciscans, and in the decades which followed wealthy Londoners provided land and money with which to expand their Newgate site. William Joynier, for example, mayor in 1239, paid for the construction of their first chapel. This was evidently quite splendid, but not in keeping with the teachings of St. Francis. It incurred the displeasure of William of Nottingham, provincial minister between 1240 and 1254, who ordered the roof to be taken down and for the bosses in the cloister to be removed.[9] And yet, as Hugh Lawrence has observed, 'the enthusiasm of patrons was not easy to resist' and Londoners continued to spend generously – even lavishly – on the expansion of the Franciscan convent.[10] Building work on the new aqueduct had begun around 1250, paid for by members of the Basing family and by the London pepperer Henry Frowyk (d. 1286), who served as mayor in 1272–3.[11] Other aldermen were important patrons: the wealthy alderman Arnold FitzThedmar, for example, bequeathed a substantial legacy of £100 to the Franciscans in his will of 1274 which enabled the friars to enlarge their site.[12] The mayor Gregory Rokesle (d. 1291) paid for the new dormitory; alderman Bartholomew de Castro, who died before 1311,

---

[8] Röhrkasten, *Mendicant Houses*, pp. 43–51.

[9] E. Gurney Salter (trans.), *The Coming of the Friars Minor to England and Germany: Being the Chronicles of Brother Thomas of Eccleston and Brother Jordan of Giano* (London, 1926), p. 63.

[10] C. H. Lawrence, *The Friars: the Impact of the Early Mendicant Movement on Western Society* (London, 1994), p. 53.

[11] Kingsford, *Grey Friars of London*, p. 48.

[12] Röhrkasten, *Mendicant Houses*, pp. 409–18; I. Stone, 'Arnold Fitz Thedmar: identity, politics and the city of London in the thirteenth century', *London Jour.*, xl (2015), 106–22.

financed the construction of the refectory, where an annual supper was to take place every St. Bartholomew's day (24 August).[13] Both men were buried in Grey Friars church and commemorated as benefactors: Rokesle as '*valens burgensis, et quondam Maior Londonie*' [a worthy burgess, and former mayor of London] and Castro as a '*valens miles et civis Londonie: fecit Refectorium*' [a worthy knight and citizen of London: he made the refectory].[14] The most important, and generous, of London patrons was Henry le Waleys, wealthy vintner, alderman, mayor of London and Bordeaux and a diplomat for Edward I, who at the end of the thirteenth century provided the money to begin construction of the nave.[15]

The popularity of the London Grey Friars was such that royal and aristocratic benefaction would match, if not exceed, civic funding during the first half of the fourteenth century.[16] But contemporary Londoners remained as involved with the Grey Friars as their forebears had been. There were, for example, at least twenty-five Londoners who commissioned glazing in the church's thirty-six windows, ten of whom were from the elite, such as the aldermen Richard de Gloucester (d. 1323), Simon de Parys (d. 1324) and Walter Mordon (d. 1351), and a number of former mayors, among whom were Richard Betoyne (d. 1341), John Lovekyn (d. 1368) and Stephen Cavendish (d. 1372).[17] The city companies, too, acted as collective donors: the Vintners, for example, provided one of the windows in the choir.[18] Testamentary evidence reveals a little about gift-giving by other wealthy Londoners, such as the bequest of £20 provided by Guy Lambyn, fishmonger, in his will of 1361.[19] Other Londoners left gifts in kind, such

---

[13] Kingsford, *Grey Friars of London*, p. 34.

[14] Kingsford, *Grey Friars of London*, p. 73 (Rokesele) and p. 85 (de Castro). The latter was not, in fact, accorded knighthood and de Castro was evidently referred as '*miles*' [knight] to mark his status as a patron of the Grey Friars.

[15] Kingsford, *Grey Friars of London*, pp. 34–5, 73 and 85; Röhrkasten, *Mendicant Houses*, pp. 419–22. On Waleys, see A. Crawford, *A History of the Vintners' Company* (London, 1977), pp. 39–41; and also F. Lachaud, 'Waleys, Henry le (d. 1302), merchant and mayor of London', in *ODNB* <https://doi.org/10.1093/ref:odnb/28460> [accessed 19 Oct. 2018].

[16] C. Steer, 'Royal and noble commemoration in the mendicant houses of London, c.1240–1540', in *Memory and Commemoration in Medieval England: Proceedings of the 2008 Harlaxton Symposium*, ed. C. M. Barron and C. Burgess (Harlaxton Medieval Studies, n.s., xx, Donington, 2010), pp. 117–42, at pp. 127–30.

[17] Kingsford, *Grey Friars of London*, pp. 36–8, 165–9; Röhrkasten, *Mendicant Houses*, pp. 433–6.

[18] Kingsford, *Grey Friars of London*, p. 68; Holder, *Friaries of Medieval London*, p. 8. In 1611 the heralds Sir Henry St. George and Nicholas Charles visited the former Grey Friars church (now Christ Church) and drew copies of the armorials they saw in the surviving medieval glass (BL, Lansdowne MS. 874, fos. 105v–106).

[19] LMA, CLA/023/DW/01/089 (186).

as the silver cup given by John Warener alias Walsyngham, armourer, in 1382 and the russet cloth bequeathed by the widow Alice Wodegate in 1388.[20] By the mid fourteenth century large-scale building work at Grey Friars had come to an end and a shift in fund-raising activities seems to have taken place thereafter.[21] Testamentary evidence, moreover, suggests that individual Franciscan friars were popular among the laity: brother John Bavel, for example, received a legacy of 2s from Maud atte Stone, widow, in 1393 and eight years later the city grocer John Vaunde left 40s to Friar John Lees to pray for him.[22] Bequests reveal the identity of friars who served as confessors and spiritual advisors to a number of testators: in 1413, for instance, Gaillard Denbidan, a merchant from Bordeaux, left 1 mark to Gerald de Crugiacha of the London Grey Friars to pray for him.[23] Other friars were particularly popular with testators: brother William Wolfe (d. 1466), for example, can be found in several wills of the 1450s, when the Franciscans enjoyed notable popularity.[24] In 1452, for example, he received three gold tablets and a silver cup from Joan Neumarche, widow, who appointed Wolfe to celebrate mass for her soul. She also named Dr. Wolfe as one of her executors.[25] Only four years later Elizabeth Rikill, a widow, left 40s to six priests of the Grey Friars who were to pray for her soul according to the instructions of William Wolfe. She also bequeathed a silver covered cup, called a 'fflattecuppe', on which the arms of her late husband Thomas Rikill were displayed, to the warden of the Grey Friars to meet the cost of general repairs to the convent. She bequeathed another

---

[20] LMA, CLA/023/DW/01/111 (117) (will of John Warener alias Walsyngham); CLA/023/DW/01/117 (44) (will of Alice Wodegate).

[21] A noted exception was the Grey Friars library, paid for by Richard Whittington and constructed between 1411 and 1415 (Holder, *Friaries of Medieval London*, pp. 86–90). There are no surviving records for daily alms-giving to the friars, but an analysis of some 2,900 wills, proved between 1349 and 1500, revealed the sustained popularity of bequests to all the mendicant orders (Röhrkasten, *Mendicant Houses*, pp. 261–76). Professor Röhrkasten's analysis was based on the probate registers of the hustings, commissary and archdeaconry courts of London and the Prerogative Court of Canterbury. Röhrkasten provided a note of caution on the completeness of testamentary evidence (as *post-mortem* acts of charity) and reminded us of the tradition practised by London testators, who often provided a standard bequest, of varying value, to all four orders of mendicant friars. It is impossible to assess the monetary value of income derived from rents or gifts in kind such as those bequeathed by John Warener or Alice Wodegate (n. 20 above), but made in the lifetime of the donor.

[22] LMA, DL/C/B/004/MS09171/001, fos. 284v–285v (will of Maud atte Stone); DL/C/B/004/MS09171/002, fo. 9r–v (will of John Vaunde).

[23] LMA, DL/C/B/004/MS09171/002, fos. 262v–263.

[24] Röhrkasten, *Mendicant Houses*, pp. 270–3, table 3. On Wolfe, see *BRUO (to A.D. 1500)*, iii. 2230.

[25] LMA, DL/C/B/004/MS09171/005, fo. 110r–v.

silver cup to William Wolfe, who, in return, was to pray for her soul.[26] The regard wealthy testators had for Friar Wolfe is revealed by the extract from the epitaph on his tombstone, copied into the Grey Friars register: *frater Willelmus Wolfe, doctor egregius, apud principes et nobiles magnificere acceptus* [brother William Wolfe, outstanding doctor, magnificently received among princes and nobles].[27] Other friars were also held in high esteem, as demonstrated by John Cutler (d. 1530), who served as warden at different times between 1505 and 1521. It was he who, in 1514, persuaded the city aldermen to resume their ancient role as 'patrons and founders' of London Grey Friars and to attend the annual procession to the church on St. Francis's day, 4 October.[28] Cutler was evidently a man of marked determination for, on 20 March 1517, he was once again before the court of aldermen procuring funds to settle a debt of £16 15s incurred in repaving the nave.[29] Five years earlier Dr. Cutler had witnessed the will of William Maryner, salter, who bequeathed the generous sum of £10 towards the repaving project in return for prayers by the friars 'among other their benefactors'.[30] Cutler was evidently a dynamic and engaging presence but also a friar trusted to serve as executor, supervisor and witness for at least six testators buried in London Grey Friars.[31]

Londoners remained steadfast supporters of the Franciscan order throughout the later middle ages. They paid for the construction of the church and its ancillary buildings and constantly supported the friars in different ways, through private legacies, bequests in return for prayers and intercession and by employing friars in the administration of their estates. The Franciscans remained popular with Londoners in life and in death and it was to them that many in the city came to entrust their commemorations.

---

[26] LMA, DL/C/B/004/MS09171/005, fo. 197.

[27] Kingsford, *Grey Friars of London*, p. 83.

[28] City of London repertories, LMA, COL/CA/01/01/002, fo. 185; see also LMA, *Letter Book M*, fo. 224. Cutler is discussed further in Steer, 'The order of St. Francis', pp. 177–9.

[29] LMA, COL/CA/01/01/003, fos. 13–14.

[30] TNA, PROB 11/12, fos. 56–57v.

[31] As executor: LMA, DL/A/A/004/MS09531/009, fos. 8v–10 (will of Katherine Langley, vowess, 1511); as overseer: TNA, PROB 11/14, fos. 217v–218v (will of Joan Hastings, Lady Willoughby and Welles, 1505); LMA, DL/C/B/004/MS09171/009, fo. 37r–v (will of Julian Maryner, widow, 1517); DL/C/B/004/MS09171/009, fo. 181v (will of Robert White, grocer, 1521); and DL/C/B/004/MS09171/009, fos. 177v–178 (will of Ralph Massy, gentleman, 1522); as witness: TNA, PROB 11/17, fos. 56–57v (will of William Maryner, salter, 1512); and LMA, DL/C/B/004/MS09171/009, fos. 177v–178 (will of Ralph Massy, gentleman, 1522).

Anniversaries of the dead

The year's mind, or anniversary, was adaptable in duration and affordable in cost.[32] At least twenty-two testators requested anniversaries to be celebrated by the Franciscans in their city church.[33] The earliest known obit was established by Thomas Cornton, a haberdasher of St. Mildred Poultry, who bequeathed 40s to the warden and convent for daily mass for one year, with a special observance on the day of his anniversary.[34] He died on 24 April 1410 and was buried in the north aisle.[35] Testators buried at the Grey Friars in the fifteenth century rarely specified the details of their obit, suggesting that they relied on other forms of agreement and probably on verbal arrangements with and trust in their executors. Neither Joan Neumarche (d. 1452) nor Joan Danvers (d. 1459), for example, set down the terms of their anniversaries, which were, presumably, left in the hands of their executors.[36] The arrangements drawn up by John Barre in 1439, however, were broadly typical of many such requests. He instructed that prayers were to be said

[32] Duffy, *Stripping of the Altars*, pp. 327–8; C. Burgess, 'A service for the dead: the form and function of the anniversary in late medieval Bristol', *Trans. Bristol and Gloucestershire Archaeol. Soc.*, cv (1987), 183–211.

[33] LMA, DL/C/B/004/MS09171/002, fos. 171–3 (will of Thomas Cornton, haberdasher, 1410); CLA/023/DW/01/167 (59) and TNA, PROB 11/3, fos. 200–202v (will of John Barre alias Markeby, skinner, 1439); TNA, C 270/32/21 (agreement made by William Cantelowe, mercer, 1460, on behalf of Thomas Gloucester, esquire (d. 1447)); LMA, DL/C/B/004/MS09171/005, fo. 110r–v (will of Joan Neumarch, widow, 1452); TNA, PROB 11/4, fos. 82v–83v (will of Joan Danvers, widow, 1457, on behalf of her husband William, esquire (d. 1439)); PROB 11/7, fo. 62r–v (will of John Fernandes, brigandine maker, 1483); PROB 11/8, fos. 124–6 (will of Lady Elizabeth Uvedale, widow, 1488); LMA, DL/C/B/004/MS09171/008, fo. 74 (will of Agnes Arnold, widow, 1490, on behalf of her husband John, brewer (d. 1470)); TNA, PROB 11/9, fos. 26v–27 (will of Robert Dauntsey, of Walden (Essex), 1491); PROB 11/9, fo. 227r–v (will of Roger Spencer, goldsmith, 1492); PROB 11/10, fos. 57v–58v (will of John Ryvers, skinner, 1493); PROB 11/12, fo. 161r–v (will of Margaret Yonge, widow, 1500); PROB 11/12, fos. 61v–62 (will of Richard Godfrey, salter, 1500); PROB 11/14, fo. 244 (will of Henry Southill, esquire, 1505); PROB 11/16, fos. 104–5 (will of John, Lord Dynham, 1509); PROB 11/16, fo. 231 (will of Thomas Pickering, gentleman, 1510); LMA, DL/A/A/004/MS09531/009, fo. 199v (will of Rowland Blount, esquire, 1509); TNA, PROB 11/20, fos. 15v–16 (will of John Tresawell, merchant tailor, 1520); LMA, CLA/023/DW/01/242 (10) (will of John Benett, merchant tailor, 1527, on behalf of Sir Stephen Jenyns, alderman (d. 1523)); DL/C/B/004/MS09171/010, fo. 79v–80 (will of Alice Baynton, widow, 1527); TNA, PROB 11/23, fos. 91v–92 (will of Stephen Lynne, haberdasher, 1529); and TNA, SC6 /HenVIII/2396, m. 62r–v (minister's accounts for the court of augmentations, 1540, payment of 70s due from the Drapers' Company for the obit of Hugh Acton at Grey Friars church).

[34] LMA, DL/C/B/004/MS09171/002, fos. 171–3.

[35] Kingsford, *The Grey Friars of London*, p. 121.

[36] LMA, DL/C/B/004/MS09171/005, fo. 110r–v (will of Joan Neumarche); TNA, PROB 11/4, fos. 82v–83v (will of Joan Danvers).

with *Placebo* and *Dirge* sung the night before his anniversary and mass of requiem celebrated the following morning. Two candles were to burn at the Grey Friars during the celebrations and, unusually, another two in his parish church of St. John Walbrook. He bequeathed 3*s* 4*d* to the Greyfriars for celebrating his memorial and a further 20*d* for the four candles. What is striking is that these arrangements were to be established after the death of Barre's widow, Alice, which suggests that she had been entrusted with the management of his obit during her lifetime.[37]

Executors were attentive to these long-term foundations. After the death of John Wood on 28 October 1487 a daily mass was to be celebrated at the Grey Friars up until his month's mind.[38] John Wood was buried in the nave, where a tombstone included an inscription for Wood and three of his four wives, Agnes, Margaret and Edith.[39] He was attentive to his commemorative wellbeing. He left, among several generous bequests, £40 for a suit of vestments and a mortuary cloth, which were to be made within three years and kept by the Fraternity of Our Lady and St. Stephen at St. Sepulchre, his parish church. They were to include the Grocers' arms and Wood's merchant mark within the morse and inscribed '*Orate pro anima Johannis Woode*' [pray for the soul of John Wood]. The mortuary cloth was to be used at the burial of the brothers and sisters of the fraternity and brought to the Grey Friars once a year, where it was to be displayed on his hearse at his year's mind (anniversary). This is a striking example of co-operation between a parish and the Grey Friars. His two executors were his widow Edith and William Maryner, salter. Ten years later 'a devout lady' named Edith (her surname was not given), who 'had a particular devotion to the monastery and friars of the house of the Friars Minor', entered into an agreement with the warden Andrew Bavard and with the brethren for a twenty-year obit for herself and her late husband John and her parents John and Agnes. The obit was to take place 'when she [Edith] quits the light'.[40] It seems likely that Widow Edith was, in fact, the widow of John Wood and it was her intention to set up another anniversary service for them both and for her parents, which the friars were to celebrate after her death. Edith was dead by 1512, when the surviving executor Maryner drew up his own will. He went to some care to ensure the continuation of their memorial and left the remaining lease of Wood's property to Christopher Norton,

---

[37] LMA, CLA/023/DW/01/167 (59) and TNA, PROB 11/3, fos. 200–202v.

[38] TNA, PROB 11/8, fo. 231r–v.

[39] Kingsford, *Grey Friars of London*, p. 112. In his will Wood referred to a fourth wife, Margaret, but evidently her name was not recorded on the inscription.

[40] BL, Harley Ch. 44 F 47, reprinted in Kingsford, *Grey Friars of London*, p. 211. The above quotations are provided in translation from Latin.

grocer of St. Sepulchre. Norton was to maintain the Wood anniversary at Grey Friars every 28 October and to spend 40s, with 3s 4d set aside for the *Dirige* and requiem mass; 3s 4d on bread and ale; and 3s 4d to the masters and brethren of the Fraternity of Our Lady and St. Stephen, who were to be present at the memorial.[41] The mortuary cloth commissioned by Wood would presumably have been laid out over his grave in the nave.

Anniversaries were not always established directly by the testator, and the case of Sir Stephen Jenyns, alderman, mayor and merchant tailor (d. 1523), is of interest. The exact circumstances surrounding the administration of the Jenyns estate are now lost, but somewhere between 1523 and 1527 his executors, John Nicholls alias Mitchell and John Kirton, both of whom were merchant tailors, enfeoffed John Benett, master of the Merchant Taylors' Company in 1528, with property in the city of London. Benett drew up his will on 24 January 1527 and bequeathed this estate to the master and wardens of the Fraternity of St. John the Baptist of the Merchant Taylors' Company, who were to endow a perpetual chantry (discussed below) and an anniversary for Sir Stephen.[42] The anniversary was to take place on 6 May with the exequies of *Placebo* and *Dirige* held in the evening before and a requiem mass the following morning. The warden of the Grey Friars was to receive 13s 4d. Benett inserted a clause whereby if the anniversary could not be performed on 6 May, it was to be celebrated within eight days and due notice of the new date given to the mayor, sheriff, the prior of the hospital of St. Mary within Cripplegate (better known as Elsingspital, that is, Elsing hospital) and to the master and wardens of the Merchant Taylors' Company, each of whom were to attend the year's mind. These city dignitaries were paid to attend the anniversary by the Fraternity of St. John the Baptist.[43] A further legacy of 6s 8d was paid to the prior of Elsingspital to attend the anniversary 'to see this my last will observed perfourmed and kept'. The attention to detail by John Benett is striking. We know that the Merchant Taylors honoured the legacy, for in the ministers' accounts in the court of augmentations for the year ending September 1540 a payment of £4 was recorded 'from the Taylors of London for the anniversary of Sir Stephen

---

[41] TNA, PROB 11/12, fos. 56–57v. William Maryner was evidently a man of some regard and administrative capabilities. He also set up a perpetual chantry for Robert Brown (d. 1483), innkeeper of St. Matthew Friday Street, in his own will and was instrumental in setting up the anniversary of Joan FitzLewes, widow, at the Minories at Aldgate; on the FitzLewes commemorations, see J. Luxford, 'The testament of Joan FitzLewes: a source for the history of the abbey of Franciscan nuns without Aldgate' in this volume.

[42] LMA, CLA/023/DW/01/242 (10).

[43] The sums are as follows: 6s 8d for the mayor; 3s 4d apiece to the sheriffs; 2s to the sword bearer; 3s 4d to the master of the Fraternity of St. John the Baptist; 20d to each of the wardens of the fraternity; and 8d to the clerk; and 8d to the beadle.

Genynnes'.[44] The Jenyns obit is revealing not only on the processes involved in founding a perpetual anniversary at London Grey Friars, but also the important role played by civic and company officials in their attendance at this ceremony.

Other testators set up anniversaries in Grey Friars church for shorter, but still long-lasting, periods. There are five known instances of twenty-year obits,[45] one for eight,[46] one for seven[47] and another for five years.[48] The arrangements made by Agnes Arnold in 1493 are notable. Her husband John, a brewer, had died in 1470 and was buried in the north aisle of the Grey Friars church close to the pietà that he had donated.[49] Agnes chose to be buried in the great cemetery of Old St. Paul's but set up a twenty-year chantry at Grey Friars church. This was to be maintained from her lease of a brewhouse called the Lamp, close to the friars' precinct. This lease was to run for a further twenty years and provide 6s 8d per annum, which was to be spent on the Arnold obit. The friars were to take 3s 4d, with the balance being distributed in alms to the poor. The bequest, over twenty years, came to £6 13s 4d (or 10 marks).[50]

Anniversaries at Grey Friars church were set up by Londoners, their widows and executors, as well as those who were visiting the city. The Franciscans were well equipped to take care of these obits since they had a constant supply of priest-friars who passed through the London convent. The Franciscans were able to complement what was on offer in the city's 100 or so parish churches, the forty-five religious houses and the cathedral of Old St. Paul's. It seems clear that patrons, or the agent acting on their behalf, took a keen interest in making sure that the anniversary was properly established and that there was complete clarity about where and when the friars were to remember their benefactors.

Short-term chantries

The Franciscan friars were as popular with Londoners as they were with royal and noble benefactors. Their ministry appealed to all. An examination

[44] TNA, SC6 /HenVIII/2396 (m. 62r–v), fo. 62v.

[45] LMA, DL/C/B/004/MS09171/008, fo. 74 (will of Agnes Arnold); TNA, PROB 11/12, fo. 161r–v (will of Margaret Yonge); PROB 11/12, fos. 61v–2 (will of Richard Godfrey); PROB 11/16, fo. 231 (will of Thomas Pickering); and PROB 11/20, fos. 15v–16 (will of John Tresawell).

[46] TNA, PROB 11/23, fos. 91v–92 (will of Stephen Lynne).

[47] TNA, PROB 11/10, fos. 57v–58v (will of John Ryvers).

[48] TNA, PROB 11/9, fo. 227r–v (will of Roger Spencer).

[49] LMA, DL/C/B/004/MS09171/006, fo. 62v.

[50] LMA, DL/C/B/004/MS09171/008, fo. 74. This may have been the 'going rate' for in 1510 the Yorkshire squire, Thomas Pickering, set up his own 20-year anniversary at 6s 8d per annum to the friars (TNA, PROB 11/16, fo. 231).

of the wills consulted in this study has revealed thirteen testators who left arrangements in their wills for short-term chantries at London Grey Friars.[51] Only one case has been identified from before 1450: Thomas Cornton, who, as well as arranging an anniversary celebration with the Greyfriars, bequeathed £2 for his one-year chantry.[52]

Temporary chantry foundation seems to have flourished in the Grey Friars church from the 1490s, with no fewer than eleven known examples identified up to 1538.[53] The will sample is small, but this apparent increase in chantry endowment might suggest a re-energized popularity. The earliest instance is found in the will of Alice Barker, who died in 1490. She was widow of John Wetwang, brewer (d. 1463), and Philip Barker, whose date of death is unknown, and left a lump sum of £10 to the Grey Friars for her burial and exequies and for a ten-year chantry for herself and her late husbands. She set down that her executors, John Hothersall, notary and stationer, and William Briggs were to appoint the friar who was to celebrate for her soul and those of her former husbands. The friar-priest was to receive 26s 8d (paid at four times of the year) and was to celebrate mass daily and to recite the *De Profundis* at the first lavatory before the elevation.[54] Widow Barker stipulated that if there were any lapse in her daily mass then the friar would answer 'before god atte the day of dome'. She certainly was determined to get what she wanted.

Other arrangements are of equal note. Thurstan Hatfield (d. 1491), a former sergeant of the crown to Edward IV, was buried in the Apostles chapel close to the king's former treasurer, Walter Blount, Lord Mountjoy (d. 1474), whom Hatfield referred to as his late master.[55] Hatfield set down

---

[51] Thomas Cornton, haberdasher (d. 1410); Alexander Crayke, lawyer (d. 1465); Alice Barker, widow (d. 1490); Thurstan Hatfield, sergeant to the crown (d. 1491); Richard Hastings, Lord Willoughby and Welles (d. 1503); John Ryvers, gentleman (d. 1506); John, Lord Dynham (d. 1509); Thomas Pickering, gentleman (d. 1510); Edward Ashley, goldsmith (d. 1518); John Tresawell, merchant tailor (d. 1520); Nicholas White, skinner (d. 1521); Robert Brown, of Walsingham (Norf.) (d. 1527); and Stephen Lynne, haberdasher (d. 1527).

[52] DL/C/B/004/MS09171/002, fos. 171–3.

[53] LMA, DL/C/B/004/MS09171/008, fos. 13v–14 (Alice Barker, widow, 1490); TNA, PROB 11/9, fos. 231v–232 (Thurstan Hatfield, sergeant to the crown, 1491); PROB 11/13, fo. 243r–v (Richard Hastings, Lord Willoughby and Welles, 1503); PROB 11/15, fo. 166r–v (John Ryvers, gentleman); PROB 11/16, fos. 104–5 (John, Lord Dynham, 1509); PROB 11/16, fo. 231 (Thomas Pickering, gentleman); PROB 11/19, fo. 59 (Edward Ashley, goldsmith, 1519); PROB 11/20, fos. 15v–16 (John Tresawell, merchant tailor, 1520); PROB 11/20, fo. 165 (Nicholas White, skinner, 1521); PROB 11/22, fo. 81 (Robert Brown, mercer, of Norfolk, 1526); and PROB 11/23, fos. 91v–92 (Stephen Lynne, haberdasher).

[54] From '*lavatorium*', washing place, in reference to the ritual hand-washing that takes place during the eucharist after the offertory of the mass and before the consecration.

[55] Kingsford, *Grey Friars of London*, p. 91.

that his chantry was to be celebrated by a Franciscan friar and was to last for a quarter of a year only, at a salary of £1 13s 4d.[56] This represents an unusually brief, short-term foundation. Hatfield's instructions for the friar are revealing in other ways, too. Once the friar had celebrated mass and recited the *De Profundis* he was 'to cast holy water apon my grave for my soule and all Christen soules ther buried'.[57] Hatfield was buried close to Lord Mountjoy and other members of the Blount family, who were to benefit from Hatfield's exequies. It is difficult to understand why this chantry was so brief: the legacies left by Hatfield suggest he enjoyed modest wealth. Nevertheless, this shows that the friars were adept at meeting the different commemorative needs of their patrons and were at ease in celebrating for whatever period was required. The recitation of the *De Profundis* at the grave was standard practice but the act of sprinkling holy water over the tomb is the only known instance of such practice at Grey Friars church.

Legacies to the Franciscans varied in value. The chantries set up by Edward Ashley, goldsmith, who died in 1518, and John Tresawell, merchant tailor, who died two years later, contrast sharply with comparable endowments set up in parish churches. Ashley left 100 marks to the Franciscans, who were to provide a friar who was to sing daily and to say a 'lowe dirige' once a week. This was to last for ten years and would have provided £6 13s 4d a year. Ashley also left an annual 10 marks (or £6 13s 4d) for a chaplain to celebrate in his parish church of St. Michael le Querne for five years.[58] Tresawell, on the other hand, left slightly less but set up his own chantry at Grey Friars for longer, seven years, at £3 6s 8d per annum out of a lump sum of £23 6s 8d.[59] The annuity would have been insufficient to meet the living costs for a parish chaplain for seven years, but the advantage of arranging this with the Franciscans meant that the testator could benefit from the resident friars at the convent, making them a cheaper alternative to a parish chaplain. But as Edward Ashley's arrangements make clear, the friars were also the happy recipients of larger sums to pay for commemorative aftercare.

There was a mixed approach to short-term chantry foundation for those buried in London Grey Friars. Some preferred to enjoy liturgical commemoration at their parish church; some set down the terms the Franciscans were to follow; but others did both. The adaptability of the friars to cater for different requests is evident, suggesting the flexibility of

---

[56] The annual equivalent would have been £6 13s 4d.

[57] TNA, PROB 11/9, fos. 231v–232. Hatfield also endowed a second temporary chantry in the parish church of Glossop (Derbyshire), which was to last for the more conventional one year.

[58] TNA, PROB 11/19, fo. 59.

[59] TNA, PROB 11/20, fos. 15v–16.

their commemorative portfolio, which could be adapted to the needs of different benefactors.

Perpetual chantries

Studies of the medieval chantry generally have focused on perpetual foundations established in parish churches. The evidence available from the 1548 chantry certificates, taken alongside testamentary evidence, churchwardens' accounts, foundation deeds preserved in municipal archives and mortmain licences recorded in the patent rolls, has revealed the process of foundation, management and maintenance and, at times, something about the chaplains who served past founders.[60] While founders would, as a matter of course, have taken great care in establishing these arrangements, only a few detailed foundation agreements survive – and, indeed, for those that were to be celebrated in the church of London Grey Friars, only one is known.[61]

Almost nothing survives for perpetual chantry foundation at Grey Friars church before the mid fifteenth century. In 1345 a London Franciscan, Thomas Heyroun, was nominated by Olive de Myngy of Norton Mandeville (Essex) to endow chantries from the proceeds of her estate. But the terms of her will are unclear and it is not known whether these were to be of perpetual or short-term duration or, indeed, whether they were to be established in the city of London or elsewhere.[62] One of the city's wealthiest merchants, alderman and mayor Sir John Philipot (d. 1384), was buried in the Apostles

---

[60] The standard work on perpetual chantries remains K. L. Wood-Legh, *Perpetual Chantries in Britain* (Cambridge, 1965). More recently see, e.g., C. Steer, '"To syng and do dommeservyce": the chantry chaplains of St. Nicholas Shambles', in *The Urban Church: Essays in Honour of Clive Burgess: Proceedings of the 2017 Harlaxton Symposium*, ed. D. Harry and C. Steer (Harlaxton Medieval Studies, n.s., xxix, Donington, 2019), pp. 449–79; *The Medieval Chantry in England*, ed. J. M. Luxford and J. McNeill (Leeds, 2011), *passim*; C. Burgess, 'Shaping the parish: St. Mary at Hill, London, in the fifteenth century', in *The Cloister and the World: Essays in Medieval History in Honour of Barbara* Harvey, ed. J. Bair and B. Golding (Oxford, 1996), pp. 246–86; R. B. Dobson, 'The foundation of perpetual chantries by the citizens of medieval York', in R. B. Dobson, *Church and Society in the Medieval North of England* (London, 1996), pp. 253–66; C. Burgess, 'Strategies for eternity: perpetual chantry foundation in late medieval Bristol', in *Religious Belief and Ecclesiastical Careers in Late Medieval England*, ed. C. Harper-Bill (Woodbridge, 1991), pp. 1–32; N. Tanner, *The Church in Late Medieval Norwich 1370–1532* (Toronto, 1984), pp. 92–8; A. Kreider, *English Chantries: the Road to Dissolution* (Cambridge, Mass., 1979); R. Hill, '"A chauntarie for souls": London chantries in the reign of Richard II', in *The Reign of Richard II: Essays in Honour of May McKisack*, ed. C. M. Barron and F. R. H. Du Boulay (London, 1971), pp. 242–55.

[61] On chantry agreements for other mendicant churches of London, see n. 7.

[62] LMA, CLA/023/DW/01/072 (89).

chapel of the Grey Friars with his first wife, Joan.[63] He is the earliest known testator buried in their church who established chantry foundations, but he sited them elsewhere, at the priory of St. Pancras, Lewes (Sussex) and another at his manor chapel at Grange near Gillingham (Kent).[64] It is unknown whether he enjoyed similar commemoration at Grey Friars church.

At least six perpetual chantries were established in Grey Friars church in the fifteenth century.[65] Of these, we know most about the earliest of them from documentation generated as the result of a protracted foundation process. This was arranged in 1458 on behalf of Thomas Gloucester, esquire, who had died eleven years before, and his wife Anne. Gloucester relied on a nuncupative will of 31 January 1447 made only six days before he died on the feast of St. Agatha. He was receiver-general of the duchy of Cornwall and cofferer to Henry VI.[66] He apparently was in charge of the king's strongboxes at the time of his death and, in a codicil to his will, requested that any debts owing to the king should be settled before all others. There were evidently delays in arranging this and, on 5 June 1448, Sir John Popham, treasurer, petitioned to recover debts of £585 14s 9d owed to the royal household and which Gloucester's executors, John Edward and Walter Gorsen, had not yet paid. Such was Sir John's concern that these debts be settled that the executors' agreement to meet their obligations was copied into the patent rolls.[67] The complexities in administering the Gloucester estate probably explain the delay in setting up his chantry in Grey Friars, where a priest was to celebrate for the testator and his wife at £6 13s 4d per annum.[68] Gloucester's executors were also to arrange a second foundation in the church of St. Nicholas, Gloucester (presumably Thomas's birthplace), where the chaplain was to celebrate daily. The celebrant was also to teach grammar to the local children, without charge; and for this

---

[63] Kingsford, *Grey Friars of London*, p. 91.

[64] LMA, CLA/023/DW/01/118 (30).

[65] TNA, C 270/32/21 (chantry agreement between William Cantelowe, on behalf of Thomas Gloucester, esquire, and the London Grey Friars, 1460); TNA, PROB 11/6, fo. 41r–v (will of John Wardall, canon and doctor of law, 1472); PROB 11/8, fos. 124–6 (Elizabeth, widow of Sir Thomas Uvedale, 1488); PROB 11/14, fos. 217v–218v (Joan, on behalf of her husband Richard Hastings, Lord Willoughby and Welles, 1505); LMA, DL/C/B/004/MS09171/009, fo. 37r–v (Julian, widow of William Maryner, 1517; her chantry was limited to 200 years but for the purpose of this discussion is considered together with the perpetual foundations of London Grey Friars); and CLA/023/DW/01/242 (10) (John Benett, on behalf of Sir Stephen Jenyns, 1527).

[66] *CPR 1446–52*, pp. 134–5; *CPR 1452–61*, pp. 30–1.

[67] *CPR 1446–52*, pp. 134–5. Gorsen was possibly dead by 1452, for on 20 Dec. Edward was pardoned of any outstanding debts due from the Gloucester estate, excluding those relating to the duchy of Cornwall (*CPR 1452–61*, pp. 30–1).

[68] Lambeth Palace Library, Reg. Stafford, fo. 146r–v.

and for celebrating the daily mass the Gloucester estate was to pay him a yearly salary of 20 marks (£13 6s 8d). The school, however, was never established.[69] It was to be ten years before any agreement was made with the London Grey Friars but neither Edward nor Gorsen was involved: it was left to William Cantelowe, alderman, mercer and former sheriff (d. 1464), to act on Gloucester's behalf.[70] On 26 March 1458 an indenture was drawn up between Cantelowe and John Kyry, warden of the London Grey Friars.[71] It was ratified by a notarial instrument two years later (see appendix).[72] This contract is remarkable, for it reveals much on the day-to-day detail of chantry commemoration as practised by the friars on behalf of friends and benefactors.

The agreement was originally drafted on 26 March 1458. It was confirmed two years later, on 27 March 1460, when it was witnessed by thirty friars present in the chapter house. It is rare to find the names of the brethren at a particular moment and their inclusion reveals the size of their community in mid fifteenth-century London. Their presence was evidently required specifically to witness the agreement previously made between William Cantelowe and John Kyry. Thomas Radnor, provincial minister of the order, presided at this ceremony together with William Goddard senior, master and guardian, and Kyry, warden. William Cantelowe promised to provide a lump sum of £200 to pay for repairs to the church and towards the running costs of the convent. In return, the friars were to celebrate a daily mass in memory of Thomas Gloucester and his wife Anne and for Cantelowe and his own wives, Margaret and Elizabeth, their respective parents, children and benefactors. The mass was to be sung near the grave of

---

[69] N. Orme, 'Education in medieval Bristol and Gloucestershire', *Trans. Bristol and Gloucestershire Archaeol. Soc.*, cxxii (2004), 9–27, at pp. 13–4.

[70] The two were close associates. See History of Parliament Trust, London, unpublished article on William Cantelowe for the 1422–61 section by M. Davies. I am grateful to the History of Parliament Trust for allowing me to see this article in draft. See also G. Holmes, 'Cantelowe, Sir William (d. 1464), merchant', in *ODNB* <https://doi.org/10.1093/ref:odnb/52243> [accessed 7 Dec. 2018].

[71] TNA, E 40/11314, printed in Kingsford, *Grey Friars of London*, pp. 208–11.

[72] TNA, C 270/32/21, printed in C. L. Kingsford, 'Additional material for the history of the Grey Friars, London', *Collectanea Franciscana II* (Manchester, 1922), pp. 61–149, at pp. 145–7. William Cantelowe also acted on behalf of his father-in-law, Laurence Pygot (d. 1450), wool merchant, and his wife Alice (d. 1453), of Dunstable (Beds.), and established their chantry at the Black Friars of Dunstable in 1460 (TNA, C 270/32/22). It is striking that a notarial instrument was used to confirm the earlier agreement, rather than an *inspeximus*, which perhaps reflects the international nature of the order and the need to have an agreement recognized across Europe. I thank Elizabeth New for this observation. See also J. L. Bolton, 'William Styfford (fl. 1437–1466): citizen and scrivener of London and notary imperial' in this volume.

Thomas and Anne Gloucester, which was located in the Lady chapel.[73] The only days when mass was not celebrated were the three days in '*ebdomada maiori*' [the greater week] before Easter Day, the *Triduum sacrum*, during which private masses were forbidden.[74] The agreement explained that it was the responsibility of the precentor of the London convent to assign on his '*tabula*' [board] the name of the friar appointed each week to celebrate at the Gloucester chantry. The appointed friar was to say, on bended knees, the *De Profundis*, either immediately before or after the mass, and to say before and after, in English, 'For the souls of Thomas Gloucester and Anne his consort and of William Cantelowe, of Margaret and Elizabeth his wives, of their parents, offspring and benefactors'. This was to be followed by the tract *Absolve Domine*. The friars were to say aloud the names of Thomas and Anne Gloucester and of William Cantelowe and his wives, Elizabeth and Margaret, every week in chapter in perpetuity. They were to be part of the friars' roll-call of benefactors. Their names were also to be read out at the feast of All Saints (1 November) when, so the agreement informs us, the number of friars present in the chapter house was at its highest and when the indenture between Cantelowe and the Franciscans was once again to be read out. This agreement was also to be copied into the friars' statute book.[75]

This agreement is particularly instructive in two respects. First, it provides evidence about the performance of chantry obligations by the Franciscan friars and particularly for one noted benefactor, Thomas Gloucester and his wife Anne. They were referred to in the register as *principui benefactores huius conventus* [principal benefactors of this convent], doubtless reflective of the generous gift of £200 forthcoming through the agency of William Cantelowe.[76] The location of the chantry mass, close to where the Gloucesters were buried, is, perhaps, not surprising, given the dovetailed relationship between the anniversaries of the dead and their tombs. What is more striking is the role of the precentor as 'duty manager' in adding the name of the friar-priest appointed to each chantry mass on a '*tabula*' displayed within the convent. Significantly, we learn that such priests were assigned on a weekly basis, reflecting, perhaps, the peripatetic nature of the friars' vocation. The use of the vernacular in naming the patrons of the chantry, immediately before and after the psalm *De Profundis* was read out, is also notable and raises questions about the audience, presumably including visitors to the friary church along with friars, friends, family

[73] Kingsford, *Grey Friars of London*, p. 80.

[74] A. Fortescue, *The Ceremonies of the Roman Rite Described* (London, 1920), pp. 285–8, at p. 285. I am grateful to Jerome Bertram for his advice on this point.

[75] This is not known to have survived.

[76] Kingsford, *Grey Friars of London*, p. 80.

and other Londoners who were present at the chantry service. The level of attention to detail on the part of Cantelowe is revealed elsewhere when, for instance, he set down the precise posture of the celebrant when the *De Profundis* was said and that the ceremony was to conclude with *Absolve Domine*. This is a good example of the care taken by patrons, either for themselves or on behalf of others, when establishing chantries.

It is curious that William Cantelowe and John Kyry felt the need to ratify their earlier agreement two years and a day after their original indenture. It can be no coincidence that the provincial minister, master and guardian and thirty members of the brethren were all gathered in the chapter house of the Franciscan church. It is notable that the provincial minister of the order attached his seal of office to validate this agreement.[77] It is also notable that all future wardens and friars of the London house were to take an oath to observe the agreement and to guarantee the continued celebration of the Gloucester-Cantelowe chantry. This important agreement was to leave nothing to chance and this, too, is suggested by the choice of witnesses, all of whom were prominent Londoners: Geoffrey Felding, alderman of Farringdon Within (the ward in which the house of the Grey Friars was established); Thomas Urswyck, the recorder of the city; and Roger Tongue, the common clerk. This suggests that Cantelowe wanted the city, as a corporate body, to have a watching brief and to ensure the terms of the contract were observed.

The detailed arrangements for the Gloucester chantry are exceptional and nothing comparable is known for other perpetual foundations at Grey Friars. A similar agreement was evidently made between John Wardall, doctor of law and canon both of St. Paul's and of Lincoln cathedral (d. 1472), and the Franciscan brethren during his lifetime. He did not set up a chantry in his will, but he referred to its existence when he charged his executors with arranging an inscription close to his grave which was to record his chantry.[78] This memorial was to be placed in the wall close to the altar of Holy Cross at the east end of the nave and to record that the brothers of the house, present and future, were to celebrate this chantry in perpetuity.[79]

---

[77] It was not unusual for the provincial minister to seal chantry agreements with notable benefactors (E. A. New, 'Speaking from the art: a reconsideration of mendicant seals in medieval England', in Harry and Steer, *The Urban Church*, pp. 222–37).

[78] TNA, PROB 11/6, fo. 41r–v; Kingsford, *Grey Friars of London*, pp. 106–7. On Wardall, see *BRUO (to A.D. 1500)*, iii. 1981.

[79] Such commemorative inscriptions were not uncommon and examples have survived, e.g., the chantry foundation of William Chapman, tailor and sheriff (d. 1446), formerly at St. Dunstan in the West and later used as a palimpsest brass for the inscription of Francis Style (d. 1646) at St. John the Baptist, Little Missenden (Bucks.) (D. C. Rutter, 'A palimpsest at Little Missenden, Bucks', *Transactions of the Monumental Brass Soc.*, viii (1) (1943), 34–6).

Not only did Wardall set up his chantry at an altar close to his grave, but he also arranged a permanent marker of its existence reminiscent of the efforts made by William Cantelowe a dozen years or so earlier. Wardall wanted any onlookers to know for whom the chantry had been established.

Lady Elizabeth Uvedale left her commemorations at the Grey Friars in the hands of her executors, who were to endow a mass for which she left £100. This was to be arranged immediately after her death.[80] She died on 21 June 1488 and was buried beneath a canopied tomb at the east end of the north aisle and close to Our Lady altar, where, according to the inscription, her chantry was celebrated.[81] Lady Elizabeth's bequest of £100 was enough to invest in property to provide a reasonable income with which to support a chaplain at an annual salary of £6 13s 4d. The friars could not own property directly, however, and Lady Elizabeth's gift was probably in cash, similar to that provided by Cantelowe, to meet the running costs and repairs of the convent and in return for perpetual commemoration. It should also be borne in mind that the friars already had priests at each convent and the greater part of the 'salary' for the celebrants in the church of the London Franciscans would be welcome funds for the general works of the friary. The bequest of 15 marks (or £10) to employ three friars at the perpetual chantry for Richard Hastings, Lord Willoughby and Welles (d. 1503), set up by his widow Joan in 1505, would likewise have provided additional income for the convent.[82] Mendicant chantries enabled patrons to enjoy the benefits of increased liturgical celebration from a larger body of priests than might be available in a parish church. Chantries established in mendicant churches could not, unlike their counterparts in the parish, rely on the same chaplain and instead benefited from an extensive clerical workforce which, for some, was an attractive alternative.

The Hastings chantry was to be celebrated at the altar in the Apostles chapel close to the grave of Lord Willoughby and Welles, where his widow later joined him. They were commemorated by sculptured alabaster effigies placed on a *tumba elevata*, a raised tomb, immediately before the altar.[83] A third widow set up a long-term chantry at Grey Friars which was to last for 200 years. Julian Maryner was widow of the wealthy salter, William Maryner,

---

[80] TNA, PROB 11/8, fos. 124–6 (Elizabeth, widow of Sir Thomas Uvedale, 1488).

[81] Kingsford, *Grey Friars of London*, pp. 107–8.

[82] TNA, PROB 11/14, fos. 217v–128v. Her husband Lord Willoughby and Welles had established a 10-year chantry in his own will of 1503 which was to be celebrated at the altar close to where he was buried and for which he left £20 (TNA, PROB 11/13, fo. 243r–v). His widow provided a perpetual arrangement.

[83] Kingsford, *The Grey Friars of London*, p. 77.

who died in 1512.[84] She outlived him by five years and in her will bequeathed a legacy of £66 13s 4d to the warden of the Franciscan convent, who was to arrange daily for a friar to celebrate for her soul and for her late husband's at an altar to be chosen by her executor, John Skevington, merchant tailor of London.[85] This bequest would be an annual equivalent of 7s 8d and was insufficient for a perpetual chaplain in one of the city's parish churches. The Franciscans provided an alternative means of commemoration through one-off, and generous, large scale payments – presumably to help with running costs – in return for which they undertook to provide permanent, or in the case of Widow Maryner long-term, chantry celebration. It was an arrangement which suited wealthy donors. The chosen friar at the Maryner chantry was to recite the *De Profundis* at the first lavatory, followed by her name and the names of her former husbands. Julian Maryner is the only patron who did not specify the altar where her chantry was to be celebrated, probably because her husband's tomb, in the centre of the north aisle, was not adjacent to any specific altar.

The final instance of perpetual chantry foundation at London Grey Friars is Sir Stephen Jenyns, merchant tailor, mayor and alderman of London. He died in 1523 and was buried under a sculptured effigy in the chapel of St. Francis.[86] His chantry was organized by John Benett, also a merchant tailor and evidently acting as a feoffee on behalf of the Jenyns estate, who set down the terms of the endowment in his own will of 1527.[87] The chantry was to be managed by the Merchant Taylors' Company, which was to arrange with the warden of Grey Friars the appointment of a friar who was to celebrate daily, between six and nine o'clock in the morning, at the altar of St. Francis – close to where Sir Stephen was buried – and a requiem mass was to be held once a week. The friar was to say before the first lavatory, and 'in audience' of those in attendance, the names of Sir Stephen, his wives Margaret, Joan and Margaret and all Christian souls, followed by the *De Profundis*. The Grey Friars were paid £2 13s 4d yearly to celebrate the chantry. The Merchant Taylors' Company was to provide the chantry with bread, wine, wax, chalice and vestments and bore responsibility for the furnishings. At the end of every day, eight young friars, one of whom was to be a priest, were to go, in perpetuity, to the hearse over Sir Stephen's

---

[84] Kingsford, *The Grey Friars of London*, p. 119. On Maryner see above and Luxford, 'The testament of Joan FitzLewes' in this volume.

[85] LMA, DL/C/B/004/MS09171/009, fos. 37r–v. Her husbands were William Boynton, Robert Lynne, John Blowboll and William Maryner.

[86] Kingsford, *Grey Friars of London*, p. 94; discussed further in Steer, 'The order of St. Francis', pp. 185–90.

[87] LMA, CLA/023/DW/01/242 (10) and above.

tomb and say the *De Profundis*.[88] The Merchant Taylors' Company was to pay the warden of the Grey Friars a further 20*s* for this. During the winter months the friars were to receive an extra 2*s* to provide for a taper to stand on the hearse when it was darker. Prayers at the tomb are well known – for example, at the York Grey Friars – and it is not surprising to find such practice in the London church.[89] But it is rare to find such details as the role to be taken by eight young friars, all but one of whom were evidently students, who were to gather at the tomb to recite *De Profundis* after the end of the day's liturgy.

John Benett, like others before him, adopted a 'belt and braces' approach when it came to securing the long-term celebration of Sir Stephen's soul, adding, 'Also I wille that the said Wardeyne of the Gray ffreers and his successoures shalle once in the yere for ever publisshe and cause to be redde this my present last wille soo that it may be hadde in a perpetuall memory'.[90] John Benett set out to secure the commemorations which his friend Sir Stephen had wanted; to this end he went into extraordinary detail in his own will to provide surety from beyond the grave so that those involved in the chantry – be it in managing the estate or celebrating the service or paying the correct fees – did so according to Sir Stephen's wishes.

Perpetual chantries established at Grey Friars reveal the care and attention to detail that patrons and executors lavished on them. The proximity of the tomb monument to the altar where the chantry was to be celebrated is notable, and this surely reflects the exceptional wealth of the benefactors concerned. Those who could afford to endow a permanent chantry could also afford to buy a grave close to an altar of their choice. It is not always clear from the Grey Friars register whether the scribe copied down details of chantries from inscriptions by the tomb or read about them in the statute book. The example of John Wardall, however, suggests that a separate inscription did, in fact, exist alongside the monument near to the grave.[91] The responsibilities of the friars themselves are also striking: the

---

[88] I thank Nigel Morgan for his comments on this daily ceremony held at the Jenyns tomb.

[89] Cf. M. Robson, who noted that every Friday the Franciscans at York gathered at the grave of Sir Brian Rocliff, where they sang the antiphon *Jhesu* ('The Grey Friars in York, *c.*1450–1540', in *The Religious Orders in Pre-Reformation England*, ed. J. G. Clark (Woodbridge, 2002), pp. 109–19, at p.116). This was also emphasized by Luxford, 'The collegiate church as mausoleum', pp. 115–6; and in C. Burgess, 'Fotheringhay church: college and community', in *The Yorkist Age: Proceedings of the 2011 Harlaxton Symposium*, ed. H. Kleineke and C. Steer (Harlaxton Medieval Studies, n.s., xxiii, Donington, 2013), pp. 347–66, at pp. 362–3.

[90] LMA, CLA/023/DW/01/242 (10).

[91] Cf. the tomb monuments for Joan FitzLewes at the Minories discussed by J. Luxford in his chapter in this volume.

oath sworn by future friars to abide by the terms of chantry agreements, the weekly duty roster for each chantry, the short-term appointment of friars at particular foundations, the times when they were to recite the *De Profundis*, the naming of the patrons and benefactors of the chantry and location of the mass are clearly specified. It is also notable that chantries set up in the friaries were cheaper than their counterparts in the parish and, more often than not, required less capital for long-term celebrations.

Conclusion

The convent of the Grey Friars remained a centre of commemoration until its surrender in 1538. Their remarkable tombscape, with 682 monuments to the dead, attests to a steady popularity. This chapter has demonstrated that tomb-monuments played an important role in the celebration of the chantry, as well as the anniversary, of past benefactors who lay buried within the walls of the Franciscan church. Testamentary evidence suggests that anniversary and chantry foundations increased from *c*.1450. It was from this date that benefactors found a way of establishing their commemorations with the London Grey Friars through cash payments rather than endowed property. Such arrangements required assurance. Testators and representatives of the dead took their responsibilities seriously: names were read out weekly in the chapter house; contracts were made and copied into the statute books; legal agreements, in the form of wills, would be read out; memorial plates (separate but complementary to the tomb monument) were set up; and the names of benefactors were recited daily with the *De Profundis*. There could be little doubt to future audiences about the identity of the patron. The sprinkling of holy water over the tomb and the gathering of friars at particular times of the day, week, month or year emphasized the close relationship between the remains of the dead and the celebration at their grave. Chantry founders, in almost all cases, chose to be buried next to the altar where their mass was to be celebrated. To meet these desires the Franciscan friars were able to provide a flexible workforce which could be adroitly managed. It was clear to Londoners, both rich and not so rich, that their souls would be safely lodged in the care of the Franciscans.

Appendix

Translation of a notarial instrument made on 27 March 1460 certifying the agreement between William Cantelowe, mercer and alderman of London, and the Grey Friars convent concerning the endowment of a perpetual chantry for Thomas Gloucester and his wife Anne, and William Cantelowe and his wives, Margaret and Elizabeth.[92]

In the translation which follows paragraph numbers and punctuation have been inserted for ease of reference.

1.   In the name of God, Amen. By the present public instrument let it be evidently clear that in the one thousandth four hundredth and sixtieth year of our Lord, in the eighth indiction, in the second year of the pontificate of our most holy father and lord in Christ the Lord by divine providence Pope Pius

2.   on the twenty-seventh day of the month of March in the Chapter House of the community of the Friars Minor of the city of London, in the presence of myself, notary public below written, and of the witnesses below written, personally appointed venerable and devout men, brothers Thomas Radnor, Minister Provincial of the aforesaid order, William Goddard, the then master and custodian, John Kyry, warden of the same community, William Wolff, Stephen Raaff, professors in sacred theology, John Boosgawyn, John Weston, William Goddard, James Wale, John Hood, William Carpentir, William Sergiant, Robert Yooll, Herman de Colonia, Anthony de Colonia, John Gulle, John Litley, Andrew Bavard, William Smyth, Henry Whithede, Thomas Pattyn, John Eversham, William Roser, John Egliston, John Pede, Robert Brown, John Stanley, William Kemys, John Nicholas, John Billyk, Thomas Bolton, William Jonson and John Gylle, friars of the aforesaid order assembled in chapter for the purpose

3.   as they declared, below written and holding their chapter or assembly, publicly stated and acknowledged, collectively and singly alike, that they had received and had from the noble William Cantelowe, mercer, citizen and alderman of London, there then present before them, two hundred pounds in sterling as alms for the repair work of their conventual church and in support of other burdens incumbent

---

[92]   TNA, C 270/32/21. An abbreviated transcript of the original Latin agreement is printed in Kingsford, 'Additional material for the history of the Grey Friars', pp. 145–7.

upon them and in return for so many great gratuitous benefactions, by genuinely and spontaneously unanimous consent assembled as reported above in chapter, they pledged on their own and their successors' behalf for all future times that one Mass daily should be specifically celebrated and dedicated in their conventual church aforesaid for the souls of Thomas Gloucester esquire and of Anne his consort, and for the souls of the aforesaid William Cantelowe and of Margaret and Elizabeth his wives, their parents, offspring and benefactors, and for the most part in that part of the aforesaid church where the bodies of the aforesaid Thomas and Anne rest interred, exceptions being three days in the Great Week which is immediately before Easter Day

4.   and that the anniversary day of the same Thomas, Anne, William, Margaret and Elizabeth will be observed with the Offices of the Dead and sung Mass every year once most holy, as the community of the aforesaid convent of friars is accustomed to do for outstanding benefactors, about the feast of St. Agatha the Virgin [5 February] each year in perpetuity

5.   and that all and each of the rest of the things they will do and observe and cause to be observed, that are contained and specified in certain indentures composed concerning and regarding the foregoing and in pursuance of them, sealed with the seals of the said Provincial and the common [seal] of the community of the aforesaid house and of the aforementioned William Cantelowe; the which same indenture was then and there read and publicly proclaimed to the same, the content of which follows in these words: 'This indenture made between brother John Kyry, warden, and the other masters and brothers of the community of Friars Minor in the city of London on the one part and the honourable William Cantelowe, citizen, mercer and alderman of the said city on the other part, bears witness that we the aforesaid brother John Kyry, warden, and the other masters and brothers have received and had from the aforesaid William two hundred pounds in sterling as alms for the repair work of our aforesaid church, or our other necessities, fully disbursed and delivered,

6.   and so being mindful of so many great gratuitous benefactions so piously gifted and bestowed on us and bound by the law of gratitude to reciprocate, by our genuinely and spontaneously unanimous consent, as much as assent, being assembled in chapter for the purpose we, on our priestly honour, with the supporting consent and approval as to permission of the reverend father brother Thomas Radnor, Provincial

Minister of our order in England, firmly promise, ordain, determine and pledge, on behalf of ourselves and our successors for all future times everlasting, that one Mass daily without interruption should be celebrated and dedicated for the souls of Thomas Gloucester esquire and of Anne his consort and for the souls of the said William and of Margaret and Elizabeth his wives, and for their parents, offspring and benefactors in our church aforesaid and for the most part in that part of the church where the bodies of the aforesaid Thomas and Anne rest interred, exceptions being three days in the Great Week which is immediately before Easter day,

7. adding and in manner and form likewise determining, that any future brother precentor of our order and house aforesaid shall be in perpetuity bound on his obedience through these presents weekly to assign on his duty board one suitable friar for the particular celebration as prescribed at Mass daily that week and any brother so assigned shall be bound under the sanction for disobedience to carry out the said directive or assignment, and should he not carry it out the community aforesaid shall nonetheless be bound in accordance with what is aforewritten.

8. Moreover the friar so assigned shall be bound under the sanction for disobedience immediately before the said Mass, or immediately after the same, to say on bended knees the *De Profundis* publicly and openly first of all announcing in the vernacular in the following form 'For the souls of Thomas Gloucester and Anne his consort and of William Cantelowe, of Margaret and Elizabeth his wives, of their parents, offspring and benefactors the *De Profundis*' and in this way shall he complete the said psalm together with the prayer *Absolve* [*Domine*]. Moreover, we pledge and in good faith promise that the names of the aforesaid Thomas Gloucester, and of Anne his consort, and of the said William Cantelow, of Margaret and Elizabeth his wives, must in perpetuity be recommended in authoritative utterance in our local chapter once every week.

9. Also, we promise that the anniversary of the death of the same shall be observed every year in perpetuity, about the feast of Saint Agatha the Virgin [5 February], with the Office of the Dead and sung Mass, as the said community is accustomed regarding outstanding benefactors.

10. And to create for the brethren for future times an ever fresh reminder, the warden or president, for the time being, shall once every year be

obliged, on his redemptive obedience, about the feast of All Saints, when the number of friars in the said community will have reached its greatest, in the friary chapter distinctly and publicly to read aloud himself, or through another brother, the contents here of the present indenture, and to enjoin upon the brethren the duties aforesaid.

11. And for the greater assurance of the foregoing, we the aforesaid warden and masters and the community, in good faith and form prescribed, promise that for the completion and fulfilment of the aforewritten, that all and each of the foregoing may in perpetuity actually be implemented, [we] have made a statute thereon binding on oath in our written statute books whereby any friar in future, and especially a warden, to be admitted amongst us shall promise, among the other undertakings, in good faith to observe and as far as in him lies to fulfil the said statute.

12. In witness of which matter, the aforesaid brother John Kyry and the friars assembled in chapter attached their common seal and William Cantelowe reciprocally his seal to these indentures. Given in London in the chapter house of the same community on the twenty-sixth day of the month of March in the one thousandth four hundredth [and] fifty-eighth year of our Lord and thirty-sixth year of King Henry the sixth after the conquest of England. And I brother Thomas Radnor Minister Provincial aforesaid, holding all and each of the foregoing as ratified and acceptable, nay, giving this matter, before it was arranged, my express consent and support that it should be ordered in the manner aforesaid, by my authority I authorize, approve and ratify by the presents all and each of the things completed in the manner and form aforesaid. In witness of which thing I have affixed to the presents the seal of my office on the day and in the year above said. After the reading and expounding of which same indenture the aforementioned brothers Thomas Radnor, William Goddard, John Kyry and the other fellow friars named with those above, being asked all and each specifically by name, promised on their plighted good faith faithfully to observe and in all things fulfil, and to cause in the future to be observed and fulfilled, all and each of the things prescribed and contained in the aforesaid indenture as far as they affect and concern them; and thus did each of the same then swear and promise in that same place.

13. All and each of these things were arranged, as they are above written and recorded, in the year of our Lord, the indiction, the pontificate, the month, on the day and in the place aforesaid, there being present

then and in that same place the noble Geoffrey Felding, alderman of the ward in Farringdon Within where the house of the friars aforesaid is situated, John Aleyn, doctor of laws, Thomas Urswyck, recorder of the city of London, Roger Tonge, common clerk of the same city of London, and other witnesses to the foregoing especially invited and requested. And I Robert Kent, bachelor in law, of the diocese of Canterbury, by apostolic authority notary public, being present together with the aforenamed witnesses, attended the aforesaid acknowledgement, pledge, promise and reading of the indenture and all and each of the other premises while they were being arranged and made in the manner thus prescribed in the year of our Lord, the indiction, the pontificate, the month, on the day and in the place aforesaid; and that all and each of them were thus done I saw and heard, caused to be written down by another, published and reduced to this public form, and I have signed it with my customary mark and name and with my own hand I have subscribed myself here, having been asked and required, as assurance and witness of all the foregoing.

14. The transformative effect:
Caroline Barron as teacher and colleague*

Clive Burgess

This book expresses many things. Most obviously, it speaks of the degree of respect that Caroline Barron commands for the role she has long played in broadening and invigorating the agendas guiding late medieval and early modern London history. The array of contributing authorities, along with the variety of their topics, only affirms this observation. But, equally, the book stands as a tribute to the continuous investment Caroline has made during her career by inspiring and instructing so many, both colleagues and students. Perhaps the most remarkable aspect concerning the latter has been her conspicuous success in guiding graduates reading for doctorates. Her ingenuity in finding and shaping viable topics and her generosity thereafter in supervising and nurturing students have both been outstanding. Her success in this area, however, resides as much with her gifts for friendship and enthusiasm as with her intellectual prowess and scholarly standards; in combination, these talents have sustained a multitude through the rigours of researching, writing and presenting.[1] To this must also be added, first, Caroline's achievement in helping to create the Medieval MA at Royal Holloway and, thereafter, in teaching on its courses, again training a host of new graduates as well as mature students keen to return to education – some of whom have subsequently opted to work for doctorates. Second, and less formally, Caroline has spread her influence and assistance yet further both through the Medieval and Tudor London seminar held in the Institute of Historical Research in summer terms and, also, in her inexhaustible willingness to see and advise any interested in, and working on, aspects of London history (or, indeed, on other aspects within the remit of her interests and expertise). The list of contributors to this volume only begins

---

* What follows is a version of a short talk that I gave as one of a series of presentations in a seminar anticipating the publication of Caroline Barron's collected essays, *Medieval London: Collected Papers of Caroline M. Barron*, ed. M. Carlin and J. T. Rosenthal (Kalamazoo, Mich., 2017), held in the Institute of Historical Research in early June 2017.

[1] As the list at the end of this volume makes plain.

to suggest the degree to which Caroline has both taught and encouraged; the number for whom this holds true more generally is, of course, very much larger and spreads internationally. And she is held universally in great affection.

In the following, however, and writing first and foremost as a colleague, it is my intention to bring a more personal perspective to bear on Caroline's achievement. I seek to celebrate her contribution both as a teacher and as a writer responsible for a remarkably influential output and – writing also from the point of view of another teacher – aim to shed light on some of the ways in which she has reached such a wide and varied audience.

When I embarked on my career at the University of London, I started as an outsider. I had not done my degrees in London, and although I was an urban historian, felt like a comparative light-weight as my work had mainly concentrated on the Church and on popular belief and behaviour. But, in the 1970s and 1980s, London history seemed like a world apart: I remember my own supervisor's comment guiding me on the choice of a doctoral topic when, rather to her surprise, I told her that I wanted to look at popular religion: 'Well', she said, 'York and Norwich have been done, London's too big – try Bristol' – ten or a dozen of the most formative words in my life. From the outside, London was both big and daunting – and, moreover, when I started teaching late medieval London history, there seemed precious little in print on which to rely for the purposes of seminar teaching.

To take an example, if one wanted to understand something as basic as the structure of London's government, this was a challenge. But I had a lucky break: while I was obliged to teach on the Royal Holloway Medieval MA, with its core course on Late Medieval London History, Caroline had also cajoled me to teach with her on the BA degree's federal offering, the London Group II – 'London Urban Society, 1400–1600'. Although she was on research leave, she was running this course because of the commitment she felt towards it and had also persuaded Vanessa Harding to lend a hand. Caroline and Vanessa dealt with the core subjects; I nervously led the proceedings on the religious topics (London both before and after the Reformation); but the students, too, were entrusted with a proportion of the topics and in these weeks both Caroline and Vanessa would get a discussion going by commenting on what had been presented. Now, out of the students in that class – held in the Royal Holloway house in Bedford Square – I have no doubt at all who learnt most during that year. Very belatedly, I must thank both Caroline and Vanessa for this: they set me on my way and I am eternally grateful.

I particularly remember the first class. Caroline, having specially donned her academic gown for the occasion, gave us a lecture on London government in the fifteenth century. Wonderful! I soaked this up like a sponge, began to think about it and also read some of the more approachable background material. Then, a week or two later, and more informally, I presented this topic to my MA class, only to be confronted by ravenous students demanding to know where on earth I had managed to glean all this so that they could read it, too. I, of course, had little option but to respond, rather airily, suggesting that this was the wisdom of the ages and, when pressed further, admitted that I had picked up some of the finer points in Caroline's doctoral thesis, a copy of which was on the shelves in her office, which I had taken over for the duration – and this was true: I had read some of her thesis. But I am not sure that I actually 'fessed up' that I had been fortunate enough to hear Caroline lecture on the topic and, as a result, been able to gain the broader perspective of how it all fitted together.

The first main point that I want to make, then, is that before Caroline published her magisterial *London in the Later Middle Ages* there was no adequate or detailed synthesis of many of the fundamental aspects of London's history in the later fourteenth and fifteenth centuries; and I would simply like to note how deeply we are all in her debt for this – particularly since the absence of any such synthesis was making a dishonest man of me. And, second, while the present volume brooks no doubt at all as to Caroline's contribution as a writer and researcher and as a galvanizer, so often setting others off on topics and assisting them in so many ways, we perhaps need to mark the fact that Caroline is a marvellous communicator. I want to pay tribute to how much I have learnt over the years, simply by listening to her in classes and lectures, as well as in the London seminar – that most congenial of classrooms. And, of course, also from reading and benefiting from her scholarly essays, many of which have recently been collected by Martha Carlin and Joel Rosenthal in *Medieval London*.

Writing as a teacher, and as one duty-bound to advise others – be they undergraduates or graduates – on what to read on various topics relating to London history, I would like very simply to emphasize the breadth of Caroline's scholarship. On topic after topic, what Caroline has written has become essential reading, and this is in addition to the monograph. Indeed, when talking things through with students as to what they might prepare for the next week's class, how often is it that the first thing I mention is by Caroline Barron? I have to admit, as a class progresses through the year the tendency grows for Professor Barron to be referred to as 'You know who' and, of course, they *do* know who. Such celebrity leads to another anecdote, because 'You know who' is not much occupied now with undergraduate or MA teaching and, as a result, has become mainly a name where undergraduates are concerned, albeit the name of *the* authority on late medieval London. And a year or two ago, when I was teaching the London Group II in the Easter Term (and this is still taught in Bedford Square), one of my students arrived for the class in what can only be described as a bit of a state. The *sal volatile* having been administered, we discovered what the matter was. The first words that she managed were: 'I've just seen Caroline Barron'. There is a signing-in book in Bedford Square and this student had signed in immediately after Caroline one Thursday afternoon – and realized who the lady was who was still standing in the vestibule. So, Caroline, your celebrity goes before you: any student, whatever stage they have reached in learning about London, holds you in high esteem, which of course reflects both on the measure and, more particularly, on the quality of your published output.

I think what I most admire is the way in which Caroline works to uncover and then explore the mechanisms, for instance, of London's government, explaining why it was as it was and why Londoners reacted and behaved as they did. Repeatedly, her work goes to the essence of a question, and this gives either me as a teacher, or my students as fledgling London historians, the key that opens the door. On this theme there are two or three of her essays that I would like briefly to mention.[2] I will start with a pair of them: these are 'The quarrel of Richard II with London, 1392–97' and 'London and the crown, 1451–61'. The first of these explores the underlying truth that London was the king's city and considers what could go wrong (like a £30,000 fine, among other things) if Londoners upset their lord – as they did with Richard II in 1392. It explains why, thereafter, the city's rulers did their utmost never to put a foot wrong – because London's all-important privileges *could* be rescinded – which helps to explain why Londoners (by comparison with city-dwellers in the Low Countries, for instance) were so careful to keep the peace and to accommodate various kings' wishes, even including keeping the city clean and putting on pageants to celebrate national occasions. The essay opens the door to many different topics, helping to shed light on the character and conditions of London in the fifteenth and early sixteenth centuries, also explaining how kings themselves regarded and used London at this time. I find myself referring to it time and again. Similarly with the second essay, which essentially concerns the city during the Wars of the Roses, when London may have had no love for Henry VI but – true to form – its governors tried for as long as possible

---

[2] All now collected together in *Medieval London*, ed. Carlin and Rosenthal.

not to step out of line, until the arrival of the Yorkist lords, who (to use an anachronism), having 'parked their tanks on London's lawn', forced their hand. Having changed sides, and to avoid grim repercussions, the city thereafter did its utmost (mainly by the strategic use of its money) to ensure that the Yorkist party should prevail, which it duly did at the Battle of Towton. Caroline helps to show here that the politics of the later 1450s and early 1460s was not simply a matter of noble faction (which was how the civil war of the mid fifteenth century was normally treated when I first encountered it), but that in this case the city played a vital role in determining the course of political events which even extended to 'king-making'. Again, I find myself referring to these principles – or mechanisms – time and again.

The final essay I want to mention is Caroline's 'The "golden age" of women in medieval London', which, when it was published (edited by Rowena Archer and Brian Ferme, appearing in the journal *Reading Medieval Studies*, xv: *Medieval Women in Southern England* (1989), 35–58), was difficult to track down. I had come to know Caroline by the time this had emerged and when it was attracting rejoinders in the early 1990s, from Judith Bennett among others, which were, understandably, both heartfelt and challenging. But what Caroline did with the 'Golden Age' was to provide undergraduates and graduates alike with the keys to open the doors onto the usually unseen half-or-more of the population; and this essay shows how the manpower shortage after the Black Death created a situation in which London's rulers had the wherewithal to 'open up' London's economy and society, to a degree, to women – for girls as apprentices, for wives as *femmes soles* and also encouraging widows to keep the family business going after their husband's death. Others may have argued for the limitations in this scenario and, more particularly, pointed out that the change was not transformative (that is, when the population eventually rose again, these advances could all too easily be reversed). But the background, the argument, the three or four main points and the response the argument has provoked – and I must also mention the women who emerge in the course of the argument (Anne Sutton will be very pleased to know how the silkwoman, Alice Claver, is enjoying a pronounced celebrity centuries after her death, along with Caroline's bell-foundresses, Johannas Hill and Sturdy) – all give students the perfect framework for an essay. So much so that the 'Golden Age' has not simply entered the mainstream, it has opened the flood-gates. And here I have a slight bone to pick, as someone obliged to set and, more to the point, mark exams, both on late medieval and early modern London and also a survey course on late medieval social and economic history. Almost all the students (especially on the survey course) tend to pick this topic. It has to be on the exam papers (were it not, I would be lynched) and is, as I say, remarkably popular. So, three or four years back, when possibly the related question was too easy, out of thirty-five students studying on the survey course, thirty-two attempted it as one of their questions; in the following year, I made the question more difficult and out of thirty-five, twenty-nine students attempted it; and last year – resigned to my fate – about thirty attempted it and generally did themselves, and the subject, justice. I feel, however, that I have come to know every nook and cranny of this topic. But it marks the extent of Caroline's contribution, even as the result of an article that first saw the light of day in a relatively obscure journal, to the topics and questions that now constitute the late medieval academic and intellectual landscape. But imagine my feelings some years back, already 'Golden-Aged-out' after exam-marking in London, when I had to turn my attention to duties as an external examiner in Lancaster: I picked up *their* late medieval exam paper, only to find … There is no escape.

Caroline has not only enlarged and enriched London history (of the city, and also in the present-day university), but her influence as a researcher and as a teacher goes much farther than this. Just think: throughout the country hundreds, possibly thousands, of history graduates are facing up to life immeasurably strengthened by a close knowledge of the debate on 'the Golden Age'. Caroline Barron's intellectual and historical contribution truly has been 'transformative' and I salute her.

Doctorates awarded under the supervision of Caroline M. Barron

1. Stephen H. Rigby, 'Boston and Grimsby in the middle ages' (1983)

2. Andrew Prescott, 'Judicial records of the rising of 1381' (1984)

3. Gervase Rosser, 'Medieval Westminster: the vill and the urban community, 1200–1540' (1984)

4. John Schofield, 'Secular buildings in the City of London c.1200 to c.1600' (1989)

5. Stephen O'Connor 'A study of the careers of Adam Fraunceys and John Pyel, 14th-century mayors of London, with an edition of their cartularies (Hatfield MS. CP 291.1 and College of Arms, MS. Vincent 64)' (1990)

6. Jenny Stratford, 'The execution of the will of John, duke of Bedford (1389–1435), with special reference to the inventories of his goods' (1991)

7. Helen Bradley, 'Italian merchants in London c.1300–1450' (1992)

8. Julia Merritt, 'Religion, government and society in early modern Westminster, c.1525–1625' (1992)

9. Matthew Davies, 'The Tailors of London and their guild, c.1300–1500' (1994)

10. Virginia Bainbridge, 'Gild and parish in late medieval Cambridgeshire, c.1350–1558' (1994)

11. Penny Tucker, 'Government and politics: London, 1461–83' (1995)

12. Anne F. Sutton, 'The mercery trade and the Mercers' Company of London, from the 1130s to 1348' (1995)

13. Elizabeth A. New, 'The cult of the Holy Name of Jesus in late medieval England, with special reference to the fraternity in St. Paul's Cathedral, c.1450–1558' (1999)

14. Roger Axworthy, 'The financial relationship between the London merchant community and Edward III, 1327–77' (2000)

15. Eleanor Quinton, 'The Drapers of London, c.1350–c.1550' (2001)

16. Matthew Groom, 'Piety and locality: studies in urban and rural religion in Surrey, c.1450–c.1550' (2001)

17. Jessica Freeman, 'The political community of fifteenth-century Middlesex' (2002)

18. Mark Forrest, 'The estates of Chertsey Abbey: land management and rural society 1300–1550' (2003)

19. John Oldland, 'London clothmaking, c.1250–c.1550' (2003)

20. Marie-Hélène Rousseau, 'Chantry foundations and chantry chaplains at St. Paul's cathedral, London, c.1200–1548' (2003)

21. Stephanie R. Hovland, 'Apprenticeship in later medieval London' (c.1300–c.1530) (2006)

22. Lauren Fogle, 'Jewish converts to Christianity in medieval London' (2006)

23. John A. McEwan, 'Medieval London: the development of a civic political community, c.1100–1300' (2007)

24. Claire Martin, 'Transport for London, 1250–1550' (2008)

25. Frank Millard, 'Politics and the creation of memory: the afterlife of Humphrey, duke of Gloucester' (2009)

26. Ann Bowtell, 'A medieval London hospital: Elsyngspital, 1330–1536' (2010)

27. Nick Holder, 'The medieval friaries of London: a topographic and archaeological history, before and after the Dissolution' (2011)

28. Jennifer Ledfors, 'The church and parish of St. Dunstan in the East London, c.1450–c.1537' (2012)

29. Robert A. Wood, 'Life and death: a study of the wills and testaments of men and women in London and Bury St. Edmunds in the late 14th and early 15th centuries' (2013)

30. Christine Winter, 'Prisons and punishments in late medieval London' (2013)

31. Christine Fox, 'The Royal Almshouse at Westminster c.1500–c.1600' (2013)

32. Christian Steer, 'Burial and commemoration in medieval London c.1140–1540' (2013)

33. Doreen Leach, 'Carpenters in medieval London c.1240–c.1540' (2017)

Tabula Gratulatoria

Jane Anghelatos
Amy Appleford
Ian Archer
Rowena E. Archer
Richard Asquith
Steve Astell
Lorraine Attreed
Taylor Aucoin
Tim Ayers
Gerry Bailey
Katie Barron
Helen Barron Williams
Seren Barron Williams
David Bates
Beresford Bell
Judith Bennett
Martin Biddle
Maggie Bolton
Michael Boon
Ann Bowtell
John Briggs
Sarah Brown
Dudley Buchanan
Mary Carruthers
Hugh and Penny Carson
Roger Catchpole
Roger Chapman
Celia Charlton
John Cherry
City of London, London
    Metropolitan Archives
John Clark
Linda Clark
Anne Clarke
Jane Clayton
Janet Clayton

Paul Cockerham
Nicola Coldstream
Joyce Coleman
Margaret Connolly
Meriel Connor
Anne Corcoran
Penelope Corfield
Antony Cox
Anne Crawford
Claire Cross
Roger Dahood
Erik Dane Wirsing
Trudi L. Darby
Giles Darkes
Catherine Delano-Smith
Anne DeWindt
Lucia Diaz Pascual
James Dixon
Gillian Draper
Martha Driver
Marie Erwood
Eric Fernie
Kathryn Fiddock
Kevin Flude
Lauren Fogle
Helen Forde
Christine Fox
Jill A. Franklin
Jessica Freeman
Katherine French
Claire Gapper
Louise Gardiner
Claire Gobbi Daunton
David Green
Francesco Guidi Bruscoli
Emmamarie Haasl

Elizabeth Hales
Jeffrey Hamilton
Louise Hampson
David Harry
Paul D. A. Harvey
Clare Hatcher
Fiona Haughey
Rosemary Haycs
Martin Henig
Marlene Hennessy
Cynthia Herrup
Alfred Hiatt
David Hogarth
Nick Holder
Peregrine Horden
Tessa Hosking
Stephanie Hovland
Leo Humphrey
Katharine Hunter
Martin Ingram
Peter Jackson
Graham Javes
Ann Kettle
Maryanne Kowaleski
Jeanne Solomon Langley
Doreen Leach
David Lepine
David Lewis
Henrietta Leyser
Janet Loengard
Ian Lonsdale
Michael Marriott
Claire Martin
Jo Mattingly
Shannon McSheffrey
Caroline Metcalfe
M. A. Michael
Linda Mitchell
Shelagh Mitchell
Linne Mooney
Gerta Moray

Marilynne Morgan
Rupert Morris
Simon Morris
Jackie Mountain
Stephen Myers
Dinah Nichols
Rebecca Oakes
Stephen O'Connor
Michael O'Donoghue
John Oldland
Deirdre Palk
Hannah Parham
Simon Polson
Susan Powell
Alice Prochaska
Records of Early English Drama
Compton Reeves
Catherine Rendón
Leah Rhys
Malcolm Richardson
Stephen Rigby
Nicholas Rogers
Susan Rose
Joel Rosenthal
Marie-Hélène Rousseau
Dean Rowland
Peter and Ann Rycraft
Sarah Salih
Lucy Freeman Sandler
Machi Sasai
Wendy Scase
Elizabeth Scudder
Martin Sheppard
Angelika Simpson
Barney Sloane
Kathryn A. Smith
Somerville College Library
Erik Spindler
Kelly Spring
Charlotte Stanford
Christopher Starr

David Stocker
Malcolm Stokes
Ian Stone
Jenny Stratford
Henry Summerson
Sheila Sweetinburgh
Adele Sykes
Norman Tanner
Tim Tatton-Brown
Melanie V. Taylor
Lynne Taylor-Gooby
Benjamin Thompson
Robert Tittler
Penny Tucker
Mio Ueno

Livia Visser-Fuchs
Linda Voigts
Susan Wabuda
Michelle Warren
Isobel Watson
Anthony Weale
Rupert Webber
Philip Whittemore
Jane Williams
Christopher Wilson
Christine Winter
Robert Wood
Kim Woods
Elizabeth Woollett
Nick Wright

Index

Lightning Source UK Ltd.
Milton Keynes UK
UKHW020647301019

352530UK00002B/14/P